Baby Names for Muslims

Traditional and Modern Boy and Girl Names from Arabic, Persian, Turkish and Other World Languages Permissible in Islam

Ikram Hawramani

2018

Copyright © Ikram Hawramani

Hawramani.com

All rights reserved. No part of this publication may be reproduced, stored in a retrieval system, or transmitted, in any form or by any means for commercial purposes without prior permission of the author. The author affirms the readers' right to share this book for personal, non-commercial purposes

Contents

Introduction 5
Permissible Names for Muslims 7
Choosing the Right Name 9
Baby Names for Girls 11
A 13
B 33
C 39
D 43
E 47
F 51
G 57
H 61
I 67
J 71
K 75
L 81
M 87
N 103
O 111
P 113
Q 117
R 119
S 125
T 139
U 143
V 145

W	147
Y	151
Z	153
Baby Names for Boys	159
A	161
B	181
C	189
D	191
E	195
F	199
G	205
H	207
I	211
J	215
K	219
L	223
M	227
N	243
O	249
P	251
Q	253
R	255
S	261
T	275
U	279
V	281
W	283
Y	287
Z	289

Introduction

This book is the result of five years of research cataloguing and describing names acceptable for use by Muslims. Great care has been taken to ensure the correctness of the meanings provided; all meanings have been validated across various dictionaries and references, such as *Taj al-Lughah wa Sihaah al-Arabiyyah* by Isma`eel bin Hammad al-Jawhari (11th century CE), *Lisaan al-Arab* by Ibn Manzur (14th century), *al-Qamoos al-Muheet* by Fairuzabadi (15th century), and contemporary sources such as the *Loghatnameh* of Dehkhoda, the *Sultan Qaboos Encyclopedia of Arab Names*, and the *Oxford Dictionary of First Names*.

Besides providing meanings, variant spellings of the names and the occasional historical note are provided. A note is provided for names that are mentioned in the Quran ("Quranic baby names"). For Western converts to Islam wishing to preserve their cultural traditions, hundreds of European names are provided whose meanings are acceptable according to Islamic criteria.

The book is arranged into two parts, the first part contains girl names and the second boy names. The language of each name is provided in brackets after the name.

A question I often get is "what is the correct English spelling of this Eastern name?" The answer, of course, is that there are no official English spellings. Parents can choose any spelling they prefer or create their own. In this book I have provided common and simple spellings, and variant spellings are provided where relevant in the variants section of the name.

The spellings provided are not meant as perfect transliterations, they are simply the most common. Sometimes "aa" is used to indicate a long "a" (as in the English word "man"), but not always.

Some sounds that cannot be expressed in English have been merged with their neighbours. For example, there are two types of "t" in Arabic, but in English both would be pronounced "t" without issue, therefore they are treated as the same sound.

Some names can be used for both boys and girls. These names are provided under both the girls' and the boys' sections.

Many names from Western cultures (French, Germany, Scandinavian, etc.) are provided. While it is often culturally unacceptable for Eastern Muslims to use these, Western converts to Islam should feel no hesitation in using them, as the various cultures of the East all use names belonging to their own local cultures. In Greater Persia, even though the majority of people are Muslim, perhaps half of all children are named Persian, rather than Arabic, names. There is no reason why a German convert to Islam should not feel proud of their own culture and use their own names, the way Persians, Turks and Malaysians do.

Not all Western names are acceptable, as some of them have pagan meanings. This book only includes those names whose meanings are perfectly acceptable according to Islamic criteria, further clarified in the next section.

Permissible Names for Muslims

In Islam, any name is permissible from any language or culture provided that it has a meaning that does not go against the principles and teachings of Islam. This is according to various fatwas (religious rulings) by respected sources, such as the Jordanian Fatwa Council (fatwa 2265), IslamWeb (a Sunnni Qatari website, fatwa 76363), IslamQA (a website managed by the conservative Saudi scholar Shaikh Muhammad Salih al-Munajjiid, fatwa 7180), IslamWay (a respected Egyptian website, fatwa 8723 by Shaikh Abdulrahaman bin Nasir al-Baraak), and Shaikh Yusuf al-Qaradhawi (a respected Egyptian scholar and president of the World Union of Islamic Scholars). All of these sources mention the permissibility of using foreign names to name Muslim children.

In fact, Islam does not have any specific texts on naming, and the prophet Muhammad himself (peace be upon him) had an Egyptian Coptic (non-Arab) wife named Maria (a non-Arabic name). The Quran does not contain any verses specifically about naming, though it prohibits the use of hurtful and offensive nicknames (Quran 49:11). The Prophet's traditions contain more specific information regarding names. For example, he specifically prohibited the use of the names Harb ("war"), Murrah ("bitter") and a name meaning "rebellious", renaming the person who had this name to "obedient". From the principles of the Quran and the Prophet's traditions we can derive the following rules:

- Names with negative meanings should not be used.
- Names that contain pagan and un-Islamic meanings should not be used, such as Mark, a reference to Mars, the Roman god of war.

Beyond these, Islam does not have any hard and fast rules about names. The Prophet (peace be upon him) had companions with names meaning "beetle", "snake", "one who suffers from night blindness", "feeble-minded", "anger", "club-footed", "squint-eyed", "bald", "one whose nose is cut", "barren" and "one who has enemies". These meanings are quite negative, or at least questionable, but the Prophet did not disallow them, because he respected the fact that these were common cultural and ancestral names.

Islam does not seek to eliminate cultural diversity, it respects the differing practices and traditions that exist among different cultures. Islam's goal is to free its followers from unjust practices. Beyond this, Muslims are free in how they express themselves. One who travels throughout the Muslim world meets a remarkable variety of practices and cultural expressions among devout Muslim societies, from Timbuktu in Mali, to Kazan in Russia, to the Maldives in the Indian Ocean, to the island of Borneo in Southeast Asia. Kurdish Muslims use mainly Kurdish words as names, Persian Muslims use Persian names, Turkish Muslims use Turkish names, and Malaysian Muslims use Malay names.

Due to the relative newness of Islam in the West, it is rare for Western Muslims to use Western names like John, William and Charles, even though these are acceptable names for Muslims. While Eastern migrants living in the West are free to avoid these, Western converts to Islam have the right to keep their Western names and pass them down to their children.

Choosing the Right Name

An argument in favor of using Western names in the West is the difficulty that the locals have with pronouncing Arabic names. *Aa`idh* is a beautiful name in Arabic, but there is no sensible reason why this name should be chosen for a child living in an English town. He will be subject to a lifetime of having to teach everyone he knows how to properly pronounce his name.

In addition to this, using strange-sounding Arabic names can exacerbate the problem of the local culture viewing Muslims as different, foreign, "other", to be mistrusted and looked down upon. A mixed child living in Britain, perhaps with a Turkish father and English mother, has a better chance of gaining the trust and friendship of his society if he has a local-sounding name than if he has a difficult foreign name. This is somewhat supported by science. A study showed that Turkish companies with simple and easy-to-pronounce names were viewed more favorably by a Western audience compared to companies with difficult-to-pronounce names. The same probably works for people's names.

This is not to scare parents away from Arabic or other Eastern names. Parents are free to choose a name that works best for their child in their particular culture and locale. An Arabic name in a cosmopolitan Western city may be less of an issue than one in a small town whose population has had little contact with Arabs and Muslims. And as the number of Muslims in the media, arts, sports and sciences increases, so will the acceptance of common Muslim names in the population.

This page intentionally left blank

Baby Names
for Girls

This page intentionally left blank

A

Aabida (Arabic)
Devoted to God - Worshiper
Variants: *Aabeda, Aabedah, Aabida, Aabidah, Abeda, Abedah, Abida, Abidah*

Aabira (Arabic)
Crossing - Passing By - Traveling
Variants: *Aabera, Aaberah, Aabirah, Abera, Aberah, Abira, Abirah*

Aadila (Arabic)
Excellent - Fair - Just - Moderate - Virtuous
Variants: *Aadela, Aadelah, Aadilah, Adela, Adelah, Adila, Adilah*

Aafa (Arabic)
Forgiver - Pardoner
Variants: *Afa, Affa, Affah*

Aafaaq (Arabic)
Horizons
The name Aafaaq is mentioned in the Quran.
Variants: *Aafaq, Afaaq, Afaq*

Aafira (Arabic)
One Who Waters a Plant
Variants: *Aafirah, Afera, Aferah, Afira, Afirah*

Aafiya (Arabic)
Good Health - Recovery

Aahoo (Persian)
Gazelle
Variants: *Ahoo, Ahu*

Aaiza (Arabic)
Replacement - Successor
Variants: *Aaidha, Aayzah, Aezah, Ayza, Ayzah*

Aakifah (Arabic)
Devoted Worshiper of God
Variants: *Aakefa, Aakefah, Aakifa, Aakifah, Akefa, Akefah, Akifa, Akifah*

Aalam (Arabic)
World
Variants: *Alam*

Aalifa (Arabic)
Amiable - Friendly
Variants: *Aalifa, Alefa, Alefah, Alifa, Alifah*

Aamad (Arabic)
Ages - Eras - Periods of Time
Variants: *Aamad, Amaad, Amad*

Aameen (Arabic)
Arabic for "Oh Allah, accept our prayer".
Variants: *Aamin, Ameen*

Aamira (Arabic)
Full of Life - Prosperous
Variants: *Aamera, Aamerah, Amira, Amirah*

Aana (Arabic)
Hours of the Night - Moments - Ocassions
Variants: *Aanaa, Ana*

Aaneseh (Arabic)
Eloquent - Virtuous

Aanil (Turkish)
Famous - Recollection
Variants: *Anil*

Aaqil (Arabic)
Discerning - Reasonable - Sensible - Wise
Variants: *Aaqel, Aqel, Aqil*

Aaqilah (Arabic)
Discerning - Reasonable - Sensible - Wise
Variants: *Aaqela, Aaqila, Aaqilah, Aaqleah, Aqela, Aqelah, Aqila*

Aaraf (Arabic)
Heights
Variants: *Aaref, Aref, Arif*

Aaribah (Arabic)
Successful
Variants: *Aareba, Arebah, Ariba*

Aarifa (Arabic)
Knowledgeable - Wise
Variants: *Aarefa, Aarifah, Arefa, Arefah, Arifa, Arifah*

Aarisha (Arabic)
Builder - Maker
Variants: *Aaresha, Aarisha, Aarishah, Aresh, Arishah*

Aasal (Arabic)
Evenings
The name Aasal is mentioned in the Quran.
Variants: *Aasaal, Asaal, Asal*

Aaseman (Persian)
Heaven - Sky
Variants: *Aasiman, Aseman, Asman*

Aasira (Arabic)
Captivator - Warrior
Variants: *Aasera, Aaserah, Asera, Aserah, Asira, Asirah*

Aatifah (Arabic)
Affection - Emotion - Feeling

Aatika (Arabic)
Generous - Pure
Variants: *Aatikah, Atika, Atikah*

Aatiq (Arabic)
Baby Pigeon - Free
Variants: *Aateq, Ateq, Atiq*

Aatiqa (Arabic)
Freed - Liberated
Aatiqa is an Arabic name for girls that means "free".
Variants: *Aatiqa, Ateqa, Ateqah, Atiqah*

Aatirah (Arabic)
Fragrant

Aatiya (Arabic)
Bestower - Giver
Variants: *Aatiyah, Atia, Atiya*

Aawaz (Kurdish)
Melody - Song - Tune
Variants: *Awaaz, Awaz*

Aaween (Kurdish)
Clean - Fresh - Pure
Literally "like water".
Variants: *Awin*

Aayizah (Arabic)
Replacement - Restitution

Aayun (Arabic)
Eyes
The name Aayun is mentioned in the Quran.
Variants: *A'yun, Ayon*

Abaal (Arabic)
Rose - Wild Rose
Variants: *Abal*

Abaasa (Arabic)
Lioness
Variants: *Abaasah, Abasa, Abasah*

Aban (Arabic)
Clear - Eloquent - Lucid
Variants: *Abaan*

Abanus (Persian, Urdu)
Ebony
Variant of Abnus.

Abbey (English, Irish)
Father of Exaltation
Pet form of Abigail

Abbie (English, Irish)
Father of Exaltation
Pet form of Abigail.

Abdaar (Arabic)
Full Moons - Moons
Plural of Badir.
Variants: *Abdar, Ebdaar*

Abdiya (Arabic)
Servant of God
Variants: *Abdeya, Abdiah, Abdiyah, Abdiyya, Abdiyyah*

Abeer (Arabic)
Perfume
Variants: *Abeir, Abir*

Abeira (Arabic)
Perfume - Saffron
Variants: *Abeera, Abeerah, Abira, Abirah*

Abigail (Hebrew)
Father of Exaltation
Name of one of prophet David's wives.

Abilene (English)
A region of the Holy Land in the New Testament, of uncertain origin.

Abinus (Persian, Urdu)
Ebony
Urdu variant of the Persian name Abnus, which means "ebony", a type of wood.
Variants: *Abeenus, Abinoos*

Abrisham (Persian)
Silk
Variants: *Abreesham*

Absaar (Arabic)
Insight - Intellect - Perception - Vision
The name Absaar is used in the Quran.
Variants: *Absar*

Aburah (Arabic)
Fragrance - Perfume

Abyah (Arabic)
Beautiful

Abyan (Arabic)
Clear - Distinct - Eloquent
Variants: *Abyen*

Ada (English)
Noble
Of uncertain origin, possibly a pet form of Adele and similar Germanic names, formed from the element adal ("noble"). It may also be used as a variant of Adah.

Adaan (Arabic)
Blissful - Happy
Variants: *Adan, Adanne*

Adah (Biblical)
Adornment

Adalah (Arabic)
Fairness - Justice

Adalgisa (Italian)
Noble Pledge
Of Germanic origin.

Adan (Arabic)
Blissful - Happy
Variants: *Eden*

Adaniyyah (Arabic)
From the City of Aden

NAMES FOR GIRLS

Adarina (Persian)
Beautiful - Fiery - Passionate
Variants: *Adareena, Adarinaa*

Adawiyah (Arabic)
Type of Plant
It is unclear what exactly this plant is, Arabic sources only say that it grows in the summer.
Variants: *Adaweyyah, Adawiyya, Adawiyyah*

Adda (German)
High-born - Noble
Pet form of Adelheid, which is the German, Dutch, and Scandinavian form Adelaide, an English name of Germanic origin.

Adeebah (Arabic)
Excellent - Good-mannered

Adeela (Arabic)
Excellent - Fair - Just - Moderate - Virtuous
Variants: *Adeelah, Adila, Adilah*

Adeen (Arabic)
Obedient - Righteou
Variants: *Adin, Azeen, Azin*

Adeena (Arabic)
Obedient - Righteou
Variants: *Adeenah, Adina, Adinah, Azeena, Azeenah, Azina, Azinah*

Adela (English)
Noble
Latinate form of Adele.

Adelaide (English)
High-born - Noble
Of Germanic origin.

Adele (English)
Noble
Of Germanic origin.

Adelheid (Dutch, German, Scandinavian)
High-born - Noble
From Adelaide.

Adelina (English)
Noble
Latinate form of Adele.

Adeline (French)
Noble
Diminutive form of Adèle.

Adineh (Persian)
Weekend
Variants: *Adeenah, Adina, Adinah*

Adlaa (Arabic)
Fair - Just

Adlah (Arabic)
Fair - Just

Adlea (Arabic)
Fair - Just
Variants: *Adlia, Adliah, Adliyah, Adliyyah*

Adn (Arabic)
Eden - Place of Everlasting Bliss
Adn is used in the Quran in verse 18:31 and others.
Variants: *Edn*

Adnanah (Arabic)
Resident - Settler

Adniyyah (Arabic)
Inhabitant - Resident

Adolphus (English, Swedish)
Noble Wolf

Adrianna (French)
From Adria
Adria refers to the area near the Adriatic Sea, which is the sea that is on the east of Italy.

Adyan (Arabic)
Creeds - Religions
Variants: *Adiaan, Adian, Adyaan*

Aeni (Arabic)
Pure - True
Variants: *Ainee, Ainy, Aynee, Ayni*

Afaf (Arabic)
Chaste - Modest - Virtuous
Variants: *Afaaf, Affaf*

Afana (Arabic)
Modest - Virtuous
Variants: *Afaana, Afaanah, Afanah*

Afeen (Arabic)
Forgiver - Pardoner
Variants: *Afin*

Afeera (Arabic)
Gazelle
Modern-day variant of Ufairah.
Variants: *Afeerah, Afira, Afirah*

Afifa (Arabic)
Chaste - Modest - Righteous
Variants: *Afeefa, Afeefah, Afefa, Afefah, Afifah*

Afiyat (Arabic)
Health - Recovery
Turkish pronunciation of Afiyah.
Variants: *Aafiyat, Afiat, Afyat*

Afkar (Arabic)
Ideas - Thoughts

Afnan (Arabic)
Spreading Branches of Trees
The name Afnan is mentioned in the Quran.
Variants: *Afnaan*

Afra (Arabic, Persian)
Maple
Variants: *Afraa*

Afraa (Arabic)
Blonde - Fair-skinned - White
Variants: *Afra*

Afrah (Arabic)
Delight - Happiness
Variants: *Afraah, Efrah*

Afreeda (Persian)
Creation - Creature
Variants: *Afreedah, Afrida, Afridah*

Afreedeh (Persian)
Creation - Creature
Variants: *Afreeda, Afreedah, Afrida, Afridah*

Afrisham (Persian)
Silk
Synonym of Abrisham.
Variants: *Afreesham*

Afrouz (Persian)
Illuminating
Variants: *Afruz*

Afrozeh (Persian)
Enlightener - Illuminator
Variants: *Afrooza, Afroozah, Afroozeh, Afroza, Afrozah, Afruzeh*

Afsah (Arabic)
Eloquent - Expressive - Fluent
The name Afsah is mentioned in the Quran.
Variants: *Efseh*

Afsaneh (Kurdish, Persian)
Fable - Myth - Story
Variants: *Afsaana, Afsaaneh, Afsana*

Afshan (Persian)
Disperser - Distributor - Spreader
Variants: *Afshaan*

Afza (Persian)
Advancer - Increaser
Variants: *Afzaa*

Afzoon (Persian)
Needlessness - Plenty
Variants: *Afzun*

Agafya (Russian)
Love
From Greek Agapia.

Agatha (English)
Good - Honorable
From Greek agathos.

Aggie (English, Scottish)
Good - Holy - Honorable - Pure
Pet form of Agnes and Agatha.

Aghla (Arabic)
Precious - Valuable
Variants: *Aghlaa*

Agna (German, Scandinavian)
Holy - Pure
Pet form of Agnethe, German and Scandinavian form of Agnes.

Agnes (Dutch, English, German, Scandinavian)
Holy - Pure

Agnethe (German, Scandinavian)
Holy - Pure

Agreen (Kurdish)
Active - Brave - Fiery - Passionate
Variants: *Agrin*

Ahbab (Arabic)
Beloved Ones
Variants: *Ahbaab*

Ahd (Arabic)
Covenant - Promise

The name Ahd is mentioned in the Quran.

Ahdaf (Arabic)
Goals - Objectives - Targets

Ahdia (Arabic)
Faithful - Sincere - True
Variants: *Ahdeyah, Ahdiya, Ahdiyyah*

Aheedah (Arabic)
Ally - Confederate

Ahida (Arabic)
Caretaker - Promiser
Variants: *Aaheda, Aahedah, Aahida, Aahidah, Aheda, Ahedah, Ahidah*

Ahina (Arabic)
Ascetic - Firm - Unshakable

Ahlam (Arabic)
Dreams
The name Ahlaam is mentioned in the Quran.
Variants: *Ahlaam*

Ahmaraan (Arabic)
Gold - Saffron
Variants: *Ahmaran*

Ahnaf (Arabic)
Upright - Worshiper of God
Variants: *Ehnef*

Ahoo (Persian)
Deer - Gazelle
Variants: *Ahu*

Ahram (Arabic)
Pyramids
Variants: *Ahraam*

Ahvaz (Persian)
[Name of a City]
Name of a city in southern Iran.
Variants: *Ahwaz*

NAMES FOR GIRLS

Ahyas (Arabic)
Brave
Variants: *Ahias*

Aida (Arabic)
Returner - Visitor
Variants: *Aidah, Ayda, Aydah*

Aidan (Arabic)
Tall Palm Tree
Variants: *Aidaan, Aydan, Eidan, Eydan*

Aidana (Arabic)
Tall Palm Tree
Variants: *Aidanah, Aydana*

Aigheen (Persian, Turkish)
Moon-like
Literally "possessor of the moon".

Aigul (Persian, Turkish)
Beautiful - Moon-like - Radiant
Literally "flower of the moon".

Aileen (English, Scottish)
Variant spelling of Eileen, from Aveline, from Avis, of uncertain meaning. In Latin avis means "bird", but the name Avis is likely from another origin.

Aileen (Turkish)
Halo of the Moon

Ailie (Scottish)
Pet form of Aileen. See Aileen.

Ailsa (Scottish)
Elfish - Supernatural - Victory
From Old Norse alf ("elf", "supernatural") and sigi ("victory").

Ain (Arabic)
Fountain - Spring
The name Ain is mentioned in the Quran, such as in verse 88:12.
Variants: *Aene, Aine, Ayn, Ayne, Eiyn*

Ainaz (Persian, Turkish)
Beautiful Like the Moon

Ainsley (English, Scottish)
One Clearing - One Wood
Originally a surname.

Aireen (Kurdish)
Fiery - Passionate
Variants: *Airin, Ayreen*

Aisana (Persian, Turkish)
Beautiful - Brilliant - Moon-like
Variants: *Aysana*

Aisha (Arabic)
Alive - Living-well - Thriving
Variants: *Aaisha, Aaishah, Aayesha, Aayeshah, Aayisha, Aayishah, Aaysha, Aayshah, Aishah, Ayesha, Ayeshah, Ayisha, Ayishah, Aysha, Ayshah*

Aisling (Irish Gaelic)
Dream - Vision

Aisooda (Turkish)
Moon-like
Literally "moon in water".

Ajaar (Arabic)
Rewards
Variants: *Ajar*

Ajab (Arabic)
Amazement - Wonder
The name Ajab is mentioned in the Quran.

Ajam (Arabic)
Date Seed - Foreign - Persian

Ajaweed (Arabic)
Acts of Kindness - Generosity

Ajeeb (Arabic)
Amazing - Wondrous
The name Ajeeb is mentioned in the Quran.

Ajwa (Arabic)
Type of Date
Ajwa is a type of date (the fruit of palm trees) that grows in al-Madinah.
Variants: *Ajua, Ajuaa, Ajwaa*

Akhtar (Persian)
Galaxy - Planet - Star - Sun

Akilina (Russian)
Eagle

Akwan (Arabic)
Cosmos - Universes
Variants: *Akuaan, Akuan, Akwaan*

Ala (Polish)
High-born - Noble
Pet form of Alicja, Polish form of Alice.
Variants: *Aala, Alaa*

Ala (Arabic)
Favors - Wonders
The name Ala is mentioned in the Quran.

Alaa (Persian)
Red - Red-colored - Rosy
Variants: *Ala*

Alaleh (Persian)
Type of Flower
Known as ranunculus in English.

Alamafruz (Arabic, Persian)
Enlightener of the World
Variants: *Alamafrooz*

Alamara (Arabic)
Beautifier of the World
Variants: *Alamaara*

Alana (English)
Rock
Feminine form of Alan.

Alanda (English)
Rock
From Alan and Amanda.

Alannah (English)
Rock
Variant spelling of Alana.

Alaya (Arabic)
Glory - Greatness
Variants: *Alaaia, Alaaya, Alaayaa, Alaia, Alayaa*

Alba (Italian)
Eflish - Supernatural - White
From Latin alba ("white") or Germanic alb ("elf", "supernatural being").

Aleefa (Arabic)
Amiable - Friendly - Kind
Variants: *Aleefah, Alifa, Alifah*

Aleema (Arabic)
Intellectual - Knowledgeable - Learned
Variants: *Aleemah, Alima, Alimah*

Aleen (Persian)
Red - Rosy
Variants: *Alin*

Aleena (Arabic)
Gentleness - Softness
Variants: *Aleeina, Aleina, Alena, Alenaa, Alinaa, Alyena, Alyina*

Aleida (German)
High-born - Noble
From Adelheid.

Alejandra (Spanish)
Defender of Humanity
From Alexandra.

Alena (Czech, German)
Short form of Magdalena (see Magdalene).

Alessandra (Italian)
Defender of Humanity
Italian form of Alexandra.

Alessia (Italian)
Defender
Italian form of Alexia.

Alethea (English)
Truth
From Greek.

Alette (French)
High-born - Noble

Alex (English)
Defender - Defender of Humanity
Short form of Alexander, Alexandra or Alexis.

Alexa (English)
Defender - Defender of Humanity
Short form of Alexandra or variant of Alexis.

Alexandra (English, Scandinavian)
Defender of Humanity
Feminine form of Alexander.

Alexandrina (English)
Defender of Humanity

Alexia (English, German)
Defender

Alexina (Scottish)
Defender - Defender of Humanity
Feminine form of Alex.

Alexis (English, German)
Defender

Aleydis (Dutch)
High-born - Noble

Aliaa (Arabic)
Highest - Uppermost
Variants: *Alea, Alia, Alya, Alyaa, Alyaa'*

Alice (English, French)
High-born - Noble
Variants: *Alys*

Alicia (English, Spanish)
Aristocratic - High in Status - Noble
A form of Alice, derived from Germanic word Adalheidis.

Alicia (English, Spanish)
High-born - Noble
A form of Alice.

Alicja (Polish)
High-born - Noble
Polish form of Alice.

Alida (Hungarian)
High-born - Noble

Alima (Arabic)
Knowledgeable - Scholar
Variants: *Alimah*

Alina (English, German)
High-born - Noble
Variant of Aline.
Variants: *Allina*

Alinda (English, German)
Noble - Soft - Tender
A combination of Alina and Linda, or a form of Adelinde.

Aline (English, French)
High-born - Noble

Alinka (Polish)
High-born - Noble
Pet form of Alicja.

NAMES FOR GIRLS

Alison (English, French, Scottish)
High-born - Noble
Norman diminutive form of Alice.

Alissa (English)
Aristocratic - High in Status - Noble
Variant of Alicia.
Variants: *Alisa, Alyssa*

Alissa (English)
High-born - Noble
Variant of Alicia.

Alix (English)
Defender - Defender of Humanity
Variant of Alex.

Aliyah (Arabic)
Exalted - High Status - Sublime and Superb
The name Alia is mentioned in the Quran in verse 69:22.
Variants: *Aaleea, Aaleia, Aaleya, Aaliyah, Alea, Aleya, Alia, Aliah, Aalia, Aliyah*

Aliyya (Arabic)
Exalted - Great - High - Sublime
Variants: *Aleyya, Aliah, Aliya, Aliyyah, Eliye*

Aliza (Jewish)
Joyful

Aliza (Hebrew)
Joyful

Allamah (Arabic)
Extremely Wise - Knowledgeable

Allegra (English, Italian)
Cheerful - Jaunty

Allie (English)
High-born - Noble
Pet form of Alison.
Variants: *Ally*

Alma (Persian, Turkish)
Apple

Alma (Spanish)
Soul

Alma (English)
Kind - Nourishing
Of uncertain origin, but can be considered the feminine form of Latin almus ("nourishing").

Almas (Persian)
Diamond
Variants: *Almaas*

Almash (Persian)
Diamond
Variant of Almas.
Variants: *Almaash*

Almaz (Persian)
Diamond
Variant of Almas.
Variants: *Almaaz*

Alnoor (Arabic)
Light
The name Alnoor is mentioned in the Quran.
Variants: *Eleanor, Elinor, Elinour, Elnoor, Elnour, Elnur, Ileanor, Ilinor*

Aloisia (English, German)
Warrior
Feminine form of Aloysius.

Alpha (English)
Excellent - Prime
Taken from the first letter of the Greek alphabet.

Altaaf (Arabic)
Gentleness - Kindness
Variants: *Altaf*

Altin (Turkish)
Variants: *Alten*

Altun (Kurdish, Turkish)
Gold
From Turkic (ancient Turkish).
Variants: *Altin, Altoon*

Aludra (Arabic)
Virgin
Variants: *Alodra, Aluza, Aluzraa*

Alvand (Persian)
Agile - Powerful - Strong
Variants: *Alvend*

Alwan (Arabic)
Colors
The name Alwan is mentioned in the Quran.
Variants: *Aluan*

Alwand (Kurdish)
Agile - Powerful - Strong
Variants: *Alwend*

Alyaanah (Arabic)
Great - High in Status

Amaal (Arabic)
Expectations - Hopes
Variants: *Aamaal, Aamal*

Amabel (English)
Lovable

Amad (Arabic)
Age - Era - Period of Time

Amal (Arabic)
Expectation - Hope
The name *Amal* is mentioned in the Quran.
Variants: *Amel, Amele, Amell, Emal, Emel, Emele, Emell, Emelle*

Amala (Arabic)
Hope - Wish
Variants: *Amalah*

Amalia (German)
Hardworking - Industrious
Variants: *Amalie*

Aman (Arabic)
Peace of Mind - Safety - Security
Variants: *Amaan*

Amana (Arabic)
Devotion - Faith - Guardianship

Amana (Aramaic)
Experienced - Skilled

Amanaat (Arabic)
Amanat
The name Amanaat is mentioned in the Quran.
Variants: *Amanat*

Amanah (Arabic)
Devotion - Guardianship - Loyalty - Trust
The name Amanah is mentioned in the Quran.
Variants: *Amaanah, Amana*

Amanat (Arabic, Persian, Turkish, Urdu)
Devotion - Guardianship - Trust
Turkish pronunciation of Amanah.

Amanatullah (Arabic)
God's Consignment

Amanda (Latin)
Lovable

Amani (Arabic)
Hope
The name Amani is mentioned in the Quran in verse 4:123.
Variants: *Amaani, Amanee, Amany*

Amanullah (Arabic)
God's Peace - God's Protection

Amara (Arabic)
Fleet - Tribe
Variants: *Amaara, Amaarah, Amarah*

Amatul Aakhir (Arabic)
Servant of God

Amatul Aala (Arabic)
Servant of God

Amatul Afuw (Arabic)
Servant of God

Amatul Ahad (Arabic)
Servant of God

Amatul Akram (Arabic)
Servant of God

Amatul Aleem (Arabic)
Servant of God

Amatul Awwal (Arabic)
Servant of God

Amatul Azim (Arabic)
Servant of God

Amatul Aziz (Arabic)
Servant of God

Amatul Baatin (Arabic)
Servant of God

Amatul Baseer (Arabic)
Servant of God

Amatul Basit (Arabic)
Servant of God

Amatul Birr (Arabic)
Servant of God

Amatul Elah (Arabic)
Servant of God

Amatul Fattah (Arabic)
Servant of God

Amatul Ghaffar (Arabic)
Servant of God

Amatul Ghafoor (Arabic)
Servant of God

Amatul Ghani (Arabic)
Servant of God

Amatul Haafiz (Arabic)
Servant of God

Amatul Hadi (Arabic)
Servant of God

Amatul Hafeez (Arabic)
Servant of God

Amatul Hai (Arabic)
Servant of God

Amatul Hakam (Arabic)
Servant of God

Amatul Hakeem (Arabic)
Servant of God

Amatul Haleem (Arabic)
Servant of God

Amatul Hameed (Arabic)
Servant of God

Amatul Haq (Arabic)
Servant of God

Amatul Haseeb (Arabic)
Servant of God

Amatul Jabar (Arabic)
Servant of God

Amatul Jaleel (Arabic)
Servant of God

NAMES FOR GIRLS

Amatul Jameel (Arabic)
Servant of God

Amatul Kabir (Arabic)
Servant of God

Amatul Kareem (Arabic)
Servant of God

Amatul Khabir (Arabic)
Servant of God

Amatul Khaliq (Arabic)
Servant of God

Amatul Khallaq (Arabic)
Servant of God

Amatul Latif (Arabic)
Servant of God

Amatul Maalik (Arabic)
Servant of God

Amatul Majeed (Arabic)
Servant of God

Amatul Maleek (Arabic)
Servant of God

Amatul Manaan (Arabic)
Servant of God

Amatul Mateen (Arabic)
Servant of God

Amatul Mawla (Arabic)
Servant of God

Amatul Mubeen (Arabic)
Servant of God

Amatul Muhaimin (Arabic)
Servant of God

Amatul Muheet (Arabic)
Servant of God

Amatul Mujeeb (Arabic)
Servant of God

Amatul Muqaddim (Arabic)
Servant of God

Amatul Muqit (Arabic)
Servant of God

Amatul Muqtadir (Arabic)
Servant of God
Variants: *Amatul Muqtader*

Amatul Musawwir (Arabic)
Servant of God
Variants: *Amatul Musawir*

Amatul Mutaal (Arabic)
Servant of God
Variants: *Amatul Mutal*

Amatul Mutaali (Arabic)
Servant of God
Variants: *Amatul Mutali*

Amatul Naseer (Arabic)
Servant of God
Variants: *Amatul Nasir*

Amatul Qadeer (Arabic)
Servant of God
Variants: *Amatul Qadir*

Amatul Qadir (Arabic)
Servant of God
Variants: *Amatul Qader*

Amatul Qahir (Arabic)
Servant of God
Variants: *Amatul Qaher*

Amatul Qareeb (Arabic)
Servant of God
Variants: *Amatul Qarib*

Amatul Qawee (Arabic)
Servant of God
Variants: *Amatul Qawi*

Amatul Qayyum (Arabic)
Servant of God
Variants: *Amatul Qayum*

Amatul Quddus (Arabic)
Servant of God
Variants: *Amatul Qudus*

Amatul Shaheed (Arabic)
Servant of God
Variants: *Amatul Shahid*

Amatul Shakoor (Arabic)
Servant of God
Variants: *Amatul Shakur*

Amatul Tawwab (Arabic)
Servant of God
Variants: *Amatul Tawab*

Amatul Wadud (Arabic)
Servant of God
Variants: *Amatul Wadood*

Amatul Wahaab (Arabic)
Servant of God
Variants: *Amatul Wahhab*

Amatul Wahid (Arabic)
Servant of God
Variants: *Amatul Waheed*

Amatul Waleei (Arabic)
Servant of God
Variants: *Amatul Wai*

Amatul Waris (Arabic)
Servant of God
Variants: *Amatul Waaris*

Amatullah (Arabic)
Servant of God
Variants: *Amat Ullah, Amatollah*

Amatur Rab (Arabic)
Servant of God
Variants: *Amatul Rab*

Amatur Raheem (Arabic)
Servant of God
Variants: *Amatul Raheem*

Amatur Rahman (Arabic)
Servant of God
Variants: *Amatul Rahman*

Amatur Raqeeb (Arabic)
Servant of God
Variants: *Amatul Raqeeb*

Amatur Razzaq (Arabic)
Servant of God
Variants: *Amatul Razzaq*

Amatus Salam (Arabic)
Servant of God
Variants: *Amatul Salam*

Amatus Samad (Arabic)
Servant of God
Variants: *Amatul Samad*

Amatus Samee (Arabic)
Servant of God
Variants: *Amatul Samee*

Amatuz Zaahir (Arabic)
Servant of God
Variants: *Amatul Zahir*

Amber (Arabic, Persian)
Amber - Ambergris
Variants: *Ambar*

Amber (English)
Amber (gemstone)

Ameena (Arabic)
Loyal - Trustworthy
Variants: *Ameeina, Ameeinah, Ameeineh, Ameenah, Ameene, Ameeneh, Ameeyna, Ameeynah, Ameeyneh, Ameina, Ameinah, Ameineh, Ameyna, Ameynah, Ameyne, Amiena, Amienah, Amiene, Amieneh, Amina, Aminah, Amineh, Amiyna, Amiynah, Amiyne,*

Amiyneh, Amyna, Amynah, Amyneh, Emeeyna, Emeina, Emeinah, Emeine, Emeineh, Emeynah, Emeyneh, Emiena, Emina, Eminah, Emine, Emineh, Emyna, Emyne

Amelia (English)
Hardworking - Industrious

Amelie (English, French)
Hardworking - Industrious
In French it is spelled with an accent (Amélie).

Amial (Arabic)
Lighthouses
Variants: *Amyaal, Amyal*

Amila (Arabic)
Hoper - Striver - Worker
Variants: *Aamila, Aamilah, Amela, Amelah, Amilah*

Amina (Arabic)
Safe
The name *Amina* is mentioned in the Quran.
Variants: *Aamena, Aamenah, Aameneh, Aamina, Aaminah, Aamine, Aamineh, Amena, Aminah, Amna, Amnah*

Aminan (Arabic)
Calm - Unafraid
Variants: *Ameenan*

Aminat (Arabic)
Faithful Ones - Trustworthy Ones
Variants: *Ameenaat*

Amira (Arabic)
Chief - Commander - Leader - Ruler
Variants: *Amirah*

Amiraa (Arabic)
Chief - Leader
Variants: *Amira*

Amita (English)
Friendship
Altered form of Amity.

Amity (English)
Friendship

Amlaas (Arabic)
Plains - Steppes

Amlahan (Arabic)
Dew

Amlas (Arabic)
Delicate - Smooth - Soft

Amman (Arabic)
Citizen - Resident
Also name of the capital of Jordan.
Variants: *Amaan, Aman*

Ammatun Naafe (Arabic)
Servant of God
Variants: *Amatul Nafi, Ammatunnafi*

Ammuna (Arabic)
Faithful - Trustworthy
Variants: *Amoona, Amoonah, Amuna*

Ammuni (Arabic)
Away From Harm - Safe
Variants: *Amuni*

Ammura (Arabic)
Beautiful - Captivating - Lovable

Ammuri (Arabic)
Beautiful - Captivating - Lovable

Amnan (Arabic)
Safe - Secure
Variants: *Amnaan*

NAMES FOR GIRLS

Amnati (Arabic)
My Hope - My Wish
Variants: *Amnaty*

Amnian (Arabic)
Safe - Secure
Variants: *Amniyan*

Amras (Arabic)
Mountains
Variants: *Amraas*

Amsal (Arabic)
Best - Exemplary - Optimal
The name Amsal is mentioned in the Quran.
Variants: *Amthal*

Amy (English)
Beloved

Amyali (Arabic)
Ambitious - Desirous
Variants: *Amialy*

Ana (Persian, Turkish)
Mother - Pillar - Principal

Ana (Spanish)
God Has Favored Me
Spanish form of Anne.

Anaa (Arabic)
Full Potential - Maturity
Variants: *Ana*

Anaat (Arabic)
Patience - Vritue
Variants: *Anat, Enaaat, Enat*

Anahid (Persian)
Blameless - Pure - Untained

Anahit (Persian)
Blameless - Pure - Untained

Anahita (Persian)
Blameless - Pure - Untained

Anan (Arabic)
Clouds
Variants: *Anaan*

Anaqat (Persian, Urdu)
Elegance
Variants: *Anaaqat*

Anar (Arabic)
Glowing - Radiant
Variants: *Anaar, Anaar*

Anar (Persian)
Pomegranate

Anarat (Arabic)
Beauty - Clarity - Radiance

Anasa (Arabic)
Comfort - Tranquility
Variants: *Anasah*

Anasat (Arabic)
Comfort - Tranquility
Turkish pronunciation of Anasa.
Variants: *Anaasat*

Anasi (Arabic)
Consoler - Goo Friend
Variants: *Anasee*

Anasiya (Arabic)
Consoler - Good Friend
Variants: *Anasia, Anasiyyah*

Anastasia (Russian)
Resurrection

Anat (Arabic)
Calmness - Composure - Forbearance - Poise
Variants: *Anatte*

Anaya (Arabic)
Care - Diligence - Protection
Variants: *Anaaya, Anaayah, Anaia, Anaiah, Anayah*

Anbarin (Persian, Urdu)
Fragrant
Variants: *Anbareen*

Andaleeb (Arabic, Urdu)
Nightingale
Variants: *Andalib*

Andalus (Arabic)
Andalusia

Andalusi (Arabic)
From Andalusia
Variants: *Andaloosi*

Andisheh (Persian)
Thinking - Thought
Variants: *Andeesha, Andeeshah, Andeesheh, Andisha, Andishah*

Andra (English, Scottish)
Warrior
In English it is the feminine form of Andrew, while in Scottish it is a male variant of Andrew.

Andrea (English)
Manliness - Virility
Feminine form of Andreas.

Andriana (English)
Silvery - Warrior
A modern creation based on Andrea, Arianna and Adriana.

Aneesa (Arabic)
Close Friend - Comforter
Variants: *Aneesah, Anesa, Anessa, Anisa, Anisa, Anisah, Anissa, Anissa, Anissah*

Aneesa (Persian)
Essence of Love - True Love

Anfa (Arabic)
Dignity - Self-respect
Variants: *Anfah*

Anfani (Arabic)
Dignified

Anfas (Arabic)
Breaths - Souls - Spirits
Variants: *Anfaas*

Anghum (Arabic)
Melodies - Tunes
Variants: *Anghom*

Anhar (Arabic)
Rivers
Variants: *Anhaar*

Anifa (Arabic)
Dignified
Variants: *Aneefah*

Aniq (Arabic)
Attractive - Elegant - Graceful - Stylish
Variants: *Aneek, Aneeq, Aneiq, Anik*

Aniqah (Arabic)
Elegant - Stylish
Variants: *Aneeqa, Aneeqah, Aniqa*

Anita (English, Spanish)
God Has Favored Me
Pet form of Ana.
Variants: *Aneeta, Anitaa*

Anita (Persian)
Kindness - Mercy

Aniyah (Arabic)
Affectionate - Caring - Consoler
Variants: *Aaniya, Aaniyah, Aneya, Aneyah*

Aniza (Arabic)
Staff - Sword
Variants: *Aneeza, Aneezah, Anizah*

Anjam (Arabic)
Star
Variants: *Anjaam*

Anjud (Arabic)
Heights - Plateaus
Variants: *Anjod*

Anjum (Arabic)
Stars
Variants: *Anjom, Anjoum*

Anjuman (Kurdish, Persian, Urdu)
Committee - Council
Variants: *Anjoman*

Anmar (Arabic)
Tigers
Variants: *Anmaar*

Ann (Arabic)
Occassion - Time
The name Ann is mentioned in the Quran.
Variants: *Aan, Aann*

Annabel (English)
Lovable
Form of Amabel or Anna.

Annali (Turkish)
Gentle - Kind
Literally "motherly", "mother-like".

Anne (English, French, German)
God Has Favored Me
Variants: *Ann, Anna*

Anneli (Scandinavian)
God Has Favored Me - My God is Bountiful
Shortened form of Anneliese.

Anneliese (German, Scandinavian)
God Has Favored Me - My God is Bountiful
From Anne and Liese.

Annella (English, Scottish)
God Has Favored Me
Variant of Anne.

Annetta (English)
God Has Favored Me
Variant of Annette.

Annette (French)
God Has Favored Me
Pet form of Anne.

Annice (English)
Holy - Pure
Variant of Annis.

Annika (Swedish)
God Has Favored Me
Pet form of Anna.

Annis (English, Scottish)
Holy - Pure
Medieval form of Agnes.
Variants: *Annys*

Anoud (Arabic)
Loved - Popular - Strong-willed

Anoush (Persian)
Eternal - Immortal
Variants: *Anoosh, Anush*

Anousha (Persian)
Eternal - Everlastin - Immortal
Variants: *Anooshah, Anoosheh, Anoushah, Anousheh, Anusha, Anusheh*

Ansab (Arabic)
Better - Worthier

Ansam (Arabic)
Breezes
Variants: *Ansaam*

Ansharah (Arabic)
Cheer - Relaxation - Relief
Non-standard pronunciation of

NAMES FOR GIRLS

Inshirah.
Variants: *Ansharaah*

Antarah (Arabic)
Brave

Antoinette (French)
Flourishing Woman
Feminine diminutive form of Antoine.

Antonia (Dutch, English, German, Italian, Portuguese, Scandinavian, Spanish)
Flourishing Woman
Feminine form of Anthony.

Anum (Arabic)
God's Blessings - God's Favors
The name Anum is mentioned in the Quran.
Variants: *Anom, Anoum*

Anumullah (Arabic)
God's Blessings - God's Favors

Anush (Arabic)
Beautiful - Handsome

Anusha (Persian)
Creed

Anushah (Persian)
Everlasting - Immortal
Anushah is a variant of the name Anusheh.

Anusheh (Persian)
Everlasting - Immortal

Anwaar (Arabic)
Lights - Radiant
Variants: *Anwar*

Anwara (Arabic)
Glow - Light - Radiance
Variants: *Anuaara, Anwaarah*

Anzar (Arabic)
Eyesight - Vision
Variants: *Andhar*

April (English)
Open
Name of the fourth month of the year, named so probably because during April buds open.

Aqeelah (Arabic)
Discerning - Reasonable - Sensible - Wise
Variants: *Aqeela, Aqila, Aqilah, Aquilleah*

Aqiba (Arabic)
Consequence - Result
The name Aqiba is mentioned in the Quran.
Variants: *Aaqibah, Aqeba, Aqebah, Aqibah*

Aqidah (Arabic)
Creed - Faith - Tenet
Variants: *Aqeeda, Aqeedah, Aqida*

Aqiq (Arabic, Persian)
Agate
Variants: *Aqeeq*

Aqrab (Arabic)
Scorpion
Variants: *Akrab*

Aqsaa (Arabic)
Farthest
Name of the third holiest site in Islam: Masjid al-Aqsa (al-Aqsa Mosque) in Palestine.
Variants: *Aksa, Aqsa*

Ara (Kurdish, Persian)
Adorner - Beautifier
Variants: *Araa*

Araa (Arabic)
Opinions - Perspectives
Variants: *Ara, Ara'*

Araarah (Arabic)
Greatness - Might - Strength

Araj (Urdu)
Fragrance
Variant of Arabic boy and girl name Arij.
Variants: *Aaraj*

Aram (Kurdish, Persian, Urdu)
Calm - Quiet
Variants: *Aaram, Araam*

Arameh (Persian)
Calm - Serene
Variants: *Araameh, Arama, Aramah*

Aramesh (Persian)
Calmness - Serenity
Variants: *Aramish*

Aran (Kurdish, Persian, Urdu)
Flat Land - Plains
Variants: *Aaran, Araan*

Arang (Persian, Urdu)
Color - Phase - State
Variants: *Aarang*

Aranka (Hungarian)
Gold

Arar (Arabic)
Lent Lily - Wild Daffodil
A type of flower.

Aras (Kurdish, Persian)
Balanced - Equal
Variants: *Aaras, Araas*

Arash (Persian)
Brilliant - Dazzling - Radiant
Variants: *Aarash, Aaresh, Aresh*

Arasteh (Persian)
Adorned - Beautiful
Variants: *Araasta, Araasteh, Arasta, Arastah*

Arax (Armenian)
Armenian name for the Aras river.

Araz (Azerbaijani)
Azerbaijani name for the Aras river.

Arbab (Arabic)
Chiefs - Masters
The name Arbab is used in the Quran.
Variants: *Arbaab*

Areebah (Arabic)
Intelligent - Wise
Variants: *Areiba, Areyba, Ariba, Aribah*

Areefa (Arabic)
Knowledgeable - Learned - Wise
Variants: *Areefah, Arifa, Arifah*

Areej (Arabic)
Fragrance
Variants: *Arij*

Areeqa (Arabic)
Deep-rooted - High-born - Noble
Variants: *Areeqah, Ariqa, Ariqah*

Areesa (Persian)
Excellent - Noble
Variants: *Areessa, Arisa, Arysa*

Areesh (Persian)
Intelligent - Wise
Variants: *Arish*

Areesha (Arabic)
Howdah
Variants: *Areeshah, Arisha, Arishah*

Areez (Persian)
Dew Drop - Leader
Variants: *Ariz*

Arf (Arabic)
Fragrance - Scent

Arfa (Arabic)
Elevated - Exalted - Great
Variants: *Arfa', Arfaa*

Arfaana (Arabic)
Spiritual Knowledge - Wisdom
Non-standard variant of the name Irfana.
Variants: *Arfaanah, Arfana, Arfanah*

Arghavan (Persian)
Judas Tree
A type of tree.

Arhaa (Arabic)
Calm - Serene
Variants: *Arhaa*

Arham (Arabic)
Compassionate - Kind - Merciful
The name Arham is mentioned in the Quran in verse 12:64.

Ariana (Persian)
Excellent - Noble
Feminine form of Aryan/Arian.
Variants: *Aariana, Aaryana, Areana, Ariaana, Aryaana, Aryana*

Arianaz (Persian)
Beautiful - Excellent
Variants: *Aryanaz*

Arinah (Arabic)
Lion's Den

Ariqaat (Arabic)
High-born - Noble

Armaghan (Persian, Urdu)
Gift
Variants: *Armagan, Armaghaan*

Armita (Persian)
Humble - Pure - Virtuous
Variants: *Armeeta, Armitaa*

Arnavaz (Persian)
Bringer of Mercy
Variants: *Arnawaz*

Arnica (Persian)
Type of Flower
Known as Arnica in the West.

Arnoush (Persian)
Eternal - Noble - Pure
Variants: *Aarnush, Arnoosh, Arnush*

Aroob (Arabic)
Cheerful - Happy - One Who Loves Her Husband
Variants: *Aroub, Arub*

Arooba (Arabic)
Cheerful - Happy - One Who Loves Her Husband
Variants: *Aroobah, Aruba, Arubah*

Aroofa (Arabic)
Knowledgeable - Patient - Wise
Variants: *Aroofah, Arufa, Arufah*

Aroos (Arabic)
Beautiful - Bride
n
Variants: *Arous, Arus*

Aroosa (Arabic)
Beautiful - Bride
Variants: *Aroosah, Arusa, Arusah*

Aroush (Persian, Urdu)
Brilliant - Dazzlig - Radiant
Variants: *Aroosh, Arush*

Arsh (Arabic)
Power - Throne
The name Arsh is mentioned in the Quran.

NAMES FOR GIRLS

Arshan (Arabic)
Thrones
Variants: *Arshaan*

Arsheeda (Persian)
Brilliant - Dazzling - Pure
Variants: *Arshida*

Arsheen (Persian)
Good Friend
Variants: *Aarshin, Arshin*

Arshi (Arabic)
Royal
Literally meaning "worthy of a throne".
Variants: *Arshee, Arshy*

Arta (Persian)
Pure - Sacred - Virtuous
Variants: *Aarta, Artaa*

Artadukht (Persian)
Righteous - Virtuous
Literally "righteous girl".
Variants: *Artadokht*

Arteena (Persian)
Pure - Virtuous
Variants: *Artina*

Arubiyyah (Arabic)
Elouent - Fluent

Arveen (Persian)
Experiment - Test
Variants: *Arvin*

Arwaa (Arabic)
Agile - Beautiful - Ibex
Variants: *Arwa*

Arya (Persian)
Excellent - Noble
Variants: *Aria, Ariaa, Aryaa*

Aryan (Persian)
Excellent - Noble
Variants: *Aarian, Aaryan, Ariaan, Arian, Aryaan*

Arz (Arabic)
Breadth - Mountain - Width

Arzandeh (Persian)
Precious - Worthy
Variants: *Arzanda*

Asa (Persian)
Adornment - Likeness - Might - Power - Similarity
Variants: *Aasa, Asaa*

Asaalat (Arabic)
Greatness - Nobleness - Originality
Turkish pronunciation of Asalah.
Variants: *Asalat*

Asadah (Arabic)
Lionness
Variants: *Asadeh*

Asah (Arabic)
Correct - Healthy - Proper
Variants: *Aseh*

Asal (Arabic)
Honey
The name Asal is mentioned in the Quran.
Variants: *Esel*

Asalah (Arabic)
Greatness - Nobleness - Originality
Variants: *Asaala, Asaalah, Asala*

Asali (Arabic)
Honey-like - Sweet
Variants: *Asalee, Asaly*

Asareer (Arabic)
Good Features of the Face
Variants: *Asarir*

Asareh (Persian)
Star
Variants: *Asaara, Asara, Asarah*

Asbah (Arabic)
Beautiful
Variants: *Esbeh*

Asdaf (Arabic)
Seashells
Variants: *Asdaaf*

Aseel (Arabic)
Creative - Deep-rooted - Evening Time - High-born - Nighttime - Original
The name Aseel is mentioned in the Quran.
Variants: *Asil, Assil*

Aseela (Arabic)
Creative - Deep-rooted - High-born - Original
Variants: *Aseelah, Asila, Asilah*

Asfa (Arabic)
Pure - Purest
Variants: *Asfaa*

Asfiya (Arabic)
Pure Ones
Variants: *Asfiaa, Asfiyaa*

Asfour (Arabic, Urdu)
Bird
Variant of Arabic Osfur.
Variants: *Asfoor, Asfur*

Asfoureh (Urdu)
Bird
Variant of Arabic Osfurah.
Variants: *Asfoora, Asfura, Asfureh*

Asha (Persian)
Adornment - Likeness - Similarity
Synonym of Asa.

Asheeqa (Arabic)
Beloved - In Love
Variants: *Asheeqah, Ashiqa, Ashiqah*

Ashena (Persian)
Acquainted - Friend
Variants: *Aashena, Aashenaa, Ashenaa*

Ashiqah (Arabic)
In Love - Obsessed

Ashiya (Urdu)
Alive - Prospering
Non-standard variant of Aisha or Asiya.

Ashley (English)
From the Meadow of Ash Trees

Ashna (Persian)
Acquainted - Friend
Variants: *Aashna, Ashnaa*

Ashofteh (Persian)
Anxious - Confused - Excited - In Love
Variants: *Aashofta, Ashofta, Ashoftah, Ashuftah, Ashufteh*

Ashti (Kurdish)
Peace
Variants: *Aashti, Ashtee, Ashty*

Ashwaq (Arabic)
Longing - Yearning
Variants: *Ashuaq, Ashwaaq*

Asifah (Arabic)
Hurricane - Storm
The name Asifah is used in the Quran.
Variants: *Aaasifah, Aasifa, Asefa, Asefah*

Asima (Arabic)
Chaste - Guardian - Protector - Virtuous
Variants: *Aasema, Aasemah, Aasima, Asema, Asemah, Asimah*

Asiya (Arabic)
Melancholic - Pensive - Wishful
Variants: *Asya*

Asiyeh (Arabic, Persian)
Melancholic - Wistful
Variants: *Aseya, Aseyah, Asiah, Asiya, Asiyah*

Asma (Arabic)
Elevated - Exalted - Great - High
Variants: *Asma', Asmaa, Asmaa'*

Asmar (Arabic)
Brown - Tan
Describes a person whose skin color is not too dark and not too light.

Asna (Arabic)
Brilliant - Radiant
Variants: *Asnaa, Esna, Esnaa*

Asrar (Arabic)
Mysteries - Secrets
Variants: *Asraar*

Asreen (Kurdish)
Drop of Tear
Variants: *Asrin*

Asu (Persian)
Agile - Gazelle - Swift

Asudeh (Persian)
At Peace - Calm - Tranquil
Variants: *Asooda, Asoodah, Asoodeh, Asuda, Asudah, Asudeh*

Asya (Kurdish, Persian)
Asia - Windmill
Variants: *Asia, Asiaa, Asyaa*

Asya (Russian)
God Has Favored Me - Resurrection
Russian pet form of Anastasia and Anna.

Atafah (Arabic)
Affectionate - Compassionate

Atanaz (Persian, Turkish)
Father's Beloved
Variants: *Ataanaz*

Atarin (Persian)
Fiery - Rosy
Variants: *Atareen*

Atarisa (Persian)
Fiery - Rosy
Variants: *Atareesa*

Ataya (Arabic)
Gifts - Gifts from God
Variants: *Ataaya, Atayaa*

Atayat (Arabic)
Gifts

Ateebah (Arabic)
Gentle - Soft

Ateef (Arabic)
Affectionate - Compassionate

Ateefah (Arabic)
Affectionate - Compassionate

Ateen (Persian)
Created - Existing - Mature
Variants: *Atin*

Ateeqa (Arabic)
Ancient - Freed - Liberated - Noble
Variants: *Ateeqah, Atiqa, Atiqah*

Ateera (Arabic)
Fragrant
Variants: *Ateerah, Atera, Atira, Atiraa, Atirah*

NAMES FOR GIRLS

Atefeh (Arabic)
Affection - Emotion - Instinct
Persian variant of Atifa.

Atfah (Arabic)
Affection - Compassion

Atfat (Arabic)
Affection - Compassion

Atheel (Arabic)
Deep-rooted - High-born - Noble
Variants: *Aseel, Asil*

Atifa (Arabic)
Affection - Emotion - Instinct
Variants: *Atefa Atefah, Atifah*

Atiyaa (Arabic)
Gift

Atiyya (Arabic)
Gift - Gift from God
Variants: *Atea, Ateya, Ateyya, Ateyyah, Atia, Atiah, Atiyah, Atiyyah, Atya, Etiye, Etiyye*

Atiyyaat (Arabic)
Gifts

Atiyyatullah (Arabic)
Gift from God

Atqaa (Arabic)
Good - Honorable - Virtuous

Attarah (Arabic)
Perfume-maker

Attawah (Arabic)
Generous - Philanthropist

Atubah (Arabic)
Delicate - Gentle - Soft

Atusa (Persian)
Learned - Skilled

Variants: *Atoosa, Atosa, Atosaa, Atusaa*

Atyaaf (Arabic)
Images in the Mind - Thoughts
Variants: *Atiaf*

Aubrey (English)
One Who Rules With Elf Wisdom

Audrey (English)
Noble Strength

Augusta (Latin)
Majestic - Venerable

Auraq (Arabic)
Dust-colored - Sand-colored
Variants: *Awraaq*

Aurelia (Latin)
Golden

Ausa (Arabic)
Gift - Help - Support
Variants: *Awsa*

Ausaq (Arabic)
Loads
Variants: *Authaq, Awthaq*

Ava (Persian)
Melody - Opinion - Song - Voice
Variants: *Aava, Aavaa, Avaa*

Avan (Persian)
Guard

Avaz (Persian)
Melody - Musical Voice
Variants: *Aavaz, Aawaz, Avaaz, Awaz*

Aveed (Persian)
Intelligence - Sense - Wisdom

Aveen (Persian)
Crystal Clear - Pure - Transparent
Variants: *Avin*

Aveen (Kurdish)
Love

Avesta (Persian)
Fellowship - Foundation - Principle
Name of a ancient language of Persia.

Avishan (Persian)
Spearmint
Variants: *Aveeshan*

Avizeh (Persian)
Earrings - Pendant
Variants: *Aveeza, Aveezeh, Aviza, Avizah*

Avril (English)
April
Variants: *Averell, Averill*

Awafita (Arabic)
Shepherdesses
Variants: *Awafetah, Awafitah*

Awaidia (Arabic)
Consoler - Visitor of the Sick
Variants: *Awayidiyyah*

Awaisha (Arabic)
Alive - Prospering

Awaiza (Arabic)
Consoler

Awamila (Arabic)
Active - Industrious
Variants: *Awamilah*

Awamira (Arabic)
Long-lived

Awarif (Arabic)
Intelligent - Wise

Awat (Kurdish)
Hope - Wish

Awatif (Arabic)
Emotions - Instincts - Passions
Variants: *Awaatef, Awaatif, Awatef*

Awayeda (Arabic)
Guide - Visitor of the Sick
Variants: *Awayidah*

Awb (Arabic)
Repentance
Variants: *Aub*

Awbi (Arabic)
Repentant
Variants: *Awby*

Awbia (Arabic)
Repentant
Variants: *Awbiyyah*

Awdaq (Arabic)
Friendly - Genial - Intimate
Variants: *Audaq*

Awdiya (Arabic)
Valleys
Variants: *Audia*

Awena (Kurdish)
Mirror
Variants: *Aawena, Awene*

Awfa (Arabic)
Faithful - True
The name Awfa is mentioned in the Quran.
Variants: *Aufa, Awfaa*

Awisa (Arabic)
Beautiful - Dimpled

Awishan (Kurdish)
Spearmint
Variants: *Aweeshan*

Awja (Arabic)
Pinnacle - Top
Variants: *Auja, Awjah*

Awla (Arabic)
Worthier
Variants: *Aulaa*

Awlya (Arabic)
Close Friends - Supporters
Variants: *Auliya*

Awqa (Arabic)
Guarding - Protective
Variants: *Auqaa*

Awsal (Arabic)
Becoming Closer to God
Variants: *Ausaal*

Awsam (Arabic)
Badges of Honor
Variants: *Awsaam*

Awsima (Arabic)
Badges of Honor
Variants: *Ausima, Awsimah*

Awwalan (Arabic)
Advanced Ones - First Ones
Variants: *Awalaan*

Awwazah (Arabic)
Restitutioner

Ayaat (Arabic)
Proofs - Signs - Verses of Scripture
The name Ayaat is mentioned in the Quran.
Variants: *Aayaat, Aayat, Ayat*

Ayah (Arabic)
Proofs - Signs - Verses of Scripture
The name Ayah is mentioned in the Quran.
Variants: *Aaya, Aayah, Aya*

Ayamin (Arabic)
Blessed Ones - Fortunate Ones
Variants: *Ayaamin, Ayamen*

Ayan (Persian)
Inspiration - Long Night
Variants: *Aayaan, Aayan, Ayaan, Ayaan, Ayyan*

Ayan (Arabic)
Era - Time
The name Ayan is mentioned in the Quran in verse 51:12.

Ayana (Arabic)
Beautiful - Perceptive
Literally means "one who has large beautiful eyes".
Variants: *Ayaana, Ayaanah, Ayanah, Ayyanah*

Ayaneh (Persian)
Inspiration - Long Night
Variants: *Ayaaneh*

Ayasha (Arabic)
Alive - Prosperous
Variants: *Ayyashah*

Ayat (Arabic)
Proof - Sign of God's Greatness - Verse of the Quran
Ayat is the Turkish pronunciation of Ayah.
Variants: *Ayet*

Ayd (Arabic)
Power - Strength
Variants: *Aid, Eyd*

Aydania (Arabic)
Slender - Tall
Variants: *Aidaniyyah, Aydaniyyah*

Ayden (Turkish)
Educated - Enlightened - Intellectual
Variants: *Aaidin, Aaydin, Aiden, Aidin, Aydin*

NAMES FOR GIRLS

Aydi (Arabic)
Hands - Power - Strength
The name Aydi is mentioned in the Quran.
Variants: *Aidi, Aidy, Aydee*

Ayeh (Arabic)
Proof of God's Greatness - Verse of the Quran
Ayeh is the Persian variant of the Arabic girl name Ayah
Variants: *Aayeh*

Ayineh (Persian)
Mirror
Variants: *Aina, Aineh, Ayena, Ayeneh, Ayina, Ayna*

Ayla (Turkish)
Halo of the Moon

Ayli (Turkish)
Moonlight

Ayna (Arabic)
Beautiful-eyed
Variants: *Aina, Ainaa, Aynaa, Eina*

Aynaa (Turkmen)
Mirror
Variants: *Ainaa*

Aynoor (Arabic, Turkish)
Moonlight
Variants: *Ainoor, Ainur, Aynur*

Ayoosh (Arabic)
Alive - Long-lived
Variants: *Ayush, Ayyoosh, Ayyush*

Aysa (Persian, Turkish)
Beautiful - Moon-like - Radiant

Aysan (Persian, Turkish)
Beautiful - Moon-like - Radiant

Ayse (Arabic)
Alive - Prosperous

Ayse, also written as Ayşe, is the Turkish variant of the Arabic girl name Aisha.
Variants: *Ayşe*

Aysen (Turkish)
Moon-like

Aysheen (Turkish)
Moon-like
Aysheen is a Turkish name for girls that means "moonlike", and figuratively it means "beautiful".

Aysoo (Turkish)
Moon-like
Literally "moon water".

Aytak (Persian, Turkish)
Beautiful - Moon-like - Radiant - Unique
Literally "lone moon".

Aytan (Persian, Turkish)
Beautiful - Brilliant - Moon-like
Variants: *Aitan*

Ayusha (Arabic)
Alive - Prosperous

Ayyam (Arabic)
Days
Variants: *Aiam, Ayaam*

Azad (Kurdish, Persian, Urdu)
Free - Sovereign
Variants: *Aazaad, Aazad, Azaad*

Azaddokht (Persian)
Free - High-born - Noble
Variants: *Azad Dokht*

Azadeh (Persian)
Free - High-born - Noble
Variants: *Azaada, Azaadah, Azaadeh, Azada, Azadah*

Azal (Arabic, Persian)
Eternity - Perpetuity

Azalia (Arabic)
Eternal - Perpertual
Variants: *Azaalia, Azalea, Azalea, Azaleah, Azaliaa, Azaliah, Azaliya, Azaliyah, Azaliyya, Azaliyyah*

Azalia (Arabic)
Dahlia

Azarakhsh (Persian)
Lightning
Variants: *Azerakhesh*

Azardokht (Persian)
Beautiful - Rose-colored - Rosy

Azari (Arabic, Persian)
Maidens - Virgins

Azarm (Persian)
Kindness - Modesty - Virtue
Variants: *Aazarm*

Azayiz (Arabic)
Mighty - Powerful

Azbah (Arabic)
Fresh Water

Azeebah (Arabic)
Fresh Water

Azeema (Arabic)
Determined - Resolved
Variants: *Azeemah, Azimah*

Azeen (Persian)
Adornment - Beautification - Creed - System
Variants: *Azin*

Azila (Arabic)
Guardian - Protector
Variants: *Aazelah, Aazila, Aazilah, Azela*

Azita (Persian)
Free - High-born - Noble

31

Variants: *Aazeeta, Aazita, Azeeta, Azitaa*

Aziza (Arabic)
Beloved - Dear - Exalted - Great - Noble
Variants: *Azeeza, Azeezah, Azizah*

Azmia (Arabic)
Brave - Determined - Resolute
Variants: *Azmeah, Azmeea, Azmeeah, Azmeya, Azmiah, Azmiya, Azmiyah*

Azra (Arabic)
Virgin
Variants: *Adhra, Adra, Adraa, Azraa, Ezra*

Azrah (Arabic)
Help - Support

Azyan (Arabic)
Adornments - Decorations - Virtues
Variants: *Azian*

Azza (Arabic)
Gazelle - Young Gazelle
Variants: *Aza, Azah, Azzah*

Azzaa (Arabic)
Gazelle

Azzat (Arabic, Turkish)
Gazelle
Turkish pronunciation of Azzah.

NAMES FOR GIRLS

B

Baan (Arabic)
Slender - Tall

Baanah (Arabic)
Slender - Tall
Variants: *Bana*

Baaqa (Arabic)
Bouquet

Badaa (Arabic)
Energy - Goal - Strength

Badawiya (Arabic)
Bedouin

Badaya (Arabic)
Beginnings - Genesis

Badeea (Arabic)
Creative - Innovative

Badeeda (Arabic)
Example - Sample - Specimen

Badeela (Arabic)
Replacement

Badhaa (Arabic)
Initiation - Start

Badiha (Arabic)
Improvisation - Instinct - Intuition
Variants: *Badeeha, Badeehah, Badihah*

Badiha (Arabic)
Creative - Intuitive - Witty

Badir (Arabic)
Full Moon - Moon
Variants: *Baader, Baadir, Bader*

Badira (Arabic)
Full Moon - Moon
Variants: *Baadera, Baaderah, Baadira, Baadirah, Badera, Baderah, Badirah*

Badra (Arabic)
Ahead - Early - Quick

Badra (Arabic)
Early - On Time

Badrah (Arabic)
Full Moon
Variants: *Badra*

Badran (Arabic)
Beautiful - Radiant
Literally "like the full moon".

Badri (Arabic)
Autumn Rain - Fullness of the Moon
In Islamic history this word means "one who took part in the Battle of Badr".
Variants: *Badry*

Badriya (Arabic)
Beautiful - Moon-like
Literally "like the full moon".
Variants: *Badriah, Badriyah, Badriyyah*

Baduah (Arabic)
Creative - Innovative

Baghisha (Arabic)
Light Rain

Bahamin (Persian)
Spring Season
Variants: *Bahameen*

Bahar (Kurdish, Persian)
Season of Spring
Variants: *Bahaar, Behar*

Bahar Banu (Persian)
Lady of Spring

Baharak (Persian)
Spring Season
Variants: *Bahaarak*

Baharan (Persian)
Spring Season - Springtime
Variants: *Beharan*

Bahareh (Persian)
Vernal
Attribution to Bahar ("spring season").

Bahasht (Kurdish)
Paradise
From Persian Behasht.

Bahayah (Arabic)
Beauty - Radiance

Baheeja (Arabic)
Beautiful - Radiant
Variants: *Baheejah, Baheja, Bahija, Bahijah*

Baheela (Arabic)
Beautiful

Baheenah (Arabic)
Beautiful

Baheerah (Arabic)
Beautiful - Radiant - Talented

Bahira (Arabic)
Brilliant - Lucid - Renowned
Variants: *Baahera, Baahira, Baahirah, Bahera, Bahirah*

Bahiri (Arabic)
Brilliant - Renowned

Bahiriya (Arabic)
Brilliant - Renowned

Bahisa (Arabic)
Researcher - Seeker

Bahiyyah (Arabic)
Beautiful - Radiant
Variants: *Bahia, Bahiah, Bahiya, Bahiyah, Bahiyya*

Bahr (Arabic)
Ocean - Sea
The name Bahr is mentioned in the Quran.

Bahraa (Arabic)
Brilliant - Lucid - Renowned
Variants: *Bahra*

Bahsa (Persian)
Good - Virtuous
Variants: *Bahsaa, Behsa, Behsaa*

Bakheeta (Arabic)
Fortunate - Lucky

Bakhshandeh (Persian)
Generous - Gracious

Bakhta (Arabic)
Good Fortunate - Luck

Bakhtia (Arabic)
Fortunate - Lucky

Bakira (Arabic)
Virgin
Variants: *Bakirah*

Balaghah (Arabic)
Eloquence

Baleegha (Arabic)
Eloquent - Far-reaching
Variants: *Baleeghah, Balighah*

Bali (Persian, Turkish)
Honey-like
Variants: *Baly*

Baljah (Arabic)
First Light of Dawn

Balooja (Arabic)
Radiant

Balqees (Arabic)
Variant of Bilqees.

Banafsha (Persian, Urdu)
Violet
Refers to a type of flower.
Variants: *Banafshah, Banafsheh*

Banan (Arabic)
Fingertips
The name Banan is mentioned in the Quran.
Variants: *Banaan*

Banazir (Persian)
Matchless - Unique
Variants: *Banazeer*

Banu (Persian)
Lady - Princess
Variants: *Banoo*

Baqaa (Arabic)
Eternity - Perpetuity
Variants: *Baqa*

Baqat (Arabic)
Bouquet
Variants: *Baqaat*

Baqiya (Arabic)
Enduring - Everlasting
The name Baqiya is mentioned in the Quran.
Variants: *Baqia, Baqiah, Baqiyah*

Baraa (Arabic)
Blameless - Healed - Innocent
The name Baraa mentioned in the Quran.
Variants: *Bara*

Baraaem (Arabic)
Fresh - Innocent - Unopened Flower Bud - Young
Variants: *Bara'im*

Baraha (Arabic)
Fair-skinned

Baraka (Arabic)
Blessings
Variants: *Baraca, Barakah, Barakeh, Barekah, Bereka, Berekah, Bereke*

Baran (Kurdish, Persian)
Rain
Variants: *Baaran*

Barayek (Arabic)
Blessed

Barbara (English, German, Polish)
Foreign Woman
Variants: *Barbra*

Bareea (Arabic)
Blameless - Innocent
Variants: *Baree'a, Bareeah, Bareeia, Bareeya, Bareeyah, Bareya, Baria*

Barhamah (Arabic)
Flower Bud

Barikaa (Arabic)
Persevering - Striving
Variants: *Barikaa*

Barikah (Arabic)
Continuous Rain - Striver
Variants: *Bareka*

Bariyya (Arabic)
The Creation
Variants: *Bareeya, Bareeyah, Bariya, Bariyyah*

Barizah (Arabic)
Prominent - Visible

The name *Barizah* is mentioned in the Quran.
Variants: *Barizah, Barizeh*

Barizia (Arabic)
Prominent - Visible
Variants: *Bariziyyah*

Barja (Persian)
Fitting - Stable - Unshakable - Worthy
Variants: *Barjaa*

Barjaa (Arabic)
Beautiful-eyed
Variants: *Barja*

Barjees (Arabic, Urdu)
Planet Jupiter
Urdu variant of Birjis.
Variants: *Barjis*

Barqah (Arabic)
Flash of Light - Flash of Lightning

Basaair (Arabic)
Clear Proofs - Clear Signs
The name Basaair is mentioned in the Quran.
Variants: *Basaaer, Basaer*

Basalah (Arabic)
Boldness - Bravery

Basama (Arabic)
Happy - Smiling
Variants: *Basaama, Basamah*

Baseemaa (Arabic)
Cheerful - Smiling

Baseemah (Arabic)
Cheerful - Smiling

Baseera (Arabic)
Insight - Proof - Wisdom
The name Baseera is mentioned in the Quran.
Variants: *Baseerah, Basira*

Bashara (Arabic)
Good News - Good Tidings
Variants: *Bashaara, Bashaarah, Basharah*

Basheera (Arabic)
Bringer of Good News - Bringer of Good Tidings
Variants: *Basheerah, Bashira, Bashirah*

Basheesha (Arabic)
Cheerful - Optimistic

Bashrah (Arabic)
Good Tidings

Bashurah (Arabic)
Cheerful - Glad - Optimistic

Bashush (Arabic)
Cheerful - Optimistic
Variants: *Bashoosh*

Bashusha (Arabic)
Cheerful - Happy

Basila (Arabic)
Brave
Variants: *Basela, Baselah, Basilah*

Basima (Arabic)
Happy - Smiling
Variants: *Baasimah, Basema, Basemah, Basimah*

Basimia (Arabic)
Happy - Smiling
Variants: *Basmiyyah*

Basiqa (Arabic)
Lofty - Outstanding - Superior - Tall
Variants: *Baaseqa, Baasiqa, Baasiqah, Baseqa, Baseqah, Basiqah*

Basiraa (Arabic)
Perceptive
Variants: *Baseeraa*

Basita (Arabic)
Generous - Gracious

Basma (Arabic)
Cheerful - Happy - Smiling
Variants: *Baasma*

Basmaa (Arabic)
Cheerful - Smiling

Basmat (Arabic)
Smile
Turkish pronunciation of Basmah.
Variants: *Besmet*

Basmin (Arabic)
Cheerful Ones - Happy Ones - Smiling Ones
Variants: *Basmeen*

Basoomah (Arabic)
Cheerful - Smiling

Bathna (Arabic)
Beautiful - Delicate
Variants: *Basna, Basnah, Bathnah*

Batia (Arabic)
Slender - Tall

Batlaa (Arabic)
Resolute - Resolved
Variants: *Batla*

Batlah (Arabic)
Independent

Batool (Arabic)
Ascetic - Virgin - Virtuous
Variants: *Batol, Batul*

Batula (Arabic)
Ascetic - Virgin
Variants: *Batoola, Batoolah*

Bawan (Kurdish)
Beloved - Darling
Variants: *Baawan*

Bawasim (Arabic)
Cheerful - Smiling

Bayan (Arabic)
Declaration - Elucidation -
Exposition - Illustration
Variants: *Baian, Bayaan*

Baydaa (Arabic)
Great Desert
Name of a place between Mecca
and Medina.

Bayyina (Arabic)
Clear Proof - Clear Sign
The name Bayyina is mentioned
in the Quran.
Variants: *Bayena, Bayenah, Bayina,
Bayinah, Bayyena, Bayyenah,
Bayyinah*

Bayyinat (Arabic)
Clear Proofs - Clear Signs
The name Bayyinat is mentioned
in the Quran.
Variants: *Bainaat, Bayenaat,
Bayinaat, Bayyinaat*

Bayzaa (Arabic)
Moonlit Night - Pure - White
The name Bayzaa is mentioned
in the Quran.
Variants: *Baiza, Baizaa*

Baza (Arabic)
Northern Goshawk
A type of bird of prey.
Variants: *Bazah*

Bazigha (Arabic)
Radiant - Shining
The name Bazigha is mentioned
in the Quran.
Variants: *Bazegha, Bazighah*

Bazija (Arabic)
Adorner - Beautifier
Variants: *Bazeja, Bazijah*

Bazira (Arabic)
Sower
One who plants seeds.
Variants: *Baazirah, Bazera*

Baziriya (Arabic)
Sower of Seeds

Beatrice (French, Italian)
One Who Blesses Others -
Voyager
Italian and French form of
Beatrix.

Beatrix (English, German)
One Who Blesses Others -
Voyager

Becky (English)
Bound to God
Pet form of Rebecca.

Beena (Kurdish, Persian)
Far-sighted - Insightful -
Percpetive
Variants: *Bina, Binaa*

Beeta (Persian)
Peerless - Unique
Variants: *Beta, Bita, Bitaa*

Behafarin (Persian)
Beautiful - Well-designed - Well-
formed - Well-made

Behasht (Persian)
Paradise
Variants: *Behesht*

Behashteh (Persian)
Heavenly
Variants: *Behashta*

Behdokht (Persian)
Good - Virtuous

Beheen (Persian)
Best - Virtuous
Variants: *Behin*

Beheena (Persian)
Best - Virtuous
Variants: *Behina*

Behnaz (Persian)
Beloved - Charming - Lovely
Variants: *Bahnaaz, Behnaaz*

Behrokh (Persian)
Beautiful - Handsome
Variants: *Behrukh*

Behshid (Persian)
Radiant
Variants: *Behsheed*

Behy (Persian)
Fortune - Goodness - Health
Variants: *Behi*

Bella (English, Italian, Scottish)
Beautiful - My God is Bountiful
Can be a short form of Isabella,
originally from Elizabeth. It can
also be an Italian adjective
meaning "beautiful".

Bernice (English, French)
Bringer of Victory

Bertha (English, German)
Bright - Famous

Beryl (English)
Precious Stone
Beryl is a pale green stone.
Emerald is a variety of beryl.

Besharat (Arabic)
Good News - Good Tidings
Turkish pronunciation of
Basharah.
Variants: *Beshaarat, Bisharat*

NAMES FOR GIRLS

Bet (English)
My God is Bountiful
Short form of Elizabeth.

Beth (English)
My God is Bountiful
Short form of Elizabeth.

Bethany (English)
House of Figs
Name of a village in the New Testament.

Betrys (Welsh)
One Who Blesses Others - Voyager
Welsh form of Beatrice.

Bettina (Italian)
Blessed
Elaboration of Benedetta.

Bettina (English)
My God is Bountiful
Elaboration of Betty, pet form of Elizabeth.

Betty (English)
My God is Bountiful
Pet form of Elizabeth.

Beverley (English)
Beaver Stream
Originally the name of a place in northern England.

Beverly (English)
Beaver Stream
Originally the name of a place in northern England.

Bianca (Italian)
Pure - White

Bice (Italian)
One Who Blesses Others - Voyager
Contracted pet form of Beatrice.

Bidar (Arabic)
Earliness - Punctuality

Bidayah (Arabic)
Beginning - Genesis - Inception

Bidayat (Arabic)
Beginning - Genesis - Inception
Turkish pronunciation of Bidayah.

Billah (Arabic)
Provision

Bilqees (Arabic)
Arabic name for the Queen of Sheba. The meaning of the name is not known.

Bionda (Italian)
Blonde - Fair-haired

Birjees (Arabic)
Planet Jupiter
Variants: *Berjees, Berjis*

Birjis (Arabic)
Planet Jupiter
Variants: *Berjees, Berjis, Birjees*

Bisharah (Arabic)
Good Tidings

Bishra (Arabic)
Good Tidings

Bishry (Arabic)
Cheerful - Glad - Optimistic

Bizrah (Arabic)
Seed

Blanche (English, French)
Pure - White

Blossom (English)
Tree Flower

Bokhur (Arabic)
Incense

Bona (Italian, Polish)
Good

Bonita (English)
Good - Pretty

Boshry (Arabic)
Gladness - Happiness

Branwen (Welsh)
Blessed Raven - White Raven

Brenda (English, Irish, Scottish)
Flaming Sword

Brianne (English)
High - Noble
Feminine form of Brian.

Bronwen (Welsh)
Blessed - Fair-skinned
Literally "fair-breasted".

Bronya (Polish)
Armor - Protection

Bryony (English)
Flowering Plant
The name of a flowering plant (bryonia in Greek).
Variants: *Briony*

Budaida (Arabic)
Example - Sample - Specimen

Budaira (Arabic)
Full Moon

Buddah (Arabic)
Fortune - Share

Budur (Arabic)
Full Moons
Variants: *Bodoor*

Buduriya (Arabic)
Beautiful - Radiant
Literally "like the full moon".

Buffy (English)
My God is Bountiful
Pet form of Elizabeth.

Buhairah (Arabic)
Lake
Variants: *Bohaira, Buhayra*

Buhur (Arabic)
Oceans - Seas
Variants: *Bohoor, Buhoor*

Bujud (Arabic)
Residence - Stay
Variants: *Bojud*

Bukrah (Arabic)
Dawn
The name Bukrah is mentioned in the Quran.

Bulainah (Arabic)
Little Pigeon

Bulbul (Arabic)
Nightingale
Variants: *Bolbol*

Bullah (Arabic)
Beauty of Youth

Bulooj (Arabic)
Radiance

Buraikaat (Arabic)
Blessings

Burhanah (Arabic)
Clue - Demonstration - Proof

Busain (Arabic)
Beautiful - Delicate - Tender

Busaina (Arabic)
Beautiful - Delicate

Variants: *Busainah, Busaynah, Buthaina, Buthainah*

Bushra (Arabic)
Glad Tidings - Good Tidings
The name Bushra is mentioned in the Quran.
Variants: *Boshra, Bushraa*

Busraq (Arabic)
Yellow Sapphire
Variants: *Busraaq*

Bustan (Persian)
Forest - Garden
Variants: *Bostan, Bustaan*

Butaila (Arabic)
Devoted to God - Pious - Virtuous

Buthainaa (Arabic)
Beautiful - Delicate - Soft
Variants: *Busainaa*

Buzur (Arabic)
Seeds

NAMES FOR GIRLS

C

Camilla (English, Italian)
Noble Virgin
Variants: *Camillia*

Candace (English)
Glowing - Queen - White
Hereditary name of a line of queens of Ethiopia.
Variants: *Candice, Candiss*

Cara (English)
Beloved - Friend

Carey (English)
River Name
Variant spelling of Cary.

Caridad (Spanish)
Generous - Loving

Carina (English, German, Scandinavian)
Beloved
Elaboration of Cara.

Carla (English, German, Italian)
Free Woman
Feminine form of Carlo, Charles or Carl.

Carlin (English)
Free Woman
Elaborated form of Carla.

Carlotta (Italian)
Free Woman
Italian form of Charlotte.

Carly (English)
Free Woman
Variant of Carla.
Variants: *Carley, Carlie*

Carmel (English)
Garden - Orchard
Name of a mountain near Haifa.

Carmela (Italian, Sicilian, Spanish)
Garden - Orchard
Form of Carmel.

Carmen (Spanish)
Garden - Orchard
Form of Carmel.

Carol (English)
Free Woman
Related to the name Charles.
Variants: *Caryl*

Carole (French)
Free Woman
French form of Carol.

Caroline (English, French)
Free Woman
From the French form of Carolina.
Variants: *Carolyn*

Carrie (English)
Free Woman
Pet form of Caroline.

Carys (Welsh)
Beloved - Loving

Catalina (Spanish)
Pure
Spanish form of Katherine

Catarina (Italian, Portuguese)
Pure
Portuguese and Italian form of Katherine.

Catherine (English)
Pure
Variants: *Catharine*

Cathleen (Irish)
Pure
Variant spelling of Kathleen, originally from Katherine.

Cathy (English)
Pure
Pet form of Catherine.

Catrin (Welsh)
Pure
Welsh form of Katherine.

Catriona (Irish, Scottish)
Pure
Originally from Katherine.

Ceinwen (Welsh)
Blessed - Lovely - White

Celeste (French)
Heavenly

Chakama (Persian)
Poem
Variants: *Chakameh*

Chaman (Persian)
Greenery - Lawn

Chamanara (Persian)
Gardener

Chamangul (Persian)
Garden Flower

Chamannaz (Persian)
Beautiful

Chand (Urdu)
Moon
Variants: *Chaand*

Charlene (English)
Free Woman
Feminine form of Charles.

39

Charlie (English)
Free Woman
Pet form of Charlotte.

Charlotte (English, French)
Free Woman
Feminine diminutive for Charles.

Charmaine (English)
Delightful
Variant of Charmian.

Charmian (English)
Delightful

Chehra (Persian)
Complexion - Face
Variants: *Chehreh*

Cheragh (Persian)
Lamp - Lantern - Light
Variants: *Charagh, Cheraagh, Chiragh*

Cherish (English)
Cherished - Dear - Treasured
Possibly originating from Cheryth, a Welsh place name, altered to match the English word "cherish".

Cherry (English)
Darling - Fruit Name
From French chéries ("darling"). Also used as a name referring to the fruit.

Cheryl (English)
Beryl - Darling
A cross between the names Cherry and Beryl.

Cheryth (English)
Darling
A cross between the names Cherry and Gwyneth.

Cheshideh (Persian)
Experienced - Learned
Variants: *Chashida, Chashidah, Cheshida*

Chevonne (Irish)
God is Gracious
From Siobhán, Irish Gaelic form of Jane.

Chiara (Italian)
Famous
Italian form of Clare.

Chiman (Kurdish, Persian)
Greenery - Lawn
Variant of Chaman.
Variants: *Cheeman*

Chole (Spanish)
Solitude
Pet form of Soledad.

Ciannait (Irish)
Ancient
Feminine diminutive for Cian.

Ciara (Irish)
Black

Claire (French)
Famous
French form of Clara.

Clara (English, German, Italian)
Famous

Clare (English)
Famous
Form of Clara.

Clarice (English)
Famous
Elaboration of Clara, or from Latin Claritia (probably "fame").

Clarinda (English)
Famous
Elaboration of Clara.

Clarissa (English)
Famous
Latinate form of Clarice.

Clemence (English)
Mercy

Clemency (English)
Mercy

Clementine (English)
Merciful
Variants: *Clementina*

Clover (English)
Flower Name
Name of a type of flower.

Colette (English, French)
Of the Victorious People
Short form of Nicolette or feminine diminutive form of Colin.
Variants: *Collette*

Colleen (English)
Girl
From an Anglo-Irish word.

Columbine (English)
Dove

Connie (English)
Steadfast
Pet form of Constance.

Conrad (English)
Bold Counsel
Variant of Konrad.

Constance (English, French)
Steadfast

Coral (English)
Precious Material
Coral is the name of a beautiful pink material found in some areas of the ocean.

NAMES FOR GIRLS

Corona (German)
Crown

Crescentia (German)
Growing

Cressida (English)
Gold
Variants: *Cressa*

Cyrille (French)
Lord
French form of Cyril.

This page intentionally left blank

D

Daaemiyyah (Arabic)
Constant - Perpetual

Dabeer (Persian)
Instructor - Teacher
Variants: *Dabir*

Dafqah (Arabic)
Burst - Gush - Surge

Dagny (Scandinavian)
New Day
Variants: *Dagne, Danga*

Dahiah (Arabic)
Intelligent - Wise

Dahiyyah (Arabic)
Intelligent - Wise

Dahlia (English)
Flower Name
Variants: *Dalya*

Daisy (English)
Flower Name
Literally meaning "day's eye".

Dale (English)
Valley

Dalia (Arabic, Kurdish, Persian)
Dahlia
Variants: *Daliaa, Dalya*

Dalilah (Arabic)
Guide - Leader

Dalkah (Arabic)
Sunset

Dalmaa (Arabic)
Extremely Dakr

Dalmah (Arabic)
Darkness

Dalu (Arabic)
Well Bucket
The name Dalu is mentioned in the Quran.

Dalwah (Arabic)
Well Bucket

Damaa (Arabic)
Ocean - Sea
Variants: *Da'maa, Daama, Dama*

Dana (Polish)
Gift from God
Short form of Bogdan.
Variants: *Daana, Daanaa, Danaa*

Dana (Persian)
Experienced - Knowledgeable - Wise

Danesh (Persian)
Knowledge - Wisdom
Variants: *Daanesh, Daanish, Danish*

Dania (Arabic)
Close - Near
The name Dania is mentioned in the Quran.
Variants: *Daaneya, Daaneyah, Daania, Daaniah, Daaniya, Daaniyah, Daniah, Daniya, Daniyah*

Daniela (Czech, Polish)
God is My Judge
Latinate feminine form of Daniel.

Danielle (French)
God is My Judge
Feminine form of Daniel.

Danika (Slavic)
Morning Star
Variants: *Danica*

Dany (French)
God is My Judge
Pet form of Danièle/Danielle.

Darakhshan (Persian, Urdu)
Brilliant - Radiant
Variants: *Darakhshaan, Derakhshan, Dirkhshan*

Dardana (Urdu)
Pearl - Precious
Variant of Dordaneh.
Variants: *Dardaana*

Dariya (Arabic)
Good-mannered - Intelligent - Lady-like - Perceptive
Variants: *Daaria, Daariyah, Darea, Daria, Dariyah*

Darlene (English)
Darling
A modern name created by altering the word darling.

Darya (Kurdish)
Ocean - Sea
Variants: *Daria, Daryaa*

Daulah (Arabic)
Power - State
Variants: *Daula, Dawla, Dawlah*

Daulat (Arabic)
Power - State
Turkish pronunciation of Daulah.
Variants: *Dawlat*

Daumaa (Arabic)
Ocean - Sea
Variants: *Dauma, Dawma*

Davina (English, Scottish)
Beloved
Feminine form of David.
Variants: *Davida, Davinia*

Dawmah (Arabic)
Hypaene thebaica
A type of palm tree.

Dawmat (Arabic)
Hypaene thebaica
A type of palm tree.

Dawn (English)
Daybreak

Dawub (Arabic)
Conscientious - Diligent
Variants: *Da'ub, Daoob, Daub, Dawood*

Dayana (Persian)
Gold
Not related to the Roman name Diana.
Variants: *Dayaana*

Deborah (English, Jewish)
Bee
Variants: *Debora, Debra*

Deema (Persian)
Beautiful - Pretty
Variants: *Dima, Dimaa*

Del (Persian)
Heart
Variants: *Dil*

Delara (Persian)
Beloved - Darling
Variants: *Delaara, Dilara*

Delaram (Persian)
Peaceful - Serene
Variants: *Dilaram*

Delbar (Persian)
Captivating - Charming
Variants: *Dilbar*

Delbaz (Persian)
Captivated - In Love
Variants: *Delbaaz, Dilbaz*

Deldar (Persian)
Beloved - Brave - In Love
Variants: *Deldaar, Dildar*

Delkash (Persian)
Captivating - Enticing
Variants: *Dilkash*

Delnavaz (Persian)
Comforter - Consoler
Variants: *Delnawaz, Dilnawaz*

Delnaz (Persian)
Beloved
Variants: *Delnaaz*

Delnia (Kurdish)
Serene
Variants: *Delnyaa, Dlnia*

Delroba (Persian)
Captivating - Enticing
Variants: *Delrobaa, Dilroba*

Delshad (Persian)
Happy - Joyful
Variants: *Delshaad, Dilshad*

Delwyn (Welsh)
Blessed - Pretty - White

Delyth (Welsh)
Pretty

Derakhshandeh (Persian)
Radiant

Desiree (French)
Desired

Detta (Italian)
Blessed
Short form of Benedetta or Bernadette.

Dewi (Welsh)
Beloved
A Welsh form of David.

Dibaaj (Arabic)
Silk Cloth
A type of silk cloth.

Didar (Persian)
Date - Meet Up - Reunion
Variants: *Deedar, Didaar*

Digna (Spanish)
Worthy

Dilafruz (Persian)
Bringer of Happiness - Gladdener - Uplifter
Variants: *Delafrooz, Delafruz*

Dilalah (Arabic)
Guidance - Instruction

Dilwen (Welsh)
Genuinely Blessed

Dilwyn (Welsh)
Genuinely Blessed - White

Dilys (Welsh)
Genuine - Steadfast

Dimah (Arabic)
Silent Rain

Dina (English)
Judgment
Variant of Dinah.

Dinah (Biblical)
Judgment
Name of one of the daughters of Jacob (prophet Ya`qub in Arabic).

Dinar (Arabic)
Gold Coin
The name Dinar is mentioned in the Quran.
Variants: *Deenar*

Dinarah (Arabic)
Gold Coin

NAMES FOR GIRLS

Diyana (Persian)
Benevolent - Giver of Gifts
Not related to the Roman name Diana.
Variants: *Deeyana*

Diyanat (Arabic)
Creed - Religion

Dominga (Spanish)
Lord
Feminine form of Domingo.

Dominica (Latin)
Lord
Feminine of Dominic.

Dominique (French)
Lord
French form of Dominica and Dominic. Used mostly for girls.

Donla (Irish)
Brown-haired Lady

Doost (Persian)
Friend

Dorcas (English)
Gazelle

Dordaneh (Arabic)
Pearl - Precious
Variants: *Dordana, Dordanah*

Dorean (Irish)
Daughter of Finn
Finn is a mythological Irish hero whose name means "white", "fair".

Doreen (Arabic)
Pearl-like
Variants: *Dorrin, Durin, Durrin*

Dorete (Danish)
Gift from God
Form of Dorothea.

Dorna (Persian)
Crane
A type of bird.
Variants: *Durnaa*

Dornaz (Arabic)
Pearl-like
Variants: *Durnaz*

Dorothea (Dutch, English, German)
Gift from God

Dorothy (English)
Gift from God
Form of Dorothea.

Dorsa (Arabic)
Pearl-like
Variants: *Dursa*

Dorte (Danish)
Gift from God
Short form of Dorete.
Variants: *Dorthe*

Dosia (Polish)
Gift from God
Pet form of Dorota (from Dorothea).

Dost (Kurdish)
Friend
From Persian Doost.

Drakhshan (Kurdish, Persian)
Brilliant - Radiant
From Persian Derakhshan.
Variants: *Dirakhshan*

Dua (Arabic)
Call - Prayer - Supplication
The name Dua is mentioned in the Quran.
Variants: *Doa, Doaa, Doua, Douaa, Dowa, Dowaa, Du`a, Du`aa', Duaa, Duwa, Duwaa*

Duhat (Arabic)
Intelligent - Sensible

Dunaa (Arabic)
Worlds

Dunya (Arabic)
Worldly Life
The name Dunya is mentioned in the Quran.
Variants: *Donyaa, Dunya, Dunyaa*

Dunya (Russian)
Beautiful
Short form of Advunya, pet form of Avdotya.

Durafshan (Persian)
Distributor of Pearls
Variants: *Dorafshan, Dur Afshan*

Durar (Arabic)
Pearls
Variants: *Dorar*

Duriya (Arabic)
Brilliant - Dazzling - Radiant
Variants: *Dorriyah, Dorriyyah, Dureya, Duria, Duriya, Duriyah, Duriyya, Durriyya, Durriyyah*

Durrah (Arabic)
Large Pearl

Duryab (Arabic)
Finder of Pearls
Variants: *Doryab, Duryaab*

This page intentionally left blank.

E

Ebony (English)
Type of Wood
Ebony refers to a deeply black wood. The name is used commonly by Blacks.

Edith (English)
Joyous - Spoils of War - Treasure
Variants: *Edythe*

Edna (English, Irish)
Kernel

Edwina (English)
Wealthy Friend
Feminine of Edwin.

Edyta (Polish)
Joyous - Spoils of War - Treasure

Eeda (Arabic)
Commitment - Consignment
Variants: *Idaa'*

Eesha (Arabic)
Life - Way of Life
The name Eesha is mentioned in the Quran in verse 69:21.
Variants: *Eisha, Esha, Eysha, Isha*

Eezah (Arabic)
Clarification - Elucidation
Variants: *Izaah*

Efah (Arabic)
Chastity - Modesty - Virtue
Variants: *Efa, Effa, Effah, Ifah, Iffa, Iffah*

Efric (Scottish)
New Speckled One
From Gaelic name Oighrig.

Eftikhar (Arabic)
Beauty - Magnificence - Stateliness
Variants: *Iftikhar*

Ehsaneh (Arabic, Persian)
Doer of Good Deeds - Virtuous
Variants: *Ehsana, Ihsaneh*

Eifa (Arabic)
Faithfulness - Loyalty
Variants: *Eefaa, Ifaa*

Eihaa (Arabic)
Inspiration - Non-verbal Communication
Variants: *Ihaa*

Eiham (Arabic)
Fantasy - Illusion
Variants: *Eyham, Iham*

Eileen (English, Irish)
Birdlike
Variants: *Eilin*

Eileen (Persian, Turkish)
Amiable - Kind

Eilnaz (Persian, Turkish)
Beautiful
Variants: *Elnaz, Ilnaz*

Eima (Arabic)
Gesture - Insignia - Mark
Variants: *Eema, Imaa*

Einas (Arabic)
Comfort - Consolation - Peace of Mind
Variants: *Eenas*

Eira (Arabic)
Kindling - Starting a Fire
Variants: *Eera, Eiraa, Eyra, Ira*

Eira (Welsh)
Snow

Eirwen (Welsh)
Blessed Snow - White Snow

Eithar (Arabic)
Love - Preferring Another Person to Yourself
Variants: *Isaar, Isar*

Eiwa (Arabic)
Guardianship - Protection
Variants: *Eewaa, Eiwaa, Eywa, Eywaa, Iwa, Iwaa, Iywa*

Elaf (Arabic)
Safety - Security Promise
The name Elaf is used in the Quran.
Variants: *Elaaf, Ilaaf, Ilaf*

Elaine (English)
Shining Light
From Helen.

Eleanor (English)
Shining Light
Derivative of Helen.
Variants: *Elinor, Ellenor*

Elen (Welsh)
Shining Light
Welsh form of Helen.
Variants: *Elin*

Elena (Italian, Spanish)
Shining Light
Italian and Spanish form of Helen.

Eleonora (Italian)
Shining Light
Italian form of Eleanor.

Eleonore (German)
Shining Light
German form of Eleanor.

Elettra (Italian)
Brilliant
Known as Electra in English.

Elfleda (English)
Noble Beauty

Elfreda (English)
Supernaturally Strong

Eliana (Turkish)
Gift
Variants: *Elyaana, Iliana*

Eliane (French)
Shining Light

Elika (Persian)
Cardamom
Variants: *Eleeka*

Elisabet (Scandinavian)
My God is Bountiful
Form of Elizabeth.

Elisabeth (English)
My God is Bountiful
Variant of Elizabeth.

Elisabetta (Italian)
My God is Bountiful
Italian form of Elizabeth.

Elise (French)
My God is Bountiful
Short form of Elisabeth.

Eliza (English)
Joyful - My God is Abundance
Eliza is the short form of Elizabeth, which comes from the Hebrew word Elisheva. It can also be a variant of the Hebrew name Aliza, which means "joyful".

Elizabeth (English)
God is My Oath

Elke (Dutch, Frisian)
High-born - Noble
Derived from Adelheid.

Ella (English)
Shining Light
Variant of Ellen, Eleanor and other names.

Ellen (English)
Shining Light
Variant of Helen.

Ellenor (English)
Shining Light
Variant of Eleanor.

Elli (German)
My God is Bountiful
Pet form of Elisabeth.

Ellie (English)
Shiing Light
Pet form of Eleanor and other names.

Elmira (Persian, Turkish)
Sacrifice
Variants: *Elmeera*

Elsa (Persian, Turkish)
Friendly - Lovable
Variants: *Elsaa, Ilsa*

Elsa (English, German, Swedish)
My God is Bountiful
Shortened form of Elisabeth.

Elsa (English, German, Swedish)
My God is Bountiful
Shortened form of Elisabeth.

Elsana (Persian, Turkish)
Friendly - Lovable - Recognizable
Variants: *Elsaana, Ilsana*

Elsie (English, Scottish)
My God is Bountiful
From Eslpeth, from Elizabeth.

Emerald (English)
Gemstone

Emilie (French, German)
Hardworking - Industrious
French form of Emily.

Emily (English)
Hardworking - Industrious

Emma (English)
Complete

Emmy (English)
Complete - Hardworking
Pet form of Emma, Emily and others.

Enfys (Welsh)
Rainbow

Engracia (Spanish)
Moderate - Temperate

Erdmute (German)
Brave Spirit
Feminine of Erdmut.

Erica (English, Scottish)
Eternal Ruler
Feminine of Eric.

Erika (German, Scandinavian)
Eternal Ruler
Cognate of Erica.

Erin (English, Irish)
Ireland

Ermine (English)
Soldier
Variant of Hermine.

Erna (German)
Determined - Serious
From Ernesta.

Eshaal (Arabic)
Excitation - Kindling
Variants: *Eshal, Ish'al, Ishaal, Ishal*

Esmeralda (English)
Emerald
Variants: *Esmerelda*

Esperanza (Spanish)
Hope

Estelle (English)
Star
Variants: *Estella*

Estrella (Spanish)
Star

Etemad (Arabic)
Reliance - Trust
Variants: *I'timad, Itimad*

Ethel (English)
Noble

Ethna (Irish)
Kernel
Form of Eithne.

Etimad (Arabic)
Dependence - Reliance
Variants: *Ettimad, Itimad*

Etna (Irish)
Kernel
Form of Eithne.

Eudora (English)
Good Gift
From Greek vocabulary elements.

Eufemia (Italian, Portuguese, Spanish)
I Speak Well
Form of Euphemia.

Eugenia (English, Italian, Spanish)
High-born - Noble
Used as the feminine form of Eugene.

Eugenie (French)
High-born - Noble
French form of Eugenia.

Eunice (English)
Good Victory

Euphemia (Latin)
I Speak Well

Eva (English, Italian, Latin, Portuguese, Scandinavian, Spanish)
Living
Latinate form of Eve.

Evangeline (English)
God Tidings - Gospel
Related to the Arabic name for the Gospels (Injil).

Eve (English, French)
Living
Name of the wife of prophet Adam, known as Hawwa in Arabic and Havva in Hebrew.

Evelina (English, Irish)
Living
Combination of Eve with -lina, or form of Evelyn.

Evita (Spanish)
Living
Spanish pet form of Eva.

Evonne (English)
Yew
Variant of Yvonne.

Ewa (Polish)
Living
Polish form of Eve.

This page intentionally left blank

F

Faahima (Arabic)
Intelligent - Understanding
Variants: *Fahema, Fahemah, Fahimah*

Faaria (Arabic)
Long-haired - Slim - Tall
Variants: *Faari'ah, Faariah, Fari'a, Fariah, Fariyah*

Faariqah (Arabic)
Differentiator - Judge

Fadia (Arabic)
Heroic - Self-sacrificing
Variants: *Fadiah, Fadiya, Fadiyah*

Fadwaa (Arabic)
Heroism - Self-sacrifice
Variants: *Faduaa, Fadwa*

Fadwah (Arabic)
Heroism - Self-sacrifice
Variants: *Fadua, Faduah, Fadwa*

Fae (English)
Fairy
Variant of Fay.

Faghira (Arabic)
Hercules' Club
A type of plant.
Variants: *Faghirah*

Fahadah (Arabic)
Leopard-trainer

Fahama (Arabic)
Intelligent - Understanding
Variants: *Fahhama*

Fahdah (Arabic)
Leopard

Faheema (Arabic)
Intelligent - Keen - Perceptive - Understanding
Variants: *Faheemah, Fahema, Fahemah, Fahima, Fahimah, Fehime*

Fahimat (Arabic)
Comprehending - Intelligent

Fahisa (Arabic)
Investigator - Tester
Variants: *Fahesa, Fahesah, Fahisah*

Fahmat (Arabic)
Comprehension - Understanding

Fahmida (Persian)
Learned - Understanding - Wise
Variants: *Fahmidah, Fahmideh*

Faiha (Arabic)
Vast Landscape - Vista
Variants: *Faihaa, Fayhaa*

Faihah (Arabic)
Scenic View

Faiqa (Arabic)
Excellent - Extraordinary - Superb
Variants: *Faaeqa, Faaiqah, Faeqa, Faiqah, Fayeka*

Fairuz (Arabic, Kurdish, Persian, Urdu)
Successful - Victor
Variants: *Fairooz, Fayrooz, Fayruz*

Fairuza (Arabic)
Turquoise
From Persian Firuzeh.
Variants: *Fairooza, Fairoozah, Fairuzah, Feeroza, Firoza*

Faitahah (Arabic)
Right Guidance

Faith (English)
Faith

Faiza (Arabic)
Successful - Winner
Variants: *Faaeza, Faaezah, Faaiza, Faaizah, Faeza, Faezah, Faizah, Fayeza, Fayezah, Fayiza, Fayizah*

Faizee (Arabic)
Abundance - Gracious - Virtuous
Variants: *Faidhi, Faizy*

Faizunnisa (Arabic)
Victor - Winner
Literally meaning "winner among women".

Fajr (Arabic)
Dawn - Daybreak
The name Fajr is mentioned in the Quran.

Fakhira (Arabic)
High Quality - Luxurious
Variants: *Faakhira, Fakhera, Fakhirah*

Fakhr (Arabic)
Glory - Honor - Pride
Variants: *Fekhr*

Fakhri (Arabic)
Cause for Pride - Glorious
Variants: *Fakhry*

Fakhrjahan (Arabic)
Pride of the World

Fakiha (Arabic)
Fruit
The name Fakiha is mentioned in the Quran.
Variants: *Fakeha, Fakehah, Fakihah*

Falak (Arabic)
Cosmos - Orbit - Ship - Space
The name Falak is used in the Quran.
Variants: *Felek*

Falak Ara (Arabic)
Beautifier of the World
Variants: *Falakara*

Falaq (Arabic)
Dawn - Daybreak
The name Falaq is used in the Quran.

Faleehah (Arabic)
Successful

Falih (Arabic)
Prosperous - Successful
Variants: *Faaleh, Faalih, Faleh*

Faliha (Arabic)
Prosperous - Successful
Variants: *Faaliha, Faalihah, Falehah, Falihah*

Fania (Italian)
Crown - Garland
Short form of Stefania.

Fannana (Arabic)
Artist
Variants: *Fannanah*

Faqeeha (Arabic)
Expert - Knowledgeable - Learned - Scholar
Variants: *Faqeehah, Faqiha, Faqihah*

Faraaid (Arabic)
Independent-minded - Unique

Farah (Arabic)
Cheer - Happiness - Joy

Farahdokht (Arabic)
Happy

Farahnaz (Arabic, Persian)
Beautiful - Happy

Farahnoush (Arabic)
Eternal Happiness
Variants: *Farahnush*

Farahrouz (Arabic)
Blessed - Fortunate
Variants: *Faharooz*

Farahzad (Arabic)
Bringer of Happiness

Farakh (Persian)
End of Fear - Relief

Faranah (Persian)
Butterfly
Variants: *Faraaneh, Farana, Faraneh*

Farangis (Persian)
Bringer of Glory
Variants: *Faranghees*

Farashah (Arabic)
Butterfly

Faraz (Persian)
Elevation - High Place - Successful - Top
Variants: *Faraaz*

Fardan (Arabic)
Unique
Variants: *Fardaan*

Fardanah (Arabic)
Intelligent - Unique - Wise

Fareea (Arabic)
Long-haired - Slim - Tall
Fareea is the name of a number of Sahabiyaat.
Variants: *Faree'ah, Fareeah, Fareeyah*

Fareeda (Arabic)
Matchless - Unique
Variants: *Fareedah, Farida, Faridah*

Fareedokht (Persian)
Blessed - Great

Fareeha (Arabic)
Fareehah - Fareha - Farehah - Fariha - Farihah

Fareen (Persian)
Blessed - Great
Variants: *Farin*

Fareenaa (Persian)
Charming - Kind - Merciful
Variants: *Farinaa*

Farha (Arabic)
Happiness - Happy Occasion
Variants: *Farhah*

Farhaa (Arabic)
Beautiful

Farhana (Arabic)
Happy - Joyful
Variants: *Farhanah*

Farhatah (Arabic)
Happiness - Joy

Farheen (Arabic, Urdu)
Happy - Joyous
Variants: *Farhin*

Fariba (Persian)
Beautiful - Captivating
Variants: *Fareeba, Fareebaa, Faribaa*

Faridaa (Arabic, Persian)
Unique
Variants: *Fareedaa*

Farihat (Arabic)
Happy

Farimaa (Persian)
Beautiful

NAMES FOR GIRLS

Farimah (Persian)
Beautiful - Blessed - Radiant
Literally "blessed moon".

Farimehr (Persian)
Blessed - Radiant
Literally "blessed sun".
Variants: *Fareemehr*

Farinaz (Persian)
Beautiful - Blessed
Variants: *Fareenaz, Farinaaz*

Farinoush (Persian)
Eternally Blessed
Variants: *Fareenoush*

Farisaa (Persian)
Beautiful

Farivash (Persian)
Blessed - Great
Variants: *Fareevash*

Farnaz (Persian)
Charming - Elegant - Great
Variants: *Farnaaz*

Farniya (Persian)
Bringer of Honor

Farokh (Persian)
Agreeable - Blessed - Fortunate - Good
Variants: *Farrokh, Farrukh, Farukh*

Farradah (Arabic)
Independent-minded - Jeweler - Original

Farrahah (Arabic)
Happy

Farrajah (Arabic)
Happy

Farrokhnaz (Persian)
Beautiful - Captivating
Variants: *Farokhnaz, Farrukhnaz*

Farshidah (Persian)
Radiance

Farvardin (Persian)
Protector of Good People
Variants: *Farvardeen, Farwardin*

Farwa (Arabic)
Crown - Wealth
Variants: *Farwa, Faruah, Farwah*

Farya (Persian)
Blessed - Magnificent
Variants: *Faria, Fariaa, Faryaa*

Farzan (Persian)
Calm - Intelligent - Sensible - Wise
Variants: *Farzaan*

Farzaneh (Persian)
Calm - Intelligent - Sensible - Wise
Variants: *Farzaana, Farzana, Farzanah*

Farzin (Persian)
Vizier
Refers to a piece in the game of shtranj (an ancestor of the game Chess).
Variants: *Farzeen*

Fatat (Arabic)
Young Man

Fateem (Arabic)
Weaned Off Breast Milk

Fateemah (Arabic)
Weaned Off Breast Milk

Fateemat (Arabic)
Weaned Off Breast Milk

Fathiyyah (Arabic)
Conqueror - Guide

Fatihah (Arabic)
Conqueror - Initiator

Fatima (Arabic)
Weaned Off Breast Milk
Name of the daughter of Prophet Muhammad PBUH.
Variants: *Fatema, Fatemah, Fatimah*

Fatin (Arabic)
Intelligent - Perceptive
Variants: *Faatin, Faten*

Fatina (Arabic)
Intelligent - Perceptive
Variants: *Faatina, Fatena, Fatenah, Fatinah*

Fatiriyyah (Arabic)
Gentle - Relaxed - Soft - Tranquil

Fatoom (Arabic)
Weaned Off Breast Milk

Fattahah (Arabic)
Conqueror - Victor

Fattuhah (Arabic)
Conquest - Guidance

Fattumah (Arabic)
Weaned Off Breast Milk

Fauz (Arabic)
Victory - Win
The name Fauz is mentioned in the Quran.
Variants: *Fawz, Fouz, Fowz*

Fawazaa (Arabic)
Successful - Winner

Fawzah (Arabic)
Success - Win

Fawziyyaa (Arabic)
Successful - Winner

Fawziyyah (Arabic)
Successful - Winner

Fay (English)
Fairy
Variants: *Faye*

Fayyah (Arabic)
Repentance

Fazar (Arabic)
Leopard

Fazeelah (Arabic)
Excellence - Merit - Virtue

Fazeelat (Arabic)
Excellence - Merit - Virtue

Fazila (Arabic)
Excellent - Generous - Praiseworth
Variants: *Faazila, Fadhila, Fadhilah, Fazela, Fazelah*

Felicia (Latin)
Lucky
Feminine form of Felix.

Felicity (English)
Good Fortune - Luck

Fenella (Scottish)
Fair-skinned - White-shouldered

Feodora (Russian)
Gift from God
Russian form of Theodora.

Fern (English)
Fern
A type of plant.

Fida (Arabic)
Bail - Bailout
Variants: *Feda, Fidaa*

Fieke (German)
Wisdom
Low German pet form of Sofie.

Fikr (Arabic)
Concept - Intellect - Thought

Fikraat (Arabic)
Concepts - Ideas - Thoughts

Fikrat (Arabic)
Concept - Idea - Thoughts
Turkish pronunciation of Fikrah.

Fikri (Arabic)
Conceptual - Perceptive - Thoughtful

Fikriyaa (Arabic)
Conceptual - Perceptive - Thoughtful

Fikriyyah (Arabic)
Intelligent - Thoughtful

Filza (Persian)
Beloved - Dear - Metal - Silver
Variants: *Felza, Felzah, Filza, Filzah, Filzeh*

Fina (Irish)
Vine
From Gaelic Fíona.

Finnian (Irish Gaelic)
Fair-skinned - White
Variants: *Finian*

Finola (Irish, Scottish)
Fair-skinned - White-shouldered

Fiona (Scottish)
Fair-skinned - White

Fionola (Scottish)
Fair-skinned - White
Variant of Finella, Finola or elaboration of Fiona.

Fiorella (Italian)
Flower

Fiorenzo (Italian)
Blossoming - Flourishing
From Florence.

Firtan (Arabic)
Cool Fresh Water

Firuz (Persian)
Successful - Victor
Variants: *Feeroz, Feeruz, Firooz, Firouz*

Firuzeh (Persian)
Turquoise
Variants: *Firooza, Firoozeh, Firuza*

Firyal (Persian)
One Who Has a Beautiful Neck

Firzah (Arabic)
Rare - Unique

Fitrah (Arabic)
Innate Nature - Instinct - Natural Disposition
The name Fitrah is mentioned in the Quran.

Fizzah (Arabic)
Silver
The name Fizzah is mentioned in the Quran.

Fizzi (Arabic)
Silvery

Fizziyah (Arabic)
Silvery

Flavia (Italian)
Golden - Yellow - Yellow-haired

Fleur (English)
Flower
From Old French.

NAMES FOR GIRLS

Florence (English, French)
Blossoming - Flourishing

Florentina (Latin)
Blossoming - Flourishing
Elaborated form of Florens.

Forough (Persian)
Glow - Radiance - Ray of Light
Variants: *Foroogh, Forugh, Furoogh, Furugh*

Forouz (Persian)
Light - Radiance
Variants: *Foruz, Furus*

Forouzan (Persian)
Brilliant - Radiant
Variants: *Foruzan, Furuzaan*

Forouzandah (Persian)
Brilliant - Radiant

Fortunata (Italian, Portuguese, Spanish)
Fortunate

Fouzhan (Persian)
Loud Call - Loud Cry

Franca (Italian)
French
Feminine of Franco.

Frances (English)
French
Feminine of Francis.

Francesca (Italian)
French
Feminine form of Francesco.

Francine (English, French)
French
Diminutive pet form of Françoise.

Freda (English)
Peaceful Ruler - Supernaturally Strong
Short form of Elfreda, Winifred and Frederica.

Frederica (German)
Peaceful Ruler
Feminine of Frederick.

Fuadah (Arabic)
Heart - Spirit

Fuhaidaa (Arabic)
Little Leopard

Fuhaidah (Arabic)
Little Leopard

Fukairaa (Arabic)
Intelligent - Thoughtful

Fulailah (Arabic)
Jasmine

Fullah (Arabic)
Jasmine

Furaihaat (Arabic)
Happy

Furaihah (Arabic)
Happy

Furaihat (Arabic)
Happy

Furat (Arabic)
Cool Fresh Water
The name Furat is mentioned in the Quran.

Furjah (Arabic)
Relief - Rescue

Fursah (Arabic)
Chance - Opportunity

Fursat (Arabic, Turkish)
Opportunity - Right Time

Futaihah (Arabic)
Beginning - Conquest - Guidance

Futaimah (Arabic)
Weaned Off Breast Milk

Fuzailah (Arabic)
Excellence - Merit - Virtue

This page intentionally left blank

G

Galawezh (Kurdish)
Canopus
Canopus is a bright star.

Gasheen (Persian)
Good - Likeable

Gemma (English, Irish, Italian)
Gem - Jewel
Variants: *Jemma*

Georgene (English)
Farmer
Altered form of Goergine.

Georgette (English)
Farmer

Georgia (English)
Farmer
Feminine of George.

Georgiana (English)
Farmer
Elaborated form of Georgia or Georgina.

Georgie (English)
Farmer
Pet form of Georgia or Georgina.

Georgina (English, Scottish)
Farmer
Feminine derivative of George.

Georgine (French)
Farmer
Variants: *Georgene*

Ghaaniyah (Arabic)
Beautiful

Ghadah (Arabic)
Gentle - Soft

Ghaddaa (Arabic)
Early Riser

Ghadinah (Arabic)
Gentle - Soft

Ghadiya (Arabic)
Early Morning Rain - Early Riser

Ghaffara (Arabic)
Forgiving
Variants: *Ghaffarah*

Ghafira (Arabic)
Forgiving
Variants: *Ghafirah*

Ghaidaa (Arabic)
Delicate - Gentle

Ghaisat (Arabic)
Rain

Ghalia (Arabic)
Dear - Respected - Valuable

Ghaliaa (Arabic)
Precious - Valuable

Ghaliba (Arabic)
Victor

Ghaniyyah (Arabic)
Needless - Rich - Self-sufficient
Variants: *Ghaneya, Ghaneyah, Ghania, Ghaniah, Ghaniya, Ghaniyah, Ghaniyya*

Gharam (Arabic)
Devotion - Infatuation - Love
The name Gharam is mentioned in the Quran.

Ghareezat (Arabic)
Instincts - Intuitions

Gharidah (Arabic)
Chanter - Singer

Gharisah (Arabic)
Newly Planted Tree - Newly Sown Seed

Gharizah (Arabic)
Instinct - Intution

Ghasina (Arabic)
Beautiful
Variants: *Ghasena, Ghasinah*

Ghawani (Arabic)
Beautiful - Needless

Ghaya (Arabic)
Ultimate Goal

Ghayat (Arabic)
Aim - End Goal

Ghaysah (Arabic)
Rain

Ghazaal (Arabic)
Gazelle - Young Gazelle
Variants: *Gazaal, Gazal, Ghazal, Ghazalle, Ghezal*

Ghazal (Arabic)
Love Poem - Song
Variants: *Gezel*

Ghazalaat (Arabic)
Gazelles

Ghazalah (Arabic)
Gazelle

Ghazia (Arabic)
Warrior

Ghaziyyah (Arabic)
Enduring - Patient

Ghaziyyat (Arabic)
Enduring - Patient

Ghazulah (Arabic)
Spindle

Gheeta (Persian)
Existence - The Creation - World

Gheeti (Persian)
Existence - The Creation - World

Gheeti Afrouz (Persian)
Enlightener of the World

Ghilara (Persian)
Pupil
The pupil is the opening in the eye through which light enters.

Ghislain (English)
Pledge
Variants: *Ghislaine*

Ghizlan (Arabic)
Gazelles

Ghonchah (Persian)
Flower Bud
Variants: *Ghoncheh*

Ghudwah (Arabic)
Early Morning

Ghufrah (Arabic)
Baby Mountain Goat

Ghufran (Arabic)
Forgiveness - Pardon
The name Ghufran is mentioned in the Quran.

Ghuraibah (Arabic)
Gold - Silver

Ghuraisah (Arabic)
Newly Planted Tree - Newly Sown Seed

Ghurrah (Arabic)
Chief - Leader - Moonrise

Ghusna (Arabic)
Tree Branch
Variants: *Ghosna, Ghusnah*

Ghuwaidah (Arabic)
Gentle - Soft

Ghuzail (Arabic, Turkish)
Beautiful

Gilda (Italian)
Sacrifice

Gill (English)
Youthful
Short form of Gillian.

Gillian (English)
Youthful
Variant of Julian.

Gina (English, Italian)
Farmer
Short form of Georgina.

Gohar (Persian)
Gem - Jewel

Goharnaz (Persian)
Beautiful - Charming

Goharshad (Persian)
Gem - Happy - Jewel

Golab (Persian)
Rosewater

Golafruz (Persian)
Beautiful

Golafshan (Persian)
Spreader of Flowers

Golala (Persian)
Tulip

Golan (Persian)
Flowers

Golara (Persian)
Adorned With Flowers

Golbahar (Persian)
Spring Flower

Golbakht (Persian)
Beautiful

Golbar (Persian)
Rose-like

Golbaran (Persian)
Rain of Flowers

Golbarg (Persian)
Flower Petal

Golbouta (Persian)
Shrub Flower

Golchaman (Persian)
Lawn Flower

Golcheen (Persian)
Select - The Best

Golchehr (Persian)
Flower-like

Goldana (Persian)
Flower

Goldar (Persian)
Flower-like

Goldees (Persian)
Flower-like

Goldokht (Persian)
Flower-like

Goleen (Persian)
Flowery - Rosy

Golesorkh (Persian)
Red Rose - Rose

Golestan (Persian)
Land of Flowers

Golestana (Persian)
Land of Flowers

Golezar (Persian)
Flower-like

Golfam (Persian)
Flower-like

Golfar (Persian)
Flower-like

Golghees (Persian)
Flower-like

Goljahan (Persian)
Flower of the World

Golkhanda (Persian)
Flower-like

Golkhandan (Persian)
Happy Flower

Golmehr (Persian)
Sunflower

Golnam (Persian)
Flower-like

Golnar (Persian)
Pomegranate Flower

Golnaz (Persian)
Moss-rose
A type of flower.

Golnisa (Arabic)
Flower Among Women

Golnoush (Persian)
Everlasting Flower

Golpaikar (Persian)
Flower-like

Golpar (Persian)
Persian Hogweed
A type of flowering plant.

Golpara (Persian)
Flower Petal

Golparee (Persian)
Flower Fairy

Golpasand (Persian)
Likable Flower

Golreez (Persian)
Adorned With Flowers

Golrokh (Persian)
Flower-like

Golsa (Persian)
Flower-like

Golseema (Persian)
Flower-like

Golsha (Persian)
Happy Flower

Golshad (Persian)
Happy Flower

Golshan (Persian)
Land of Floewrs

Golsheed (Persian)
Radiant Flower

Golshekar (Persian)
Sweet Flower

Goltala (Persian)
Golden Flower

Golzaar (Persian)
Land of Flowers

Golzad (Persian)
Flower-like

Golzar (Persian)
Golden Flower

Golzari (Persian)
Golden Flower

Gord (Persian)
Brave - Hero

Gouzal (Turkish)
Beautiful

This page intentionally left blank

H

Haalah (Arabic)
Halo

Hababah (Arabic)
Affectionate - Loving

Habaq (Arabic)
Basil - Ocimum
A type of plant.

Habibah (Arabic)
Beloved
Variants: *Habeeba*

Habibiyyah (Arabic)
Beloved

Habiyyah (Arabic)
Little Girl

Habriyah (Arabic)
Blessed - Scholar - Virtuous
Variants: *Habriyyah*

Hadahid (Arabic)
Hoopoes

Hadal (Arabic)
Mistletoe
A type of plant.

Hadees (Arabic)
Hadeeth - Hadis - Hadith - Hedis
The name Hadees is mentioned in the Quran.

Hadfah (Arabic)
Aim - Target

Hadiqah (Arabic)
Garden
Variants: *Hadeeqa*

Hadiya (Arabic)
Guide
Variants: *Hadiyah, Hadye, Hadyeh*

Haelah (Arabic)
Beautiful - Exceptional

Hafifah (Arabic)
Rustle - Swish
Variants: *Hafeefah*

Hafizah (Arabic)
Protector
Variants: *Hafeedha, Hafeezah*

Haibaa (Arabic)
Greatness - Majesty

Haibah (Arabic)
Greatness - Majesty

Haida (Persian)
Clear - Lucid
Variants: *Haideh, Haydeh*

Hajirah (Arabic)
Midday Heat
Variants: *Haajera, Haajerah, Haajira, Haajirah, Hajera, Hajerah, Hajira*

Hajraa (Arabic)
Independent - Needless - Self-sufficient
Variants: *Hajra*

Hakeema (Arabic)
Decisive - Wise
Variants: *Hakeeima, Hakeemah, Hakeima, Hakema, Hakemah, Hakiema, Hakima, Hakimah, Hakimeh, Hakymah, Hekeema, Hekeeyma, Hekeima, Hekeimah, Hekeimeh, Hekiema, Hekima, Hekimah, Hekime, Hekimeh, Hekiyma, Hekyma, Hekymah, Hekyme, Hekymeh*

Hala (Persian)
Halo
Variants: *Haaleh, Haleh*

Halaa (Arabic)
Sweet

Halaat (Arabic)
Sword Gems

Halawah (Arabic)
Sweetness

Haliyah (Arabic)
Adorned

Hallamah (Arabic)
Enduring - Forbearing - Lenient

Hallumah (Arabic)
Forbearing - Lenient - Patient

Halul (Arabic)
Pouring - Torrential

Hamamah (Arabic)
Dove - Pigeon

Hamasah (Arabic)
Ardency - Eagerness - Zeal

Hamda (Arabic)
Noble - Praiseworthy
Variants: *Hamda', Hamdaa, Hemda, Hemdaa*

Hamdam (Persian)
Close Friend - Companion

Hamdanah (Arabic)
Praise - Praiser

Hamdat (Arabic, Turkish)
Praise
Turkish pronunciation of Hamdah.

Hamdiya (Arabic)
Admirable - Noble -

Praiseworthy
Variants: *Hamdeya, Hamdia, Hamdiah, Hamdiyah, Hamdiyya, Hamdiyyah, Hemdye*

Hameda (Arabic)
Praiser of God - Thankful
Variants: *Haameda, Haamedah, Hamedah, Hamida, Hamidah*

Hameeda (Arabic)
Praiser of God - Thankful
Variants: *Hameedah, Hamida, Hamidah*

Hamidat (Arabic)
Praiseworthy
Turkish pronunciation of Hamidah.

Hamim (Arabic)
Close Friend
The name Hamim is mentioned in the Quran.
Variants: *Hameem*

Hamimah (Arabic)
Devoted - Loyal

Hammadah (Arabic)
Praiser
Variants: *Hamada*

Hammadiyyah (Arabic)
Praiseworthy

Hammatah (Arabic)
Extremely Sweet

Hammudah (Arabic)
Praiseworthy

Hammuzah (Arabic)
Lion

Hamraa (Arabic)
Fair-skinned

Hamraz (Persian)
Close Friend - Intimate Friend

Hamta (Persian)
Companion - Partner - Soul Mate
Variants: *Hamtaa*

Hamyaa (Arabic)
Defender - Protector

Hamziyyah (Arabic)
Brave

Hanaa (Arabic)
Happiness - Peace
Variants: *Hana, Hanaa'*

Hanan (Arabic)
Love - Sympathy
The name Hanan is mentioned in the Quran.
Variants: *Hanaan*

Haneen (Arabic)
Desire - Longing - Love - Nostalgia
Variants: *Hanin*

Hangama (Persian)
Amazing - Marvelous - Moment - Season
Variants: *Hangaameh*

Hanifaa (Arabic)
Devout Believer - Monotheist
Variants: *Haneefaa*

Hanifah (Arabic)
Devout Believer - Monotheist
Variants: *Haneefa, Hanifa*

Hanifiyyah (Arabic)
Monotheism
Variants: *Haneefiyah*

Hanita (Persian)
Happy - Joyous
Variants: *Haneetaa*

Haniya (Arabic)
Happy - Joyful - Peaceful
Variants: *Haneya, Haneyah, Hania, Haniah, Haniyah, Hanya, Hanyah*

Haniyya (Arabic)
Delighted - Happy - Joyful
Variants: *Hanea, Haneeah, Haneeia, Haneeya, Hania, Haniyah, Haniyya, Haniyyah, Heneea, Heneia, Heniye, Henyye*

Hannah (Arabic)
Kind - Loving - Sympathetic
Variants: *Hana, Hanah, Hanna*

Hannanah (Arabic)
Affectionate - Caring - Sympathetic

Hannufah (Arabic)
Devout Believer - Monotheist

Hanoon (Arabic)
Affectionate - Sympathetic
Variants: *Hanoun, Hanun*

Hansaa (Arabic)
Brave Warrior

Hanunah (Arabic)
Affectionate - Tender

Hanwa (Arabic)
Xeranthemum
A type of flowering plant.

Haqqaat (Arabic)
Privileges - Rights - Truths

Harayir (Arabic)
Free - Generous - Pure
Variants: *Haraayer*

Hareem (Arabic)
Sanctuary - Sanctum
Variants: *Harim*

NAMES FOR GIRLS

Haritha (Arabic)
Cultivator - Farmer - Lion
Variants: *Haaretha, Haarethah, Haaritha, Haarithah, Haresah, Haretha, Harethah, Harithah*

Haroona (Arabic)
Mountain
Haroona is the Arabic feminine form of Harun. Harun is not an Arabic word, some Arabic sources say it means "mountain".
Variants: *Haroonah, Haruna, Harunah*

Harz (Arabic)
Guardianship - Protection

Harzanah (Arabic)
Guardian - Protector
Variants: *Harzana*

Hasana (Arabic)
Good Deed
The name Hasana is mentioned in the Quran.
Variants: *Hasanah*

Hasanaa (Arabic)
Beautiful

Haseemah (Arabic)
Assiduous - Diligent - Persevering
Variants: *Haseema*

Haseena (Arabic)
Beautiful - Good
Variants: *Haseenah, Hasina, Hasinah*

Hashimah (Arabic)
Modest - Reserved - Virtuous
Variants: *Hasheema*

Hasinah (Arabic)
Beautiful

Hasisah (Arabic)
Inspired - Rapid - Swift
Variants: *Haseesa*

Hasnaa (Arabic)
Beautiful
Variants: *Hasna, Hasnaa', Hesna, Hesnaa*

Hasnaat (Arabic)
Beautiful

Hasnah (Arabic)
Beautiful
Variants: *Hasna*

Hasnaw (Arabic)
Beautiful

Hassunah (Arabic)
Beautiful
Variants: *Hassoona*

Hastee (Persian)
Existence - The Creation

Hatima (Arabic)
Decisive - Wise
Variants: *Haatima, Haatimah, Hatema, Hatemah, Hatimah, Hatyma*

Hattabah (Arabic)
Woodcutter

Hattal (Arabic)
Heavy Rain

Hawa (Arabic)
Tree With Dark Leaves
Variants: *Hawaa*

Hawraa (Arabic)
Fair-skinned - White
Variants: *Haura, Hauraa, Hawra*

Hayaa (Arabic)
Chastity - Modesty - Virtue
Variants: *Haia, Haya*

Hayat (Arabic)
Life
The name Hayat is mentioned in the Quran.
Variants: *Hayaat*

Haydaraa (Arabic)
Lioness
Variants: *Haidara*

Haydarah (Arabic)
Lioness
Variants: *Haidara*

Hayiyyah (Arabic)
Bashful - Modest

Hayyin (Arabic)
Facilitated - Lenient
The name Hayyin is mentioned in the Quran.

Hazarah (Arabic)
Civilization - Culture
Variants: *Hadaara, Hadharah*

Hazeem (Arabic)
Continuous Rain - Thunder

Hazeemah (Arabic)
Intelligent - Wise
Variants: *Hazima*

Haziqa (Arabic)
Brilliant - Excellent - Sagacious - Skillful
Variants: *Haazeqa, Haaziqa, Hazeqah, Haziqah*

Hazmiyah (Arabic)
Determined - Resolute
Variants: *Hazmiyyah*

Heba (Arabic)
Bestowal - Blessing - Gift - Gift from God
Variants: *Hebah, Heiba, Hiba, Hibah, Hybah*

Hedi (Kurdish)
Calm - Serene
Variants: *Hedy*

Hend (Arabic)
Group of 100 to 200 Camels - India - Indian

Hezha (Kurdish)
Respected

Hiddah (Arabic)
Activity - Swiftness
Variants: *Hidda*

Hijra (Arabic)
Asceticism - Avoidance of Sin - Migration
Variants: *Hejra, Hejrah, Hijrah*

Hikma (Arabic)
Wisdom
The name Hikma is mentioned in the Quran.
Variants: *Hekma, Hekmah, Hikmah*

Hikmat (Arabic)
Wisdom
Variants: *Hekmat, Hikmet*

Hilf (Arabic)
Alliance - Treaty

Hillah (Arabic)
Downpour - Show of Rain

Hilyah (Arabic)
Adornment - Jewelry - Virtues

Himaa (Arabic)
Harbor - Haven - Hideaway

Himayah (Arabic)
Care - Guardianship - Safekeeping

Himayat (Arabic, Turkish)
Care - Defense - Protection - Safekeeping
Turkish pronunciation of Himayah.

Hishmah (Arabic)
Modesty - Virtue
Variants: *Hishma*

Hishmat (Arabic, Turkish)
Modesty - Virtue
Variants: *Heshmat*

Hobb (Arabic)
Affectionate - Love
The name Hobb is mentioned in the Quran.

Homa (Persian)
Blessed - Fortuntae
Also the name of a mythical bird that flew higher than all birds.
Variants: *Homaa, Huma, Humaa*

Homadokht (Persian)
Blessed - Fortunate

Hoor (Arabic)
Beautiful - Beautiful-eyed - Companion of Paradise
The name Hoor is mentioned in the Quran.
Variants: *Hour, Hur*

Hoori (Arabic)
Beautiful - Beautiful-eyed - Companion of Paradise
Variants: *Hoory, Houri, Huri, Huriy*

Hooriyah (Arabic)
Beautiful - Beautiful-eyed - Companion of Paradise
Variants: *Hooria, Hooriah, Hooriya, Huriya, Huriyah*

Hounia (Persian)
Good - Noble - Virtuous
Variants: *Honya, Hunia*

Hubab (Arabic)
Beloved

Hubabah (Arabic)
Beloved

Hubaibah (Arabic)
Beloved

Hubbah (Arabic)
Loving

Huda (Arabic)
Guidance
The name Huda is mentioned in the Quran.
Variants: *Hoda, Hodaa, Hudaa*

Hufaizah (Arabic)
Protector
Variants: *Hofaidhah*

Hulaa (Arabic)
Jewelry
Variants: *Holaa*

Hullah (Arabic)
Costume - Dress

Hulou (Arabic)
Sweet
Variants: *Hulu*

Hulwah (Arabic)
Sweet

Hulwi (Arabic)
Sweet

Huma (Arabic)
Guardian - Protectors
Huma is the plural of the boy name Hamee.
Variants: *Homa, Homaa, Homaat, Houma, Houmaa, Howma, Howmaa, Humaa, Humaat, Huwma, Huwmaa*

NAMES FOR GIRLS

Humaira (Arabic)
Healthy - Red-colored - Rosy
Variants: *Homairaa, Humairaa, Humayra, Humayraa*

Hunaifah (Arabic)
Devout Believer - Monotheist
Variants: *Honaifa*

Hunain (Arabic)
Hunain is the name of a valley between at-Taif and Mecca in which a battle took place. The literal meaning of the word is not known.
Variants: *Honain, Honayn, Hunayn*

Hunoon (Arabic)
5th Month of the Islamic Calendar
Synonym for Jamad al-Ula.
Variants: *Honoon, Hunoun*

Huraira (Arabic)
Cat - Kitten

Variants: *Horaira, Horairah, Hurairah, Hurayrah*

Huriaa (Persian)
Woman of Paradise
Variants: *Huryaa*

Hurvash (Arabic)
Beautiful
Variants: *Hoorvash*

Husaimah (Arabic)
Assiduous - Diligent - Persevering
Variants: *Hosaima*

Husainah (Arabic)
Beautiful
Variants: *Hosaina*

Husamah (Arabic)
Sharp Sword - Sword Blade
Variants: *Husama*

Hushaimah (Arabic)
Modesty - Virtue
Variants: *Hoshaima*

Husna (Arabic)
Best - Most Beautiful
The name Husna is mentioned in the Quran.
Variants: *Hosnaa, Husnaa*

Husniyyah (Arabic)
Beautiful

Huveida (Persian)
Apparent - Clear - Lucid - Prominent
Variants: *Hovaida, Hovaidaa, Hoveida, Huveidaa, Huweidaa, Hwaida, Hwaidaa*

Huwainaa (Arabic)
Composure - Leniency - Serenity

This page intentionally left blank

I

Iba (Arabic)
Dignity - Reserve - Self-respect
Variants: *Eba, Ebaa, Eibaa, Iba', Ibaa*

Ibadaat (Arabic)
Acts of Worship

Ibadah (Arabic)
Worship
The name Ibadah is mentioned in the Quran.

Ibhar (Arabic)
Breadth - Graciousness
Variants: *Ebhar, Ibhaar*

Ibrah (Arabic)
Interpretation - Lesson - Wisdom
The name Ibrah is mentioned in the Quran.
Variants: *Ebrah, Ibra*

Ibrat (Arabic)
Interpretation - Lesson - Wisdom
Ibrat is the Turkish pronunciation of the Arabic name Ibrah.
Variants: *Ebrat*

Ibreez (Arabic)
Gold
Variants: *Ebreez, Ebriz, Ibriz*

Ibtihal (Arabic)
Humble Prayer - Supplication
Variants: *Ebtehal*

Ibtisam (Arabic)
Smile
Variants: *Ebetesam, Ebtesaam, Ibtesam, Ibtisaam*

Ibtisama (Arabic)
Smile
Variants: *Ebtesama, Ebtisama, IBtisamah, Ibtesama*

Idrak (Arabic)
Maturation - Perception - Understanding
Variants: *Edraak, Edrak, Idraak*

Iffat (Arabic)
Chastity - Modesty
Turkish pronunciation of Iffah.

Ifra (Arabic)
Enjoining of Good
Variants: *Efra, Efraa, Ifraa*

Ifrah (Arabic)
Gladdening - Heartening - To Make Someone Happy - Uplifting
Variants: *Efraah, Efrah, Ifraah*

Ihdaf (Arabic)
Closeness - Proximity
Variants: *Ihdaaf*

Ihkam (Arabic)
Decisiveness - Mastery
Variants: *Ehkaam, Ehkam, Ihkaam*

Ihlal (Arabic)
Clarity - Radiance
Variants: *Ehlal*

Ihram (Arabic)
Prohibition
The word ihram is used to refer to a pilgrim's entering into a state of prohibition once he starts his pilgrimage, in which many things are prohibited to him, such as hunting or wearing perfume.

Ihsan (Arabic)
Generosity - Good Deeds - Graciousness - Kindness
The name Ihsan is mentioned in the Quran.

Ihtiram (Arabic)
Consideration - Esteem - Regard
Variants: *Ehteram, Ehtiram, Ihteram*

Ihtisham (Arabic)
Modesty - Virtue
Variants: *Ehtisham, Ihtesham, Ihtishaam*

Ijada (Arabic)
Excellence - Proficiency - Skill
Variants: *Ejada, Ejadah, Ijaada, Ijaadah, Ijadah*

Ijlal (Arabic)
Greatness - Majesty
Variants: *Ejlaal, Ejlal, Ijlaal*

Ikha (Arabic)
Brotherhood - Friendship
Variants: *Ekha, Ekhaa, Ikhaa, Ikhaa'*

Ikhlas (Arabic)
Faithfulness - Loyalty - Sincerity
Variants: *Ekhlaas, Ekhlas, Ikhlaas*

Ikleel (Arabic)
Crown
Variants: *Iklil*

Ilan (Arabic)
Announcement - Proclamation
Variants: *Elaan, Ilaan*

Ilana (Arabic)
Gentleness - Softness
Variants: *Elaana, Elana, Ilaana, Ilanah*

Ilham (Arabic)
Inspiration - Muse
Variants: *Elhaan, Elham, Ilhaam*

Ilhan (Arabic)
Eloquence
Variants: *Elhaan, Elhan, Ilhaan*

Iliya (Arabic)
Great - High in Status - Noble
Variants: *Eliyah, Eliyyah, Iliyah, Iliyya, Iliyyah*

Illiyeen (Arabic)
Best Place in Paradise - Highest of Rank - Paradise - Sublime
The name Illiyeen is mentioned in the Quran in verse 83:18.
Variants: *Elienne, Eliyeen, Eliyin, Elliyeen, Elyeanne, Elyinne, Iliyeen, Illiyin, Ilyeen*

Ilm (Arabic)
Knowledge - Science
The name Ilm is mentioned in the Quran.

Ilya (Arabic)
Great - High in Status - Noble
Variants: *Elia, Eliah, Ilia, Iliah, Ilyah*

Ilyana (Arabic)
Gentleness - Leniency - Softness
Non-standard derivation from Liyana and Ilan.
Variants: *Eliana, Elyaanah, Elyana, Ilyaana, Ilyaanah*

Imama (Arabic)
Command - Leadership
Variants: *Imamah*

Iman (Arabic)
Faith
The name Iman is mentioned in the Quran.
Variants: *Eemaan, Eimaan, Eiman, Emaan, Eman, Imaan*

Imaneh (Persian)
Faithful
From Arabic Iman.

Variants: *Emana, Emaneh, Imaan, Imaaneh*

Imani (Arabic)
Faithful
Variants: *Imaani, Imaany, Imany*

Imhal (Arabic)
Forbearance - Leniency
Variants: *Emhal, Imhaal*

Imtisal (Arabic)
Adoration - Imitation - To Follow
Variants: *Emtisal*

Inab (Arabic)
Grape
The name Inab is mentioned in the Quran.

Inabah (Arabic)
Grape Seed - Vine

Inam (Arabic)
Blessings - God's Favors
Variants: *Enaam, In'am, Inaam*

Inan (Arabic)
Grade - Level - Rank - Status
Variants: *Enan, Inaan*

Inara (Arabic)
Enllightenment - Illumination
Variants: *Einara, Enara, Enarah, Eynara, Inaara, Inaarah, Inarah*

Inaya (Arabic)
Care - Diligence - Protection
Variants: *Enaaya, Enaya, Enayah, Inaaya, Inayah*

Inayaat (Arabic)
Care - Consideration - Protection

Inayatullah (Arabic)
God's Care and Protection

Inbihaj (Arabic)
Cheerfulness - Delight - Mirth
Variants: *Enbihaj, Inbehaaj*

Inbisat (Arabic)
Cheerfulness - Joyfulness - Relaxation
Variants: *Enbisat, Inbesaat*

Infisal (Arabic)
Distance - Divergence - Separation
Variants: *Infesal*

Inhal (Arabic)
Pouring of Rain
Variants: *Enhal*

Injah (Arabic)
Success
Variants: *Injaah*

Injeel (Arabic)
Messenger - The Gospels
The name Injeel is mentioned in the Quran.
Variants: *Enjil*

Injeela (Arabic)
Messenger
Variants: *Enjila, Injila*

Inji (Arabic, Turkish)
Pearl

Insaf (Arabic)
Fairness - Justice
Variants: *Insaaf*

Insha (Arabic)
Creation - Expression
Variants: *Ensha*

Inshad (Arabic)
Chanting - Singing
Variants: *Enshad, Inshaad*

NAMES FOR GIRLS

Inshiraf (Arabic)
Glory - Greatness - Honor
Variants: *Insheraaf*

Inshirah (Arabic)
Cheer - Relaxation - Relief
Variants: *Ensherah, Insheraah, Insherah, Inshiraah*

Insijam (Arabic)
Harmony - Symmetry
Variants: *Ensejam, Insejam*

Intibah (Arabic)
Alertness - Attention - Care - Vigilance
Variants: *Entebah, Entibah, Intibaah*

Intiha (Arabic)
Completion - Conclusion - End
Variants: *Intehaa*

Intisar (Arabic)
Triumph - Victory
Variants: *Entisar, Intesaar*

Intishal (Arabic)
Healing - Recovery
Variants: *Entishal, Intishaal*

Intizar (Arabic)
Anticipation - Expectation - Wait
Variants: *Intezaar*

Iqra (Arabic)
Read - Recite
The name Iqra is mentioned in the Quran in verse 96:1. The name is in the form of a command (to read or recite).
Variants: *Eqra, Iqraa*

Irfa (Arabic)
Knowledge - Recognition - Wisdom
Variants: *Erfa, Erfah, Irfah*

Irfana (Arabic)
Knowledge - Wisdom
Variants: *Erfaana, Erfaanah, Erfana, Erfanah, Irfaana, Irfaanah, Irfanah*

Irhaa (Arabic)
Calm - Serene

Irtiqa (Arabic)
Ascension - Ascent - Improvement - Promotion
Variants: *Ertiqa, Ertiqaa, Irteka, Irteqa, Irtika, Irtiqaa*

Isabel (English, French, Spanish)
God is My Oath
Variant of Elizabeth.

Isabella (English)
God is My Oath
From Isabel, variant of Elizabeth.

Isam (Arabic)
Bond - Connection - Promise
Variants: *Esaam, Esam, Isaam*

Ishrah (Arabic)
Companionship - Fellowship

Ishraq (Arabic)
Daybreak - Emergence - Illumination - Sunrise - Vividness
The name Ishraq is mentioned in the Quran.
Variants: *Eshraaq, Eshraq, Ishraaq*

Ismat (Arabic)
Majesty - Purity - Virtue
Variants: *Esmat, Ismet*

Israa (Arabic)
Night Journey
Variants: *Esra*

Israr (Arabic)
Determination - Insistence - Resolve

Istiqlal (Arabic)
Independence - Sovereignty
Variants: *Esteqlal, Estiqlal, Istiqlaal*

Itaa (Arabic)
Growth - Maturing - Yield
Variants: *Eta, Etaa, Ita*

Ithath (Arabic)
Plenty - Splendor
Variants: *Esaas, Esas, Ethaat, Ethath, Isaas, Isas, Ithaath*

Itqan (Arabic)
Mastery - Proficiency - Skill

Ivaz (Persian)
Adorned - Beautified
Variants: *Eewaz, Eiwaz, Evaz, Ewaz, Ivaaz, Iwaaz*

Iyan (Arabic)
Era - Time
The name Iyan is mentioned in the Quran. It is an alternate reading of the word Ayyan used in verse 27:65.
Variants: *Eyaan, Eyan, Eyyan, Iyaan, Iyyan*

Izaan (Arabic)
Acceptance - Obedience - Submission
Variants: *Ezaan, Iz'an*

Izdihar (Arabic)
Blossoming - Flourishing
Variants: *Ezdihar*

Izma (Arabic)
Greatness - Importance - Might
Variants: *Ezma, Ezmah, Izmah*

Izmat (Arabic)
Greatness - Importance - Might
Variants: *Ezmat*

Izzaa (Arabic)
Greatness - Might - Power

Izzat (Arabic)
Greatness - Majesty - Might

Izzi (Arabic)
Mighty - Powerful - Strong

J

Jabaa (Arabic)
Slender - Slim

Jabbadah (Arabic)
Attractive - Charming

Jabeehah (Arabic)
Beautiful

Jabira (Arabic)
Fixer - Improver - Mender
Variants: *Jaabera, Jaaberah, Jaabira, Jaabirah, Jabera, Jaberah, Jabirah*

Jablah (Arabic)
Power - Strength

Jabraa (Arabic)
Mender

Jabrah (Arabic)
Brave

Jadirah (Arabic)
Deserving - Essence - Nature

Jafeerah (Arabic)
River

Jafurah (Arabic)
River

Jahan (Persian)
World
Variants: *Jahaan, Jehaan, Jehan, Jihaan, Jihan*

Jahdaa (Arabic)
Striver

Jahidah (Arabic)
Striver

Jahizah (Arabic)
Prepared - Ready

Jahudah (Arabic)
Striver

Jamalah (Arabic)
Beauty

Jamila (Arabic)
Beautiful - Radiant
Variants: *Gamilah, Jameela, Jameelah, Jameeleh, Jameila, Jameilah, Jameileh, Jameyleh, Jamilah, Jamyla, Jemeela, Jemeelah, Jemeila, Jemeilah, Jemila, Jemilah, Jemile, Jemileh, Jemylah, Jemyleh*

Jamilaa (Arabic)
Beautiful

Jamlaa (Arabic)
Beautiful
Variants: *Gemla*

Jamlah (Arabic)
Beautiful

Janafruz (Persian)
Consoling - Soothing

Janan (Persian)
Beloved - Good
Variants: *Jaanan, Janaan*

Janina (Arabic)
Garden - Silk Chador
Variants: *Janeena, Janeenah, Janinah*

Jannaat (Arabic)
Gardens - Paradise
The name Jannaat is mentioned in the Quran.
Variants: *Janaat, Janat, Jannat, Jennat*

Jannah (Arabic)
Garden - Paradise
The name Jannah is mentioned in the Quran.
Variants: *Jana, Janah, Janna, Jena, Jenah, Jenna, Jennah*

Jasimah (Arabic)
Hulking - Muscular - Strong
Variants: *Jasemah, Jasima*

Javaneh (Persian)
New - Young

Jawahar (Arabic)
Jewels - Precious Stones
Alternative form of Jawahir.
Variants: *Jawaahar, Joaahar, Joahar, Jowahar*

Jawahir (Arabic)
Jewelry - Jewels - Precious Stones
Plural of Jawharah.
Variants: *Jawaaher, Jawaahir, Jawaher, Jowaher, Jowahir*

Jawd (Arabic)
Torrential Rain

Jawdah (Arabic)
Goodness - Virtue

Jawdat (Arabic)
Goodness - Virtue

Jawhar (Arabic)
Essence - Jewel - Precious Stone
Variants: *Johar, Jouhar, Jowhar*

Jawhara (Arabic)
Essence - Jewel - Precious Stone
Variants: *Jawharah, Johara, Joharah*

Jayidah (Arabic)
Good - Gracious

Jazaa (Arabic)
Recompense - Reward
The name Jazaa is mentioned in the Quran.
Variants: *Jaza, Jaza', Jeza, Jezaa*

Jazal (Arabic)
Delight - Happiness

Jazilaa (Arabic)
Great - Tremendous

Jazilah (Arabic)
Great - Majestic

Jewel (English)
Gemstone

Jibal (Arabic)
Mountains
The name Jibal is mentioned in the Quran.
Variants: *Jebaal, Jebal, Jibaal*

Jibalah (Arabic)
Mountains

Jidah (Arabic)
Generosity - Graciousness

Jihadah (Arabic)
Strife - Struggle

Jinan (Arabic)
Gardens - Paradises

Jinani (Arabic)
Heavenly

Joanna (Latin)
God is Gracious
Used as a feminine of John.

Joanne (English)
God is Gracious
Feminine of John, from Old French.

Jodd (Arabic)
Beach - Coast - Fortunate - Side

Joelle (English)
Yahweh is God
Used as a feminine of Joel, taken from French Joëlle.

Johan (Scottish)
God is Gracious
Older Scottish spelling of Joan.

Johana (Czech)
God is Gracious
Form of Joanna.

Johanna (Dutch, German, Scandinavian)
God is Gracious
Feminine of Johannes.

Johd (Arabic)
Strife - Struggle

Jonna (Danish)
God is Gracious
Contracted form of Johanna.

Josefa (Czech, Portuguese, Scandinavian, Spanish)
God Shall Add
Feminine form of Joseph.

Josephine (English)
God Shall Add
English form of Joséphine, feminine of Joseph.

Joud (Arabic)
Generosity - Graciousness

Joudah (Arabic)
Generosity - Graciousness

Joy (English)
Joy

Joyce (English)
Lord

Juana (Spanish)
God is Gracious
Feminine form of Juan.

Juanita (Spanish)
God is Salvation
Feminine pet form of Juan.

Jubaihah (Arabic)
Face

Jublah (Arabic)
Essence - Nature

Judiyah (Arabic)
Generous - Selfless

Judy (Arabic)
The name *Judy* is mentioned in the Quran.
Variants: *Joodi, Joody, Joudi, Judi*

Juhainah (Arabic)
Young Woman

Julia (Latin)
Youthful
Feminine form of Julius.

Juliana (Latin)
Youthful

Julianne (English)
God Has Favored Me - Youthful
Combination of Julie and Anne.
May also be used as a form of Juliana.

Julie (French)
Youthful
French form of Julia.

Julienne (French)
Youthful
Feminine of Julien.

Juliet (English)
Youthful
Anglicized form of Juliette or Guilietta (both of which have the same meaning).

Juliette (French)
Youthful
Diminutive of Julie.

Jumalaa (Arabic)
Beautiful

Jumanah (Arabic)
Pearl

Jumlanah (Arabic)
Nightingale

Junaina (Arabic)
Garden

Variants: *Jonaina, Jonainah, Junainah, Junayna, Junaynah*

Juniper (English)
Juniper
A type of plant.

Justine (English)
Fair - Just

Juwayriya (Arabic)
Damask Rose - Rose - Young Woman
Variants: *Jouaria, Jowairiah, Juairia, Juairiyah, Juwayriyyah, Jwairiyyah*

This page intentionally left blank

NAMES FOR GIRLS

K

Kaarima (Arabic)
Excellent - Generous - Gracious - Noble
Variants: *Kaarema, Kaaremah, Kaarimah, Karema, Karemah, Karima, Karimah*

Kabira (Arabic)
Chief - Great - Powerful
The name Kabira is mentioned in the Quran.
Variants: *Kabeera, Kabeerah, Kabirah*

Kafiyah (Arabic)
Sufficient

Kahal (Arabic)
One Who Has Beautiful Dark Eyelids

Kahhalah (Arabic)
Kohl-wearer

Kahlaa (Arabic)
One Who Has Beautiful Black Eyes

Kaina (Arabic)
Being - Event - Existing - Happening
Variants: *Caena, Caina, Cainah, Cayena, Ka'ina, Kaena, Kainah*

Kainaat (Arabic)
The Creation
Variants: *Kaenat, Kainat*

Kalifah (Arabic)
Adorer - Lover

Kalima (Arabic)
Word
The name Kalima is mentioned in the Quran.
Variants: *Kalema, Kalemah, Kalimah*

Kalsum (Arabic)
Beautiful
Lterally "one who has full, healthy cheeks". Variant of Kulsum.

Kalsumah (Arabic)
Beautiful
Variant of Kulsumah.

Kamalah (Arabic)
Completeness - Perfection - Wholeness

Kamaliyyah (Arabic)
Complete - Perfect - Whole

Kamayilah (Arabic)
Complete - Perfect - Whole

Kamilaa (Arabic)
Complete - Whole

Kamilah (Arabic)
Complete - Flawless - Perfect - Whole
The name Kamilah is mentioned in the Quran in verse 2:196.
Variants: *Camilla, Kaamila, Kaamilah, Kamela, Kamelah, Kamella, Kamellah, Kamila, Kamilla, Kamillah*

Kamilat (Arabic)
Complete - Perfect - Whole

Kamillaa (Arabic)
Complete - Perfect - Whole

Kandus (Arabic)
Magpie
A type of bird.

Kani (Persian)
Precious - Valuable
Variants: *Kaani, Kany*

Kani (Kurdish)
Fountain - Spring

Kania (Persian)
Fountain - Spring

Kaniaw (Kurdish)
Spring Water

Kanza (Arabic)
Treasure
Variants: *Kanzah, Kenza, Kenzah, Kinza*

Karam (Arabic)
Generosity - Graciousness

Karamah (Arabic)
Graciousness - Honor

Karawan (Arabic)
Curlew
A type of bird.

Kareema (Arabic)
Excellent - Generous - Gracious - Noble
Variants: *Kareemah, Karima, Karimah*

Kareen (Persian)
Distant - Faraway
Variants: *Karin*

Karen (Danish)
Pure
Danish form of Katherine.

Kari (Norwegian)
Pure
Norwegian form of Katharine.

Karin (Swedish)
Pure
Swedish form of Katherine.

Karita (Scandinavian)
Affection
Scandinavian form of Charity.

Karlotte (German)
Free Woman
Form of Charlotte.

Karolina (Czech, Polish, Scandinavian)
Free Woman
Form of Caroline.

Karoline (Danish, German)
Free Woman
Form of Caroline.

Kashaaf (Arabic)
Discoverer - Finder
Variants: *Kashaaf, Kashshaf, Keshaf*

Kasia (Polish)
Pure
Pet form of Katarzyna, Polish form of Katherine.

Katana (Persian)
Beautiful - Fresh
Variants: *Kataneh*

Katarina (Swedish)
Pure
Swedish form of Katherine.

Katarzyna (Polish)
Pure
Polish form of Katherine.

Kate (English)
Pure
Short form of Katherine.

Kateebah (Arabic)
Battalion - Regiment

Katerina (Russian)
Pure
Russian form of Katherine.

Katharine (English)
Pure
Variant of Katherine.

Katherine (English)
Pure
The original meaning of this name is unknown, but it is often used by association with the Greek word katharos ("pure").

Kathleen (English, Irish)
Pure
Form of Gaelic Caitlín, itself from Katherine.

Kathryn (English)
Pure
American form of Katherine.

Katibah (Arabic)
Writer

Katie (English)
Pure
Pet form of Kate.
Variants: *Katy*

Katinka (Russian)
Pure
Pet form derived from Katya.

Katrien (Dutch)
Pure
Dutch form of Katherine.
Variants: *Katrijn*

Katrine (Danish, German)
Pure
Contracted form of Katharine.

Katriona (English)
Pure
Variant spelling of Catriona, itself from Katherine.

Kattamah (Arabic)
Keeper of Secrets

Katya (Russian)
Pure
Pet form of Yekatarina, Russian form of Katherine.

Kawkab (Arabic)
Star
The name Kawkab is mentioned in the Quran in verse 6:76.
Variants: *Kaukab, Kokab*

Kawkabah (Arabic)
Planet - Star - Venus
Variants: *Kaukabah, Kawkabah, Kokaba, Kowkaba*

Kawnaa (Arabic)
Existing - Hapening

Kawnah (Arabic)
Existing - Hapening

Kawnain (Arabic)
Beings - Existences - Universes

Kayaneh (Arabic, Persian)
Queen-like - Royal
Variants: *Kaianeh, Kayaaneh*

Kazhal (Persian)
Black-eyed

Kazimah (Arabic)
One Who Controls His Own Anger

Kaziwa (Persian)
Dawn
Variants: *Kazeewa*

Keelin (Irish)
White and Slender

Keihana (Persian)
Cosmos - Universe - World
Variants: *Kayhaneh, Kihaneh*

Keivandokht (Persian)
Beautiful

Kestrel (English)
Kestrel
A type of bird.

NAMES FOR GIRLS

Keyanaz (Persian)
Elite - High-born - Noble
Variants: *Kianaz*

Keyandokht (Persian)
Elite - High-born - Noble

Kezia (Biblical)
Tree
Name of one of the daughters of Job (prophet Ayyub in the Quran).

Khabirah (Arabic)
Experienced - Expert

Khadijah (Arabic)
Born Preterm
Variants: *Hadija, Hedije, Kadija, Khadeeja, Khadeejah, Khadija*

Khadujah (Arabic)
Preterm Giver of Birth
Pet form of Khadijah.

Khafifah (Arabic)
Nimble - Sprightly
Variants: *Khafeefa*

Khaira (Arabic)
Beautiful - Virtuous
Variants: *Caira, Cairah, Caire, Caireh, Hairah, Kaireh, Kayra, Kayrah, Kayre, Kayreh, Keira, Keirah, Keire, Keireh, Kerah, Keyrah, Keyre, Keyreh, Khairah, Khaireh, Khayrah, Kheirah, Kheireh, Khera, Kheyra, Kheyrah, Kheyre, Kheyreh*

Khairaat (Arabic)
Beauty - Goodness
The name Khairaat is mentioned in the Quran in verse 55:70.
Variants: *Khairat, Khayraat, Khayrat, Kheirat*

Khaldaa (Arabic)
Immortal

Khaleedah (Arabic)
Immortal

Khaleef (Arabic)
Leader - Successor
Variants: *Kaleef, Khaleif, Khalif*

Khaleefa (Arabic)
Leader - Successor
The name Khaleefa is mentioned in the Quran.
Variants: *Kalifa, Kalifah, Khaleefah, Khalifa, Khalifah*

Khaleela (Arabic)
Companion - Friend
Variants: *Helile, Kaleela, Kalila, Kalilah, Kalyla, Khaleelah, Khalilah, Khalyla, Khelile*

Khalidah (Arabic)
Immortal
Variants: *Khaleda, Khalida*

Khalisah (Arabic)
Pure
The name Khalisah is mentioned in the Quran.
Variants: *Khalesa*

Khaliyah (Arabic)
Bygone - Solitary
The name Khaliyah is mentioned in the Quran.

Khalsat (Arabic)
Purity - Safety

Khalulah (Arabic)
Nimble - Sprightly

Khamrah (Arabic)
Fragrance

Kharaman (Persian)
Charming - Elegant - Graceful

Khasabah (Arabic)
Blessed
Variants: *Khasaaba*

Khasibah (Arabic)
Blessed - Fertile - Productive

Khatereh (Persian)
Memory - Recollection

Khatibah (Arabic)
Orator - Speaker

Khatrah (Arabic)
Idea - Notion - Occurrence

Khavar (Persian)
East - Orient

Khawatir (Arabic)
Ideas - Notions - Thoughts

Khawdan (Arabic)
Delicate - Good-mannered

Khawlah (Arabic)
Gazelle

Khayal (Arabic)
Fantasy - Imagination - Vision

Khayriyyah (Arabic)
Charitable - Good
Variants: *Kahyriyya, Khayrea, Khayria, Khayriah, Khayriya, Khayriyah*

Khayyira (Arabic)
Beautiful - Virtuous
Variants: *Cayyera, Cayyira, Hayyire, Kayera, Kayerah, Kayyerah, Khaiyrah, Khayera, Khayerah, Khayirah, Khayyera, Khayyerah, Khayyirah*

Khazraa (Arabic)
Green - Green-colroed

Khazrat (Arabic)
Green - Softness

Khazzarah (Arabic)
Green - Soft

Kheer (Arabic)
Generosity - Honor - Virtue

Khibrah (Arabic)
Deep Knowledge - Expertise

Khilal (Arabic)
Companionship - Friendship
The name Khilal is mentioned in the Quran in verse 14:31.
Variants: *Kelal, Khelaal, Khelal, Khilaal, Khylal, Kilal*

Khilfah (Arabic)
Successor

Khilfat (Arabic)
Successor

Khimar (Arabic)
Cover - Scarf - Veil

Khimrah (Arabic)
Fragrance - Scarf - Veil

Khiraa (Arabic)
Purification - Selection

Khisbah (Arabic)
Blessed

Khojasteh (Persian)
Blessed - Fortunate

Khorshid (Persian)
Sun

Khubchehr (Persian)
Beautiful

Khulaifah (Arabic)
Successor

Khulaisah (Arabic)
Pristine - Wholesome

Khullah (Arabic)
Friendship - Love

Khulud (Arabic)
Immortality
Variants: *Kholood, Kholud, Khulood*

Khusaibah (Arabic)
Blessed - Fruitful - Productive

Khuta (Arabic)
Steps

Khuwaid (Arabic)
Delicate - Good-mannered - Tender

Khuwairah (Arabic)
Good - Virtuous

Khuzaimah (Arabic)
Gabal Elba Dragon Tree
A type of tree.

Khuzarah (Arabic)
Ocean - Sea

Khuzrah (Arabic)
Green - Softness

Kiana (Persian)
Essence

Kiara (Persian)
Pica
Pica refers to a desire for eating non-nutritious things, such as ice.

Kifah (Arabic)
Strife - Struggle
Variants: *Kefaah, Kefah, Kifaah*

Kifahah (Arabic)
Strife - Struggle

Kifayah (Arabic)
Adequacy - Contentment - Satisfaction

Kifayatullah (Arabic)
God's Contentment
Contentment that is bestowed by God.

Kilina (Ukranian)
Eagle-like
Form of Akilina.

Kilya (Russian)
Eagle-like
Pet form of Akilina.

Kimia (Persian)
Elixir
Variants: *Keemya*

Kina (Scottish)
Defender of Humanity
Short form of Alickina, originally from Alexander.

Kinanah (Arabic)
Quiver
A container that holds arrows.

Kindiyyah (Arabic)
Mountain-dweller

Kiram (Arabic)
Gracious Ones - Honorable Ones
The name Kiram is mentioned in the Quran.

Kiswa (Arabic)
Clothing - Garment
Refers to the black silk cloth that covers the Kaaba in Mecca, Saudi Arabia.
Variants: *Keswa, Keswah, Kiswah*

Klara (Dutch, German, Polish, Russian, Scandinavian)
Famous
Form of Clara.

Klementyna (Polish)
Merciful
Form of Clementina.

Kohl (Arabic)
Kohl

Kufah (Arabic)
Mound of Sand

Kukka (Finnish)
Flower

Kulaisim (Arabic)
Beautiful - Full-cheeked

Kulbahar (Arabic)
Flower of Spring
From Persian Gulbahar.

Kulfah (Arabic)
Burden - Charge - Tan Color

Kulfat (Arabic)
Burden - Charge - Tan Color

Kulsoom (Arabic)
Beautiful - Full-cheeked

Kulsumah (Arabic)
Beautiful - Full-cheeked

Kulya (Russian)
Eagle-like
Pet form of Akilina.

Kumailah (Arabic)
Complete - Perfect - Whole

Kumailiyah (Arabic)
Complete - Perfect - Whole

Kunaizah (Arabic)
Little Treasure

Kundas (Arabic)
Magpie
A type of bird.

Kuram (Arabic)
Gracious Ones - Honorable Ones

Kyle (English)
Narrow Strait
From a Scottish surname, from the name of a region.

Kyra (English)
Lord
Variant of Cyra, feminine of Cyrus.

This page intentionally left blank

L

Laaiqah (Arabic)
Eligible - Qualified - Suitable

Labeebaa (Arabic)
Intelligent

Labeebah (Arabic)
Intelligent - Sagacious

Labisah (Arabic)
Wearer

Ladeenaa (Arabic)
Gentle

Ladeenah (Arabic)
Gentle - Good-mannered

Lahjah (Arabic)
Dialect

Lahzah (Arabic)
Blink of an Eye - Instance - Moment
Variants: *Lahza, Lahzeh*

Lail (Arabic)
Night
The name Lail is mentioned in the Quran.
Variants: *Layl, Leil, Leyl*

Laila (Arabic)
Ecstasy - Intoxication
Name of a Sahabiyyah.
Variants: *Lailaa, Layla, Laylaa, Leila, Leyla*

Lailah (Arabic)
Night
The name Lailah is used in the Quran.
Variants: *Laila, Layla, Laylah*

Lailan (Arabic)
Two Nights

Lailat (Arabic)
Nights

Laily (Arabic)
Belonging to the Night - Nightly

Laithaa (Arabic)
Lioness

Laithah (Arabic)
Lioness

Lala (Persian)
Tulip
Variants: *Laala, Laalah, Laaleh, Lalah, Laleh*

Lalaa (Arabic)
Glimmer - Shine

Lalee (Arabic)
Pearls
Variants: *La'aali, La'ali, Laalee, Laalei, Laali, Laaly, Lalei, Lali, Laly*

Lalezar (Persian)
Field of Tulips
Variants: *Laalehzar, Laalezar, Lalezaar*

Lamaah (Arabic)
Glimmer - Shine

Lamaan (Arabic)
Glimmer - Shine

Lamihah (Arabic)
One Who Glances

Lana (Arabic)
Gentle - Lenient - Soft
Variants: *Laana*

Lara (English)
Famous

Short form of Klara. It can also be short for the Russian name Larissa, whose meaning is not known.

Larisaa (Persian)
Precious - Valuable
Variants: *Lareesa, Larisa*

Lark (English)
Lark
A type of bird.

Lasiniyyah (Arabic)
Eloquent - Fluent

Lasnaa (Arabic)
Eloquent - Fluent

Latafat (Arabic)
Gentleness - Kindness

Latayif (Arabic)
Gentle - Kind

Lateefa (Arabic)
Gentle - Kind
Variants: *Lateefah, Latifa, Latifah*

Laura (English, Italian, Spanish)
Laurel

Laurel (English)
Laurel
A type of tree.
Variants: *Laurelle*

Lauretta (Italian)
Laurel
Diminutive form of Laura.

Laveen (Persian)
Name of a place near the Western border of Iran.
Variants: *Laaveen, Laavin, Lavin*

Lavender (English)
Lavender

A type of herb with purple flowers.

Lawahiz (Arabic)
Eyes - One Who Glances

Laweeh (Arabic)
Apparent - Manifest - Visible

Layaal (Arabic)
Nights
The name Layaal is mentioned in the Quran.

Layan (Arabic)
Gentleness - Softness
Variants: *Laean, Laian, Laiane, Layaan, Layane, Layanne*

Layana (Persian)
Radiant - Shining
Variants: *Layaana, Layanaa*

Layliyyah (Arabic)
Belonging to the Night - Nightly

Layyanah (Arabic)
Affable - Friendly - Gentle

Layyasah (Arabic)
Brave

Layyin (Arabic)
Delicate - Soft - Tender
The name *Layyin* is mentioned in the Quran.
Variants: *Layen, Layene, Layinne, Layyen, Layyene, Layyine, Leine, Leyin, Leyinne, Leyyin*

Layyina (Arabic)
Delicate - Soft - Tender
Variants: *Layena, Layenah, Layene, Layeneh, Layineh, Layyena, Layyenah, Layyinah, Layyineh, Leinah, Leyina, Leyyina*

Lazimah (Arabic)
Desired - Wished For

Leah (Biblical)
Languid
Name of the first wife of Jacob (prophet Ya`qub in the Quran).
Variants: *Lea*

Leanne (Arabic)
Delicate - Gentle - Soft
Variants: *Leane, Leyanne, Lian, Liyan, Liyane, Liyanne, Lyan*

Leanne (English)
Clearing - God Has Favored Me - Shining Light - Wood
Combination of Lee ("wood", "clearing") and Anne ("God has favored me"), or variant spelling of Liane ("shining light").

Lee (English)
Clearing - Wood
From a surname referring to various places.

Leen (Arabic)
Delicate - Gentle - Soft - Tender
Variants: *Leein, Leene, Leeyn, Lein, Leine, Leine, Lene, Leyn, Leyne, Liene, Lin, Liyne, Lyn, Lyne*

Leena (Arabic)
Delicate - Gentle - Soft - Tender
The name Leena is mentioned in the Quran in verse 59:5.
Variants: *Leeinah, Leenah, Leina, Leinah, Lenah, Leineh, Lenah, Liena, Lina, Linah, Liynah, Lyna, Lynah, Lyneh*

Leeniyyah (Arabic)
Friendly - Gentle

Leesa (English)
My God is Bountiful
Variant of Lisa, originally form Elizabeth.

Lempi (Finnish)
Love

Lena (Dutch, English, German, Scandinavian, Scottish)
Shining Light
Derived from names ending with lena or lina, such as Helena.

Lene (Danish, German)
Shining Light
Short form of Helene or Magdalene.

Lenora (English)
Shining Light
From Leonora or Lena.
Variants: *Lennora, Lennorah, Lenorah*

Leocadia (Spanish)
Bright - Clear - Light

Leona (English, German)
Lion
Feminine of Leon.

Leonora (English)
Shining Light
From Eleonora, from Helen.

Leontina (Italian)
Lion

Letizia (Italian)
Happiness
Italian form of Lettice.

Lettice (English)
Happiness

Lexine (English, Scottish)
Defender of Humanity
Elaboration of Lexy, pet form of Alexandra.

Lexy (English)
Defender of Humanity
Pet form of Alexandra.

NAMES FOR GIRLS

Lia (Italian)
Languid - Rose
From Leah or Rosalia.

Liane (English, French)
Shining Light
Short form of Éliane.
Variants: *Lianne*

Lida (Czech)
Woman From Lydia
Lydia is a region in Asia Minor (today's Turkey).

Lidia (Polish)
Woman From Lydia
Lydia is a region in Asia Minor (today's Turkey).

Lidmila (Czech)
Grace of the Tribe
Form of Ludmila

Liduina (Italian)
Friend of the People
Form of Lidwina.

Lidwina (Dutch)
Friend of the People

Liese (German)
My God is Bountiful
German pet form of Elisabeth.

Lieselotte (German)
My God is Bountiful
From Liese and the suffix -lotte used for diminution.

Lila (English)
Night
Variant of Arabic Laila or Leila.

Lilac (English)
Lilac
The name of a flowering shrub.
Originally from Persian.

Lili (German)
My God is Bountiful
Pet form of Elizabeth.

Lilia (Persian)
Nigth
Variants: *Lilya*

Lilian (English)
My God is Bountiful
Probably derived from Elizabeth.
Variants: *Lillian*

Lilo (German)
My God is Bountiful
Pet form of Lieselotte.

Lilufar (Persian)
Waterlily
Variant of Nilufar.
Variants: *Leelufar, Lilofar*

Lily (English)
Lily
A type of flower.

Liona (English)
Lion
Altered form of Leona.

Lipa (Romanian)
Horse-lover
Short form of Filipa.

Liqa (Arabic)
Meeting
The name Liqa is mentioned in the Quran.
Variants: *Leqa, Liqaa*

Lis (English)
My God is Bountiful
Variant of Liz.

Lis (Scandinavian)
My God is Bountiful
Shortened form of Elisabet.

Lisa (English)
My God is Bountiful
Variant of Liza, short for Eliza, short for Elizabeth.

Lisbet (English, Scandinavian)
My God is Bountiful
Short form of Elizabeth or Elisabet.

Lisette (French)
My God is Bountiful
Diminutive form of Lise, short for Elisabeth.
Variants: *Lysette*

Lisha (English)
Delightful - Lucky
Shortened form of Delicia, and Felicia.

Lissa (English)
Bee
Short form of Melissa. May also be used as a variant of Lyssa.

Liv (Scandinavian)
Defense - Protection
May also be used as a variant of Elisabet, in which case it would mean "My God is Bountiful".

Livia (English)
Olive
Often a short form of Olivia, though originally from the Roman family name Livius, which may have had a meaning close to "bluish".

Liwaa (Arabic)
Banner - Ensign - Flag

Liyana (Arabic)
Gentleness - Softness - Tenderness
Variants: *Leana, Leeanah, Liana, Lianna, Liannah, Liyanah*

Liz (English)
My God is Bountiful
Short form of Elizabeth.

Liza (English)
My God is Bountiful
Short form of Eliza.

Lizzie (English)
My God is Bountiful
Pet form of Liz.
Variants: *Lizzy*

Lora (German)
Laurel
German form of Laura.
Variants: *Lore*

Loredana (Italian)
Laurel Grove
Originally from the place name Loreo.

Loreen (English)
Laurel
Elaboration of Lora.

Lorelle (English)
Laurel
Elaboration of Lora.

Lorene (English)
Laurel
Variant of Loreen.

Loretta (English)
Laurel
Variant of Lauretta.

Lorinda (English)
Laurel
Elaboration of Lora.

Lorraine (English, Scottish)
From the Land of Famous Warriors
Refers to a migrant from Lorraine in France. Lorraine itself means "territory of the Lothar", and "Lothar" means "famous warrior(s)".
Variants: *Lorane*

Lothar (German)
Famous Warrior

Lottelore (German)
Free Woman - Shining Light
From Karlotte and Lore.

Lou (English)
Famous Warrior
Short form of Louis or Louise.

Louella (English)
Famous Warrior
From Louise, feminine of Louis.

Louisa (English)
Famous Warrior
Feminine of Louis.

Louise (English, French)
Famous Warrior
Feminine of Louis.

Lova (Swedish)
Famous Warrior
Pet form of Lovisa.

Lovisa (Latin)
Famous Warrior
Form of Louise.

Lubabaa (Arabic)
Affluence - Pure

Lubabah (Arabic)
Pure

Lubaibah (Arabic)
Pure

Lucetta (English)
Illuminated - Radiant
Elaboration of Lucia or Lucy.

Lucia (English)
Illuminated - Radiant
Feminine of Lucius.

Luciana (Italian, Portuguese, Spanish)
Illuminated - Radiant
Feminine of Luciano.

Luciella (Italian)
Illuminated - Radiant
Diminutive form of Lucia.

Lucilla (Latin)
Illuminated - Radiant
Pet form of Lucia.

Lucille (French)
Illuminated - Radiant
French form of Lucilla.

Lucinda (French)
Illuminated - Radiant
Derivative of Lucia.

Lucy (English)
Illuminated - Radiant
From Lucia.

Ludmila (Czech, Russian)
Grace of the Tribe

Ludovica (Dutch, German)
Famous Warrior
Feminine of Ludovic.

Luella (English)
Famous Warrior
Variant of Louella.

Lughah (Arabic)
Language

Luha (Arabic)
Amount - Measure

Luham (Arabic)
Great

Luisa (Spanish)
Famous Warrior
Feminine of Luis.

Luise (German)
Famous Warrior
Form of Louise.

Lujain (Arabic)
Silver

Luluah (Arabic)
Bead of Pearl - Pearl

Lumaihah (Arabic)
Glance
Lumaihah is an Arabic name for girls that means "glance".

Lutaifah (Arabic)
Gentle - Kind

Lutfah (Arabic)
Gentleness - Kindness - Leniency

Luwaihah (Arabic)
Painting Canvas

Luzdivina (Spanish)
Divine Light

Lydia (English)
Woman From Lydia
Lydia is an area in Asia Minor (modern day Turkey).

Lysette (English)
My God is Bountiful
Variant of Lisette.

Lyssa (English)
High-born - Noble
Short form of Alyssa.

Lyubov (Russian)
Love

This page intentionally left blank

M

Maab (Arabic)
Place of Return
The name Maab is mentioned in the Quran in verse 13:29. The Quran uses this name to refer to Paradise.
Variants: *Ma'aab, Ma'ab, Mab*

Maadah (Arabic)
Recurrence - Return

Maadulah (Arabic)
Balanced - Rectified - Tuned

Maanah (Arabic)
Easy

Maarib (Arabic)
Destiny - Goal
The name Maarib is mentioned in the Quran in verse 20:18.
Variants: *Ma'aareb, Ma'arib, Maareb, Mareb, Mareyb, Mareybe, Marib*

Maarifah (Arabic)
Awareness - Knowledge - Wisdom

Maarifatuddin (Arabic)
Knowledge of the Faith

Maarij (Arabic)
Ascents - Routes of Ascent - Stairs
The name Maarij is mentioned in the Quran.

Maash (Arabic)
Livelihood - Sustenance
The name Maash is mentioned in the Quran.

Maawa (Arabic)
Refuge - Sanctuary

The name Maawa is mentioned in the Quran.
Variants: *Ma'wa, Maawaa, Mawaa*

Maazah (Arabic)
Affection - Honor - Love - Respect
Variants: *Maaza, Maazza, Mazzah*

Maazuzah (Arabic)
Powerful - Strong

Mabel (English)
Lovely
From Old French amabel.
Variants: *Mable*

Mabelle (English)
Lovely
Variant of Mabel.

Mabrukah (Arabic)
Blessed

Madeehaa (Arabic)
Praise

Madeehah (Arabic)
Praise

Madihah (Arabic)
Praiser

Madina (Arabic)
City
Madina is the name of the city of the Prophet (pbuh) in Arabia.
Variants: *Madeenah, Madeina, Madinah, Madyna, Medina, Medyna*

Madinaa (Arabic)
City
Variant of Madinah.

Mae (English)
Drop of the Sea - Hawthorn - Pearl
Variant of May.

Maeen (Arabic)
Fountain - Spring - Water Stream
The name Maeen is mentioned in the Quran.
Variants: *Maein, Main*

Maeena (Arabic)
Helper - Supporter
Variants: *Maeeneh, Maeyna, Maiena, Maina, Mayina, Mayna*

Mafalda (Italian, Portuguese)
Strength in Battle
Variant of Matilda.

Mafaz (Arabic)
Salvation - Success
The name Mafaz is mentioned in the Quran.
Variants: *Mafaaz, Maphaz, Mefaz*

Mafazah (Arabic)
Salvation - Success
The name Mafazah is mentioned in the Quran.
Variants: *Mafaaza, Mafaza, Mefaaza, Mefaza, Mefaze, Mephaze*

Maftooh (Arabic)
Free - Open
Variants: *Maftuh*

Mafzalah (Arabic)
Graciousness

Maghdah (Arabic)
Gentle - Soft

Maghfira (Arabic)
Forgiveness - Pardon
The name Maghfira is mentioned in the Quran.
Variants: *Magfira, Maghfera, Maghferah, Maghfirah*

Mah (Persian)
Moon
Variants: *Maah*

Maha (Persian)
Moon-like
Variants: *Mahaa*

Mahaada (Arabic)
Comforter - Facilitator
Variants: *Mahaadah, Mahada, Mahadah*

Mahabad (Persian)
City of the Moon
Name of a city in Kurdistan of Iran.

Mahabbat (Arabic)
Affections

Mahafrin (Persian)
Moon-like

Mahak (Persian)
Little Moon
Variants: *Maahak*

Mahan (Persian)
Moon-like
Variants: *Mahaan*

Mahana (Persian)
Moon-like
Variants: *Mahaana*

Mahara (Arabic)
Expertise - Skill - Talent
Variants: *Mahaara, Mahaarah*

Mahasen (Arabic)
Beauty - Good Qualities - Virtues
Variants: *Mahaasen, Mahaasin, Mahasin*

Mahasta (Persian)
Elite - Great

Mahasti (Arabic, Persian)
Moon Lady
Variants: *Mahastee*

Mahban (Persian)
Guardian of the Moon
Variants: *Mahbaan*

Mahbub (Arabic)
Adored - Loved

Mahbubah (Arabic)
Adored - Loved

Mahd (Arabic)
Cradle - Place of Comfort - Starting Point
The name Mahd is mentioned in the Quran.
Variants: *Mehd*

Mahdah (Arabic)
Flat Land - Plain

Mahdia (Arabic)
Rightly-guided - Well-guided
Variants: *Madiah, Mahdeya, Mahdiya, Mahdiyah*

Mahdis (Persian)
Moon-like
Variants: *Mahdees*

Mahdisa (Persian)
Moon-like
Variants: *Mahdeesa*

Mahdokht (Persian)
Moon Girl

Mahfam (Persian)
Moon-colored
Variants: *Mahfaam*

Mahfuzah (Arabic)
Guarded - Protected

Mahgol (Persian)
Moon Flower
Variants: *Maahgol, Mahgul*

Mahia (Persian)
Great

Variants: *Mahiaa, Mahiaa, Mahya, Mahya, Mahyaa, Mahyaa*

Mahia (Arabic)
Life - Lifetime
The name Mahia is mentioned in the Quran in verse 6:162 and others.

Mahida (Arabic)
Comforter - Facilitator
Variants: *Maaheda, Maahedah, Maahida, Maahidah, Maheda, Mahedah, Mahidah*

Mahin (Persian)
Moon-like
Variants: *Maahin, Maheen*

Mahindokht (Persian)
Moon-like Girl
Variants: *Maheendokht*

Mahirah (Arabic)
Adept - Proficient - Skilled

Mahisa (Persian)
Moon-like
Variants: *Maheesa, Mahisaa, Mahissa*

Mahjabeen (Arabic)
Moon-like

Mahjahan (Persian)
Moon of the World

Mahkamah (Persian)
Moon-like
Variants: *Maahkameh, Mahkama*

Mahlaa (Arabic)
Forbearing - Lenient

Mahmudah (Arabic)
Praiseworthy

Mahmunir (Arabic, Persian)
Radiant Moon

Mahnam (Persian)
Moon-like
Variants: *Mahnaam*

Mahnegar (Persian)
Moon-like

Mahnisa (Arabic)
Moon Among Women

Mahnoor (Arabic, Persian)
Moonlight
Variants: *Maahnoor, Maahnur, Mahanoor, Mahenoor, Mahinoor, Mahnur, Mehnor, Mehnur*

Mahnush (Persian)
Everlasting Moon
Variants: *Mahnoosh*

Mahpaikar (Persian)
Moon-like

Mahpari (Persian)
Fairy of the Moon
Variants: *Mahpary*

Mahpasand (Persian)
Beloved Moon

Mahrokh (Persian)
Moon-like

Mahrou (Persian)
Moon-like
Variants: *Maahru, Mahroo*

Mahrouz (Persian)
Moon Day
Variants: *Mahrooz*

Mahrukhsar (Persian)
Moon-like

Mahrusah (Arabic)
Guarded - Protected

Mahsa (Persian)
Moon-like
Variants: *Mahsaa*

Mahsan (Persian)
Moon-like
Variants: *Mahsaan*

Mahshad (Persian)
Happy Moon
Variants: *Mahshaad*

Mahshid (Persian)
Moonlight
Variants: *Mahsheed*

Mahsima (Arabic)
Moon-like
Variants: *Maahsimaa*

Mahsumah (Arabic)
Decided - Determined - Resolved

Mahsunah (Arabic)
Beautified - Improved

Mahta (Persian)
Moon-like
Variants: *Mahtaa*

Mahtab (Persian)
Moonlight
Variants: *Maahtab, Mahtaab*

Mahtaban (Persian)
Shining Moon

Mahtaj (Persian)
Crown of the Moon
Variants: *Mahtaaj*

Mahulah (Arabic)
Beautiful

Mahvar (Persian)
Moon-like
Variants: *Maahvar*

Mahvash (Persian)
Beautiful Like the Moon

Mahyas (Persian)
Moon Jasmine
Variants: *Mahias, Mahyaas*

Mai (Swedish)
Drop of the Sea - Pearl
Pet form of Maria and Margit (from Margaret).

Maidan (Arabic)
Arena - Plaza

Mair (Welsh)
Drop of the Sea
Welsh form of Mary.

Maira (Arabic)
Nimble - Swift
Variants: *Ma'irah, Maaera, Maaerah, Maaira, Maairah, Maera, Maerah, Mairah*

Maisarah (Arabic)
Affluence
The name Maisarah is mentioned in the Quran.

Maisie (Scottish)
Pearl
From the Gaelic form of Margaret.

Maithah (Arabic)
Flat Land
Variants: *Maisah*

Maiza (Arabic)
Distinguisher
Variants: *Maaeza, Maaezah, Maaiza, Maaizah, Maeza*

Maja (German, Scandinavian)
Drop of the Sea
Pet form of Maria

Majal (Arabic)
Chance - Elbowroom - Opportunity - Space

Majd (Arabic)
Distinction - Glory - Honor
Variants: *Mejd*

Majdah (Arabic)
Glorious - Praiseworthy

Majdiyah (Arabic)
Laudable - Praiseworthy
Majdiyah is an Arabic name for boys that means "praiseworthy", "commendable", "glorious".

Majeedah (Arabic)
Glorious - Laudable - Praiseworthy

Majidaa (Arabic)
Praiseworthy

Majidah (Arabic)
Praiseworthy

Makaana (Arabic)
Greatness - Highness of Status

Makeen (Arabic)
Deep-rooted - Firmly Established - Honored - Powerful
The name Makeen is mentioned in the Quran.
Variants: *Mackein, Macken, Mackene, Mackeyne, Makeene, Makein, Makeine, Makene, Makin, Mekeen, Mekein, Mekeine, Mekene, Mekin, Mekyn, Mekyne*

Makeenah (Arabic)
Influential - Powerful

Makkiyah (Arabic)
Meccan

Makramah (Arabic)
Generosity - Graciousness - Honor

Makrumah (Arabic)
Generous - Good Deeds - Gracious

Malahah (Arabic)
Beauty - Good Looks

Maleekah (Arabic)
Lady - Owner - Queen

Maleknaz (Arabic)
Queen of Beauty - Queen of Charm

Malene (Danish)
Woman From Magdala
Danish form of Magdalene.

Maliha (Arabic)
Beautiful - Eloquent - Happy
Variants: *Maleeha, Maleehah, Malihah*

Malikaat (Arabic)
Queen

Malikah (Arabic)
Queen

Malkah (Arabic, Jewish)
Queen
Hebrew for "queen". It can also be a colloquial Arabic pronunciation of the name Malikah, which also means "queen".

Mamduhah (Arabic)
Praiseworthy

Mana (Persian)
Everlasting
Variants: *Maana, Manaa*

Manal (Arabic)
Achievement - Attainment - Success
Variants: *Manaal, Menaal, Menal, Menale, Menall*

Manaliaa (Arabic)
Achievement - Attainment

Manar (Arabic)
Illuminating - Radiant
Variants: *Manaar, Menaar, Menar*

Manara (Arabic)
Illuminating - Lighthouse - Radiant
Variants: *Manaara, Manaareh, Manarah, Manare, Manareh, Menaara, Menara, Menarah, Menareh*

Manari (Arabic)
Radiant

Mandegar (Persian)
Everlasting
Variants: *Mandegaar*

Mandy (English)
Lovable
Pet form of Amanda.

Maneehah (Arabic)
Gift from God

Manhal (Arabic)
Fountain - Spring - Water Well

Manhiyyah (Arabic)
Generous - Giving

Manizha (Persian)
Name of a character in the Shahnameh.

Manja (Arabic)
Place of Safety

NAMES FOR GIRLS

Mansurah (Arabic)
Backed - Supported - Victor

Manusriyyah (Arabic)
Vicor

Manya (Russian)
Drop of the Sea
Pet form of Maria.

Manzurah (Arabic)
Anticipated - Foreseen - Seen - Visible

Maqbulah (Arabic)
Accepted - Approved

Maqsurah (Arabic)
Affluent

Marab (Arabic)
Destiny - Goal
Variants: *Marabb, Marabbe, Marabe, Mareb, Mareb, Marebb, Marebbe, Marebe, Merab, Merabb, Merabbe, Merabe, Mereb, Merebb, Merebbe, Merebe*

Marah (Arabic)
Activity - Fun - Joy
The name Marah is mentioned in the Quran.

Maram (Arabic)
Goal - Intention
Variants: *Maraam*

Maranat (Arabic, Turkish)
Gentleness - Softness

Marea (English)
Drop of the Sea
Altered spelling of Maria.

Mareekh (Arabic)
Lead Monoxide
A chemical used in Medieval times in alchemy and medicine.

Mareerah (Arabic)
Resolved - Strong

Margaret (English)
Pearl

Marghaa (Arabic)
Garden - Meadow

Marghah (Arabic)
Garden - Meadow

Marguerite (French)
Pearl
French form of Margaret.

Marhaa (Arabic)
Exuberant - Lively

Mari (Welsh)
Drop of the Sea
Welsh form of Mary.

Maria (Latin)
Drop of the Sea
Latin form of Mary.

Mariam (Arabic)
Wished for Child
The name *Mariam* is mentioned in the Quran.
Variants: *Maream, Mariem, Mariemme, Marium, Mariyam, Mariyem, Maryam, Maryem, Maryeme, Maryum, Meream, Meriam, Meriem, Meriemme, Merium, Meriyam, Meriyem, Merryum, Meryame, Meryamm, Meryamme, Meryem, Meryemme*

Marian (English)
Drop of the Sea - God Has Favored Me
Variant of Marion (itself originally from Mary), or a combination of Mary and Ann.

Marianna (English)
Drop of the Sea
Variant of French Marianne.

Marianne (French)
Drop of the Sea
French form of Mariamne, itself originally from Mary.

Marianne (English)
Drop of the Sea - God Has Favored Me
Alternate form of Marian.

Maribel (Spanish)
Drop of the Sea - My God is Bountiful
Form of Maria Isabel, or simplified form of Maribella.

Maribella (English)
Drop of the Sea - My God is Bountiful
Combination of Maria and Bella.

Marica (Hungarian)
Drop of the Sea
Form of Maria.

Marie (French)
Drop of the Sea
French form of Maria.

Mariel (English)
Drop of the Sea
Shortened form of Mariella.

Mariella (Italian)
Drop of the Sea
Italian form of Maria.

Marielle (French)
Drop of the Sea
Diminutive form of Marie.

Marietta (Italian)
Drop of the Sea
Diminutive form of Maria.

Marigold (English)
Drop of the Sea - Gold - Marigold
Refers to a type of flower, itself from the words gold and Mary.

Marihaat (Arabic)
Exuberant - Lively

Marilene (English)
Drop of the Sea
Elaboration of Mary or variant of Marilyn.

Marilyn (English)
Drop of the Sea
Elaboration of Mary.

Marion (English)
Drop of the Sea
From French Marie.

Marisa (English, Italian, Spanish)
Drop of the Sea
Elaboration of Maria.

Marisol (Spanish)
Radiant Drop of the Sea
Made up of Maria and Sol.

Marita (Spanish)
Drop of the Sea
Pet form of Maria.

Mariwah (Arabic)
Type of Plant
Known as Maerua scientifically.

Marjan (Arabic)
Pearl - Red Coral
The name *Marjan* is mentioned in the Quran.
Variants: *Marjan, Marjanne, Merjaan, Merjan*

Marjana (Arabic)
Pearl - Red Coral

Variants: *Marjaana, Marjaanah, Merjaanah, Merjana*

Marjani (Arabic)
Coral-like - Pearl-like

Marjia (Arabic)
Desirable - Desired - Wished For
Variants: *Marjiyah, Marjeya, Marjeyah, Marjiah*

Marjina (Arabic)
Pearl - Red Coral
Marjina is a non-standard modification of the name Marjana.
Variants: *Marjeena, Marjinah*

Marjuwwah (Arabic)
Desired

Marketta (Finnish)
Pearl
Finnish form of Margaret.

Marlene (German)
Drop of the Sea - Woman From Magdala
Contracted form of Maria Magdalene.

Marmar (Persian)
Marble
Variants: *Mermer*

Marmaraa (Arabic)
Heavy Rain - Marble

Marmari (Arabic)
Heavy Rain - Marble-like

Marmuri (Arabic)
Marble-like

Martha (Aramaic)
Lady

Martita (Spanish)
Lady

Marwa (Arabic)
The name *Marwa* is mentioned in the Quran.
Variants: *Marwah, Marweh, Merua, Meruah, Merva, Mervah, Merve, Merveh, Merwa, Merwah, Merweh*

Marwanah (Arabic)
Quartz

Mary (English)
Drop of the Sea
From French Marie, from Latin Maria, form of Miriam. Known in Arabic as Maryam.

Marylyn (English)
Drop of the Sea
Variant of Marilyn.

Maryvonne (French)
Drop of the Sea - Yew
Combination of Marie and Yvonne.

Marzia (Arabic)
Content - Pleasing to God
The name *Marzia* is mentioned in the Quran in verse 89:28.
Variants: *Mardeyah, Mardheyya, Mardhiyyah, Mardia, Mardiah, Mardiyah, Mardiyeh, Mardya, Marzea, Marzeya, Marziah, Marziyah, Marziyeh, Marziyyah, Merziah, Merziyah, Merziyeh*

Marzuqah (Arabic)
Blessed by God - Given Provision

Masakin (Arabic)
Habitation - Residence
The name Masakin is mentioned in the Quran.

Masar (Arabic)
Path - Road
Variants: *Masaar, Mesaar, Mesar*

NAMES FOR GIRLS

Masarra (Arabic)
Delight - Good Tidings - Joy
Variants: *Masara, Masarrah, Mesarrah*

Masarrat (Arabic)
Gladness - Happiness - Joy

Masbubah (Arabic)
Poured

Masha (Russian)
Drop of the Sea
Pet form of Marya.

Mashaa (Arabic)
Willpower

Mashael (Arabic)
Lanterns - Lights - Torches
Variants: *Masha'il, Mashaael, Mashaail, Mashail*

Mashahirah (Arabic)
Famous - Popular

Mashal (Arabic)
Lantern - Light
Variants: *Mash'al, Mashaal*

Mashar (Arabic)
Honeycomb Cell

Mashara (Arabic)
Honeycomb Cell

Mashariqah (Arabic)
Eastern - Oriental

Mashiyat (Arabic)
Will - Willpower
Variants: *Masheat, Masheeat, Mashi'at, Mashiat, Mashiyyat*

Mashta (Arabic)
Winter Resort

Mashurah (Arabic)
Long-hiared
Variants: *Mash'ura*

Masla (Arabic)
Comfort - Consolation

Maslamah (Arabic)
Peace - Safety

Mason (English)
Mason

Masrur (Arabic)
Glad - Happy
The name Masrur is mentioned in the Quran.

Massat (Arabic)
Contact - Touch

Mastana (Persian)
Happy - Joyous
Variants: *Mastaanah, Mastaneh*

Mastoor (Arabic)
Covered - Hidden - Modest
The name Mastoor is mentioned in the Quran.

Mastoorah (Arabic)
Covered - Hidden - Modest

Masudah (Arabic)
Glad - Happy

Masudiyyah (Arabic)
Glad - Happy

Masus (Arabic)
Unripe Date

Masyunah (Arabic)
Guarded - Protected

Mataf (Arabic)
Place of Tawaf - Place of Visitation
Variants: *Mataaf*

Matahir (Arabic)
Cleansers - Purifiers

Mataraa (Arabic)
Rain

Matarah (Arabic)
Bout of Rain - Rain

Mateerah (Arabic)
Rainy

Matheelah (Arabic)
Exemplary - Ideal - Model

Mathlaa (Arabic)
Exemplary - Ideal - Model

Mathnawi (Arabic)
Binary - Couplet
Usually refers to a type of poetry.

Mathwa (Arabic)
Abode - Home
The name Mathwa is mentioned in the Quran.

Matia (Arabic)
Excellent - Superb
Variants: *Maateah, Maatia, Maatiah, Matea, Mati'a, Mati'ah, Matiah*

Matilda (Latin)
Strength in Battle
Variants: *Mathilda*

Matlubah (Arabic)
Desired - Sought

Matrona (Russian)
Lady
Variants: *Matryona*

Matthew (English)
Gift of God

Matyusha (Russian)
Lady
Pet form of Matrona.

Maud (English)
Strength in Battle
Form of Matilda

Maureen (English, Irish)
Drop of the Sea
Form of Irish Gaelic Máirín,
form of Mary.
Variants: *Maurene, Maurine*

Mawaadah (Arabic)
Affection - Love

Mawadda (Arabic)
Affection - Love
Mawadda is mentioned in the Quran.
Variants: *Mauada, Mawada, Mawadah, Mawadda, Mawaddah*

Mawfaa (Arabic)
Faithful - Loyal

Mawiyyah (Arabic)
Fair-skinned White-skinned

Mawiza (Arabic)
Admonition - Guidance - Word
of Encouragement
The name Mawiza is mentioned
in the Quran.
Variants: *Maweza, Mawezah, Mawizah*

Mawjudah (Arabic)
Accessible - Existing - Obtainable

Mawmah (Arabic)
Great Success

Mawoudah (Arabic)
Appointed - Determined - Promisee

Mawsim (Arabic)
Festival Day - Season - Time

Maxi (German)
Great
Short form of masculine
Maximilian or feminine
Maximiliane.
Variants: *Maxie*

Maxine (English)
Great
Feminized form of Max.

May (English)
Drop of the Sea - Hawthorn - Pearl
Pet form of Margaret and Mary,
and also a type of flower.
Muslims shouldn't use this name
with the meaning of "fifth
month of the year" as this
derives from a pagan goddess's
name (Maia).

Maya (Persian)
Graciousness
Variants: *Maaya, Maayaa, Mayaa*

Maybelle (English)
Lovely
Alternation of Mabel.

Maymun (Arabic)
Blessed - Prosperous
Variants: *Maimoon, Maimun, Maymoon*

Maymuna (Arabic)
Blessed - Prosperous
Variants: *Maimoona, Maimoonah, Maimuna, Maimunah, Maymoona, Maymoonah, Maymunah*

Maysura (Arabic)
Needless - Prosperous
Variants: *Maysurah, Meisoura, Meisura, Meysora, Meysura*

Maziyyah (Arabic)
Complete - Good Quality - Perfect - Virtue - Whole

Mazna (Arabic)
Beautiful - Rain-Bearing Cloud
Variants: *Maazina, Maazinah, Maazna, Maaznah, Mazena, Mazenah, Mazina, Mazinah, Maznah*

Mazyunah (Arabic)
Adorned - Beautified

Meehan (Persian)
Homeland
Variants: *Mehan, Mihan*

Meeno (Persian)
Heaven - Paradise
Variants: *Meenu, Mino, Minu*

Meg (English)
Pearl
Short form of Margaret.

Megan (Welsh)
Pearl
Pet form of Meg.

Meha (Persian)
Elite - Great - Noble
Variants: *Mehaa, Miha*

Mehbanu (Persian)
Elite - High-born - Lady-like - Noble

Mehniya (Persian)
Elite - High-born - Noble
Variants: *Mahniyaa, Mehnyaa*

Mehra (Persian)
Affectionate - Kind
Variants: *Mehraa, Mihra, Myhra*

Mehrab (Persian)
Beautiful - Radiant
Variants: *Mehraab, Mihrab*

NAMES FOR GIRLS

Mehrabah (Persian)
Beautiful - Radiant

Mehraban (Persian)
Affectionate - Kind

Mehrafarin (Persian)
Affectionate - Kind

Mehrafruz (Persian)
Affectionate - Kind

Mehrak (Persian)
Radiant - Sun-like
Variants: *Mihrak*

Mehrana (Persian, Turkish)
Beautiful - Radiant
Variants: *Mehraana*

Mehrandokht (Persian)
Affectionate - Kind

Mehranghiz (Persian)
Affectionate - Kind

Mehranoush (Persian)
Eternal Kindness

Mehrara (Persian)
Affectionate - Kind
Variants: *Mehraara*

Mehrasa (Persian)
Beautiful - Radiant
Variants: *Mehraasa*

Mehravah (Persian)
Beautiful - Radiant

Mehrayeen (Persian)
Affectionate - Kind

Mehrazar (Persian)
Affectionate - Kind

Mehrazin (Persian)
Affectionate - Kind
Variants: *Mehradin, Mehrazeen*

Mehrbanu (Persian)
Kind - Lady of the Sun

Mehrdokht (Persian)
Affectionate - Kind

Mehrgan (Persian)
Autumn
Variants: *Mihrgaan*

Mehrgol (Persian)
Flower of Mercy - Sunflower
Variants: *Mihrgol*

Mehri (Persian)
Compassionate - Kind

Mehrin (Persian)
Compassionate - Kind
Variants: *Mehreen*

Mehrjahan (Persian)
Radiant - Sun of the World

Mehrjan (Persian)
Autumen

Mehrnaz (Persian)
Beautiful - Charming
Variants: *Mehrnaaz, Mihrnaz*

Mehrnegaar (Persian)
Beautiful - Radiant
Variants: *Mihrnegar*

Mehrnesa (Arabic)
Beautiful Among Women
Variants: *Mehrnisa, Mihrnisaa*

Mehrnia (Persian)
Compassionate - Kind
Variants: *Mihrnia*

Mehrnoush (Persian)
Eternally Beautiful
Variants: *Mihrnoosh*

Mehrsa (Persian)
Radiant - Sun-like
Variants: *Mehrsaa*

Mehrshid (Persian)
Sun
Variants: *Mehrsheed*

Mehzad (Persian)
Elite - High-born - Noble
Variants: *Mehzaad*

Meinwen (Welsh)
Fair-skinned - Slender - White

Melinda (English)
Bee - Black - Dark
From Melanie and Melissa.

Melissa (Greek)
Honey-bee
n
Variants: *Melisa, Melisaa, Melysaa*

Melissa (English)
Bee

Melody (English)
Melody

Mercedes (English)
Mercy - Reward

Mercia (English)
Mercy - Reward
Elaboration of Mercy.

Mercy (English)
Mercy - Reward

Mererid (Welsh)
Pearl
Form of Margaret.

Merete (Danish)
Pearl
Form of Margaret.

Meriel (English)
Bright Sea
Variant of Muriel.

Mia (Danish, Swedish)
Drop of the Sea
Pet form of Maria.

Mibkar (Arabic)
Drivenn - Motivated

Micheline (French)
Who is Like God?
French diminutive of Michèle,
ultimately from a feminine of
Michael.

Michelle (French)
Who is Like God?
Variant of Michèle, ultimately
feminine of Michael.

Midhah (Arabic)
Poem of Praise

Midhat (Arabic, Turkish)
Poem of Praise

Miesha (Arabic)
Life - Livelihood
The name Miesha mentioned in
the Quran in verse 28:58.
Variants: *Ma'ishah, Maisha,
Mayeesah, Mayeesha, Maysha,
Myesha, Myiesha, Mysha*

Mietaa (Arabic)
Generous

Mifrah (Arabic)
Happy - Joyous
Variants: *Mefraah, Mefrh, Mifraah*

Miftah (Arabic)
Guide - Key

Miftahah (Arabic)
Guide

Mihad (Arabic)
Cradle - Place of Comfort - Plain
The name Mihad is mentioned in
the Quran.
Variants: *Mehaad, Mehad, Mihaad*

Mildred (English)
Gentle Strength

Milena (Czech)
Favor - Grace
Short form of many names
containing mil ("grace", "favor").

Milhaan (Arabic)
Pure White Color
Variants: *Melhaan, Melhan, Milhan*

Millicent (English)
Hardworking - Industrious

Mina (Persian)
Daisy
Variants: *Minaa*

Mina (Scottish)
Dove
Short form of Calumina.

Minbarah (Arabic)
Dais - Platform - Pulpit - Stage

Minhaj (Arabic)
Clear Path - Clear Way -
Curriculum - Method
The name Minhaj is mentioned
in the Quran.

Minhal (Arabic)
Generous - Honorable

Minna (Arabic)
Charity - Gift from God
Variants: *Menna, Mennah, Mina,
Minah, Minnah*

Minnatullah (Arabic)
God's Blessings - God's Bounty

Minudokht (Persian)
From Paradise - Heavenly
Variants: *Meenudokht, Minodokht*

Mirabella (Italian, Latin)
Lovely - Wondrous
Variant of Mirabelle.

Mirabelle (English, French)
Lovely - Wondrous

Miral (Turkish)
Gazelle

Miranda (English)
Admirable - Lovely
Invented by Shakespeare, from
Latin roots.

Miriam (Biblical)
Drop of the Sea
Form of Hebrew Maryam (also
Maryam in Arabic).

Mirsalah (Arabic)
Message-bearer - Messenger

Mirwaa (Arabic)
Beautiful

Misam (Arabic)
Beautiful
Variants: *Meesam, Meysam,
Miesam, Mysam*

Misaq (Arabic)
Covenant
The name Misaq is mentioned in
the Quran.
Variants: *Meesaq, Meethaq, Misaaq,
Mithaaq, Mithaq*

Misbah (Arabic)
Lamp - Lantern - Light - Oil
Lamp
The name Misbah is mentioned
in the Quran.
Variants: *Mesbaah, Mesbah,
Misbaah*

NAMES FOR GIRLS

Misbahah (Arabic)
Lamp

Misha (Persian)
Marigold
A type of flower.
Variants: *Meesha, Meeshaa, Mesha, Mishaa*

Mishaali (Arabic)
Kindler - Lighter

Mishal (Arabic)
Lantern - Light
Variants: *Mesh'al, Meshaal, Meshal, Mish'al, Mishaal*

Mishkat (Arabic)
Niche
The name Mishkat is mentioned in the Quran.
Variants: *Meshkaat, Meshkat, Mishkaat*

Misia (Polish)
Who is Like God?
Pet form of Michalina (from Michael).

Miskah (Arabic)
Musk

Miskiyyah (Arabic)
Musk-like

Mislafah (Arabic)
Advanced - Ahead

Misriyyah (Arabic)
Egyptian

Misty (English)
Misty

Mitchell (English)
Who is Like God?
From a form of Michael.

Mitra (Persian)
Promise - Sun
Variants: *Metra, Metraa, Mitraa, Mytra*

Mitzi (German, Swiss)
Drop of the Sea
Pet form of Maria.

Mizn (Arabic)
Rain-Bearing Cloud - White Cloud

Mizna (Arabic)
Rain-Bearing Cloud - White Cloud
Variants: *Mezna, Meznah, Miznah*

Mizyan (Arabic)
Beautiful

Modest (Russian)
Moderate - Modest - Obedient - Restrained
From Latin Modestus.

Moeza (Arabic)
One Who Honors Others - One Who Values Others
Variants: *Moeizah, Muizza, Muizzah*

Moira (English, Irish, Scottish)
Drop of the Sea
From an Irish Gaelic form of Mary.
Variants: *Moyra*

Molly (English, Irish)
Drop of the Sea
Pet form of Mary.

Mona (English, Irish)
Noble
From Gaelic Muadhnait.

Mona (Arabic)
Desired - Wanted

Moonam (Arabic)
Given Blessings
Variants: *Mounam, Mun'am, Munam*

Moreen (Irish)
Great
From Gaelic, not related to Maureen.

Morna (Irish, Scottish)
Beloved
Variant of Myrna.

Morvarid (Persian)
Pearl
Variants: *Morvareed*

Morven (English)
Big Gap - Big Peak
From place names.

Morwenna (Cornish, Welsh)
Maiden

Motya (Russian)
Lady - Twin
The masculine name is from Matthew ("twin") while the feminine name is from Matrona ("lady").

Moujabah (Arabic)
Amazed - Impressed - Pleased

Moujibah (Arabic)
Amazing - Impressive

Mouminat (Arabic)
Believers
The name Mouminat is mentioned in the Quran.
Variants: *Mominat, Mu'minat*

Mouminin (Arabic)
Believers
The name Mouminin is mentioned in the Quran.

Moutazah (Arabic)
Honored - Majestic - Powerful

Moutiyah (Arabic)
Generous

Mozhda (Persian)
Good News - Good Tidings
Variants: *Mozhdah, Mozhdeh*

Mozhgan (Persian)
Eyelashes
Variants: *Muzhgan*

Muammeerah (Arabic)
Long-lived
Variant of Muammirah.

Muantirah (Arabic)
Bold - Brave
Variants: *Mo'antira*

Muarrifah (Arabic)
Guide

Muawadah (Arabic)
Recurrence - Return

Muawidah (Arabic)
Returner

Muayadah (Arabic)
Resurgence - Return

Muayyadaa (Arabic)
Backed - Supported

Muayyadah (Arabic)
Backed - Supported

Muayyid (Arabic)
Eid Celebrator

Muayyidah (Arabic)
Eid Celebrator

Muayyidah (Arabic)
Advocate - Supporter

Muazzirah (Arabic)
Helper - Supporter

Mubaraka (Arabic)
Blessed
The name Mubaraka is mentioned in the Quran in verse 24:35.
Variants: *Mobaraka, Mobarakah, Mubaaraka, Mubarakah*

Mubdia (Arabic)
Creative - Innovative - Inventive
Variants: *Mobdia, Mobdiah, Mubdi'ah, Mubdiah*

Mubin (Arabic)
Apparent - Clear - Self-evident
The name Mubin is mentioned in the Quran.
Variants: *Mobeen, Mobin, Mubeen*

Mubinaa (Arabic)
Apparent - Clear - Distinct - Manifest

Mubinah (Arabic)
Apparent - Clear - Distinct - Manifest

Mudassira (Arabic)
Clothed - Covered - Dressed
Variants: *Modasira, Modasirah, Modassira, Modassirah, Mudasera, Mudaserah, Mudasirah, Mudassirah, Mudathera, Mudathira, Mudathirah*

Mueena (Arabic)
Helper - Supporter
Variants: *Moeina, Moeinah, Mueenah, Muina, Muinah*

Mueidah (Arabic)
Experienced - Skilled

Mufazzalah (Arabic)
Gracious

Mufazzilah (Arabic)
Gracious

Mufidah (Arabic)
Beneficial

Mufizah (Arabic)
Gracious

Mufliha (Arabic)
Prosperous - Successful
Variants: *Mofliha, Moflihah, Mufleha, Muflehah, Muflihah*

Mughithah (Arabic)
Rescuer - Savior

Muhairah (Arabic)
Skilled

Muhajira (Arabic)
Ascetic - Avoider of Sin - Migrator
Variants: *Muajera, Muhaajera, Muhaajerah, Muhaajira, Muhaajirah, Muhajerah, Muhajirah*

Muhandamah (Arabic)
Beautiful

Muhannaa (Arabic)
Congratulated - Well Greeted

Muhannadah (Arabic, Persian)
Indian-made Sword

Muhannah (Arabic)
Congratulated - Well Greeted

Muhassanah (Arabic)
Beautified - Improved

Muhassinah (Arabic)
Beautifier - Improver

Muhdah (Arabic)
Flat Land - Plain

NAMES FOR GIRLS

Muhibbat (Arabic)
Lovers

Muhizzat (Arabic, Turkish)
Gracious - Honorable

Muhjaa (Arabic)
Blood - Heart - Soul

Muhjah (Arabic)
Blood - Heart - Soul

Muhlah (Arabic)
Forbearance - Leniency

Muhsinah (Arabic)
Doer of Good Deeds

Muhtaramah (Arabic)
Honored - Respected

Muhtarimah (Arabic)
Respectful

Muiddah (Arabic)
Preparer

Muireall (Scottish Gaelic)
Bright Sea

Muireann (Irish Gaelic)
Fair Sea - White Sea

Mujahidah (Arabic)
Striver

Mujeedah (Arabic)
Doer of Good Deeds

Mujibah (Arabic)
Answerer - Responder
Mujibah means "a person who answers other's calls for help".

Mujiddah (Arabic)
Conscientious - Striving

Mujillah (Arabic)
Great - Strong

Mujirah (Arabic)
Rescuer - Savior

Mujtahidah (Arabic)
Striver

Mukafat (Arabic)
Recompense - Reward

Mukarramah (Arabic)
Honored - Respected

Mukawwinah (Arabic)
Builder - Creator

Mukhallisah (Arabic)
Chosen - Excellent - Fine - Superior

Mukhlasah (Arabic)
Chosen - Purified - Selected

Mukhlisah (Arabic)
Faithful - Loyal - Sincere

Mukhtarah (Arabic)
Chosen - Excellent - Fine - Superior

Mulan (Arabic)
Gentle - Soft

Mulhah (Arabic)
Quip - Witticism

Mulhat (Arabic)
Quip - Witticism

Mulukah (Arabic)
Queen

Muminah (Arabic)
Believer in God
The name Muminah is mentioned in the Quran.

Mumtazah (Arabic)
Excellent - Exceptional

Munadiyah (Arabic)
Caller

Munadiyat (Arabic)
Callers

Munajidah (Arabic)
Helper - Supporter

Munamirah (Arabic)
Leopard-like

Munaqqaa (Arabic)
Pure

Munar (Arabic)
Bright - Well-lit

Mundiyah (Arabic)
Generous - Giving

Muneeba (Arabic)
One Who Turns to God - Virtuous
Muneebah is an Arabic name for girls that means "one who turns t God", "one who does not insist on sinning".
Variants: *Moneeba, Moniba, Monibah, Muneiba, Muniba, Munibah*

Munia (Arabic)
Hope - Wish

Muniah (Arabic)
Hope - Wish

Munifah (Arabic)
Great - High in Status

Munira (Arabic)
Brilliant - Enlightening - Illuminating - Radiant
Variants: *Moneearh, Moneera, Monira, Monirah, Muneera, Muneerah, Munirah*

99

Munisa (Arabic)
Affable - Friendly
Variants: *Monisa, Moonesah, Mounesa, Mounisa, Mu'nisah, Munesa, Munesah, Munisah*

Munjidah (Arabic)
Rescuer - Savior

Munshidah (Arabic)
Reciter of Poetry

Muntasiriyyah (Arabic)
Victorious - Winning

Muradat (Arabic)
Beloved - Desired

Muraihah (Arabic)
Joyfulness - Liveliness

Muraziyah (Arabic)
Gainer of Approval - Satisfier

Muridah (Arabic)
Desirous - Seeker

Murihah (Arabic)
Gentle - Lenient

Mursalah (Arabic)
Message-bearer - Messenger

Mursalin (Arabic)
Messengers
The name Mursalin is mentioned in the Quran.
Variants: *Morsalin, Mursaleen*

Murshidaa (Arabic)
Guide

Murshidah (Arabic)
Guide

Mursilah (Arabic)
Dispatcher

Murzaqah (Arabic)
Blessed - Fortunate

Murziqah (Arabic)
Giver of Provision

Murziyah (Arabic)
Pleaser - Satisfier

Musabbihah (Arabic)
Glorifier of God

Musadah (Arabic)
Glad - Happy

Musafah (Arabic)
Helped - Rescued

Musamma (Arabic)
Definite - Determined - Specified
The name Musamma is mentioned in the Quran.
Variants: *Mosamma, Musamaa*

Musawiyah (Arabic)
Equal - Equivalent

Musawwarah (Arabic)
Formed - Imagined - Pictured - Shaped

Musdiyah (Arabic)
Bestower - Giver - Granter

Musefah (Arabic)
Helper - Rescuer

Musfira (Arabic)
Beautiful - Happy - Joyous
The name Musfira is mentioned in the Quran.
Variants: *Mosfera, Mosferah, Mosfira, Mosfirah, Musfera, Musferah, Musfirah*

Mushaa (Arabic)
Gentle Walker

Musharrafah (Arabic)
Honorable

Musharrafi (Arabic)
Honorable

Mushiah (Arabic)
Radiant

Mushilah (Arabic)
Kindler - Lighter
Variants: *Mush'ila*

Mushirah (Arabic)
Gesturer - Guide

Mushrifah (Arabic)
Overlooking - Overseer - Towering

Mushtaq (Arabic)
Desirous - Eager - Yearning

Mushtari (Arabic)
Planet Jupiter

Musidah (Arabic)
Helper

Muskah (Arabic)
Intelligence - Sense

Muslihah (Arabic)
Doer of Good Deeds - Improver - Reformer

Muslimaa (Arabic)
Muslim
Variant of Muslimah.

Muslimah (Arabic)
Muslim

Mutairah (Arabic)
Rain

Muteeah (Arabic)
Obedient

Muthailah (Arabic)
Exemplary - Ideal - Model

Muthalaa (Arabic)
Ideal - Model

Muthlaa (Arabic)
Exemplary - Ideal - Model

Mutmaanah (Arabic)
At Peace - Tranquil

Mutmainnah (Arabic)
At Peace - Tranquil
The name Mutmainnah is mentioned in the Quran.

Muyassarah (Arabic)
Facilitated - Successful

Muyassirah (Arabic)
Facilitator

Muzainah (Arabic)
Rain-Bearing Cloud

Muzammil (Arabic)
Wrapped in Garments
The name Muzammil is mentioned in the Quran.
Variants: *Mozammil, Muzamel, Muzamil*

Muzayyanah (Arabic)
Adorned - Beautified

Muzdalifa (Arabic)
Variants: *Muzdalefa, Muzdalefah, Muzdalifah*

Muzeeah (Arabic)
Radiant

Muzhirah (Arabic)
Blooming

Muzn (Arabic)
Rain-Bearing Cloud - White Cloud
The name Muzn is mentioned in the Quran.

Muzna (Arabic)
Rain-Bearing Cloud - White Cloud

Myriam (English, French)
Drop of the Sea
Variant of Miriam.

Myrna (English, Irish)
Beloved
Anglicized form of Gaelic Muirne.

Myrtle (English)
Myrtle
Denotes the plant of the same name.

This page intentionally left blank

NAMES FOR GIRLS

N

Naaima (Arabic)
Blessed - Gentle - Living in Luxury - Soft
Variants: *Naaema, Naaimah, Naema, Naemah, Naima, Naimah*

Naba (Arabic)
Announcement - News - Tidings

Nabahat (Arabic)
Vigilance - Wakefulness

Nabeela (Arabic)
Dignified - Gracious - Noble
Variants: *Nabeelah, Nabila, Nabilah*

Nabhanah (Arabic)
Aware - Vigilant - Wakeful

Nabighah (Arabic)
Brilliant - Outstanding

Nabihah (Arabic)
Aware - Honorable - Vigilant - Wakeful

Nada (Arabic)
Blessedness - Dew - Goodness - Rain
Variants: *Nadaa*

Naddaa (Arabic)
Generous
Variants: *Nada, Nadaa, Nadda*

Naddaa (Arabic)
Caller - Charitable - Generous - Pleader

Nadeerah (Arabic)
Eloquent - Fluent

Nadezhda (Russian)
Hope

Nadia (English, French)
Hope
From Russian Nadya, from Nadezhda.

Nadiaa (Arabic)
Caller

Nadine (French)
Hope
Elaboration from Nadia.

Nadirah (Arabic)
Rare - Unique

Nadiyah (Arabic)
Caller

Nadja (German)
Hope
Variant of French and English Nadia.

Nadraa (Arabic)
Rare - Unique

Nadrah (Arabic)
Piece of Gold - Piece of Iron - Rare - Unique

Naeema (Arabic)
Blessed - Blissful
Variants: *Na'eemah, Na'ima, Na'imah, Naeemah, Naeemeh, Naima, Naimah, Nayima*

Naeemaat (Arabic)
Blessings - Bliss

Nafahat (Arabic)
Fragrant - Gifts - Presents

Nafeesa (Arabic)
Desired - Precious
Variants: *Nafeesah, Nafisa, Nafisah*

Nafizah (Arabic)
Influential - Powerful

Naghmat (Arabic)
Melody - Tune

Nahad (Arabic)
Honorable - Mighty - Strong

Nahala (Persian)
Sapling - Young Tree
Variants: *Nahaaleh, Nahaleh*

Nahar (Arabic)
Daytime
The name Nahar is mentioned in the Quran.
Variants: *Nahaar, Nehar*

Nahid (Persian)
Venus
Variants: *Naahid, Naheed*

Nahida (Persian)
Venus
Variants: *Naheedeh, Nahideh*

Nahizah (Arabic)
Diligent - Elevated - Energetic - High - Lofty

Nahjah (Arabic)
Apparent - Clear

Nahran (Arabic)
Rivers

Nahwah (Arabic)
Intelligence - Wisdom

Naifah (Arabic)
Elevated - High - Towering

Nailawfir (Arabic, Persian)
Lily

Nailufar (Arabic, Persian)
Lily

Naira (Arabic)
Brilliant - Radiant

Naizak (Arabic)
Meteor - Shooting Star - Short Spear

Najat (Arabic)
Rescue - Salvation
The name Najat is used in the Quran.
Variants: *Najaat*

Najdah (Arabic)
Bravery - Rescue

Najeedah (Arabic)
Lion

Najeemah (Arabic)
Radiant

Najhah (Arabic)
Success

Najibah (Arabic)
Excellent - High-born
Variants: *Najeeba*

Najidaa (Arabic)
Rescuer - Supporter

Najihah (Arabic)
Prosperous - Successful

Najiyah (Arabic)
Rescued - Survivor

Najiyyah (Arabic)
Rescuer - Savior
Variants: *Najia*

Najlaa (Arabic)
Beautiful-eyed - Long Night

Najlah (Arabic)
Offspring - Progeny - Scion

Najlan (Arabic)
Beautiful-eyed

Najlat (Arabic, Turkish)
Offspring - Progeny - Scion

Najm (Arabic)
Star
The name Najm is mentioned in the Quran.
Variants: *Nejm*

Najma (Arabic)
Star
Variants: *Najmah*

Najmaa (Arabic)
Star

Najmiyyah (Arabic)
Star-like

Najud (Arabic)
Intelligent - Sensible - Wise

Najumah (Arabic)
Radiant

Najwa (Arabic)
Intimate Conversation - Whispered Speech
The name Najwa is mentioned in the Quran.

Nakheel (Arabic)
Date Palms

Nakhlah (Arabic)
Date Palm
The name Nakhlah is mentioned in the Quran.

Namaa (Arabic)
Affluence

Namiyah (Arabic)
Developing - Growing - Increasing

Nanna (Scandinavian)
Daring

Naomi (Biblical)
Pleasantness

Naoum (Arabic)
Blessed

Naqaawa (Arabic)
Cleanliness - Purity

Naqeeba (Arabic)
Leader - Representative
Variants: *Nakibah, Naqeebah, Naqiba, Naqibah*

Naqil (Arabic)
Copyist - Transporter

Naqilah (Arabic)
Copyist - Transporter

Naqsheen (Persian)
Adorned - Decorated
Variants: *Naqshin*

Naratain (Arabic)
Flowers - White Flowers

Nardana (Persian)
Pomegranate Bead
Variants: *Nardaneh*

Nardeen (Persian)
Spikenard
A type of flowering plant.
Variants: *Nardin*

Nareen (Arabic)
Fresh - Passionate - Rosy
Variants: *Narin*

Nargol (Persian)
Pomegranate Flower
Variants: *Nargul*

Narina (Persian)
Fresh - Passionate - Rosy
Variants: *Nareeneh, Narineh*

Narinaa (Persian)
Fresh - Passionate - Rosy

Narmeen (Persian)
Gentle - Kind - Soft
Variants: *Narmin*

Naroon (Arabic)
Pomegranate Tree
Variants: *Narun*

Narvan (Arabic)
Elm Tree
Variants: *Narwan*

Nasar (Persian)
Shade - Shaded
Variants: *Nasaar*

Nasayir (Arabic)
Helper - Supporter

Naseeba (Arabic)
Fitting - Lady-like - Proper
Variants: *Naseebah, Nasiba, Nasibah, Nesibe*

Naseefa (Arabic)
Secretly Spoken Words
Variants: *Naseefah, Nasifa, Nesife*

Naseeraa (Arabic)
Helper - Supporter

Nashia (Arabic)
Young Generation - Young Woman
The name Nashia is mentioned in the Quran.

Nashidah (Arabic)
Praiser - Reciter of Poetry

Nashmeel (Persian)
Adorable - Enegetic
Variants: *Nashmil*

Nashwan (Arabic)
Delirious - Ecstatic
Variants: *Nashuan, Nashwaan*

Nasihah (Arabic)
Giver of Advice - Guide

Nasikah (Arabic)
Worshiper

Nasikhah (Arabic)
Clerk - Copyist - Editor

Nasima (Persian)
Soft Breeze
From Arabic.
Variants: *Naseemah, Naseemeh, Nasimeh*

Nasimaa (Persian)
Soft Breeze
Variants: *Naseemaa*

Nasirah (Arabic)
Helper - Supporter

Nasrat (Arabic)
Help - Support

Nasreen (Arabic, Kurdish, Persian)
White Narcissus
Variants: *Nasrin*

Nastya (Russian)
Resurrection
Pet form of Anastasia.

Nauratan (Arabic)
Flowers - White Flowers

Nava (Persian)
Melody - Song
Variants: *Navaa*

Navida (Persian)
Good News - Good Tidings
Variants: *Naveedah, Navideh*

Nawal (Arabic)
Bestowal - Blessing - Gift
Variants: *Nawaal, Newaal, Newal*

Nawat (Arabic)
Core - Kernel - Pip - Seed

Nawfaa (Arabic)
Great - High

Nawfah (Arabic)
Great - High

Nawfalah (Arabic)
Beautiful - Generous

Nawlaa (Arabic)
Gift - Present

Nawr (Arabic)
Radiance - White Flower

Nawraa (Arabic)
Beautiful - Radiant

Nawrah (Arabic)
Flower

Nawras (Arabic, Persian)
Blossoming - Budding - Young

Nawroz (Kurdish, Persian)
New Day
Name of the Persian New Year's Day.
Variants: *Nawrooz, Norooz, Noruz, Nouroz*

Nawwal (Arabic)
Generous - Noble

Nawwar (Arabic)
Glowing - Radiant

Nawwarah (Arabic)
Brilliant - Dazzling

Nawzaa (Arabic)
Glowing - Shimmering

Nayamee (Arabic)
Affluent - Blissful

Nayir (Arabic)
Brilliant - Radiant

Nayla (Arabic)
Charitable - Gracious - Winner
Variants: *Na'ilah, Naa'ila,
Naayela, Naayla, Naela, Naila,
Nayela, Nayelah, Nayila, Naylah*

Naylaa (Arabic)
Gift

Naylaa (Arabic)
Achiever - Acquirer

Nayyirah (Arabic)
Brilliant - Radiant

Nazaara (Arabic)
Beauty - Happiness - Radiance
Variants: *Nadaarah, Nadara,
Nadhaara, Nadhara, Nazaarah,
Nazara, Nazarh*

Nazee (Persian)
Beautiful - Charming

Nazeef (Arabic)
Clean - Virtuous

Nazeek (Turkish)
Delicate - Slender
Variants: *Nazik*

Nazeela (Persian, Turkish)
Attractive - Charming
Variants: *Nazilaa*

Nazeemah (Arabic)
Orderly - Organized

Nazeerah (Arabic)
Beautiful - Delicate

Nazeerah (Arabic)
Cautioner - Warner

Nazeeta (Persian)
Beautiful - Charming
Variants: *Nazita*

Nazimah (Arabic)
Adjuster - Arranger - Organizer

Nazira (Arabic)
Beautiful - Radiant
The name *Nazira* is mentioned
in the Quran.
Variants: *Naazerah, Naazira,
Naazirah, Nadherah, Nadhira,
Nadhirah, Nazerah, Nazirah*

Nazlar (Persian, Turkish)
Beautiful - Charming
Variants: *Nazlaar*

Nazli (Turkish)
Beloved - Charming - Delicate -
Rose-water
Variants: *Naazli, Naazly, Nazlee,
Nazly*

Nazmiyyah (Arabic)
Orderly - Organized - Systematic

Nazneen (Persian)
Beautiful - Beloved - Dear -
Precious
Variants: *Naznin*

Nazra (Arabic)
Beauty - Radiance
Nazra is used in the Quran in
verse 76:11.
Variants: *Nadhra, Nadra, Nadrah,
Nazrah, Nazreh, Nezra, Nezrah,
Nezre, Nezreh*

Neeka (Persian)
Good - Kind - Virtuous
Variants: *Nika, Nikaa, Nyka*

Neekdokht (Persian)
Good - Kind - Virtuous

Neeki (Persian)
Goodness - Kindness - Virtue
Variants: *Neeky, Niki*

Neeknaz (Persian)
Good - Kind - Virtuous
Variants: *Niknaz*

Neekta (Persian)
Good - Kind - Virtuous
Variants: *Nikta*

Neeku (Persian)
Good - Kind - Virtuous
Variants: *Neekou, Nikou, Niku*

Neelgoun (Persian)
Navy-blue Colored

Neelu (Persian)
Navy-blue Colored
Variants: *Nilu*

Neem (Arabic)
Affluence

Negaah (Persian)
Eyesight - Glance
Variants: *Negah*

Negaara (Persian)
Form - Painting - Shape
Variants: *Negareh*

Negaarin (Persian)
Beautiful - Charming
Variants: *Negareen*

Neghin (Persian)
Gem - Precious Stone
Variants: *Negheen*

Nehal (Persian)
Sapling - Young Tree
Variants: *Nihal, Nyhal*

Nehrin (Arabic, Turkish)
River
Variants: *Nehreen*

Neima (Arabic)
Blessing - Favor - Gift from God
The name Neima is mentioned in the Quran.
Variants: *Nemah, Ni'mah, Nimah*

Neimaat (Arabic)
Blessings

Neimat (Arabic)
Blessing

Nelee (Persian)
Navy-blue Colored
Variants: *Neely*

Nell (English)
Shining Light
Short form of Eleanor, Ellen and Helen.

Nelya (Russian)
Shining Light
Pet form of Yelena.

Nemoona (Persian)
Example - Model - Paragon
Variants: *Nemooneh, Nemuneh*

Niam (Arabic)
Blessings - God's Favors
The name Niam is mentioned in the Quran.

Niamullah (Arabic)
God's Blessings - God's Favors

Nida (Arabic)
Call - Plea - Prayer
The name Nida is mentioned in the Quran in verse 2:172 and others.
Variants: *Neda, Nidaa, Nidaa', Niyda, Nyda*

Niddat (Arabic)
Equivalent - Opponent

Nihlah (Arabic)
Belief - Creed - Gift
The name Nihlah is mentioned in the Quran.

Nijarah (Arabic)
Carpentry

Nijarat (Arabic, Turkish)
Carpentry

Nijat (Urdu)
Rescue - Salvation
Variant of Najat.
Variants: *Nejaat, Nejat, Nijaat*

Nijdah (Arabic)
Rescuer - Supporter

Nila (Persian)
Navy-blue Colored
Variants: *Neela*

Nilaa (Arabic)
Water Hyacinth
A group of flowering plants.

Nilah (Arabic)
Water Hyacinth
A group of flowering plants.

Nilia (Persian)
Navy-blue Colored
Variants: *Neelya, Nilya*

Niliyyah (Arabic)
Beautiful

Nilsine (Swedish)
Of the Victorious People
Feminine of Nils.

Nilufar (Persian)
Waterlily
Variants: *Neelofar, Neelufar, Nilofar, Niloufar, Nilufer*

Nimatullah (Arabic)
God's Blessings - God's Favors

Ninon (French)
God Has Favored Me
Pet form of Anne.

Nisa (Arabic)
Women

Nisbah (Arabic)
Connection - Harmony - Relationship

Nisbat (Arabic)
Connection - Harmony - Relationship

Nisbi (Arabic)
Comparative - Proportional

Nismah (Arabic)
Soft Breeze

Nismat (Arabic, Turkish)
Soft Breeze

Niswah (Arabic)
Women

Niyayesh (Persian)
Prayer - Supplication
Variants: *Neyaayesh, Niayesh, Nyayesh*

Niyaz (Persian)
Desire - Intention
Variants: *Neyaz, Niaz, Niyaaz, Nyaz*

Niyazi (Arabic)
Beloved - Desired

Niyusha (Persian)
Hearer - Intelligent - Perceptive
Variants: *Niusha*

Niyyat (Arabic)
Aims - Goals - Intentions

Nizalah (Arabic)
Strife - Struggle

Nobahar (Persian)
Early Spring - Spring Flower
Variants: *Noubahaar*

Nobar (Persian)
Early Harvest - First Harvest of a Crop
Variants: *Noubar*

Noemi (Italian)
Pleasantness
Form of Naomi.

Nogul (Persian)
New Flower
Variants: *Nougol*

Nola (Australian, Irish)
Descendant of a Champion
Feminine of Nolan.

Nolene (Australian)
Descendant of a Champion
Feminine of Nolan.
Variants: *Noleen*

Nona (English)
Ninth
From Latin, originally used for a ninth child if it was a girl, or the ninth girl born to a family.

Noon (Arabic)
Sword Blade
The name Noon is mentioned in the Quran.

Nooni (Arabic)
Sharp

Noqra (Persian)
Silver
Variants: *Noqreh, Nuqrah, Nuqreh*

Nora (English, Irish, Scandinavian, Scottish)
Honor - Shining Light
Short form of Eleanora (ultimately from Helen) or Honora.
Variants: *Norah*

Norma (English, Italian)
North Woman - Rule - Standard
In Italian it is used with the Latin meaning of "rule", "standard". In Britain it is used as a feminine equivalent of Norman.

Norosta (Persian)
Fresh - New
Variants: *Norosteh, Nourosteh*

Noum (Arabic)
Affluence

Nouran (Persian)
Radiant
Variants: *Nouraan, Nuraan, Nuran*

Nouranghiz (Arabic)
Radiant

Noursaba (Persian)
Dawn Breez - Ray of Inspiration
Variants: *Nursabaa*

Nousha (Persian)
Everlasting
Variants: *Nousheh, Nusheh*

Noushaa (Persian)
Intelligent - Perceptive
Variants: *Nushaa*

Noushafarin (Persian)
Blessed - Fortunate

Noushin (Persian)
Adorable
Variants: *Nusheen, Nushin*

Nouzhan (Persian)
Flood - River
Variants: *Nuzhaan*

Nouzhin (Persian)
Beautiful - Fresh

Literally "like a pine tree".
Variants: *Nuzheen*

Nuaim (Arabic)
Delicate - Soft

Nuaimaat (Arabic)
Delicate - Soft

Nuaimah (Arabic)
Delicate - Soft

Nuala (Irish)
Fair-shouldered
Short form of Gaelic name Fionnuala.

Nubla (Arabic)
Chivalry - Graciousness - Nobleness

Nudairah (Arabic)
Rareness - Uniqueness

Nudriyyah (Arabic)
Rare - Unique

Nuha (Arabic)
Intellect - Intelligence - Reason
The name Nuha is mentioned in the Quran.
Variants: *Noha, Nohaa, Nouha, Nuhaa*

Nuhiah (Arabic)
Intelligence - Wisdom

Nujaidah (Arabic)
Rescue

Nujaimah (Arabic)
Little Star

Nujud (Arabic)
Clarity - Elevation - Highness

Numou (Arabic)
Growth - Increase

NAMES FOR GIRLS

Nuqawah (Arabic)
Best - Finest

Nuqrah (Arabic)
Piece of Gold - Precious - Valuable

Nur (Arabic)
Light - Radiance
The name *Nur* is mentioned in the Quran.
Variants: *Noor, Nour*

Nura (Arabic)
Light - Radiance
Variants: *Nurah, Nure, Nureh*

Nuraa (Arabic)
Light

Nurahan (Arabic, Persian, Turkish)
Good Tidings - Radiant King

Nuralain (Arabic)
Bringer of Happiness - Consoler - Remover of Sadness
Literally means "light of the eyes".
Variants: *Nooralain, Noorulain, Nurul Ain, Nurulain*

Nurat (Arabic, Turkish)
Light

Nureen (Arabic, Persian)
Brilliant - Radiant

Nuril (Aramaic)
Light of God

Nuriyah (Arabic)
Brilliant - Radiant
Variants: *Nooria, Nooriah, Nooriya, Nooriyah, Nuria, Nuriah, Nuriya*

Nurshah (Arabic)
Light of the King

Nurtaj (Arabic)
Crown of Light

Nusaiba (Arabic)
Fitting - Lady-like - Proper
Variants: *Nosaiba, Nosaibah, Nosayba, Nusaibah, Nusayba, Nusaybah*

Nusaimah (Arabic)
Soft Breeze

Nusairah (Arabic)
Triumph - Victory

Nushur (Arabic)
Resurrection
The name Nushur is mentioned in the Quran.

Nusrah (Arabic)
Defense - Fortification - Support
Variants: *Nosra, Nosrah, Nusra*

Nusrat (Arabic)
Defense - Fortification - Support

Nusrat is the Turkish pronunciation of the Arabic name Nusrah.
Variants: *Nosrat*

Nutou (Arabic)
Elevation - Greatness - Loftiness

Nuwairah (Arabic)
Light - Radiance

Nuwwar (Arabic)
Blossoms - Flowers

Nuwwarah (Arabic)
Blossoms - Flowers

Nuzairah (Arabic)
Flourishing - Radiant

Nuzairah (Arabic)
Cautioner - Warner

Nuzhaa (Arabic)
Purity - Virtue

Nuzhah (Arabic)
Chastity - Stroll - Virtue

Nuzhat (Arabic, Turkish)
Chastity - Virtue

This page intentionally left blank

O

Octavia (English)
Eighth
From Latin origins.

Odette (French)
Prosperous

Odile (French)
Prosperous

Ohda (Arabic)
Care - Custody - Guardianship -
Responsibility - Trusteeship
Variants: *Ohdah, Uhdah*

Olalla (Spanish)
Eloquence
Spanish form of Eulalia.

Olena (Ukrainian)
Shining Light
Form of Helen.

Olga (Russian)
Prosperous - Successful
Feminine form of Oleg.

Olive (English)
Olive

Olivia (English)
Olive

Olka (Turkish)
Homeland

Olwen (Welsh)
One Whose Footprint is Blessed
- One Whose Footprint is White

Olya (Russian)
Prosperous - Successful
Pet form of Olga.

Omaimiya (Arabic)
Affectionate - Kind - Loving
Literally "mother-like".
Variants: *Umaymiyyah*

Omideh (Persian)
Hope
Variants: *Omeedeh, Umideh*

Omniati (Arabic)
My Hope - My Wish
Variants: *Umniati, Umniyyati*

Onaifa (Arabic)
Dignified
Variants: *Unaifah, Unayfah*

Onaitarah (Arabic)
Brave

Onaysa (Arabic)
Consoler - Good Friend
Variants: *Unaysah*

Onshuda (Arabic)
Chant - Hymn
Variants: *Unshuda*

Onsiyah (Arabic)
Bringer of Calm and Gladness
Variants: *Unsia*

Opal (English)
Opal
Opal is a type of gemstone.

Opaline (English)
Opal
Elaboration of Opal.

Oraib (Arabic)
Intelligent - Keen - Perceptive
Variants: *Uraib*

Oraiba (Arabic)
Intelligent - Keen - Perceptive
Variants: *Uraibah*

Oraibia (Arabic)
Intelligent - Keen - Perceptive
Variants: *Uraibiyyah*

Orla (Irish)
Golden Lady - Golden Princess

Ornella (Italian)
Flowering Ash Tree

Ornetta (Italian)
Flowering Ash Tree

Orzah (Arabic)
Competent - Proactive

Otilie (Czech)
Prosperous
Form of Ottilie.

Ottilie (French, German)
Prosperous

Ottoline (English, French)
Prosperous
Diminutive form of Ottilie.

Otylia (Polish)
Prosperous
Form of Ottilie.

Ouhood (Arabic)
Promises
Variants: *Ohood*

Oula (Arabic)
First - Foremost
The name Oula is mentioned in
the Quran.
Variants: *Oola, Oulaa, Ulaa*

Owaiba (Arabic)
Repentant
Variants: *Uwaibah*

Owaidat (Arabic)
Consoler - Visitor of the Sick

Owaiqiba (Arabic)
Recompense - Reward

Owaiza (Arabic)
Replacement

Owaria (Arabic)
Water Well

Oyaina (Arabic)
Beautiful-eyed

NAMES FOR GIRLS

P

Padida (Persian)
Marvelous - Phenomenon
Variants: *Padideh*

Paivand (Persian)
Connection - Kin - Oath - Promise
Variants: *Payvand*

Paloma (Spanish)
Dove

Pania (Persian)
Guardian - Protector

Paniz (Persian)
Sugar

Paola (Spanish)
Small
Feminine of Paolo.

Parand (Persian)
Silk

Parandis (Persian)
Silk-like

Parang (Persian)
Gleam of a Jewel - Gleam of a Sword

Paransa (Persian)
Silk-like

Parastesh (Persian)
Worship

Parastu (Persian)
Swallow
A type of bird.

Pardees (Persian)
Paradise

Paree (Persian)
Fairy
Variants: *Pari*

Pareechehr (Persian)
Fairy-like
Variants: *Parichehr*

Pareechehra (Persian)
Fairy-like
Variants: *Parichehreh*

Pareedokht (Persian)
Fairy-like
Variants: *Paridokht*

Pareerokh (Persian)
Fairy-like
Variants: *Parirokh*

Pareesa (Persian)
Fairy-like
Variants: *Parisaa*

Pareesan (Persian)
Fairy-like
Variants: *Parisaan*

Pareesima (Arabic)
Fairy-like

Pareezad (Persian)
Fairy-like
Variants: *Parizad*

Paria (Persian)
Fairy-like
Variants: *Paryaa*

Parigol (Persian)
Flower Fairy
Variants: *Pareegul*

Parimah (Persian)
Moon Fairy
Variants: *Pareemah*

Parina (Persian)
Delicate - Soft
Variants: *Pareenaa*

Parinaz (Persian)
Beautiful - Charming
Variants: *Pareenaz*

Parinoush (Persian)
Eternal Fairy
Variants: *Pareenush*

Parishad (Persian)
Happy Fairy
Variants: *Pareeshad*

Parivash (Persian)
Beautiful - Fairy-like
Variants: *Pareevash*

Pariwash (Kurdish, Persian)
Beautiful - Fairy-like
Variants: *Pareewash*

Parla (Persian)
Radiant

Parmeen (Persian)
Crystal

Parna (Persian)
Silk Cloth

Parnia (Persian)
Silk Canvas

Parnian (Persian)
Silk Canvas

Partou (Persian)
Radiance - Ray of Light

Parva (Persian)
Concentration - Focus

Parvana (Persian)
Butterfly
Variants: *Parvaneh*

Parvar (Persian)
Nurture

Parveen (Persian)
Pleione
Pleione is a star.
Variants: *Parvin*

Parveendokht (Persian)
Pleione-like
Pleione is a star.

Paryan (Persian)
Fairy-like
Variants: *Parian*

Parzheen (Persian)
Fence - Hedge of Flowers

Pastora (Spanish)
Shepherd
Feminine of Pastor.

Patricia (English)
Noble - Patrician
Feminine of Patrick and Patricio.

Paula (English, German)
Small
Feminine of Paul.

Paulene (English)
Small
Variant of Pauline.

Paulette (French)
Small
Diminutive feminine of Paul.

Paulina (Latin)
Small
Feminine of Paulinus.

Pauline (French)
Small
French form of Paulina.

Pearl (English)
Pearl

Pegah (Persian)
Dawn
Variants: *Pegaah*

Pelagia (Polish)
Open Sea
Form of Greek Pelagius.

Pelayo (Spanish)
Open Sea
Spanish form of Greek Pelagius.

Perla (Spanish)
Pearl
Spanish form of Pearl.

Perlita (Spanish)
Pearl
Pet form of Perla.

Persis (English)
Persian Woman
Name of a woman mentioned in the New Testament.

Peta (English)
Rock - Stone
Feminine of Peter.

Petra (English)
Rock - Stone
Feminine of Peter.

Philippa (English, German)
Horse-lover
Feminine of Philip.

Philippina (English, German)
Horse-lover
Elaboration of Philippa.
Variants: *Philipina*

Pia (English, Italian, Polish, Scandinavian)
Honorable - Pious - Respectful
From the feminine form of Latin pius.

Piedad (Spanish)
Piety

Pierce (English, Irish)
Rock - Stone
Variant of Piers.

Pierrette (French)
Rock - Stone
French feminine diminutive of Pierre.

Pinar (Persian)
Fountain - Spring
Variants: *Peenar*

Piraya (Persian)
Adornment - Gold - Jewels
Variants: *Peerayeh, Pirayeh*

Piruza (Persian)
Turquoise
Variants: *Piroozah, Piruzeh*

Poppy (English)
Poppy

Porgul (Persian)
Adorned With Flowers

Porushat (Persian)
Happy - Joyful

Pounaa (Persian)
Pennyroyal
A fragrant plant.
Variants: *Punaa*

Pounah (Persian)
Pennyroyal
A fragrant plant.
Variants: *Pouneh, Puna, Puneh*

Pouran (Persian)
Beautiful
Variants: *Puran*

Prudence (English)
Provident - Prudence

From a Latin word meaning "provident", and also used in referral to the English word.

Prunella (English)
Prunella
Refers to a type of plant.

Purandokht (Persian)
Beautiful
Variants: *Pourandokht*

Purnush (Persian)
Beautiful - Sweet

Pursa (Persian)
Inquirer

Puyah (Persian)
Aim - Goal
Variants: *Puyeh*

This page intentionally left blank

NAMES FOR GIRLS

Q

Qabilaa (Arabic)
Accepter - Approver - Endorser

Qabilah (Arabic)
Accepter - Approver - Endorser

Qaddarah (Arabic)
Arranger - Organizer

Qadduraa (Arabic)
Able - Capable - Powerful

Qaddurah (Arabic)
Able - Capable - Powerful

Qadeerah (Arabic)
Able - Capable - Powerful

Qadri (Arabic)
Able - Powerful

Qadriyyah (Arabic)
Able - Capable - Powerful

Qadumah (Arabic)
Bold - Brave

Qaisah (Arabic)
Firmness - Strength

Qaleeb (Arabic)
Water Well

Qamar (Arabic)
Moon
The name Qamar is mentioned in the Quran.
Variants: *Qemer*

Qamaraat (Arabic)
Moons

Qamari (Arabic)
Moon-like

Qamariyyah (Arabic)
Moon-like

Qamirah (Arabic)
Moonlit

Qamrun (Arabic)
Moon

Qanita (Arabic)
Devoted to God - Worshiper
Variants: *Kanita, Kanitah, Qaanita, Qaneta, Qanetah, Qanitah*

Qareen (Arabic)
Companion - Friend
The name Qareen is mentioned in the Quran.

Qarirah (Arabic)
Calm - Glad - Happy - Tranquil

Qarurah (Arabic)
Tranquil

Qaseemah (Arabic)
Beautiful - Dawn

Qasmaa (Arabic)
Beautiful

Qassamah (Arabic)
Distributor - Divider

Qasumah (Arabic)
Beautiful

Qayyimah (Arabic)
Good - Proper - Upright

Qiblah (Arabic)
Direction - Direction of the Kaaba
The name Qiblah is mentioned in the Quran.

Qiladah (Arabic)
Necklace

Qindil (Arabic)
Oil Lamp

Qindilah (Arabic)
Oil Lamp

Qiraat (Arabic)
Recitation - Recitation of the Quran
Variants: *Qeiraat, Qeraat, Qira'ah, Qira'at*

Qismah (Arabic)
Fortune - Luck

Qismat (Arabic)
Fortune - Luck

Qiyadah (Arabic)
Leadership

Qiyam (Arabic)
Night-long Worship
The name Qiyam is mentioned in the Quran.

Qudairah (Arabic)
Ability - Capacity - Power

Qudrah (Arabic)
Ability - Capacity - Power

Qudwah (Arabic)
Exemplar - Ideal - Model

Qumr (Arabic)
Fair-skinned

Qumrah (Arabic)
Moonlight

Qumri (Arabic)
Dove
Specifically the European turtle dove.

Qunnah (Arabic)
Tall Mountain

Qurb (Arabic)
Closeness - Nearness

Qurrah (Arabic)
Comfort - Consolation
Qurrah is mentioned in the Quran in verse 28:9. The name is used with the meaning of "a child who brings comfort and consolation to her parents".
Variants: *Qorah, Qorra, Qura, Qurah, Qurra*

Qurrat (Arabic)
Consolation
Qurrat is the Turkish pronunciation of the Arabic word *Qurrah*m which means "consolation", "comfort", a child who brings comfort and consolation to her parents.
Variants: *Qorat, Qorrat, Qurat*

Qurratul Ain (Arabic)
Consolation
Qurratul Ain means "a child who brings comfort and consolation to her parents".
Variants: *Qurat Alain, Qurat al-Ain, Quratulain, Qurrat Alain, Qurrat al-Ain, Qurratolain, Qurratul `ain, Qurratulain*

Qusaimah (Arabic)
Fortune - Luck

Quwa (Arabic)
Strength
The name Quwa is mentioned in the Quran.
Variants: *Qowa, Quah, Quwwa, Quwwah*

R

Raahima (Arabic)
Compassionate - Kind - Merciful
Variants: *Raahema, Raahemah, Raahimah, Rahema, Rahemah, Rahima, Rahimah*

Rabaa (Arabic)
Grace - Kindness

Rabab (Arabic)
White Cloud
Variants: *Rabaab*

Rabeeba (Arabic)
Queen
Variants: *Rabeebah, Rabibah*

Rabeehah (Arabic)
Earner - Winner

Rabiah (Arabic)
Constant - Fertile - Firmly Set in Place - Fourth - Rainy - Stable

Rabihaat (Arabic)
Earners - Winners

Rabihah (Arabic)
Earner - Winner

Rabwah (Arabic)
Highland - Small Hill

Rachel (English, French, German)
Ewe
Name of the wife of Jacob (prophet Ya`qub), mother of Joseph (prophet Yusuf) and Benjamin.
Variants: *Rachelle*

Radih (Arabic)
Strong - Tough

Raeda (Arabic)
Guide - Leader - Pioneer
Variants: *Ra'eda, Ra'ida, Raaeda, Rayeda, Rayida*

Raeefah (Arabic)
Compassionate - Merciful

Raeesa (Arabic)
Chief - Leader
Variants: *Raeesah, Raesa, Raisa, Raisah*

Rafa (Arabic)
Compassion - Kindness - Sympathy
Rafa is mentioned in the Quran in verse 57:27.
Variants: *Ra'fah, Raafa, Raafah, Rafaa*

Rafahiyyah (Arabic)
Affluence - Ease - Luxury

Rafeea (Arabic)
High - Lofty - Sublime
Variants: *Rafeeah, Rafi'ah, Rafiah*

Rafeedah (Arabic)
Generous - Gracious

Rafeeqa (Arabic)
Companion - Gentle - Kind
Variants: *Rafeeka, Rafeeqah, Rafika, Rafiqa, Rafiqah*

Rafida (Arabic)
Helper - Supporter
Variants: *Raafida, Raafidah, Rafeda, Rafedah*

Rafifah (Arabic)
Brilliance - Gloss - Luster

Rafou (Arabic)
Exalted - Great - Mighty

Raghaad (Arabic)
Abundance - Ease - Luxury - Wealth

Raghdah (Arabic)
Delicate - One Who Lives in Affluence and Luxury - Soft - Sweet

Raghdiyyah (Arabic)
Delicate - One Who Lives in Affluence and Luxury - Soft - Sweet

Ragheebah (Arabic)
Desired - Wished For

Raghibah (Arabic)
Aspiring - Desirous - Seeking

Raghidah (Arabic)
Delicate - One Who Lives in Affluence and Luxury - Soft - Sweet

Raghubah (Arabic)
Aspiring - Desirous

Raha (Arabic)
Comfort - Peace of Mind - Rest
Variants: *Raaha, Raahah, Rahah*

Rahaa (Arabic)
Serene - Tranquil - Vast
Variants: *Raha, Raha*

Rahaa (Kurdish)
Free - Uninhibited

Rahayef (Arabic)
Delicate - Gentle
Variants: *Rahaif*

Rahbat (Arabic)
Vast Expanse of Land

Rahd (Arabic)
Delicate - Soft

Raheebah (Arabic)
Generous

Raheef (Arabic)
Gentle - Tender
Variants: *Rahif*

Raheel (Arabic)
Departure - Journey
Variants: *Rahil*

Raheela (Arabic)
Departure - Journeying - Traveling
Variants: *Raheelah, Rahila, Rahilah*

Raheema (Arabic)
Compassionate - Kind - Merciful
Variants: *Raheemah, Raheemeh, Raheima, Raheyma, Rahiema, Rahima, Rahimah, Rahiyma, Rahyma*

Rahifaa (Arabic)
Gentle - Tender
Variants: *Rahaefa*

Rahila (Arabic)
Journeyer
Variants: *Rahilah*

Rahimaa (Arabic)
Compassionate - Merciful

Rahma (Arabic)
Compassion - Grace - Kindness - Mercy
The name Rahma is mentioned in the Quran.
Variants: *Rahmah, Rehma*

Rahmanah (Arabic)
Compassionate - Merciful

Rahmi (Arabic)
Compassionate - Merciful

Rahmiyyah (Arabic)
Compassionate - Merciful

Rahqah (Arabic)
Nectar

Rahumah (Arabic)
Compassionate - Merciful

Raifa (Arabic)
Compassion - Kind - Softhearted
Variants: *Ra'ifa, Ra'ifah, Raa'ifah, Raaifah, Raefa, Rayefa, Rayfa, Rayifa*

Raima (Arabic)
Woman Who Loves Her Baby
Variants: *Ra'imah, Raaemah, Raaima, Raaymah, Raema, Raimah, Rayma*

Rajayah (Arabic)
Hope - Wish

Rajihah (Arabic)
Predominant - Superior

Rajwaa (Arabic)
Hope - Wish

Rakeenah (Arabic)
Composed - Dignified

Rakhaa (Arabic)
Ease of Living - Luxury

Rakhamah (Arabic)
Compassion - Kindness

Rakhimah (Arabic)
Loving - Soft-spoken

Rakhs (Arabic)
Delicate - Soft

Rakhshan (Persian)
Radiant

Rakhshandeh (Persian)
Radiant

Rakhumah (Arabic)
Gentle - Soft-spoken

Rakidah (Arabic)
Calm - Tranquil

Raknah (Arabic)
Residence - Stay

Rama (Persian)
Happy - Joyous - Jubilant
Variants: *Raama*

Ramesh (Persian)
Delight - Happiness - Joy
Variants: *Raamesh, Ramish*

Ramina (Persian)
Happy - Joyous - Jubilant
Variants: *Raminaa*

Ramineh (Persian)
Happy - Joyous - Jubilant
Variants: *Ramina, Raminah*

Ramlaa (Arabic)
Benefit - Good Things of Life

Ramlah (Arabic)
Grain of Sand

Ramlat (Arabic, Turkish)
Grain of Sand

Ramzah (Arabic)
Gesture - Mark - Symbol

Ramzia (Arabic)
Gesture - Sign - Symbl
Variants: *Ramziya, Ramziyah, Ramziyya, Ramziyyah*

Rana (Arabic)
Beautiful
Variants: *Ra'naa, Raana, Raanaa, Ranaa*

NAMES FOR GIRLS

Ranada (Arabic)
Fragrant Tree
Variants: *Rannada*

Randah (Arabic)
Fragrant Tree
Variants: *Randa*

Ranin (Arabic)
Buzz - Resonance
Variants: *Raneen*

Ranya (Arabic)
One Who Has a Loving Gaze
Variants: *Raneya, Rania, Raniah, Raniya, Raniyah, Ranyah*

Raoofah (Arabic)
Compassionate - Merciful

Raqeema (Arabic)
Intelligent - Knowledgeable - Perceptive - Wise
Variants: *Rakeemah, Rakeimah, Rakima, Rakimah, Raqeemah, Raqima, Raqimah*

Raqiah (Arabic)
Ascension - Elevation

Raqqah (Arabic)
Flat Land With Soft Dust

Raquel (Spanish)
Ewe
Spanish form of Rachel.

Rasaan (Arabic)
Intermittently Falling Raindrops

Raseena (Arabic)
Deep-rooted - Stable - Upstanding
Variants: *Raseenah, Rasina, Rasinah*

Rashaa (Arabic)
Baby Gazelle

Rashadah (Arabic)
Right Guidance - Right Path

Rashdaa (Arabic)
Mature - Rightly-guided

Rashidaa (Arabic)
Rightly-guided

Rashidah (Arabic)
Rightly-guided

Rashiqah (Arabic)
Graceful - Nimble - Slender - Slim

Rasifah (Arabic)
Composed - Dignified

Rasiyah (Arabic)
Stable - Tall - Towering

Ratiyah (Arabic)
Scholar - Wise

Rawaa (Arabic)
Refreshing Water
Variants: *Rawa*

Rawashed (Arabic)
Rightly-guided
Variants: *Rawashid*

Rawashedah (Arabic)
Rightly-guided
Variants: *Rawashida*

Rawayeh (Arabic)
Fragrance
Variants: *Rawayih*

Raweeha (Arabic)
Good Scent - Happiness - Relaxation
Variants: *Raweehah, Rawiha, Rawihah*

Rawfiyyah (Arabic)
Mercy - Tranquility
Variants: *Rawfiya*

Rawh (Arabic)
Cool Breeze - Mercy - Relaxation
Variants: *Rauh*

Rawhah (Arabic)
Fragrance - Fresh Breeze
Variants: *Rauha*

Rawhiya (Arabic)
Consolation - Fragrance - Rest
Variants: *Rauhia, Rauhiah, Rauhiyyah, Rawhiyyah*

Rawsan (Arabic)
Light Rain
Variants: *Rausan*

Raya (Persian)
Thinking - Thought
Variants: *Rayaa*

Raydaa (Arabic)
Soft Breeze
Variants: *Raida*

Raydah (Arabic)
Soft Breeze
Variants: *Raida*

Rayhan (Arabic)
Fragrance
The name Rayhan is mentioned in the Quran.
Variants: *Raihaan, Raihan, Rayhaan, Reehan, Reihan, Reyhan, Rihan*

Rayyaa (Arabic)
Fragrance - Quenched (not thirsty)
Variants: *Rayaa*

Rayyan (Arabic)
Quenched - Watered
Name of one of the gates of

Paradise.
Variants: *Raiaan, Raian, Rayaan, Rayan, Reyan, Reyyan, Ryan*

Razan (Persian)
Vineyard
Variants: *Razaan*

Razanah (Arabic)
Composure

Razeen (Arabic)
Calm - Composed - Dignified

Razinah (Arabic)
Composed - Dignified

Raznah (Arabic)
Composure - Dignity

Razwaa (Arabic)
[Name of a Mountain in al-Madinah]
Variants: *Radhwa, Radhwaa, Radwa, Radwaa, Razwa, Rezwa, Rezwaa*

Rebab (Arabic)
Covenant - Oath - Promise
Variants: *Rebaab, Reibab, Ribaab, Ribab*

Reem (Arabic)
White Gazelle
Variants: *Rim*

Reema (Arabic)
White Gazelle
Variants: *Reemah, Rima, Rimah*

Regina (English)
Queen

Rehab (Arabic)
Generous - Open-hearted - Open-minded - Spacious - Vast
Variants: *Rehaab, Reihaab, Reihab, Reyhaab, Reyhab, Rihaab, Rihab, Ryhab*

Reine (French)
Queen

Reyah (Arabic)
Power - Scents - Victory - Winds
Variants: *Reyaah, Riah, Riyaah, Riyah, Ryah*

Rhoda (English)
Rose
From Greek.

Rhonwen (Welsh)
White Lance - White-haired

Rhys (Welsh)
Ardor

Rifa (Arabic)
Concord - Harmony - Tranquility

Rifaah (Arabic)
Greatness - Highness of Status

Rifaat (Arabic)
Greatness - Highness of Status

Rifaq (Arabic)
Companions - Friends

Rifqah (Arabic)
Gentleness - Kindness - Leniency

Rifqat (Arabic, Turkish)
Gentleness - Leniency
Turkish pronunciation of Rifqah.

Riham (Arabic)
Light Rain
Variants: *Reham*

Rihanna (Arabic)
Fragrance
Variants: *Raehanah, Raehaneh, Raihaanah, Raihaaneh, Raihanah, Raihaneh, Rayhaana, Rayhana,*

Rayhanah, Reihana, Reihannah, Rihana, Rihannah

Riqqah (Arabic)
Gentleness - Kindness - Leniency

Risliyyah (Arabic)
Gentle - Lenient

Rita (English, Scandinavian)
Pearl
From the Spanish or Italian form of Margaret.

Riza (Arabic)
Contentment - Having God's Approval
Variants: *Reda, Redaa, Redha, Redhaa, Reza, Rida, Ridaa, Ridha, Ridhaa, Rizaa*

Rizqaa (Arabic)
Blessing - Gift

Rizqah (Arabic)
Blessing - Gift

Rizwan (Arabic)
Contentment - Having God's Approval
The name Rizwan is mentioned in the Quran in verse 57:20.
Variants: *Redhwan, Rezwaan, Rezwan, Ridhwaan, Ridhwan, Ridwaan, Ridwan, Rizwaan*

Robin (English)
Bright With Fame - Robin
Pet form Robert, or a reference to the bird.

Rohina (Persian)
Bejeweled Steel
Variants: *Ruheena*

Romina (Persian)
Pure
Variants: *Ruminaa*

NAMES FOR GIRLS

Ros (English)
Lovely Rose - Pure Rose
Short form of Rosalind and Rosamund

Rosa (Italian, Latin, Spanish)
Rose
Form of Rose.

Rosalba (Italian)
White Rosa

Rosaleen (English)
Lovely Rose
Variant of Rosalyn.

Rosalie (French)
Rose
French form of Latin Rosalia, from rosa ("rose").

Rosalind (English)
Lovely Rose
Originally Germanic with the meaning of "tender horse", later derived from Latin rosa linda ("lovely rose").

Rosaline (English)
Lovely Rose
Variant of Rosalind.

Rosalyn (English)
Lovely Rose
Form of Rosalind.
Variants: *Rosalynne*

Rosamund (English)
Pure Rose
Originally from Germanic roots, later derived from Latin.

Rosanne (English)
God Has Favored Me - Rose
From Rose and Anne.

Rose (English)
Rose

Roselle (English)
Rose
Elaboration of Rose.

Rosemary (English)
Rosemary
From the herb name, literally meaning "sea dew".

Rosetta (Italian)
Rose
Pet form of Rose.

Rosha (Persian)
Cheerful - Happy
Variants: *Rusha*

Roshaan (Persian)
Radiant
Variants: *Rushaan*

Roshan (Persian)
Radiant
Variants: *Rowshan*

Roshna (Kurdish)
Radiant

Rosie (English)
Rose
Pet form of Rose.

Rosita (Spanish)
Rose
Pet form of Rosa.

Roswitha (German)
Famous Strength
Variants: *Roswithe*

Roubita (Persian)
Unique

Roushanak (Persian)
Radiant

Rouyaa (Arabic)
Dream

The name Rouyaa is mentioned in the Quran.

Rouza (Persian)
Radiant
Variants: *Rouzaa, Ruzaa*

Rowan (English)
Rowan
Refers to a type of tree.

Rowley (English)
Famous Land
Variant of Roly, pet form of Roland.

Roz (English)
Lovely Rose - Pure Rose
Variant of Ros.

Roza (Kurdish, Persian)
Radiant
Variants: *Rozaa*

Rozanne (English)
God Has Favored Me - Rose
Variant of Rosanne.

Rozha (Kurdish)
Radiant
Variants: *Rozhaa*

Rozhan (Kurdish)
Days of Life - Time
Variants: *Rozhaan*

Rozhbin (Kurdish)
Enlightener - Guide
Variants: *Rozhbeen*

Rozhin (Kurdish)
Radiant like the Sun
Variants: *Rozheen*

Rozhya (Kurdish)
Daylight
Variants: *Rozhia*

Rozhyar (Persian)
Daytime
Variants: *Rozhiar*

Ruaydaa (Arabic)
Gentle
Variants: *Rouaida, Ruadaa, Ruaida, Rueyda, Rwaida*

Ruaydah (Arabic)
Gentle
Variants: *Roaidah, Ruaida, Runvaida, Ruwaidah, Rwaida, Rwayda*

Rubaa (Arabic)
Blessings - Highlands - Hills - Virtue

Rubab (Arabic)
Blessings - Bond - Good Deeds
Variants: *Robaab, Robab, Rubaab*

Rubaihah (Arabic)
Earner - Winner

Ruby (English)
Ruby
Refers to a type of gemstone.

Rudabeh (Persian)
Heavenly Gift

Rufaa (Arabic)
Affectionate - Kind
Variants: *Rofa*

Rufah (Arabic)
Affectionate - Sympathetic
Variants: *Roofa*

Rufaidah (Arabic)
Helper - Supporter
Variants: *Rofaida, Rufaida, Rufaydah*

Rufaidiyyah (Arabic)
Helper - Supporter

Rughaidah (Arabic)
Delicate - One Who Lives in Affluence and Luxury - Soft - Sweet

Ruhab (Arabic)
Forbearing - Generous - Open-minded
Variants: *Rohaab, Rohab, Ruhaab*

Ruhaibah (Arabic)
Vast Expanse of Land

Ruhaila (Arabic)
Departer - Journeyer
Variants: *Rohailah, Ruhailah, Ruhayla*

Ruhaimah (Arabic)
Compassionate - Merciful
Variants: *Rohayma, Ruhaima*

Ruhaimah (Arabic)
Light Rain

Ruhan (Arabic)
Kind - Spiritual
Variants: *Rohaan, Rohan, Rouhaan, Rouhan, Ruhaan*

Ruhana (Arabic)
Soul - Spirit
Variants: *Rohana*

Rukhaa (Arabic)
Soft Breeze
The name Rukhaa is mentioned in the Quran.

Rumaisaa (Arabic)
Sirius
Sirius is the name of a star.
Variants: *Romaisaa, Rumaisa*

Rumaisah (Arabic)
Dispersing Wind

Runa (Scandinavian)
Secret Lore

Runak (Kurdish)
Radiant
Variants: *Roonak*

Ruqayya (Arabic)
Ascending - Elevated - Exalted - Great
Variants: *Roqayah, Roqayya, Roqayyah, Ruqaia, Ruqaya, Ruqayah, Ruqayyah*

Ruqayyat (Arabic)
Elevated Ones

Rushadaa (Arabic)
Mature Ones - Rightly Guided Ones

Rusul (Arabic)
Little Girl - Messengers

Ruwaa (Arabic)
Beautiful Appearance - Beautiful View

Ruwaid (Arabic)
Leniency - Soft Breeze
Variants: *Rowaid*

Ruwaiha (Arabic)
Fragrance - Relaxation - Rest
Variants: *Rowaiha, Ruaiha, Ruayha, Ruayhah, Rueiha, Ruwaihah*

Ruwaizah (Arabic)
Beautiful Garden
Variants: *Rowaiza*

Ruwayyifah (Arabic)
Kind - Sympathetic
Variants: *Rowayfiah*

Ruzainah (Arabic)
Composed - Dignified

S

Saadaa (Arabic)
Happy - Successful
Variants: *Sa'adaa*

Saadah (Arabic)
Happy - Successful
Variants: *Sa'ada*

Saadanah (Arabic)
Dove - Pigeon
Variants: *Sa'dana*

Saadat (Arabic)
Happy - Successful
Variants: *Sa'adat*

Saadat (Arabic)
Leaders - Lords

Saadunah (Arabic)
Happy - Successful
Variants: *Sa'duna*

Saaebah (Arabic)
Intelligent - Rational - Sensible

Saaedah (Arabic)
Great - Majestic
Variants: *Saedah*

Saaf (Arabic)
Pure

Saafah (Arabic)
Frond
Variants: *Sa'fah*

Saafia (Arabic)
Blameless - Pure - Virtuous
Variants: *Saafeya, Saafeyah, Saafiyah, Safiya, Safiyah*

Saaiha (Arabic)
Flowing Water - Traveler
Variants: *Saaehah, Saaihah, Saeha, Saihah*

Saairah (Arabic)
Avenger - Excited - Revolutionary
Variants: *Thaira*

Saakinah (Arabic)
Tranquil
Variants: *Saakena*

Saalima (Arabic)
Intact - Pure - Virtuous
Variants: *Saalema, Saalemah, Saalimah*

Saama (Persian)
Oath - Promise - Vow
Variants: *Saameh, Samah, Sameh*

Saamiah (Arabic)
Hearer - Obedient - Understanding
Variants: *Saamia*

Saatarah (Arabic)
Thyme - Thymus
Variants: *Sa'tara*

Saayah (Arabic)
Effort - Labor

Saayerah (Arabic)
Returner

Saayidah (Arabic)
Happy - Successful
Variants: *Sa'ayida*

Saayidah (Arabic)
Chief - Dominant

Saba (Arabic)
Soft Breeze
Variants: *Sabaa*

Sabah (Arabic)
Complete - Whole
Variants: *Thaba*

Sabahah (Arabic)
Brilliance - Radiance

Sabbaghah (Arabic)
Dyer

Sabbarah (Arabic)
Enduring - Patient

Sabeel (Arabic)
Path - Road - Way
The name Sabeel is mentioned in the Quran in verse 27:24 and others.
Variants: *Sabil, Sabyll, Sebil, Sebill, Sybil*

Sabeela (Arabic)
Path - Road - Way
Variants: *Sabeelah, Sabilah, Sebeelah, Sebila, Sebylla*

Sabella (English)
My God is Bountiful
Derived from Isabella (ultimately from Elizabeth).

Sabhaa (Arabic)
Beautiful - Bright

Sabia (Irish)
Sweet
From Gaelic Sadhbh.

Sabibah (Arabic)
Poured Water

Sabihah (Arabic)
Beautiful - Bright

Sabiqa (Arabic)
Advanced - Ahead
Variants: *Saabeqah, Saabiqa, Saabiqah, Sabeqa*

Sabirah (Arabic)
Enduring - Patient

Sabitah (Arabic)
Deep-rooted - Established
Variants: *Thabita*

Sabri (Arabic)
Enduring - Patient

Sabriyyah (Arabic)
Enduring - Patient

Sabuah (Arabic)
Lioness
Variants: *Saboah, Sabua*

Saburah (Arabic)
Enduring - Patient

Sadaaqah (Arabic)
Affection - Friendship

Sadadah (Arabic)
Rationality - Sense
Variants: *Sadada*

Sadaf (Arabic)
Seashell
Variants: *Sedef*

Sadafah (Arabic)
Conch - Shell

Sadaqaat (Arabic)
Acts of Charity
The name Sadaqaat is mentioned in the Quran.

Sadaqah (Arabic)
Charity - Something Given As Charity
The name Sadaqah is mentioned in the Quran.

Sadeeqah (Arabic)
Friend

Sadia (Arabic)
Blessed - Successful
Variants: *Sadiah, Sadiya, Sadiyah, Sadya*

Sadinah (Arabic)
Maintainer of the Kaaba
Variants: *Sadeena*

Sadiqah (Arabic)
Sincere - Truthful

Saeedaa (Arabic)
Happy - Successful
Variants: *Sa'ida*

Saeedah (Arabic)
Happy - Successful
Variants: *Sa'idah*

Saeedanah (Arabic)
Happy - Successful
Variants: *Su'idana*

Safaa (Arabic)
Innocence - Purity
The name Safaa is mentioned in the Quran.
Variants: *Safa, Sapha, Saphaa, Sefa, Sefaa, Sepha, Sephaa*

Safawaat (Arabic)
Best - Finest - Prime

Safee (Arabic)
Pure
Variants: *Safi, Safy*

Safeenah (Arabic)
Ship
Variants: *Safeena, Safina*

Safeerah (Arabic)
Ambassador

Safeeya (Arabic)
Blameless - Chosen - Pure - Virtuous

Variants: *Safeeiah, Safeeyah, Safiyya, Safiyyah*

Saffanah (Arabic)
Pearl - Shipwright
Variants: *Safaana, Saffana*

Safwah (Arabic)
Best - Finest - Prime

Safwana (Arabic)
Bright Day - Pure - Rock
Variants: *Safwaana, Safwaanah, Safwanah*

Safwat (Arabic)
Best - Finest - Prime

Sahargul (Persian)
Flower of Dawn
Variants: *Sahargol*

Saharl (Arabic)
Deserts

Saharnaz (Persian)
Charm of Dawn
Variants: *Sharanaaz*

Sahbah (Arabic)
Companionship - Friendship

Sahela (Arabic, Persian)
Beach - Coast
Variants: *Saheleh*

Sahibah (Arabic)
Companion - Friend
The name Sahibah is mentioned in the Quran.

Sahira (Arabic)
Moon - Unsleeping - Wakeful
The name Sahira is mentioned in the Quran in verse 79:14.
Variants: *Saahera, Saahira, Saahirah, Sahera, Saherah*

NAMES FOR GIRLS

Sahiyah (Arabic)
Awake - Sober - Vigilant

Sahlah (Arabic)
Gentle - Lenient

Sahlat (Arabic)
Gentle - Lenient

Saihah (Arabic)
Flow - Streaming - Travel

Sairan (Kurdish, Persian)
Expedition - Picnic - Trip
Variants: *Sayran*

Sajdaa (Arabic)
Prostrator - Worshiper of God
Variants: *Sajda*

Sajeedah (Arabic)
Prostrator - Worshiper
Variants: *Sajeeda*

Sajida (Arabic)
Prostrator - Worshiper of God
Variants: *Saajeda, Saajedah, Saajida, Saajidah, Sajeda, Sajedah, Sajidah*

Sakeenah (Arabic)
Composure - Dignity - Tranquility
Variants: *Sakeena, Sakina, Sakinah, Sekina*

Sakhiyyah (Arabic)
Generous - Noble
Variants: *Sakhia*

Sal (English)
Princess
Short form of Sally.

Salaat (Arabic)
Litany - Prayer
The name Salaat is mentioned in the Quran.

Salama (Arabic)
Safety - Security
Variants: *Salaama, Salaamah, Salamah*

Salawaat (Arabic)
Formal Prayer
The name Salawaat is mentioned in the Quran.

Saleehah (Arabic)
Good - Pious

Saleema (Arabic)
Intact - Pure - Safe - Virtuous
Variants: *Saleemah, Salima, Salimah*

Saleemaa (Arabic)
Safe - Unharmed

Saleemaat (Arabic)
Safe - Unharmed

Saleena (Persian, Turkish)
Flood-like - Torrential
Variants: *Saleenaa, Salina*

Sali (Arabic)
Amused - Cheerful
Variants: *Saly*

Saliha (Arabic)
Virtuous
Variants: *Saaleha, Saaliha, Saleha, Salehah, Saliha, Salihah, Salihe, Salyheh*

Salihat (Arabic)
Good Deeds - Pious Ones
The name Salihat is mentioned in the Quran.
Variants: *Salehaat, Salehat, Salihaat, Saulihat*

Salikah (Arabic)
Follower of a Path
Variants: *Saleka, Salika*

Salitaa (Arabic)
Eloquent - Tall

Salitah (Arabic)
Eloquent - Tall

Sally (English)
Princess
Pet form of Sarah.

Salma (Arabic)
Purity - Safety - Security - Virtue
Variants: *Salmaa, Selma, Selmaa*

Salome (English, German)
Peace
Ultimately from an Aramaic name meaning "peace".

Saloofah (Arabic)
Advancer

Saloomah (Arabic)
Safe - Unharmed

Salsabil (Arabic)
Refreshing and Tasy Drink
Variants: *Salsabeel*

Salsabilah (Arabic)
Refreshing and Tasy Drink
Variants: *Salsabeela*

Saltanah (Arabic)
Power - Rule - Sultanate
Variants: *Saltana*

Saluhah (Arabic)
Good - Pious

Salwa (Arabic)
Comfort - Consolation
The name Salwa is mentioned in the Quran.
Variants: *Salua, Salwaa*

Salwah (Arabic)
Consolation

Sama (Arabic)
Elevated - Lofty
Variants: *Samaa*

Samaa (Arabic)
Heaven - Sky
The name Samaa is mentioned in the Quran.

Samaanah (Arabic)
Hearer

Samaaraa (Arabic)
Nighttime Conversation
Alternate form of Samaarah.
Variants: *Samara*

Samaarah (Arabic)
Nighttime Conversation Companion
Variants: *Samaara, Samara, Samarah*

Samaee (Arabic)
Heavenyl

Samah (Arabic)
Leniency - Pardon

Samahaa (Arabic)
Generosity - Leniency

Samahah (Arabic)
Generosity - Leniency

Saman (Persian)
Jasmine

Saman Naz (Persian)
Elegant Like a Jasmine Flower
Variants: *Samannaz*

Saman Rokh (Persian)
Jasmine-like

Samanta (Aramaic)
Listener

Samantha (English)
He (God) Has Hearkened
From Sam (short for Samuel) and the arbitrary suffix -antha.

Samar (Arabic)
Darkness of the Night - Night - Nighttime Conversation
Variants: *Summer*

Samara (Arabic)
Nighttime Conversation Companion

Samarah (Arabic)
Fruit - Product

Samawah (Arabic)
Elevation - Greatness

Samawat (Arabic)
Heavens - Skies
The name Samawat is mentioned in the Quran.
Variants: *Samaawat*

Samawi (Arabic)
Heavenly

Sameeka (Arabic)
Elevated - High in Status - Majestic
Variants: *Sameekah, Samika, Samikah*

Sameera (Arabic)
Friend - Night Conversation Partner
Variants: *Sameerah, Sameira, Samira, Samirah, Semira, Semire*

Samhaa (Arabic)
Forgiving - Lenient

Samhah (Arabic)
Forgiveness - Leniency

Samhiyyah (Arabic)
Forgiving - Lenient

Sami (Arabic)
Great - Lofty - Sublime
Variants: *Saami, Saamy, Samee, Samy*

Samiha (Arabic)
Forgiving - Gracious
Variants: *Samihah*

Samika (Arabic)
Elevated - High in Status - Majestic
Variants: *Saameka, Saamika, Saamikah, Sameka, Samikah*

Samina (Persian)
Beautiful - Daisy-like
Variants: *Sameena, Sameenaa*

Samiyyan (Arabic)
Great - High in Status

Sammadah (Arabic)
Determined - Persevering - Steadfast

Sammarah (Arabic)
One Who Continues Conversation Long Into the Night

Samraa (Arabic)
Mature - Ripe
Variants: *Thamraa*

Samreen (Arabic)
Beneficial - Fruitful - Productive
Variants: *Samrin*

Samtah (Arabic)
Beauty

Samyaa (Arabic)
Great - Honored

Sana (Arabic)
Flare - Flash - Glow - Shine - Spark
The name Sana is mentioned in

NAMES FOR GIRLS

the Quran in verse 24:43.
Variants: *Sanaa, Sanaa, Sena*

Sana (Persian)
Easy - Simple

Sanaa (Arabic)
Glory - Greatness - Honor
Variants: *Sanaa', Sena, Senaa*

Sanaa (Arabic)
Craft - Work
Name of the capital of Yemen.

Sanabel (Arabic)
Ears of Corn - Ears of Wheat - Plant Spikes
The name Sanabel is mentioned in the Quran.
Variants: *Sanaabel, Sanaabil, Sanabil*

Sanai (Arabic)
Praise
Variants: *Thanay*

Sanan (Arabic)
Tradition - Way of Life

Sanaya (Arabic)
Honorable - Honored - Noble
Variants: *Sanaaya, Sanaayaa, Sanayaa, Senaia*

Sanayah (Arabic)
Flash of Light - Radiance
Variants: *Sanaaya, Sanaiya, Sanaya*

Sanaz (Persian)
Rose - Unique
Variants: *Saanaz, Sanaaz*

Sandah (Arabic)
Climb - Dependence - Reliance

Sandra (English, Italian)
Defender of Humanity
Short form of Alessandra, Italian form of Alexandra.

Sandy (English)
Defender of Humanity
Pet form of Alexandra or Sandra.
Variants: *Sandie*

Saniyya (Arabic)
Honored - Noble - Sublime - Superb
Variants: *Saneyah, Sania, Saniya, Saniyyah, Sanyah*

Saniyyaat (Arabic)
Exalted - High in Status

Sanna (Scandinavian)
Lily
Short form of Susanna.

Sannah (Arabic)
Bear - Leopard

Sanubar (Arabic)
Cypress

Sanya (Russian)
Defender of Humanity
Pet form of Alexander and Alexandra.
Variants: *Saanya, Sanyaa*

Sanya (Persian)
Bright Forest Shade

Saqibah (Arabic)
Piercing - Sharp
Variants: *Thaqiba*

Saqrah (Arabic)
Falcon

Saqriyyah (Arabic)
Falcon-like

Sara (Persian)
Pure - Untainted
The is also the Persian pronunciation of *Sarah*, the name of the wife of Prophet Ibrahim peace be upon him.
Variants: *Saara, Saara, Saaraa, Saaraa, Saraa, Saraa*

Sara (English)
Princess
Variant of Sarah.

Sara (Arabic)
Delighted - Happy - Joyous
Non-standard derivation from the Arabic name Sarah.

Saraab (Arabic)
Mirage
The name Saraab is mentioned in the Quran.
Variants: *Sarab*

Sarah (Arabic)
Delighted - Happy - Joyous
Sarah is also the Arabic name for the wife of Prophet Ibrahim peace be upon him.
Variants: *Saara, Saarah*

Saran (Persian)
Beginning - Start
Variants: *Saaran, Saraan*

Sarayaa (Arabic)
Army Company - Brigade
Variants: *Saraya*

Sarayah (Arabic)
Army Company - Brigade
Variants: *Saarayah, Saraya*

Sareema (Arabic)
Firm Decision - Resolution
Variants: *Sareemah, Sarima, Sarimah*

Sargol (Persian)
Yellow Rose
Variants: *Sargul*

Sarihah (Arabic)
Shepherdess
Variants: *Saariha*

Sarima (Arabic)
Decisive - Resolute - Strong-willed
Variants: *Sarimah*

Sarina (Persian)
Calm - Tranquil

Sariya (Arabic)
Night Cloud - Night Rain - Night Traveler
Variants: *Saariya, Saariyah, Sareya, Sareyah, Saria, Sariah, Sariyah*

Sarraa (Arabic)
Ease and Abundance - Happy Times
The name Sarraai is mentioned in the Quran.
Variants: *Saraa, Sarra*

Sarraat (Arabic)
Ease and Abundance - Happy Times
Variants: *Saraat, Sarat*

Sarv (Persian)
Cypress
A type of tree.

Sarveen (Persian)
Elegant - Tall
Literally "like a pine tree".
Variants: *Sarvin*

Sarvgul (Persian)
Elegant - Tall
Literally "pine flower".

Sarvi (Persian)
Elegant - Tall
Literally "like a pine tree".
Variants: *Sarvy*

Sarvnaz (Persian)
Elegant - Tall
Literally "like a pine tree".

Sarwah (Arabic)
Cypress - Generosity - Selflessness
Variants: *Sarwa, Tharwa, Tharwah*

Sarwah (Arabic)
Affluence - Fortune - Wealth

Sarwat (Arabic, Kurdish, Persian, Turkish, Urdu)
Affluence - Fortune - Wealth
Turkish pronunciation of Sarwah.
Variants: *Tharwat*

Sasha (English)
Defender of Humanity
Pet form of Alexander or Alexandra.

Sateerah (Arabic)
Modest
Variants: *Satira*

Sattarah (Arabic)
Hider
Variants: *Satarah*

Sauba (Arabic)
Reward
Variants: *Saubah, Sawba, Sawbah, Soba, Sobah, Souba*

Sauda (Arabic)
Blessed - Fortunate - Happy
Variants: *Saudah*

Sawa (Arabic)
Equal - Similar

Sawab (Arabic)
Repentant - Reward
Variants: *Thawab*

Sawaba (Arabic)
Repentant
Variants: *Thawabah*

Sawalih (Arabic)
Pious - Virtuous

Sawalihah (Arabic)
Pious - Virtuous

Sawbat (Arabic, Turkish)
Repentance
Turkish pronunciation of Sawbah.
Variants: *Thawbat*

Sawda (Arabic)
Land With Many Palm Trees
Name of one of the wives of Prophet Muhammad PBUH.
Variants: *Sauda, Saudah, Sawdah, Sowda, Sowdah*

Sawlah (Arabic)
Ascendancy - Domination - Power

Sawrah (Arabic)
Revolution - Uprising
Variants: *Thawrah*

Sawrat (Arabic)
Revolution - Uprising
Turkish pronunciation of Sawrah.
Variants: *Thawrat*

Sawsan (Persian)
Lily
Variants: *Sosan*

Sawsanah (Arabic)
Lily

Saya (Persian, Turkish)
Honest - Sincere
Variants: *Saaya, Saaya, Saayah, Saayeh, Sayaa, Sayah, Sayeh*

NAMES FOR GIRLS

Saya (Kurdish, Persian)
Shade - Shadow

Sayibah (Arabic)
Rational - Sensible - Wise

Sayna (Persian)
Serene - Silent
Variants: *Saina, Sainaa, Saynaa*

Sayyadah (Arabic)
Hunter

Sazgar (Kurdish, Persian)
Friendly - Harmonious
Variants: *Saazgar*

Scarlett (English)
Scarlet
Refers to a brilliant red color.
Variants: *Scarlet*

Semaara (Arabic)
Nighttime Conversation
Variants: *Semaarah, Semara, Simaara, Simara, Simarah*

Senbal (Arabic)
Spike of Corn

Sepida (Persian)
Dawn
Variants: *Sepeedah, Sepeedeh, Sepidah, Sepideh, Speeda, Spideh*

Serena (Persian)
Calm - Serene - Tranquil

Setara (Persian)
Fortunte - Star
Variants: *Setaara, Setaareh, Setarah, Setareh, Stara, Starah*

Setayesh (Persian)
Praise
Variants: *Setayish*

Setoudeh (Persian)
Laudable - Praiseworthy
Variants: *Setoodah, Setoodeh, Setuda*

Shaan (Arabic)
Greatness - Rank - Status
The name Shaan is mentioned in the Quran.
Variants: *Sha'n, Shan*

Shababah (Arabic)
Young Age - Youth

Shabahang (Persian)
Canopus - Nightingale
Canopus is the name of a bright star.
Variants: *Shabaahang*

Shabibah (Arabic)
Young Woman

Shabinah (Arabic)
Beautiful Young Woman

Shabirah (Arabic)
Beautiful - Gracious

Shabiyyah (Arabic)
Great - High in Status

Shablaa (Arabic)
Lion Cub

Shabnam (Persian)
Dew
Variants: *Shabnem*

Shadab (Persian)
Fresh - Happy - Joyous
Variants: *Shaadab*

Shadan (Kurdish, Persian)
Happy - Joyous
Variants: *Shaadan*

Shadi (Persian)
Happiness - Joy
Variants: *Shaadi, Shadee, Shady*

Shadiah (Persian)
Happiness - Joy
Variants: *Shadiyeh*

Shadiyyah (Arabic)
Seeker of Knowledge

Shadleen (Arabic, Persian)
Delicate - Happy
Variants: *Shadlin*

Shafaq (Arabic)
Affection - Dawn - Pity - Sympathy - Twilight

Shafaqat (Arabic)
Affection - Pity - Sympathy

Shafeefah (Arabic)
Translucent - Transparent

Shafiqa (Arabic)
Compassioante - Sympathetic
Variants: *Shafeeqa, Shafeeqah, Shafiqah*

Shafiyat (Arabic)
Healer

Shafiyyah (Arabic)
Healer

Shafyaa (Arabic)
Healer

Shaghf (Arabic)
Strong Love

Shahada (Arabic)
Martyrdom - Testimony
The name Shahada is mentioned in the Quran.
Variants: *Shahadah*

Shahbaa (Arabic)
Gray

Shahdokht (Persian)
Princess

Literally "king's daughter".
Variants: *Shaahdukht*

Shaheen (Persian)
Magnificent - Royal - Stately
Variants: *Shahin*

Shaheera (Arabic)
Distinguished - Well-known
Variants: *Shaheerah, Shahera, Shaherah, Shahira, Shahirah*

Shahgul (Persian)
Beautiful - Royal Flower
Variants: *Shaahgol*

Shahidah (Arabic)
Witness

Shahin (Arabic, Persian)
Peregrine Falcon
A type of bird.
Variants: *Shaheen*

Shahirah (Arabic)
Populizer

Shahla (Arabic)
Dark Blue-eyed
Variants: *Sahlaa*

Shahmah (Arabic)
Intelligent - Rational - Sensible

Shahnaz (Persian)
Beautiful - Beloved - Princess
Variants: *Shaahnaz, Shahnaaz*

Shahparee (Persian)
Beautiful
Literally "king's fairy".

Shahrbanu (Persian)
Queen
Literally "lady of the city".
Variants: *Sehrbanu, Shahrbano*

Shahro (Persian)
Imperious - Magnificent - Stately
Variants: *Shahru, Shehru*

Shahrzad (Persian)
Cosmopolitan
Literally "city-born".
Variants: *Shahrazad, Shahrezad, Shahrzaad*

Shahzad (Persian)
Princess
Variants: *Shaahzad*

Shaima (Arabic)
One Who Has Many Beauty Marks

Shaiqah (Arabic)
Beautiful

Shajaa (Arabic)
Brave - Strong

Shajarah (Arabic)
Tree
The name Shajarah is mentioned in the Quran.

Shajeeah (Arabic)
Brave - Strong

Shakiba (Persian)
Enduring - Patient
Variants: *Shakeeba, Shakibaa*

Shakila (Arabic, Persian)
Beautiful - Well-formed
Variants: *Shakeela, Shakeelaa, Shakilaa*

Shakirat (Arabic)
Thankful

Shakiriyyah (Arabic)
Thankful

Shakkarah (Arabic)
Thankful

Shakura (Arabic)
Appreciative - Thankful
Variants: *Shakoora, Shakoorah, Shakurah*

Shalal (Arabic)
Waterfall

Shamikha (Arabic)
Great - High - Lofty - Towering
Variants: *Shamekhah, Shamikhah*

Shamisah (Arabic)
Bright - Sunlit

Shamkhah (Arabic)
Greatness - Highness of Status

Shammam (Arabic)
Muskmelon

Shammamah (Arabic)
Muskmelon

Shamra (Arabic)
Fennel
Variants: *Shamrah*

Shams (Arabic)
Light and Radiance
The name *Shams* is mentioned in the Quran.

Shams Jahan (Arabic)
Radiant
Literally "sun of the world".

Shamsa (Arabic)
Radiant - Sun
Variants: *Shamsah, Shemsa, Shemsah, Shemse*

Shanaz (Kurdish, Persian)
Beautiful - Beloved - Princess
Variants: *Shaanaz, Shanaaz*

Shaqaaiq (Arabic)
Heavy Rain

NAMES FOR GIRLS

Shaqayeq (Persian)
Poppy
A type of flower.
Variants: *Shaqaayeq, Shaqayiq*

Shaqeerah (Arabic)
Fair-skinned

Shaqhaa (Arabic)
Fair-skinned

Shaqhah (Arabic)
Fair-skinned

Shaqrah (Arabic)
Fair-skinned

Shaqriyyah (Arabic)
Fair-skinned

Sharaa (Arabic)
Beautiful

Sharah (Arabic)
Beautiful

Shararah (Arabic)
Flare - Spark

Shari (Arabic)
Beautiful

Sharifah (Arabic)
Glorious - High in Status - Honored

Shariqah (Arabic)
Variants: *Glowing, Radiant*

Sharmeen (Persian)
Bashful - Modest
Variants: *Sharmin, Shermin*

Sharminah (Persian)
Bashful - Modest
Variants: *Sharmeena, Sharmeeneh, Sharmina, Sharmineh*

Sharraqah (Arabic)
Bright - Briliant

Sharufah (Arabic)
Glorious - Honorable - Noble

Shauna (English)
God is Gracious
Feminine of Shaun.

Shawab (Arabic)
Young Woman

Shawq (Arabic)
Desire - Longing

Shawqat (Arabic, Turkish)
Desire - Longing

Shawqiyyah (Arabic)
Desirous - Longing

Shawraa (Arabic)
Beautiful

Shayaa (Persian)
Deserving - Worthy

Shayan (Kurdish)
Deserving - Worthy
Variants: *Shaayan, Shayaan*

Shayestah (Persian)
Capable - Deserving - Worthy
Variants: *Shaaistah, Shaaysta, Shaista, Shayesta, Shayista*

Shayiqah (Arabic)
Beautiful

Shaykhaa (Arabic)
Great - High in Status

Shazad (Kurdish)
Princess
Variants: *Shaazad, Shazaad*

Shazah (Arabic)
Special - Unique

Shazrah (Arabic)
Little Pearl - Lump of Gold

Sheeda (Persian)
Brilliant - Sun-like
Variants: *Sheedeh, Shidah, Shideh*

Sheedrokh (Persian)
Beautiful - Brilliant - Sun-like
Variants: *Shidrokh*

Sheefa (Arabic)
Cure - Healing

Sheefta (Persian)
In Love - Infatuated - Obsessed
Variants: *Sheeftah, Sheefteh, Shifta, Shifteh*

Sheela (Persian)
[Name of a River]
A river in the Sistan and Baluchistan province of Iran.
Variants: *Shila*

Sheemah (Arabic)
Character - Natural Disposition - Nature

Sheena (Irish, Scottish)
God is Gracious
From forms of Jane (from John).

Sheeva (Persian)
Attraction - Charm - Expressive - Vidid
Variants: *Sheva, Shiva, Shivaa*

Sheida (Persian)
In Love - Infatuated
Variants: *Shaida, Sheyda, Sheydaa*

Shell (English)
Who is Like God?
Short form of Michelle.

Shemshad (Persian)
Boxwood
A type of plant.

Sheree (English)
Darling
Respelling of Chérie.

Sherry (English)
Darling
Respelling of Chérie.

Sheryl (English)
Beryl - Darling
Variant of Sheryl.
Variants: *Sherill, Sherrill*

Shevaun (English, Irish)
God is Gracious
Ultimately from Jane, from John.

Shewa (Kurdish)
Form - Shape

Shiblah (Arabic)
Lion Cub

Shifa (Arabic)
Cure - Healing - Remedy
The name Shifa is mentioned in the Quran.
Variants: *Shefa, Shefaa, Shifaa*

Shilan (Kurdish, Persian, Turkish)
Feast - Food - Jujube - Lunch
Jujube is a type of tree.

Shira (Arabic)
Beautiful

Shireen (Persian)
Sweet

Shirin (Persian)
Sweet
Variant of Shireen.
Variants: *Shirrin*

Shokouh (Persian)
Glory - Greatness
Variants: *Shokuh, Shukuh*

Shokufa (Persian)
Tree Flower
Variants: *Shokoofah, Shokufah, Shokufeh, Shukufah, Shukufeh*

Shokufaa (Persian)
Blossoming - Flourishing - Thriving
Variants: *Shokufa, Shukufaa*

Shoulah (Arabic, Persian)
Flame
Variants: *Sholeh, Shouleh, Shu'lah, Shuleh*

Shufafah (Arabic)
Clear - Translucent - Transparent

Shufaiqah (Arabic)
Mercy - Pity

Shuhada (Arabic)
Martyrs - Witnesses
The name Shuhada is mentioned in the Quran.
Variants: *Shohada, Shohadaa, Shuhadaa*

Shuhaibah (Arabic)
Little Shooting Star

Shuhaidah (Arabic)
Witness

Shuhairah (Arabic)
Famous - Month

Shuhbah (Arabic)
Grayness

Shuhdah (Arabic)
Hony-containing Honeycomb

Shujayaah (Arabic)
Brave - Strong

Shukranah (Persian)
Gratitude

Variants: *Shokraana, Shokraneh, Shukraneh*

Shulaikhah (Arabic)
Origin - Root

Shuqairaa (Arabic)
Fair-skinned

Shuqrah (Arabic)
Fairness of Skin

Shuqriyyah (Arabic)
Fair-skinned

Shuqur (Arabic)
Blondness - Fairness of Skin
Variants: *Shoqur*

Shuraa (Arabic)
Consultation - Council - Honeycomb Cell - View

Shurafaa (Arabic)
High in Status - Honorable

Shurah (Arabic)
Beauty

Shuruq (Arabic)
Sunrise

Shuwaihah (Arabic)
Artemisia
A group of plants that include tarragon.

Siaad (Arabic)
Helper
Variants: *Sead*

Siba (Arabic)
Childhood - Emotion - Enthusiasm - Youthfulness
Variants: *Seba, Sebaa, Sibaa, Syba*

Sibgha (Arabic)
Color - Dye - Hue
The name Sibgha is mentioned

in the Quran.
Variants: *Sebgha, Sebghah, Sibga, Sibghah*

Siddiqah (Arabic)
Saintly - Truthful - Virtuous
The name Siddiqah is mentioned in the Quran.
Variants: *Sediqa, Sediqah, Siddeeqah, Siddika, Siddiqa, Sideekah, Sideeqah, Sidika, Sidiqah*

Sidra (Arabic)
Lote Tree
The name Sidra is mentioned in the Quran in verses 53:14 and 53:16. It is the name of a the name of a tree in heaven.
Variants: *Sedra, Sedrah, Sidrah*

Sidratul Muntaha (Arabic)
Lote Tree of the Utmost Boundary
The name Sidratul Muntaha is mentioned in the Quran. It is the name of a tree in or near Paradise.
Variants: *Sidrat Ul Muntaha, Sidratulmuntaha*

Sifah (Arabic)
State - Trait

Signy (Scandinavian)
New Victory
Variants: *Signe, Signi*

Sigrid (Scandinavian)
Beautiful Victory

Sihab (Arabic)
Deep Water Well

Silaam (Arabic)
Peace-making
Variants: *Selam*

Silver (English)
Fair-haired - Silver

Sima (Arabic)
Appearance - Complexion - Countenance
Variants: *Seema, Simaa*

Simab (Persian)
Mercury
Refers to the liquid metallic element.
Variants: *Seemab*

Simmaa (Arabic)
Brave - Lion

Simmah (Arabic)
Mark - Sign - Token - Trait

Simone (French)
Hearkening
Feminine of Simon.

Sineen (Arabic)
Mountain Sinai
The name Sineen is mentioned in the Quran.
Variants: *Senin, Sinin*

Sinnah (Arabic)
Coulter - Double-headed Axe

Siraa (Arabic)
Tradition - Way of Life

Siraayah (Arabic)
Night Journey
Variants: *Seraya, Siraaya*

Sirah (Arabic)
Tradition - Way of Life

Siraj (Arabic)
Cresset - Lamp - Light
Variants: *Seraa, Seraj, Siraaj*

Siranoush (Persian)
Eternally Content - Eternally Pleased
Variants: *Siraanush*

Sirat (Arabic)
Path
The name Sirat is mentioned in the Quran.
Variants: *Serat, Siraat*

Siri (Scandinavian)
Beautiful Victory
Pet form of Sigrid.

Sitr (Arabic)
Cover Up - Hiding
Variants: *Setr*

Sitya (Persian)
The Universe - The World
Variants: *Setya, Setyaa*

Sive (Irish)
Sweet

Siwa (Arabic)
Flat Land With Soft Sand

Siyadah (Arabic)
Glory - Greatness - Honor - Leadership

Siyam (Arabic)
The name Siyam is mentioned in the Quran.
Variants: *Fasting*

Siyaq (Arabic)
Articulation - Context

Sodad (Arabic)
Great - Honorable
Variants: *Saudad, Sawdad, So'dad, Soudad, Sudad*

Sofia (Norwegian, Swedish)
Wisdom
Form of Sophia

Sofie (Danish, Dutch, German)
Wisdom
Form of Sophia.

Sol (Spanish)
Sun

Solange (French)
Religious - Solemn

Sonbol (Arabic)
Ear of Corn - Ear of Wheat - Plant Spike
The name Sonbol is mentioned in the Quran.
Variants: *Sonbol, Sonbul, Sunbol, Sunbul*

Sonbula (Arabic)
Ear of Corn - Ear of Wheat - Plant Spike
The name Sonbula is mentioned in the Quran.
Variants: *Sonbulah, Sunbula, Sunbulah*

Sondra (English)
Defender of Humanity
Altered form of Sandra.

Sonia (English)
Wisdom
Variant of Sonya.

Sonja (German, Scandinavian)
Wisdom
Variant of Sonya.
Variants: *Sonje*

Sonya (Arabic)
Exalted - High in Status

Sonya (Russian)
Wisdom
Pet form of Sofya.

Sophia (Greek)
Wisdom

Sophie (French)
Wisdom
Variant of Sophia.

Sormeh (Persian)
Kohl
Variants: *Sorm, Surmeh*

Sorrel (English)
Sorrel
Refers to a type of plant.

Sougand (Persian)
Oath - Vow
Variants: *Sogand*

Souma (Persian)
Moonlight
Variants: *Sumaa*

Souna (Persian)
Gold
Variants: *Sunaa*

Sounai (Persian, Turkish)
End of the Month - One Who Prays
Variants: *Sunay*

Souzan (Persian)
Enthusiastic - Passionate
Variants: *Suzan*

Speda (Kurdish)
Dawn
From Persan Sepida.

Star (English)
Star

Stefania (Italian)
Crown - Garland
Form of Stephanie.

Steffany (English)
Crown - Garland
Variant of Stephanie.

Steffi (German)
Crown - Garland
Pet form of Stephanie.

Stella (English)
Star
From Latin stella ("star").

Steph (English)
Crown - Garland
Short form of Stephanie.

Stephanie (English, German)
Crown - Garland
From French Stéphanie.

Stevi (English)
Crown - Garland
Pet form of Stephanie.

Stevie (English)
Crown - Garland
Pet form of Stephen and Stephanie.

Storm (English)
Storm

Stuart (English, Scottish)
Steward
Originally an occupational name for someone serving a steward in a royal or noble household.

Suadaa (Arabic)
Happy - Successful
Variants: *Suaydaa*

Suaidah (Arabic)
Happy - Joyful

Subahah (Arabic)
Beautiful - Bright

Subahah (Arabic)
Beautiful - Flame of a Lamp

Subaibah (Arabic)
Lover

Subaihah (Arabic)
Morning Arriver

Subail (Arabic)
Pouring Rain - Spike of Corn
Variants: *Sobail*

Subhah (Arabic)
Beautiful - Bright

Sudainah (Arabic)
Maintainer of te Kaaba
Variants: *Sodaina*

Sudaiqah (Arabic)
Sincere - Truthful

Sudur (Arabic)
Hearts
The name Sudur is mentioned in the Quran.
Variants: *Sodur, Sudoor*

Sue (English)
Lily
Short form of Susan.
Variants: *Soo, Su*

Suffah (Arabic)
Plaza - Square

Suha (Arabic)
Little Star

Suhad (Arabic)
Insomnia

Suhaibah (Arabic)
Red-brown-haired

Suhailaa (Arabic)
Gentle - Lenient - Soft

Suhailah (Arabic)
Gentle - Lenient - Soft

Suhaima (Arabic)
Arrow
Variants: *Sohaima, Sohaimah, Suhaimah*

Suhaira (Arabic)
Unsleeping - Wakeful
Variants: *Sohaira, Sohayra, Sohayrah, Suhairah, Suhayra, Suhayrah*

Suhbah (Arabic)
Companionship - Friendship

Sujaydah (Arabic)
Prostrator - Worshiper
Variants: *Sojaida*

Sukainah (Arabic)
Adorable - Cute - Energetic - Sprightly
Variants: *Sokaina*

Sukkar (Arabic)
Sugar
Variants: *Sokar, Sukar*

Suknah (Arabic)
Tranquility
Variants: *Sokna*

Sukniyyah (Arabic)
Tranquil
Variants: *Soknia*

Sulaimaa (Arabic)
Safe - Unharmed

Sulaimaat (Arabic)
Safe - Unharmed

Sulaimah (Arabic)
Safe - Unharmed

Sulaiwah (Arabic)
Consolation

Sulamaa (Arabic)
Safe Ones - Whole Ones
Variants: *Solama*

Sultanah (Arabic)
Queen - Ruler
Variants: *Soltana*

Sulufah (Arabic)
Advancement

Sulwan (Arabic)
Consolation - Solace
Variants: *Soluan*

Sumaihah (Arabic)
Forgiving - Gracious - Lenient

Sumaira (Arabic)
Companion - Nighttime Conversation Partner
Variants: *Somaira, Somairah, Sumairah, Sumayra*

Sumairaa (Arabic)
Tan-skinned

Sumama (Arabic)
Rescue - Salvation
Variants: *Sumamah, Thumama, Thumamah*

Sumayya (Arabic)
Birthmark - Special - Unique
Variants: *Somaya, Somayyah, Sumaia, Sumaya, Sumayah, Sumayyah*

Summer (English)
Summer

Sumou (Arabic)
Elevation - Greatness

Sunan (Arabic)
Traditions - Ways of Life
The name Sunan is mentioned in the Quran.

Sundus (Arabic)
Fine Silk - Silk Brocade
The name Sundus is mentioned in the Quran.

Sunnah (Arabic)
Tradition - Way of Life

The name Sunnah is mentioned in the Quran.

Sunud (Arabic)
Climb - Dependence - Reliance

Suraa (Persian)
Powerful - Strong
Variants: *Soura, Sura*

Surah (Arabic)
Chapter of the Quran - Greatness - Highness of Rank
The name Surah is mentioned in the Quran.

Surina (Persian)
Happy - Joyous
Variants: *Sureena*

Surma (Kurdish)
Kohl

Susan (English)
Lily
Variants: *Suzan*

Susan (English)
Lily
Anglicized form of Susanna.

Susanna (Biblical)
Lily
Variants: *Suzanna*

Susie (English)
Lily
Pet form of Susan and Susanna.
Variants: *Suzie, Suzy*

Sutait (Arabic)
Little Lady
Variants: *Sotayt*

Suwaib (Arabic)
Reward
Variants: *Thuwaib*

Suwaiba (Arabic)
Reward
Variants: *Soaiba, Souaibah, Suaiba, Suwaibah, Swaiba, Thuwaibah*

Suwaida (Arabic)
Land With Many Palm Trees
Variants: *Sowaida, Sowaidah, Suwaidah, Suwaydah*

Suwaidis (Arabic)
Sixth

Suwaimah (Arabic)
Bamboo - Gold - Mark - Symbol

Suwairaa (Arabic)
Pure Gold

Suzanne (French)
Lily
French form of Susanna.

Suzette (French)
Lily
Pet form of Suzanne.

Swanhild (German)
Battle Swan
Variants: *Swanhilda, Swanhilde*

T

Taal (Arabic)
Ascending - Come
The name can be a command ("come!") or a description of the state of something that ascends.

Taaliah (Arabic)
Reciter
Variants: *Talalia, Taliya, Taliyah*

Taazaz (Arabic)
Honor - Might - Power

Taban (Persian)
Shining
Variants: *Taaban, Tabaan*

Tabandeh (Persian)
Radiant - Shining
Variants: *Taabandah, Tabanda*

Tabarak (Arabic)
Blessed

Tabarruk (Arabic)
Blessedness

Tabiah (Arabic)
Follower - Successor

Tabith (Aramaic)
Gazelle

Tabseer (Arabic)
Education - Enlightenment

Tadbir (Arabic)
Contrivance - Organization - Procurement

Tadris (Arabic)
Research - Study

Tafheem (Arabic)
Elaboration - Illustration
Variants: *Tafhim, Tefhim*

Taflah (Arabic)
Delicate - Gentle - Soft

Tafli (Arabic)
Delicate - Gentle - Soft

Taghrid (Arabic)
Singing

Tahani (Arabic)
Congratulations

Taheerah (Arabic)
Pure - Virtuous

Tahillah (Arabic)
Gladness - Happiness

Tahira (Arabic)
Pure
Variants: *Taahera, Taahira, Tahera*

Tahmeed (Arabic)
Praising of God
Variants: *Tahmid, Tehmid*

Tahmineh (Persian)
Powerful - Strong
Variants: *Tahmeenah, Tahmina*

Tahrir (Arabic)
Liberation

Tahsin (Arabic)
Beautification - Improvement
Variants: *Tahseen, Tehsin*

Tahzeeb (Arabic)
Edification - Purification - Rectification - Refinement

Taiba (Arabic)
Repentant - Virtuous
Variants: *Ta'ibah, Taaebah, Taaiba, Taaibah, Taeba, Taebah, Taibah*

Taibah (Arabic)
Good - Wholesome
Also another name for the city of Medina.
Variants: *Teibah*

Taidah (Arabic)
Compassion - Kindness

Taihaa (Arabic)
Vast
Variants: *Taiha, Tayha, Tayhaa, Teiha, Teihaa*

Tajallah (Arabic)
Crown of God
Variants: *Taj Ullah, Tajullah*

Tajdar (Persian)
Crowned

Takreem (Arabic)
Graciousness - Honor - Respect
Variants: *Takrim, Tekrim*

Talaah (Arabic)
Aspect - Countenance - Face

Talaat (Arabic, Turkish)
Aspect - Countenance - Face
Turkish pronunciation of Talaah.

Talibah (Arabic)
Pursuer - Seeker - Seeker of Knowledge
Variants: *Taaliba, Taleba, Talebah, Taliba*

Talitha (Biblical)
Little Girl
From Aramaic.

Talulla (Irish)
Abundance - Lady - Princess

Tamanna (Arabic)
Hope - Wish
Variants: *Tamana, Tamanaa, Tamannaa*

Tamassuk (Arabic)
Adherence

Tamasul (Arabic)
Similarity

Tamheed (Arabic)
Facilitation - Preparation

Tamirah (Arabic)
Date Merchant

Tammamah (Arabic)
Date Merchant

Tamsin (English)
Twin
Contracted form of Thomasina.

Taneem (Arabic)
Blessedness
Variants: *Tan'im, Taneim, Tanim*

Tansy (English)
Tansy
A flower name.

Taqadum (Arabic)
Advancement - Progress

Tara (Persian)
Most Brilliant Star
Variants: *Taara*

Tara (English)
Hill

Taraneh (Persian)
Beautiful Young Person
Variants: *Taraaneh, Tarana, Taranah*

Tarashud (Arabic)
Guidance

Tareefah (Arabic)
Exquisite - Quaint - Rare

Tarheeb (Arabic)
Graciousness - Spaciousness - Vastness

Tariqa (Arabic)
Star
Variants: *Taareqa, Taareqah, Taariqa, Taariqah, Tareqa, Tareqah, Tariqah*

Tarkheem (Arabic)
Mellowing - Softening

Tarkhunah (Arabic)
Tarragon

Tarqiyah (Arabic)
Ascension

Tasaad (Arabic)
Happy - Successful

Tasahir (Arabic)
Vigils

Tasamuh (Arabic)
Forbearance - Forgiveness - Pardon

Taskeen (Arabic)
Tranquility

Tasmia (Arabic)
Naming
The name Tasmia is mentioned in the Quran.
Variants: *Tasmiah, Tasmiya, Tasmiyah*

Tasmira (Arabic)
Fruit - Investment - Product - Profit
Variants: *Tasmirah, Tathmira*

Tasneem (Arabic)
Falling Water - Fountain in Paradise
Variants: *Tasnim*

Tasteer (Arabic)
To Author - To Write

Tasweer (Arabic)
To Describe - To Paint - To Picture

Tatheer (Arabic)
Purification
The name Tatheer is mentioned in the Quran.
Variants: *Tateheer, Tathir*

Tawadud (Arabic)
Affection - Love

Tawaf (Arabic)
Circumambulation
Variants: *Tawaaf, Tewaf*

Tawaqur (Arabic)
Calmness - Composure - Solemnity

Tawbaat (Arabic)
Repntance

Tawfiqah (Arabic)
Success

Tawhidah (Arabic)
Monotheism

Tawilah (Arabic)
Long - Tall

Tawlah (Arabic)
Elevation - Highland

Tawny (English)
Tawny-haired
Variants: *Tawney*

Tawus (Arabic)
Beautiful - Peafowl

Tawwabah (Arabic)
Repenting

NAMES FOR GIRLS

Tawwad (Arabic)
Affection - Love

Tayibat (Arabic)
Acts of Virtue - Good Things - Pure Things
The name Tayibat is mentioned in the Quran.
Variants: *Taibaat, Tayebat, Tayyebat, Tayyibaat, Tayyibat*

Tayilah (Arabic)
Generous - Great

Taymurah (Arabic, Turkish)
Iron

Taysirah (Arabic)
Ease - Facilitation

Tayyibah (Arabic)
Good - Virtuous - Wholesome
The name Tayyibah is mentioned in the Quran.

Taza (Arabic, Persian)
Active - Fresh - Happy

Tazayyun (Arabic)
Adornment - Beautification

Tazeen (Arabic)
Adornment - Beautification
Variants: *Tazieen, Tazyeen, Tazyin*

Tazkiah (Arabic)
Growth - Improvement - Purification

Teal (English)
Teal
Refers to a type of bird.
Variants: *Teale*

Teeha (Arabic)
Vast
Variants: *Teehah, Tiha, Tihah*

Tegwen (Welsh)
Blessed - Fair-skinned - Lovely

Teodora (Italian, Polish, Portuguese, Spanish, Swedish)
Gift of God
Form of Theodora.

Thameenah (Arabic)
Precious - Valable
Variants: *Sameenah*

Thamirah (Arabic)
Fruit-bearing - Productive
Variants: *Samirah*

Thanaa (Arabic)
Praise
Variants: *Sanaa*

Tharaa (Arabic)
Affluence - Prosperity - Wealthiness
Variants: *Saraa'*

Thayeba (Arabic)
Repentant
Variants: *Thayebah, Thayiba*

Thea (English)
Gift of God
Short form of Dorothea.

Thecla (English)
Glory of God
From Greek Theokleia.

Theodora (English)
Gift of God
Feminine of Theodore.

Theodosia (Greek)
Gift of God

Thurayya (Arabic)
Chandelier - Pleiades
Pleiades is a group of stars.
Variants: *Soraia, Surayya*

Thurayyat (Arabic)
Chandeliers
Variants: *Surayyat*

Tibhaj (Arabic)
Beauty - Radiance

Tibrah (Arabic)
Gold Ore

Tilda (English)
Strength in Battle
Short form of Matilda.

Tilde (Danish)
Strength in Battle
Short form of Matilda.

Tina (Persian)
Rose
Variants: *Teena, Teena, Tinaa, Tinaa*

Tina (Arabic)
Fig

Tinat (Arabic)
Figs

Tinjal (Arabic)
Beauty of the Eyes

Tirhab (Arabic)
Graciousness - Spaciousness - Vastness

Tiyam (Kurdish, Persian)
Beloved - Darling
Variants: *Tiam*

Tiymah (Arabic)
Beautiful

Toivo (Finnish)
Hope

Tooba (Arabic)
The name Tooba is mentioned in the Quran.

Variants: *Blessedness, Bliss, Goodness*

Topaz (English)
Topaz
Type of gemstone.

Tricia (English)
Noble - Patrician
Short form of Patricia.

Trina (English)
Pure
Short form of Katrina.

Trine (Danish)
Pure
Short form of Katrine.

Trinette (English)
Pure
Elaboration of Trina.

Trisha (English)
Noble - Patrician
Respelling of Tricia.

Tufan (Arabic)
Cataclysm - Deluge - Flood
The name Tufan is mentioned in the Quran.

Turaifah (Arabic)
Blessing - Luxury

Turan (Persian)
Name of an area of Persia and an ancient kingdom that used to be in today's Turkmenistan and parts of Afghanistan.
Variants: *Touran, Turaan*

Turas (Arabic)
Inheritance
The name Turas is mentioned in the Quran.

Turfah (Arabic)
Blessings - Luxuries

Tutia (Persian)
Echinus - Zinc
Variants: *Tutya*

U

Ubaidah (Arabic)
Servant of God - Worshiper of God

Ubayaa (Arabic)
Beautiful

Ubayaat (Arabic)
Beautiful

Udaina (Arabic)
Eden - Place of Everlasting Bliss
Variants: *Odaina, Odainah, Odayna, Odeina, Udainah*

Ufairah (Arabic)
Gazelle
Variants: *Ofaira, Ofairah, Ofayra, Ofayrah, Ufaira, Ufayrah*

Uhaidah (Arabic)
Covenant - Promise

Ulrika (German, Scandinavian)
Power of Prosperity
Variant of Ulrike.

Ulrike (Danish, German)
Power of Prosperity
Feminine of Ulrich.

Ulya (Arabic)
Highest - Sublime - Supreme
Ulya is mentioned in the Quran in verse 9:40.
Variants: *Oliaa, Olya, Olyaa, Ulia, Uliaa, Ulyaa*

Umaima (Arabic)
Mother
Diminutive form of umm ("mother").
Variants: *Omaima, Oumaima, Umaimah, Umayma*

Umaira (Arabic)
Performer of Umrah - Pilgrim
Variants: *Omaira, Omairah, Umairah, Umayra, Umayrah*

Umamah (Arabic)
Three Hundred Camels
Variants: *Oumama, Umaama, Umama*

Umm Aiman (Arabic)
Blessed

Umm Hamdi (Arabic)
Grateful - Thankful

Ummah (Arabic)
Community - Nation
The name Ummah is mentioned in the Quran.
Variants: *Omma, Ommah, Uma, Umah, Umma*

Ummul Hanaa (Arabic)
Happy - Peaceful
Variants: *Ummulhana*

Umniya (Arabic)
Hope
The name Umniya is mentioned in the Quran in verse 22:52.
Variants: *Omniya Umnia, Umnea, Umneya*

Umrah (Arabic)
Minor Pilgrimage - Overhaul - Restoration - Revival
The name Umrah is mentioned in the Quran.

Unayzee (Arabic)
Agile - Beautiful - Gazelle
Variants: *Onaizee, Onayzi, Unayzi*

Unity (English)
Unity

Uraifah (Arabic)
Fragrant - Good Scent

Ursula (English, German, Scandinavian)
Bear-cub

Urwah (Arabic)
Ever-green Tree - Handhold - Lion
The name Urwah is mentioned in the Quran in verse 31:22.
Variants: *Orwa, Orwah, Urwa*

Usko (Finnish)
Faith

Usmanah (Arabic)
Baby Houbara - Baby Snake

Usraat (Arabic)
Refuge - Shelter

Utaiqah (Arabic)
Generosity - Virtue

Utairah (Arabic)
Fragrant

Uzaibah (Arabic)
Fresh Water

Uzaizah (Arabic)
Honor - Might - Power

Uzrat (Arabic)
Virginity

This page intentionally left blank

V

Val (English)
Healthy - Strong
Short form of Valerie or Valentine.

Valda (English)
Healthy - Strong
Elaboration of Val.

Valdemar (Scandinavian)
Famous Rule
Variant of Waldemar.

Valene (English)
Healthy - Strong
Elaboration of Val.

Valentine (English)
Healthy - Strong

Valeri (Russian)
Healthy - Strong

Valerie (English)
Healthy - Strong

Valetta (English)
Healthy - Strong
Elaboration of Val.

Vanda (Persian)
Desire - Wish - Worshiper
Variants: *Vaandaa*

Vanja (Scandinavian)
God is Gracious
From Russian Vanya.

Varda (Jewish)
Rose
Cognate of Arabic Wardah.
Variants: *Vardah*

Varvara (Russian)
Foreign
Form of Barbara.

Vashti (Persian)
Beauty - Goodness - Happiness - Kindness
Variants: *Vashtee, Vashty*

Veesta (Persian)
Acquirer - Discoverer - Finder
Variants: *Vista*

Vera (Russian)
Faith

Verity (English)
Truth

Vibeke (Danish, Norwegian)
War Fortress
Form of Wibeke.

Vicky (English)
Victory
Pet form of Victoria.
Variants: *Vicki, Vickie, Vikki*

Victoire (French)
Victory
French form of Victoria.

Victoria (English, Spanish)
Victory

Vida (Persian)
Acquirer - Finder - Prominent - Visible
Variants: *Veeda*

Viktoria (German, Scandinavian)
Victory
Form of Victoria.

Vilhelmina (Swedish)
Determined Protector
Form of Wilhelmina.

Vilhelmine (Danish, Norwegian)
Determined Protector
Form of Wilhelmina.

Vina (Persian)
Perception - Recognition
Variants: *Veena*

Viola (English, Italian, Scandinavian)
Violet
A type of flowering plant.

Violet (English)
Violet
A type of flower.

Vita (Danish, English)
Life

Vitale (Italian)
Alive

Vittoria (Italian)
Victory
Form of Victoria.

Vivien (English)
Alive
Form of Vivian.
Variants: *Vivean, Vivianne*

Vivienne (French)
Alive
Feminine form of Vivien.

Viyana (Persian)
Sensibility - Wisdom
Variants: *Veeyana, Viana*

This page intentionally left blank

NAMES FOR GIRLS

W

Waad (Arabic)
Promise
The name Waad is mentioned in the Quran.
Variants: *Wa'd, Wad*

Waafiyah (Arabic)
Faithful - Loyal - Perfect - Whole

Waaliyah (Arabic)
Governor - Ruler

Waddaa (Arabic)
Affection - Love

Waddah (Arabic)
Affection - Love

Wadida (Arabic)
Affectionate - Loving
Variants: *Wadeeda, Wadeedah, Wadidah*

Wadiyah (Arabic)
Valley

Waelah (Arabic)
Clan - Tribe

Wafa (Arabic)
Completion - Faithfulness - Fulfillment - Loyalty

Wafeeqah (Arabic)
Appropriate - Companion - Friend - Harmonious

Wafiyyah (Arabic)
Faithful - Loyal
Variants: *Wafeeya, Wafiya, Wafiyah*

Wafqah (Arabic)
Accord - Harmony

Wahbah (Arabic)
Bestowal - Gift

Wahbiyyah (Arabic)
Bestowal - Gift

Wahdah (Arabic)
Alliance - Unity
Variants: *Wahda*

Wahdat (Arabic)
Wahdat is the Turkish pronunciation of Wahdah.

Waheebah (Arabic)
Bestowal - Gift

Waheeda (Arabic)
Peerless - Singular - Unique
Variants: *Waheedah, Wahida, Wahidah*

Wahibah (Arabic)
Bestower - Giver

Wahida (Arabic)
Singular - Unique
The name Wahida is mentioned in the Quran.
Variants: *Waheda, Wahedah, Wahidah*

Wajahah (Arabic)
Distinction - Glory - Honor - Prestige

Wajahat (Arabic)
Distinction - Prominence

Wajeedaa (Arabic)
Affectionate - Loving

Wajeedah (Arabic)
Affectionate - Loving

Wajeehah (Arabic)
Honorable - Noble - Prestigious

Wajibah (Arabic)
Essential - Imperative - Obligatory

Walburg (German)
Foreign Fortress - Fortress of Power

Waleedah (Arabic)
Girl - Infant - New - Newborn

Waleeya (Arabic)
Caretaker - Companion - Custodian - Patron
Variants: *Waleeyah, Walia, Waliah, Waliya, Waliyah, Waliyya, Waliyyah*

Wanawsha (Kurdish, Persian)
Violet
Refers to a type of flower.
Variants: *Wanausha*

Waniya (Arabic)
Breeze - Gentle Breeze
Variants: *Waaniya, Wanea, Waneya, Wania, Waniyah*

Waqida (Arabic)
Brilliant - Kindled
Variants: *Waqidah*

Waqqaa (Arabic)
Guardian - Protector - Shield

Ward (Arabic)
Flower - Rose
Variants: *Werd*

Wardaa (Arabic)
Flower - Rose
Variants: *Warda*

Wardah (Arabic)
Flower - Rose
The name Wardah is mentioned in the Quran.
Variants: *Warda*

Wardiyyah (Arabic)
Rose-like - Rosy

Wareefah (Arabic)
Blooming - Flourishing

Warida (Arabic)
Aware - Experienced - Learned
Variants: *Waareda, Wareda, Waredah, Waridah*

Waritha (Arabic)
Inheritor - Long-lived
Variants: *Waarisah, Waretha, Warisa, Warithah*

Warqaa (Arabic)
Female Pigeon
Variants: *Warqa*

Wasamah (Arabic)
Beauty

Wasaya (Arabic)
Behests - Teachings Precepts - Tenets

Waseela (Arabic)
Instrument - Path - Route - Track
The name Waseela is mentioned in the Quran.
Variants: *Waseelah, Wasila, Wasilah*

Waseema (Arabic)
Beautiful
Variants: *Waseemah, Wasima, Wasimah*

Wasfah (Arabic)
Description - Praise

Wasfia (Arabic)
Praiseworthy
Variants: *Wasfia, Wasfiah, Wasfiyya, Wasfiyyah*

Washan (Arabic)
Elevated Land - Highland

Washana (Arabic)
Elevated Land - Highland

Wasifa (Arabic)
Describer - Praiser
Variants: *Waasefa, Waasifa, Waasifah, Wasefa, Wasefah, Wasifah*

Wasiya (Arabic)
Gracious - Patient
Variants: *Wasi'ah, Wasia, Wasiah, Wasya*

Wasiyyah (Arabic)
Behest - Tenet - Will

Wasmaa (Arabic)
Beautiful

Wathiqa (Arabic)
Confident - Sure
Variants: *Waseqa, Wasiqa, Wathiqah*

Wazeenah (Arabic)
Creative - Original

Wazhaa (Arabic)
Beautiful

Wazhah (Arabic)
Clarity - Prominence

Wazia (Arabic)
Distributor - Protector
Variants: *Wazi'ah, Waziyah*

Wazihaa (Arabic)
Apparent - Clear - Visible

Wazihah (Arabic)
Apparent - Clear - Visible

Wazin (Arabic)
Collator - Comparer - Weigher

Wazira (Arabic)
Assistant - Helper - Minister
Variants: *Wazeera, Wazeerah, Wazirah*

Waznah (Arabic)
Intelligent - Petite

Wazzaa (Arabic)
Beautiful - Clean - Radiant

Wera (Polish)
Faith
Form of Vera.
Variants: *Wiara, Wiera*

Wiam (Arabic)
Concord - Harmony - Peace - Rapport
Variants: *Wi'am, Wiaam*

Wid (Arabic)
Affection - Harmony Love
Variants: *Widd*

Widad (Arabic)
Affection - Harmony - Love
Variants: *Wedaad, Wedad, Widaad*

Wifaq (Arabic)
Harmony - Sympathy - Unity
Variants: *Wefaaq, Wefaq, Wfaaq*

Wijdan (Arabic)
Affection - Conscience - Fondness - Soul - Tenderness
Variants: *Wejdaan, Wejdan, Wijdaan*

Wilhelmina (German)
Determined Protector
Feminine of Wilhelm.
Variants: *Wilhelmine*

Willa (English)
Determined Protector
Feminine of William.

NAMES FOR GIRLS

Willow (English)
Willow

Wilma (German)
Determined Protector
Contracted form of Wilhelmina, or used as a feminine of William.

Wiqaa (Arabic)
Protection - Shield

Wirad (Arabic)
Flowers - Roses
Variants: *Werad, Wiraad*

Wisal (Arabic)
Communion - Reunion
Variants: *Wesal, Wisaal*

Wisama (Arabic)
Attractiveness - Beauty
Variants: *Wesama, Wesamah, Wisaama, Wisaamah, Wisamah*

Wuhaibah (Arabic)
Bestowal - Gift

Wuraidah (Arabic)
Little Flower

Wurud (Arabic)
Flowers - Roses
Variants: *Worud, Wurood*

This page intentionally left blank

Y

Yagana (Persian)
Peerless - Unique
Variants: *Yaganeh*

Yakta (Persian)
Peerless - Unique

Yalina (Arabic)
Gentleness - Leniency - Softness
Variants: *Yaleena, Yaleenah, Yaleina, Yalinah, Yelina, Yelinah*

Yamam (Arabic)
Dove
Variants: *Yamaam*

Yamama (Arabic)
Dove
Variants: *Yamaama, Yamaamah, Yamama*

Yamar (Arabic)
Alive - Life - Long-lived
Variants: *Ya'mar, Yaamar, Yaamer, Yamer*

Yameena (Arabic)
Blessed - Prospering - Righteous
Variants: *Yameenah, Yamina, Yaminah*

Yameenaa (Arabic)
Blessed - Favored

Yaminah (Arabic)
Blessed

Yana (Persian)
Doer of Good Deeds

Yaqeen (Arabic)
Certainty
The name Yaqeen is mentioned in the Quran.
Variants: *Yaqin*

Yaqeena (Arabic)
Certain
Variants: *Yaqeenah, Yaqina, Yaqinah*

Yaqoot (Arabic)
Ruby
The name Yaqoot is mentioned in the Quran.
Variants: *Yaqut*

Yaquta (Arabic)
Ruby
Variants: *Yaooqtah, Yaqoota, Yaqutah*

Yar (Persian)
Companion - Friend
Variants: *Yaar*

Yara (Persian)
Capability - Courage - Power
Variants: *Yaara, Yaaraa, Yaraa*

Yaroq (Turkish)
Brilliant - White

Yas (Persian)
Jasmine
Variants: *Yaas*

Yasaal (Persian)
Garland - Wreath
Variants: *Yasal*

Yasaman (Persian)
Jasmine
Variants: *Yaasaman, Yaseman*

Yaseera (Arabic)
Blessed - Easy
Variants: *Yaseerah, Yasira, Yasirah*

Yashal (Arabic)
Brilliant - Radiant
Variants: *Yash'al*

Yasira (Arabic)
Lenient
Variants: *Yaasira, Yaasirah, Yaserah, Yasirah*

Yasm (Arabic, Persian)
Jasmine
Variants: *Yaasm*

Yasma (Arabic, Persian)
Jasmine
Variants: *Yaasmah, Yasmah, Yasmeh*

Yasmin (Arabic, Persian)
Jasmine
Variants: *Yasmeen*

Yasmina (Arabic, Persian)
Jasmine
Variants: *Yaasmina, Yasminah, Yasmineh*

Yasminaa (Persian)
Jasmine

Yasmoon (Persian)
Jasmine
Variants: *Yasmoun, Yasmun*

Yasna (Persian)
Prayer - Supplication

Yawer (Persian)
Companion - Friend
Variants: *Yawar*

Yazeedah (Arabic)
Growth - Increase

Yelisaveta (Russian)
My God is Bountiful
Form of Elizabeth.

Yumna (Arabic)
Blessed
Variants: *Yiumna, Yomna, Yomnaa, Youmna, Youmnaa, Yowmna, Yowmnaa, Yumna, Yumnaa, Yuwmna, Yuwmnaa*

Yumnaat (Arabic)
Blessedness - Blessings

Yumnah (Arabic)
Blessed - In the Grace of God
Variants: *Yomna, Yomnah, Yumna*

Yusma (Persian)
Beautiful - Beloved
From colloquial Persian.

Yusra (Arabic)
Blessedness - Comfort - Ease
The name Yusra is mentioned in the Quran.
Variants: *Yosra, Yosraa, Yousra, Yusraa*

Yusraat (Arabic)
Affluence

Yusrah (Arabic)
Affluence

Yusriya (Arabic)
Living in Luxury - Needless - Rich
Variants: *Yosriyah, Yosriyya, Yosriyyah, Yusria, Yusriah, Yusriyah, Yusriyya, Yusriyyah*

Yusrullah (Arabic)
God's Blessing

Yvette (French)
Yew
Feminine diminutive of Yves.

Yvonne (French)
Yew
Feminine diminutive of Yves.

Z

Zaada (Arabic)
Increasing - Prosperous
Variants: *Zaadah, Zadah*

Zaakiyah (Arabic)
Blessed - Virtuous
Variants: *Zakiah*

Zaaria (Kurdish)
Ocean
Variants: *Zaaryaa*

Zabi (Arabic)
Gazelle

Zabira (Arabic)
Knowledgeable - Wise
Variants: *Dhabira, Zaabirah, Zabirah*

Zabiyyah (Arabic)
Gazelle

Zabreen (Persian)
Highest - Lofty
Variants: *Zabrin*

Zafaa (Arabic)
Growth - Increase - Proximity - Side

Zafar (Arabic)
Triumph - Victory - Win
Variants: *Dafar, Dhafar, Zafer*

Zafeera (Arabic)
Successful
Variants: *Dhafeera, Dhafeerah, Dhafirah, Zafeerah, Zafira, Zafirh*

Zafira (Arabic)
Successful
Variants: *Dhafirah, Zaafira, Zaafirah, Zafirah*

Zaghalil (Arabic)
Adorable
Variants: *Zaghaleel*

Zaghlula (Arabic)
Baby Pigeon
Variants: *Zaghloola, Zaghloolah, Zaghlulah, Zagloolah*

Zahaa (Arabic)
Morning

Zahab (Arabic)
Gold
The name *Zahab* is mentioned in the Quran.
Variants: *Dahab, Dehab, Dhahab, Zehab*

Zahabia (Arabic)
Golden
Variants: *Dahabia, Dahabiyyah, Dhahabia, Zahabeya, Zahabiah, Zahabiyah, Zahabiyyah*

Zaheena (Arabic)
Intellectual - Intelligent - Sagacious
Variants: *Daheena, Dahina, Zahina, Zahinah*

Zaheera (Arabic)
Brilliant - Radiant
Variants: *Zaheerah, Zahira, Zahirah*

Zaheeraa (Arabic)
Radiant
Variants: *Zahira*

Zahia (Arabic)
Beautiful - Breeze - Radiant
Variants: *Zaheya, Zaheyah, Zahiah, Zahiya, Zahiyah*

Zahian (Arabic)
Bright Day - Brilliant
Variants: *Dhahian, Zahiaan, Zahyaan, Zahyan*

Zahidah (Arabic)
Ascetic
Variants: *Zaheda*

Zahira (Arabic)
Bright Star - Glowing - Radiant
Variants: *Zahirah*

Zahou (Arabic)
Beautiful View - Blooming Plant
Variants: *Zahu, Zahu*

Zahou (Arabic)
Beautiful View - Blooming Plant

Zahraa (Arabic)
Brilliant - Radiant
Variants: *Zahra, Zahraa', Zehra, Zehraa*

Zahrah (Arabic)
Flower
The name *Zahrah* is mentioned in the Quran.
Variants: *Zahra, Zahreh, Zehra, Zehrah, Zehre, Zehreh*

Zahriyyah (Arabic)
Flower-like
Variants: *Zahria*

Zahwah (Arabic)
Beauty - Freshness - Vista
Variants: *Zahua, Zahuah, Zahwa*

Zahyaa (Arabic)
Bright - Moonlit Night - Pure

Zaida (Arabic)
Generous
Variants: *Zaaeda, Zaaedah, Zaaida, Zaaidah, Zaayda, Zaaydah, Zaayeda, Zaayedah, Zaeda, Zayda, Zaydah, Zayeda, Zayedah*

Zaigham (Arabic)
Lion
Variants: *Zaygham*

Zaighama (Arabic)
Lioness
Variants: *Zaighamah*

Zaina (Arabic)
Adornment - Beauty - Excellence
Variants: *Zainah, Zayna, Zaynah, Zeinah, Zeineh*

Zainabah (Arabic)
The name of a tree with fragrant flowers. It is unclear what tree it is exactly.
Variants: *Zainaba*

Zaira (Arabic)
Guest - Visitor
Variants: *Zaaera, Zaaerah, Zaaira, Zaairah, Zaera, Zaerah, Zayra*

Zaitun (Arabic)
Olive - Olive Tree
The name Zaitun is mentioned in the Quran.
Variants: *Zaitoon, Zaytoon, Zaytun, Zeitoon, Zeitun, Zeytun*

Zaituna (Arabic)
Olive - Olive Tree
The name Zaituna is mentioned in the Quran.
Variants: *Zaitoona, Zaitoonah, Zaitunah, Zaytoona, Zaytoonah, Zaytuna, Zaytunah*

Zakaa (Arabic)
Intelligence - Keenness
Arabic for "intelligence", "cleverness".
Variants: *Zaka*

Zakat (Arabic)
Alms - Purification
The name Zakat is mentioned in the Quran.
Variants: *Zakaat, Zekat*

Zakawat (Arabic, Turkish)
Intelligence - Keenness
Turkish pronunciation of Zakawah.
Variants: *Zakaawat*

Zakhira (Arabic)
Rich - Wealthy - Wise
Variants: *Zaakhira, Zaakhirah, Zakhera, Zakherah, Zakhirah*

Zakiya (Arabic)
Fragrant - Innocent - Pure
Variants: *Zakeyah, Zakeyyah, Zakia, Zakiah, Zakiyah, Zakiyya, Zakiyyah*

Zaluj (Arabic)
Nimble - Sprightly
Variants: *Zalooj*

Zamaair (Arabic)
Consciences - Hearts - Minds
Variants: *Zamaaer, Zamaer, Zamair*

Zamaneh (Persian)
Day and Age - Epoch
Variants: *Zamaaneh, Zamana, Zamanah*

Zameela (Arabic)
Colleague - Companion
Variants: *Zameelah, Zamila, Zamilah*

Zameer (Arabic)
Conscience - Heart - Mind
Variants: *Dameer, Dhamir, Zamir, Zemir*

Zaminah (Arabic)
Guarantor - Surety

Zamira (Arabic)
Fit - Lean
Variants: *Damira, Zaamera, Zaamerah, Zaamira, Zaamirah, Zamera, Zamerah, Zamirah*

Zanbaqi (Arabic)
Lily-like
Variants: *Zanbaqy*

Zanera (Arabic, Persian)
Intelligent - Sensible
Variants: *Zaneereh, Zanireh*

Zanna (English)
Lily
Short form of Suzanna.

Zanurah (Arabic)
Intelligent - Keen
Variants: *Zanoora*

Zar (Persian, Turkish)
Gold
Variants: *Zer*

Zara (Arabic)
Excellent - Pinnacle - Top
Plural of Zirwah.
Variants: *Daraa, Dharaa, Zaraa*

Zara (English)
Flower
Possibly from Arabic Zahrah ("flower"), used in Britain, Italy, Spain and Portugal.

Zarab (Persian)
Colloidal Gold - Golden Water
Variants: *Zaraab*

Zarafshan (Persian)
Beautiful - Spreader of Gold
Variants: *Zar Afshan, Zarafshaan*

Zareefa (Arabic)
Charming - Intelligent - Witty
Variants: *Dharifah, Zareefah, Zarifa, Zarifah*

Zareera (Arabic, Persian)
Fragrant Plant
Known as Reseda in English.
Variants: *Zareerah, Zarira, Zarirah*

NAMES FOR GIRLS

Zarfaat (Arabic)
Courteous - Elegant - Refined - Witty

Zarghama (Arabic)
Brave - Lionness - Warrior
Variants: *Zarghamah*

Zargonaa (Kurdish)
Beautiful
Literally "golden faced".
Variants: *Zargona*

Zargoon (Persian)
Beautiful - Percious
Literally "gold-colored", "like gold".
Variants: *Zargun*

Zargoona (Persian)
Beautiful - Percious
Literally "gold-colored", "like gold".
Variants: *Zarguna, Zargunaa*

Zargul (Persian)
Golden Flower
Variants: *Zargol, Zergul*

Zaria (Kurdish)
Ocean
Variants: *Zarya*

Zarin (Persian)
Golden
Variants: *Zareen*

Zarina (Persian)
Golden
Variants: *Zareena, Zareenah, Zarinah*

Zariya (Arabic)
Scattering Wind
Variants: *Dhariya, Zarea, Zareia, Zaria, Zarya*

Zarnab (Arabic, Persian)
Fragrant Plant

Scientific name: Taxus baccata.
Variants: *Zarnaab*

Zarqa Bano (Arabic)
Blue-eyed Lady
Variants: *Zarqaa Banu*

Zarqa Habiba (Arabic)
Blue-eyed Beloved

Zarqa Sultana (Arabic)
Blue-eyed Queen

Zarqaa (Arabic)
Blue-eyed
Arabic for "blue eyed".
Variants: *Zarqa*

Zarra (Arabic)
Pilgrim - Visitor
Arabic for "visitor", "pilgrim".
Variants: *Zaraa, Zarraa*

Zaryan (Urdu)
Gold Finder
Variants: *Zarian, Zaryaan*

Zaufishan (Arabic, Persian)
Radiant - Spreader of Light
Variants: *Zaufeshan, Zaufishaan, Zofishan, Zowfishan*

Zawal (Arabic)
Sundown
Variants: *Zawaal*

Zawala (Arabic)
Sundown
Variants: *Zawaala, Zawaalah, Zawalah*

Zaweela (Arabic)
Motion - Movement
Variants: *Zaweelah, Zawila, Zawilah*

Zayana (Arabic)
Adorner - Beautifier - Decorator
Variants: *Zayaana, Zayaanah,*

Zayyana, Zayyanah, Zeyaana, Zeyana, Zeyyana, Zeyyanah

Zayanaa (Arabic)
Adorner - Beautifier
Variants: *Zayaana*

Zayda (Arabic)
Fortune - Increase - Progress
Variants: *Zaayedah, Zaayida, Zaayidah, Zaydah Zayida, Zayeda, Zayidah*

Zayirah (Arabic)
Roaring Lion
Variants: *Zayera*

Zayn (Arabic)
Adornment - Beauty - Excellence - Grace - Virtue
Variants: *Zain, Zaine, Zane, Zayne, Zein, Zeine, Zeyn, Zeyne*

Zayyan (Arabic)
Adorner - Beautifier - Decorator
Variants: *Zaiaan, Zaian, Zaiane, Zayaan, Zayan, Zayyaan, Zayyaane, Zayyane, Zeyan, Zeyyan*

Zeeana (Arabic)
Adornment - Beautification
Variants: *Zeana, Zeanah, Ziana, Zianah, Ziyaana, Ziyaanah, Ziyana, Ziyanah, Zyaanah, Zyana, Zyanah*

Zeeb (Persian)
Beauty
Variants: *Zib, Zib*

Zeeb (Persian)
Beauty - Elegance

Zeenah (Arabic)
Adornment - Beauty
The name Zeenah is mentioned in the Quran in verse 57:20.
Variants: *Zeena, Zeinah, Zeinah, Zeineh, Zienah, Zinah, Zynah*

Zehak (Arabic)
Laughter
Variants: *Dhihak, Zeihak, Zihak*

Zehn (Arabic)
Intellect - Psyche - Reason
Variants: *Zihn*

Zeifa (Arabic)
Guest
Variants: *Zaifa, Zaifah, Zayfa, Zayfah*

Zephyrine (English)
West Wind
Ultimately from Greek Zephyros ("west wind").

Zewar (Kurdish, Persian)
Adornment - Beautification

Zhaleh (Persian)
Dew
Variants: *Zhaaleh, Zhala, Zhalah*

Zhasman (Persian)
Jasmine

Zhasmin (Persian)
Jasmine

Zheela (Persian)
Hail

Zheena (Persian)
Alive - Vibrant

Zheeno (Persian)
Alive - Vibrant

Zhenya (Russian)
High-born - Noble
Pet form of Yevgeni (male) and Yevgenia (female).

Zia ul Qamar (Arabic)
Moonlight
Variants: *Ziaul Qamar, Ziyaul Qamar*

Ziara (Arabic)
Visit - Visitation
Variants: *Ziaara, Ziaarah, Ziarah, Ziyara, Ziyarah, Zyaara, Zyaarah, Zyara, Zyarah*

Ziba (Persian)
Beautiful
Variants: *Zeeba, Zeebaa, Zibaa*

Ziba Talaat (Persian)
Beautiful
Literally meaning "one with a beautiful complexion".

Zibaa (Arabic)
Gazelles

Zibandeh (Persian)
Adorned - Beautified - Worthy

Zibaru (Persian)
Beautiful
Variants: *Zeebaru*

Zibriqan (Arabic)
Crescent - Moon

Zifaf (Arabic)
River Bank - Shore - Side

Zihaka (Arabic)
Happy - Laughing
Arabic for "one who laughs often", "happy".
Variants: *Zehaakah, Zehaka, Zihaaka*

Zihni (Arabic)
Intellectual - Reasonable - Understanding
Arabic for "intellectual", "understanding", "reasonable", "deep thinker".
Variants: *Dhehni, Zehni, Zihnee, Zihny*

Zihniyyah (Arabic)
Intelligent - Wise

Zikr (Arabic)
Mention - Remembrance
The name Zikr is mentioned in the Quran.
Variants: *Dhekr, Dhikr, Dikr, Zekr*

Zikra (Arabic)
Memory - Recollection - Remembrance
The name Zikra is mentioned in the Quran.
Variants: *Dekra, Dekraa, Dhikra, Dhikraa, Dikra, Dikraa, Zekra, Zekraa, Zikraa, Zykra*

Zikrayat (Arabic)
Memories - Recollections - Reminiscences

Zil Allah (Arabic)
God's Mercy - God's Protection
Literally meaning "shade of God".
Variants: *Zell Allah, Zilallah*

Zil Elahi (Arabic, Urdu)
God's Mercy - God's Protection
Literally meaning "shade of God".
Variants: *Zill Elahi*

Zil Yazdan (Arabic, Persian, Urdu)
God's Mercy - God's Protection
Literally meaning "shade of God".
Variants: *Zil Yazdaan*

Zil-e-Qamar (Arabic)
Dark Side of the Moon
Urdu for "the dark side of the moon". Arabic version is Zil al-Qamar or Zilil Qamar. In Urdu it can also be written as Zili Qamar and Zil e Qamar.
Variants: *Zil E Qamar, Zilleqamar*

NAMES FOR GIRLS

Zilal (Arabic)
Shade
The name Zilal is mentioned in the Quran.
Variants: *Zelaal, Zelal, Zilaa, Zylal*

Zill (Arabic)
Shade - Shadow
Variants: *Zel, Zell, Zil*

Zilla (Arabic)
Shade - Shadow
Variants: *Zella, Zellah, Zila, Zilah, Zillah*

Zimal (Arabic)
Garment - Robe
Variants: *Zemaal, Zemal, Zimaal, Zymaal, Zymal*

Zirwa (Arabic)
Pinnacle - Superb - Top
Variants: *Dherwa, Dhirwa, Thirwa, Zerwa, Zirua, Zyrua, Zyrwa*

Zivanka (Slavic)
Full of Life

Zivar (Persian)
Adornment - Beautification
Variants: *Zeevar, Ziver*

Ziya (Arabic)
Light - Radiance
The name Ziya is mentioned in the Quran.
Variants: *Dea, Deea, Deia, Deya, Deyya, Dhea, Dheea, Dheia, Dheya, Dhia, Dhiaa, Dhiya, Dhiyaa', Dhiyya, Dhiyyaa, Dhya, Dhyya, Dia, Diaa, Diea, Diya, Dya, Dyaa, Zea, Zeea, Zeia, Zeiya, Zeya, Zeyaa, Zia, Ziaa, Ziea, Zieya, Ziya, Ziyaa, Zya*

Ziyada (Arabic)
Increase - Progress
The name Ziyada is mentioned in the Quran.

Variants: *Ziaada, Ziada, Ziadah, Ziyaada, Ziyaadah*

Zoe (English)
Life
From Greek.

Zoeya (Arabic)
Brilliant - Radiant
Variants: *Zaw'iyyah, Zawiyah, Zawiyyah, Zoeyah, Zouiyyah*

Zofia (Polish)
Wisdom
Polish form of Sofia.

Zohra (Arabic)
Bright White Color - Radiant - Venus
Variants: *Zohrah, Zohreh, Zuhra, Zuhrah*

Zonera (Arabic)
Variant of Zunairah.
Variants: *Zonerah, Zuneera, Zunera, Zunerah*

Zoona (Arabic)
Adornment - Beautification
Variants: *Dhuna, Doona, Zona, Zonah, Zoonah, Zouna, Zounah, Zuna, Zunah*

Zoona (Arabic)
Gazelle

Zoraiz (Arabic, Persian)
Enlightener - Spreader of Light
Variants: *Dhuraiz, Zoreez, Zoriz, Zouraiz, Zuriz*

Zoreza (Arabic)
Radiant
Literally "spreader of light".
Variants: *Zooriza, Zoureza, Zourizah, Zureeza, Zuriza, Zurizah*

Zosia (Polish)
Wisdom
Pet form of Zofia.

Zryan (Kurdish)
Storm
Variants: *Zriaan, Zrian, Zryaan*

Zubaida (Arabic)
Excellent - Soft-bodied - Superb
Variants: *Zobaida, Zobaidah, Zobayda, Zobaydah, Zubaidah, Zubayda, Zubaydah*

Zubi (Arabic)
Gazelle

Zuha (Arabic)
Forenoon
The name Zuha is mentioned in the Quran.
Variants: *Doha, Duha, Zohaa, Zuhaa*

Zuhaa (Arabic)
Radiance

Zuhaibah (Arabic)
Lump of Gold

Zuhaira (Arabic)
Flower - Radiant
Variants: *Zohaira, Zohairah, Zuhairah, Zuhayra, Zuhayrah*

Zuhairaa (Arabic)
Little Flower - Radiant
Variants: *Zohaira*

Zuhayyah (Arabic)
Radiant
Variants: *Zohaya*

Zuhdiyyah (Arabic)
Ascetic
Variants: *Zohdia*

Zuhniyyah (Arabic)
Intelligent - Wise

Zuhr (Arabic)
Radiant
Variants: *Zohr*

Zuhriyyah (Arabic)
Florid - Pink - Rosy
Variants: *Zohria*

Zuhur (Arabic)
Flowers
Variants: *Zohur, Zuhoor*

Zulfaa (Arabic)
Closeness - Nearness - Rank - Station
The name Zulfaa is mentioned in the Quran.
Variants: *Zolfa, Zolfaa, Zulfa*

Zulhijjah (Arabic)
12th Month of the Hijri Calendar

Zulla (Arabic)
Shade
The name Zulla is mentioned in the Quran.
Variants: *Zolla, Zollah, Zula, Zulah, Zullah*

Zultan (Arabic, Urdu)
King - Leader
Urdu variant of Arabic Sultan.
Variants: *Zultaan*

Zultana (Arabic, Urdu)
Leader - Queen
Urdu variant of Arabic Sultana.
Variants: *Zultanana*

Zumar (Arabic)
Groups - Throngs
The name Zumar is mentioned in the Quran.
Variants: *Zomar, Zomer, Zumer*

Zumard (Arabic, Urdu)
Emerald
Urdu variant of the Arabic word

Zumurrud.
Variants: *Zomard*

Zumurrud (Arabic)
Emerald
Variants: *Zomorrud, Zumurud*

Zumurruda (Arabic)
Emerald
Variants: *Zomorrudah, Zumrudah, Zumurrdah, Zumurudah*

Zurafaa (Arabic)
Beautiful - Elegant - Graceful
Variants: *Dhurafa, Zorafa, Zorafaa, Zurafa*

Zurfah (Arabic)
Charm - Elegance - Wit

Zurmah (Arabic)
Lavender

Zuwaila (Arabic)
Motion - Movement
Variants: *Zuwailah, Zuwaylah*

Zuwailah (Arabic)
Adorable

Zuwainah (Arabic)
Blessing

Zuwaiten (Arabic)
Little Olive
Variants: *Zowayten*

Zuzana (Czech)
Lily
Form of Susanna.

Zuzanna (Polish)
Lily
Polish form of Susanna.

Zyan (Arabic)
Adornment - Beautification - Decoration

Variants: *Zeyan, Ziyaan, Ziyan, Zyaan*

Baby Names for Boys

This page intentionally left blank

A

Aabid (Arabic)
Devoted to God - Worshiper
The name Aabid is mentioned in the Quran.
Variants: *Aabed, Abed, Abid*

Aabidullah (Arabic)
Servant of God - Worshiper of God
Variants: *Abidulla, Abidullah*

Aabir (Arabic)
Crossing - Passing By - Traveling
Variants: *Aaber, Aber, Abir*

Aabis (Arabic)
Fierce - Grim
Variants: *Aabes, Abes, Abis*

Aadil (Arabic)
Excellent - Fair - Just - Moderate - Virtuous
Variants: *Aadel, Adel, Adil*

Aaf (Arabic)
Forgiver - Pardoner
Variants: *Aaff, Af*

Aafaaq (Arabic)
Horizons
The name Aafaaq is mentioned in the Quran.
Variants: *Aafaq, Afaaq, Afaq*

Aafiq (Arabic)
Generous - Great - Superb - Wise
Variants: *Aafeq, Aafiq, Afiq*

Aaidun (Arabic)
Returning Ones
The name Aaidun is mentioned in the Quran.

Aaiz (Arabic)
Replacement - Successor
Variants: *Aa'idh, Aaez, Aedh, Aez*

Aakif (Arabic)
Devoted Worshiper of God
The name Aakif is mentioned in the Quran.
Variants: *Aakef, Aakif, Akef, Akif*

Aala (Arabic)
Exalted - High in Status - Supreme
The name Aala is mentioned in the Quran.
Variants: *A'la, Alaa*

Aalam (Arabic)
World
Variants: *Alam*

Aali (Arabic)
Great - Lofty - Sublime
The name Aali is mentioned in the Quran.
Variants: *Aalee, Aaly, Alee, Aly*

Aalif (Arabic)
Amiable - Friendly
Variants: *Aalef, Alef, Alif*

Aamad (Arabic)
Ages - Eras - Periods of Time
Variants: *Amaad, Amad*

Aameen (Arabic)
Arabic for "Oh Allah, accept our prayer".
Variants: *Aamin, Ameen*

Aamin (Arabic)
Safe - Secure - Unharmed
Variants: *Amen, Amin*

Aamir (Arabic)
Full of Life - Prosperous
Variants: *Aamer, Amer, Amir*

Aaqil (Arabic)
Discerning - Reasonable - Sensible - Wise
Variants: *Aaqel, Aqel, Aqil*

Aaraf (Arabic)
Heights
Variants: *Aaref, Aref, Arif*

Aarib (Arabic)
Successful
Variants: *Aareb, Areb, Arib*

Aariz (Arabic)
Rain-Bearing Cloud
The name Aariz is mentioned in the Quran.
Variants: *Aaredh, Aarez, Aaridh, Arez, Aridh, Ariz*

Aaron (Ancient Egyptian)
Of uncertain origin and meaning, possibly Egyptian. Name of the brother of prophet Musa (Moses).
Variants: *Aron, Arron*

Aasal (Arabic)
Evenings
The name Aasal is mentioned in the Quran.
Variants: *Aasaal, Asaal, Asal*

Aasir (Arabic)
Captivator - Warrior
Variants: *Aaser, Aser, Asir*

Aatami (Finnish)
Earth
Finnish form of Adam, probably from Hebrew adama ("earth").

Aati (Arabic)
Bestower - Giver
Variants: *Aatee, Aaty, Atee*

Aatik (Arabic)
Generous - Pure
Variants: *Atek, Atik*

Aatiq (Arabic)
Baby Pigeon - Free
Variants: *Aateq, Ateq, Atiq*

Aayiz (Arabic)
Replacement - Restitution

Aazam (Arabic)
Great - Mighty
Variants: *A'zam, Aadham*

Aazz (Arabic)
Great - Mighty
Variants: *A'az, Aaz*

Ababil (Arabic)
Bundles - Crowds - Flocks - Groups
Variants: *Abaabil, Ababeel*

Aban (Arabic)
Clear - Eloquent - Lucid
Variants: *Abaan*

Abanus (Persian, Urdu)
Ebony
Variant of Abnus.

Abbad (Arabic)
Servant of God - Worshiper of God
Variants: *Abaad, Abad, Abbaad*

Abbas (Arabic)
Lion
Variants: *Abaas, Abas*

Abbondio (Italian)
Abundant - Copious

Abbood (Arabic)
Servant of God - Worshiper of God
Variants: *Abbud, Abood, Abud*

Abda (Arabic)
Power - Strength
Variants: *Abdah, Abduh*

Abdaal (Arabic)
Replacements - Successors
Variants: *Abdal*

Abdar (Arabic)
Early - Full Moon - Moon - Quick
Variants: *Abder, Ebder*

Abdul Aakhir (Arabic)
Servant of God

Abdul Aala (Arabic)
Servant of God

Abdul Afuw (Arabic)
Servant of God

Abdul Ahad (Arabic)
Servant of God
Variants: *Abdulahad*

Abdul Akram (Arabic)
Servant of God

Abdul Aleem (Arabic)
Servant of God

Abdul Awwal (Arabic)
Servant of God

Abdul Azim (Arabic)
Servant of God

Abdul Aziz (Arabic)
Servant of God

Abdul Baatin (Arabic)
Servant of God

Abdul Baseer (Arabic)
Servant of God

Abdul Basit (Arabic)
Servant of God

Abdul Birr (Arabic)
Servant of God

Abdul Elah (Arabic)
Servant of God

Abdul Fattah (Arabic)
Servant of God

Abdul Ghaffar (Arabic)
Servant of God

Abdul Ghafoor (Arabic)
Servant of God

Abdul Ghani (Arabic)
Servant of God

Abdul Haafiz (Arabic)
Servant of God

Abdul Hadi (Arabic)
Servant of God
Variants: *Abdolhadi, Abdul Hady, Abdulhadi*

Abdul Hafee (Arabic)
Servant of God

Abdul Hafeez (Arabic)
Servant of God

Abdul Hai (Arabic)
Servant of God

Abdul Hakam (Arabic)
Servant of God

Abdul Hakeem (Arabic)
Servant of God

Abdul Halim (Arabic)
Servant of God

Abdul Hameed (Arabic)
Servant of God

Abdul Haq (Arabic)
Servant of God

Abdul Haseeb (Arabic)
Servant of God

NAMES FOR BOYS

Abdul Jabar (Arabic)
Servant of God

Abdul Jaleel (Arabic)
Servant of God

Abdul Jameel (Arabic)
Servant of God

Abdul Kabir (Arabic)
Servant of God

Abdul Karim (Arabic)
Servant of God

Abdul Khabir (Arabic)
Servant of God

Abdul Khaliq (Arabic)
Servant of God

Abdul Khallaq (Arabic)
Servant of God

Abdul Latif (Arabic)
Servant of God

Abdul Maalik (Arabic)
Servant of God

Abdul Majeed (Arabic)
Servant of God

Abdul Maleek (Arabic)
Servant of God

Abdul Manaan (Arabic)
Servant of God

Abdul Mateen (Arabic)
Servant of God

Abdul Mawla (Arabic)
Servant of God

Abdul Mubeen (Arabic)
Servant of God

Abdul Muhaimin (Arabic)
Servant of God

Abdul Muheet (Arabic)
Servant of God

Abdul Mujeeb (Arabic)
Servant of God

Abdul Muqaddim (Arabic)
Servant of God

Abdul Muqit (Arabic)
Servant of God

Abdul Muqtadir (Arabic)
Servant of God

Abdul Musawwir (Arabic)
Servant of God

Abdul Mutaal (Arabic)
Servant of God

Abdul Mutaali (Arabic)
Servant of God

Abdul Naseer (Arabic)
Servant of God

Abdul Qadeer (Arabic)
Servant of God

Abdul Qadir (Arabic)
Servant of Allah
Variants: *Abdulqaadir, Abdulqader*

Abdul Qahir (Arabic)
Servant of God

Abdul Qareeb (Arabic)
Servant of God

Abdul Qawee (Arabic)
Servant of God

Abdul Qawi (Arabic)
Servant of Allah
Variants: *Abdolqawee, Abdulqawi*

Abdul Qayyum (Arabic)
Servant of God

Abdul Quddus (Arabic)
Servant of Allah
Variants: *Abd Ul Quddus, Abd e Quddus, Abdol Quddus, Abdulquddus*

Abdul Shaheed (Arabic)
Servant of God

Abdul Shakoor (Arabic)
Servant of God

Abdul Tawwab (Arabic)
Servant of God

Abdul Wadud (Arabic)
Servant of God

Abdul Wahaab (Arabic)
Servant of God

Abdul Wahid (Arabic)
Servant of God

Abdul Wakeel (Arabic)
Servant of God

Abdul Waleei (Arabic)
Servant of God

Abdul Waris (Arabic)
Servant of God

Abdulbary (Arabic)
Servant of God

Abdullah (Arabic)
Servant of Allah
The name Abdullah is mentioned in the Quran.
Variants: *Abdollah*

Abdur Rab (Arabic)
Servant of God

Abdur Raheem (Arabic)
Servant of God

Abdur Rahman (Arabic)
Servant of God

Abdur Raoof (Arabic)
Servant of God

Abdur Raqeeb (Arabic)
Servant of God

Abdur Razzaq (Arabic)
Servant of God

Abdus Salam (Arabic)
Servant of Allah
Variants: *Abd Ul Salam, Abd al-Salam, Abdosalam, Abdossalam, Abdul Salam, Abdusalam, Abdussalam*

Abdus Samad (Arabic)
Servant of God

Abdus Samee (Arabic)
Servant of God

Abduz Zaahir (Arabic)
Servant of God

Abe (English, Jewish)
Father
Either from Aramaic abba ("father"), or an English and Jewish short form of Abraham.

Abeed (Arabic)
Servant of God - Worshiper of God

Abel (Biblical)
Breath - Vapour
The younger son of Adam and Eve in the Bible, from Hebrew Hevel.

Abhaj (Arabic)
Better - Brilliant - Successful

Abhar (Arabic)
Brilliant - Lucid - Renowned
Variants: *Abher*

Abi (Arabic)
Dignified - Reserved
Variants: *Abee, Abeei, Abeey, Abei*

Abidain (Arabic)
Worshipers

Abideen (Arabic)
Servant of God - Worshiper of God
Variants: *Aabidin, Abedin*

Abinus (Persian, Urdu)
Ebony
Urdu variant of the Persian name Abnus, which means "ebony", a type of wood.
Variants: *Abeenus, Abinoos*

Abkar (Arabic)
Early - On Time
Variants: *Abker*

Ablagh (Arabic)
Eloquent - Mature

Ablaj (Arabic)
Brilliant - Clear - Lucid

Abner (Biblical)
Father of Light
Name of a relative of King Saul.

Abou (Arabic)
Beauty - Radiance

Abqar (Arabic)
Extraordinary - Supernatural

Abraham (Biblical)
Father of a Multitude (of Nations)
Known as Ibrahim in Arabic.

Abraj (Arabic)
Beautiful-eyed

Abram (Biblical)
High Father
Either an independent name, or a contracted form of Abraham.

Abraq (Arabic)
Brilliant - Radiant
Variants: *Abrak, Abreq*

Absaar (Arabic)
Insight - Intellect - Perception - Vision
The name Absaar is used in the Quran.
Variants: *Absar, Ahsar*

Absaar (Arabic)
Eye-sights - Insights - Perceptions - Visions
The name Absaar is mentioned in the Quran

Abu Bakr (Arabic)
Young - Young Man - Youthful
The name Abu Bakr is from Abu ("father of", "like") and Bakr (ancient name of Arabian tribes, "young man").
Variants: *Abubaker, Abubakir, Abubakr*

Abu Firas (Arabic)
Lion
Variants: *Abu Feras, Abu Firaas, Abufiras*

Abuda (Arabic)
Servant of God - Worshiper of God
Variants: *Abooda, Aboodah, Abudah*

Abudain (Arabic)
Worshiper

Abudi (Arabic)
Worshiper

Abul Fazl (Arabic)
Gracious
Variants: *Abulfazl*

Abwan (Arabic)
Handsome - Radiant

Abyan (Arabic)
Clear - Distinct - Eloquent
Variants: *Abyen*

Abyaz (Arabic)
Bright - Pure - White
Variants: *Abyad, Abyez*

Adalat (Arabic)
Fairness - Justice
Turkish pronunciation of Adalah.
Variants: *Adaalat*

Adam (Arabic)
Dust
The name Adam is mentioned in the Quran. According to some scholars it is related to Adeem, which means "dust", since God created prophet Adam from dust.

Adam (Biblical)
Earth
Known as Adam in Arabic as well, though the Arabic pronunciation is different.

Addal (Arabic)
Fair - Just

Adeel (Arabic)
Excellent - Fair - Just - Moderate - Virtuous
Variants: *Adil*

Adeen (Arabic)
Obedient - Righteou
Variants: *Adin, Azeen, Azin*

Adham (Arabic)
Black - Dark
Variants: *Adhem, Adhum, Edhem*

Adie (Scottish)
Earth
Pet form of Adam.

Adl (Arabic)
Fairness - Justice
The name Adl is mentioned in the Quran.
Variants: *Edl*

Adlan (Arabic)
Fair - Just

Adli (Arabic)
Fair - Just
Variants: *Adlee, Adly*

Adnan (Arabic)
Inhabitant - Resident
Variants: *Adnaan*

Adr (Arabic)
Heavy Rain

Adwam (Arabic)
Eternal - Everlasting - Lasting - Stable
Variants: *Aduam*

Adyan (Arabic)
Creeds - Religions
Variants: *Adiaan, Adian, Adyaan*

Afanasi (Russian)
Immortal

Afeen (Arabic)
Forgiver - Pardoner
Variants: *Afin*

Affan (Arabic)
Chaste - Modest - Virtuous
Variants: *Afaan, Afan, Affaan*

Afif (Arabic)
Chaste - Modest - Righteous
Variants: *Afeef, Afef*

Afnan (Arabic)
Spreading Branches of Trees
The name Afnan is mentioned in the Quran.
Variants: *Afnaan*

Afonso (Portuguese)
Battle - Noble - Prompt - Struggle
From Spanish Alfonso. The exact meaning is not known and is probably a mixture of the mentioned meanings.

Afonya (Russian)
Immortal
Pet form of Afanasi.

Afrad (Arabic)
Matchless - Unique

Afrasiab (Persian)
Fearsome - Mighty
Variants: *Afraasiab, Afrasyaab, Afrasyab*

Afraz (Persian)
Loftiness - Nobleness
Variants: *Afraaz*

Afsah (Arabic)
Eloquent - Expressive - Fluent
The name Afsah is mentioned in the Quran.
Variants: *Efseh*

Afseruddin (Arabic)
Supporter of Islam
Literally "crown of the faith".

Afshan (Persian)
Disperser - Distributor - Spreader
Variants: *Afshaan*

Afshar (Persian, Turkish)
Companion - Friend
Variants: *Aafshar, Afshaar*

Aftabuddin (Arabic, Persian)
Supporter of Islam
Literally "sun of the faith".

Afza (Persian)
Advancer - Increaser
Variants: *Afzaa*

Afzaal (Arabic)
Good Deeds - Kind Deeds
Variants: *Afdhaal, Afdhal, Afzal*

Agha (Turkish)
Chief - Lord - Master
Variants: *Aagha, Aghaa*

Aghla (Arabic)
Precious - Valuable
Variants: *Aghlaa*

Aghlab (Arabic)
Conqueror - Superior - Victor

Agostinho (Portuguese)
Great - Magnificent
Form of Augustine.

Agostino (Italian)
Great - Magnificent
Form of Augustine.

Agreen (Kurdish)
Active - Brave - Fiery - Passionate
Variants: *Agrin*

Ahad (Arabic)
One - Peerless - Unique
The name Ahad is mentioned in the Quran.

Ahbab (Arabic)
Beloved Ones
Variants: *Ahbaab*

Ahdaf (Arabic)
Goals - Objectives - Targets

Ahdawi (Arabic)
Faithful - Loyal

Ahdee (Arabic)
Faithful - Loyal
Variants: *Ahdy*

Ahibun (Arabic)
Prepared - Ready

Ahid (Arabic)
Caretaker - Promiser
Variants: *Aahed, Aahid, Ahed*

Ahin (Arabic)
Ascetic
Variants: *Aahen, Aahin, Ahen*

Ahkam (Arabic)
Decisive - Wise
The name Ahkam is mentioned in the Quran.
Variants: *Ahkem, Ehkem*

Ahmad (Arabic)
Noble - Praiseworthy
One of the names of Prophet Muhammad (pbuh). The name *Ahmad* is mentioned in the Quran.
Variants: *Ahmat, Ahmed, Ahmet, Ehmet*

Ahmar (Arabic)
Red - Red-colored
Variants: *Ahmer*

Ahnaf (Arabic)
Upright - Worshiper of God
Variants: *Ehnef*

Ahram (Arabic)
Pyramids
Variants: *Ahraam*

Ahsan (Arabic)
Beautiful - Best - Handsome
The name Ahsan is mentioned in the Quran.
Variants: *Ehsen*

Ahvaz (Persian)
[Name of a City]
Name of a city in southern Iran.
Variants: *Ahwaz*

Ahwas (Arabic)
Brave
Variants: *Ahuas*

Ahyam (Arabic)
Starless Night
Variants: *Ahiam*

Ahyan (Arabic)
Moments - Times
Variants: *Ahiaan, Ahian, Ahyaan*

Ahyas (Arabic)
Brave
Variants: *Ahias*

Aidan (Arabic)
Tall Palm Tree
Variants: *Aidaan, Aydan, Eidan, Eydan*

Ailean (Scottish Gaelic)
Rock

Ain (Arabic)
Fountain - Spring
The name Ain is mentioned in the Quran, such as in verse 88:12.
Variants: *Aene, Aine, Ayn, Ayne, Eiyn*

NAMES FOR BOYS

Aindrea (Scottish Gaelic)
Man - Warrior
Form of Andrew.

Ainsley (English, Scottish)
One Clearing - One Wood
Originally a surname.

Aish (Arabic)
Life - Livelihood
Variants: *Aysh*

Ajaar (Arabic)
Rewards
Variants: *Ajar*

Ajab (Arabic)
Amazement - Wonder
The name Ajab is mentioned in the Quran.

Ajam (Arabic)
Date Seed - Foreign - Persian

Ajaweed (Arabic)
Acts of Kindness - Generosity

Ajeeb (Arabic)
Amazing - Wondorous
The name Ajeeb is mentioned in the Quran.

Ajeel (Arabic)
Quick
Variants: *Ajil*

Ajiad (Arabic)
Generous - Gracious - Noble
Variants: *Ajyad*

Ajmal (Arabic)
Beautiful - Delightful
Variants: *Ajmel*

Ajmi (Arabic)
Intelligent - Wise

Akbar (Arabic)
Great - Magnificent
The name Akbar is mentioned in the Quran.
Variants: *Akber, Ekber*

Akfah (Arabic)
Black
Akfah refers to the color "black".

Akhas (Arabic)
Excellent - Special
Akhas is an indirect Quranic name for boys that means "special", "excellent". It is derived from the KH-SAAD-SAAD root which is used in the Quran.
Variants: *Excellent, Special*

Akhlaq (Arabic)
Decency - Integrity - Morality
Akhlaq is an indirect Quranic name for boys that means "morality", "integrity", "decency". It is derived from the KH-L-Q root which is used in many places in the Quran.
Variants: *Akhlaaq*

Akhmad (Arabic)
Calm - Silent - Tranquil

Akhtab (Arabic)
Falcon

Akhtaf (Arabic)
Slender - Slim
Akhtaf is an indirect Quranic name for boys that means "slender", "slim". It is derived from the KH-T16-F root which is used in the Quran.

Akhtar (Persian)
Galaxy - Planet - Star - Sun

Akhyar (Arabic)
Good - Virtuous
The name Akhyar is mentioned in the Quran.
Variants: *Akhiar, Akhyaar*

Akhzam (Arabic)
Serpent - Snake
Ancient Arabic name.

Akhzar (Arabic)
Green - Green-colored

Aki (Arabic)
Textile Merchant
Variants: *Akee, Aky*

Akim (Russian, Scandinavian)
Established by God
From Joachim.

Akmal (Arabic)
Complete - Perfect - Whole
Variants: *Akmel*

Aknan (Arabic)
Covers - Shelters
The name Aknan is mentioned in the Quran.
Variants: *Aknaan*

Akram (Arabic)
Gracious - Honorable - Honored
The name Akram is used in the Quran.
Variants: *Ekrem*

Akrama (Arabic, Urdu)
Female Pigeon
Akrama is the Urdu variant of the Arabic name Ikrimah.
Variants: *Akramah*

Akwan (Arabic)
Cosmos - Universes
Variants: *Akuaan, Akuan, Akwaan*

Akyas (Arabic)
Intelligent - Wise
Variants: *Akias*

Alaa (Arabic)
Greatness - Highness
Variants: *Ala*

Aladdin (Arabic)
Supporter of Islam
Literally "supremacy of the faith".

Alain (French)
Rock
French form of Alan.

Alamat (Arabic)
Emblem - Gesture - Sign - Symbol
Turkish pronunciation of Alamah.
Variants: *Alaamat*

Alamgir (Arabic)
World Conqueror
Variants: *Alamgeer, Alamghir*

Alamguir (Arabic, Persian)
World Conqueror
Variants: *Alam Ghir, Alamgeer, Alamghir*

Alan (English, Scottish)
Rock
Of Celtic origin.
Variants: *Aalan*

Alan (Kurdish)
Flag-bearer

Alaqat (Persian, Turkish, Urdu)
Attachment - Devotion - Relationship
Turkish pronunciation of Alaqah.
Variants: *Alaaqat*

Alasdair (Scottish Gaelic)
Defender of Humanity
Form of Alexander.

Alastar (Irish Gaelic)
Defender of Humanity
Form of Alexander.

Albert (English, French)
Bright - Famous - Noble

Alborz (Persian)
Great Mountain - High Mountain
Variants: *Alburz*

Albrecht (German)
Bright - Famous - Noble
Form of Albert.

Alec (English, Scottish)
Defender of Humanity
From Alexander.

Aleef (Arabic)
Compassionate - Friendly - Good Friend - Kind
Variants: *Alif*

Aleem (Arabic)
Intellectual - Knowledgeable - Learned
The name Aleem is mentioned in the Quran.
Variants: *Alim*

Aleix (Catalan)
Defender
From Alexius.

Aleixandre (Catalan)
Defender of Humanity
From Alexander.

Aleixo (Portuguese)
Defender
From Alexius.

Alejandro (Spanish)
Defender of Humanity
From Alexander.

Alejo (Spanish)
Defender
Form of Alexius.

Aleksander (Polish)
Defender of Humanity
Form of Alexander.

Aleksandr (Russian)
Defender of Humanity
Roman-alphabet spelling of the Russian form of Alexander.

Aleksei (Russian)
Defender
Russian form of Alexius.

Aleksy (Polish)
Defender
Polish form of Alexius.

Alessandro (Italian)
Defender of Humanity
Italian form of Alexander.

Alessio (Italian)
Defender
Italian form of Alexius.

Alex (English)
Defender - Defender of Humanity
Short form of Alexander, Alexandra or Alexis.

Alexander (Dutch, English, German, Hebrew)
Defender of Humanity
Latin form of the Greek name Alexandros.

Alexej (Czech)
Defender - Defender of Humanity
Czech form of Alexius or pet form of Alexander.

Alexis (English, German)
Defender

NAMES FOR BOYS

Alexius (Latin)
Defender

Alhasan (Arabic)
Gentle - Good - Handsome - Virtuous

Alhusain (Arabic)
Good-looking - Handsome - Virtuous
Variants: *Alhosain*

Ali (Arabic)
Exalted - Great - High - Sublime - Superb
The name Ali is mentioned in the Quran.
Variants: *Alee, Aleei, Aliy, Aliyy*

Alim (Arabic)
Knowledgeable - Scholar

Alis (Czech, German)
Warrior
German and Czech form of Aloysius.

Alistair (Scottish)
Defender of Humanity
Variant of Alasdair, a form of Alexander.

Alke (German)
High-born - Noble

Allaam (Arabic)
Extremely Wise - Knowledgeable
The name Allaam is mentioned in the Quran.

Allamah (Arabic)
Extremely Wise - Knowledgeable

Allan (English, Scottish)
Rock
Variant of Alan.

Allaster (Scottish)
Defender of Humanity
Variant of Alistair, a form of Alexander.

Allen (English, Scottish)
Rock
Variant of Alan.

Alois (Czech, German)
Warrior
German and Czech form of Aloysius.

Alojzy (Polish)
Warrior
Polish form of Aloysius.

Aloysius (Dutch, English, German)
Warrior

Alpha (English)
Excellent - Prime
Taken from the first letter of the Greek alphabet.

Altaaf (Arabic)
Gentleness - Kindness
Variants: *Altaf*

Altaf (Arabic)
Gentle - Kind
Variants: *Altaaf*

Alvand (Persian)
Agile - Powerful - Strong
Variants: *Alvend*

Alvin (English)
Elfish Friend - Supernatural Friend
Variants: *Alwyn, Aylwin*

Alyan (Arabic)
Great - High - Sublime
Variants: *Aliaan, Alian, Alyaan*

Alyosha (Russian)
Defender
Pet form of Aleksei.

Amad (Arabic)
Age - Era - Period of Time

Amadeus (Latin)
Lover of God

Amado (Spanish)
Beloved

Amador (Spanish)
Lover

Aman (Arabic)
Peace of Mind - Safety - Security
Variants: *Amaan*

Amanat (Arabic, Persian, Turkish, Urdu)
Devotion - Guardianship - Trust
Turkish pronunciation of Amanah.
Variants: *Amanaat*

Amancio (Spanish)
Loving

Amans (Catalan)
Loving

Amara (Arabic)
Fleet - Tribe
Variants: *Amaara, Amaarah, Amarah*

Amato (Italian)
Beloved

Ambrose (English)
Immortal

Amdad (Arabic)
Expansion - Gain - Growth - Increase

Amedeo (Italian)
Lover of God

Ameed (Arabic)
Chief - Leader - Prefect
Variants: *Amid*

Ameen (Arabic)
Loyal - Trustworthy - Virtuous
The name *Ameen* is mentioned in the Quran.
Variants: *Amein, Amin, Amyne, Emeen, Emin, Umeen*

Amerigo (Italian)
Ruler of the House

Amial (Arabic)
Lighthouses
Variants: *Amyaal, Amyal*

Amil (Arabic)
Hoper - Striver - Worker
Variants: *Aamel, Aamil, Amel*

Amir (Arabic)
Chief - Commander - Leader - Ruler
Variants: *Ameer, Emeer, Emir*

Amiri (Arabic)
Leader
Variants: *Ameeri, Ameree, Ameri, Amiree, Amiry*

Amiri (Arabic)
Enlivener - Reviver

Amiruddin (Arabic)
Supporter of Islam
Literally "leader of the faith".
Variants: *Amir Uddin*

Amjaad (Arabic)
Distinction - Glory - Honor
Variants: *Amjad*

Amjad (Arabic)
Distinguished - Glorious - Honorable
Variants: *Amjed*

Amlas (Arabic)
Delicate - Smooth - Soft

Ammam (Arabic)
Leader

Amman (Arabic)
Citizen - Resident
Also name of the capital of Jordan.
Variants: *Amaan, Aman*

Ammar (Arabic)
Long-lived - Pious - Reviver
Variants: *Amaar, Amar, Ammaar*

Ammuni (Arabic)
Away From Harm - Safe
Variants: *Amuni*

Amnan (Arabic)
Safe - Secure
Variants: *Amnaan*

Amooz (Persian)
Instructor - Teacher
Variants: *Amuz*

Amr (Arabic)
Life - Revival

Amrullah (Arabic)
God's Command
Variants: *Amr Ullah*

Amsal (Arabic)
Best - Exemplary - Optimal
The name Amsal is mentioned in the Quran.
Variants: *Amthal*

Amyali (Arabic)
Ambitious - Desirous
Variants: *Amialy*

Anaqat (Persian, Urdu)
Elegance
Variants: *Anaaqat*

Anar (Arabic)
Glowing - Radiant
Variants: *Anaar*

Anas (Arabic)
Comforter - Consoler - Friend

Anasat (Arabic)
Comfort - Tranquility
Turkish pronunciation of Anasa.
Variants: *Anaasat*

Anasi (Arabic)
Consoler - Goo Friend
Variants: *Anasee*

Anatole (French)
Dawn - Sunrise

Anatoli (Russian)
Dawn - Sunrise

Anbas (Arabic)
Lion

Andaleeb (Arabic, Urdu)
Nightingale
Variants: *Andalib*

Andalus (Arabic)
Andalusia

Andalusi (Arabic)
From Andalusia
Variants: *Andaloosi*

Anders (Scandinavian)
Manly - Warrior
Scandinavian form of Andrew.

Andoni (Basque)
Flourishing Man
Basque form of Anthony.

NAMES FOR BOYS

Andra (English, Scottish)
Warrior
In English it is the feminine form of Andrew, while in Scottish it is a male variant of Andrew.

Andras (Welsh)
Manly - Warrior
Welsh form of Andrew.

Andre (Portuguese)
Manly - Warrior
Portuguese form of Andrew.

Andrea (Italian)
Manly - Warrior
Italian form of Andrew.

Andreas (English, German, Greek, Latin)
Manliness - Virility
New Testament Greek form of Andrew.

Andrei (Russian)
Manly - Warrior
Russian form of Andrew.

Andrej (Czech)
Manly - Warrior
Czech form of Andrew.

Andrew (English)
Manly - Warrior

Andy (English, Scottish)
Manly - Warrior
Scottish and English pet form of Andrew.

Anees (Arabic)
Close Friend - Comforter
Variants: *Aneis, Anis*

Anfa (Arabic)
Dignity - Self-respect
Variants: *Anfah*

Anfani (Arabic)
Dignified

Anfas (Arabic)
Breaths - Souls - Spirits
Variants: *Anfaas*

Anhar (Arabic)
Rivers
Variants: *Anhaar*

Aniq (Arabic)
Attractive - Elegant - Graceful - Stylish
Variants: *Aneek, Aneeq, Aneiq, Anik*

Anjam (Arabic)
Star
Variants: *Anjaam*

Anjud (Arabic)
Heights - Plateaus
Variants: *Anjod*

Anjum (Arabic)
Stars
Variants: *Anjom, Anjoum*

Anjuman (Kurdish, Persian, Urdu)
Committee - Council
Variants: *Anjoman*

Anmar (Arabic)
Tigers
Variants: *Anmaar*

Anoush (Persian)
Eternal - Immortal
Variants: *Anoosh, Anush*

Anoushiravan (Persian)
Eternal - Everlasting - Immortal
Variants: *Anooshirvan, Anoshiravan, Anushiravan, Anushirvan*

Ansab (Arabic)
Better - Worthier

Ansam (Arabic)
Breezes
Variants: *Ansaam*

Ansar (Arabic)
Advocates - Defenders - Supporters - Upholders
The name Ansar is mentioned in the Quran.
Variants: *Ansaar*

Ansari (Arabic)
Supporter of Islam
Variants: *Ansaari, Ansary*

Antar (Arabic)
Brave

Anthony (English)
Flourishing Man
Variants: *Antony*

Antoine (French)
Flourishing Man
French form of Anthony.

Antoni (Catalan, Polish)
Flourishing Man
Catalan and Polish form of Anthony.

Antonio (Italian, Spanish)
Flourishing Man
Italian and Spanish form of Anthony.

Anum (Arabic)
God's Blessings - God's Favors
The name Anum is mentioned in the Quran.
Variants: *Anom, Anoum*

Anumullah (Arabic)
God's Blessings - God's Favors

Anush (Arabic)
Beautiful - Handsome

Anushah (Persian)
Everlasting - Immortal
Anushah is a variant of the name Anusheh.
Variants: *Anoosha, Anusha, Anushah*

Anusheh (Persian)
Everlasting - Immortal
Variants: *Anoosheh*

Anwaar (Arabic)
Lights - Radiant
Variants: *Anwar*

Anwaaraddin (Arabic)
Supporter of Islam
Literally "radiance of the faith".
Variants: *Anwaruddin*

Anwar (Arabic)
Clear - Eloquent - Enlightened
Variants: *Anwer*

Anwari (Arabic)
Radiant
Variants: *Anuari*

Aqeeb (Arabic)
Follower
Variants: *Aqib*

Aqeed (Arabic)
Aqid
Variants: *Under Oath*

Aqeel (Arabic)
Discerning - Reasonable - Sensible - Wise
Variants: *Aqil, Aquil, Aquille*

Aqiq (Arabic, Persian)
Agate
Variants: *Aqeeq*

Aql (Arabic)
Intelligence - Mind - Sense - Thought - Wisdom
Variants: *Akl*

Aqlan (Arabic)
Intelligent - Keen

Aqrab (Arabic)
Scorpion
Variants: *Akrab*

Aqsaa (Arabic)
Farthest
Name of the third holiest site in Islam: Masjid al-Aqsa (al-Aqsa Mosque) in Palestine.
Variants: *Aksa, Aqsa*

Aqsad (Arabic)
Achiever - Moderate - Modest - Righteous
Variants: *Aksad, Eqsed*

Aqwa (Arabic)
Strong - Strongest
Variants: *Aqua, Aqwaa*

Ara (Kurdish, Persian)
Adorner - Beautifier
Variants: *Aara, Aaraa, Araa*

Araabi (Arabic)
Eloquent - Fluent

Arad (Persian)
Angel's Name
Name of an angel in Zoroastrianism.

Araj (Urdu)
Fragrance
Variant of Arabic boy and girl name Arij.
Variants: *Aaraj*

Aram (Biblical)
Height
Name of a grandson of prophet Noah.
Variants: *Aaram, Araam*

Aram (Kurdish, Persian, Urdu)
Calm - Quiet

Aran (Kurdish, Persian, Urdu)
Flat Land - Plains
Variants: *Aaran, Araan*

Arandas (Arabic)
Fierce Lion

Arang (Persian, Urdu)
Color - Phase - State
Variants: *Aarang*

Arar (Arabic)
Lent Lily - Wild Daffodil
A type of flower.

Aras (Kurdish, Persian)
Balanced - Equal
Variants: *Aaras, Araas*

Aras (Turkish)
Name of a river taht flows through Turkey, Armenia, Iran and Azerbaijan.

Arash (Persian)
Brilliant - Dazzling - Radiant
Variants: *Aarash, Aaresh, Aresh*

Arastoo (Persian)
Lover of Wisdom
Persian variant of Aristotle.
Variants: *Arastu*

Arax (Armenian)
Armenian name for the Aras river.

Araz (Azerbaijani)
Azerbaijani name for the Aras river.

Arbab (Arabic)
Chiefs - Masters

NAMES FOR BOYS

The name Arbab is used in the Quran.
Variants: *Arbaab*

Arbad (Arabic)
Lion - Snake

Arban (Arabic)
Eloqent - Fluent

Ardal (Irish)
Having a Bear's Valor

Ardalan (Kurdish, Persian)
Goodness - Virtue
Variants: *Adalaan*

Ardas (Arabic)
Lion

Ardavan (Persian)
Guardian - Protector
Literally "protector of the virtuous people".
Variants: *Ardavaan, Ardawan*

Ardeshir (Persian)
Brave - Fearless
Variants: *Arashir, Ardasheer, Ardesheer*

Ardin (Persian)
Pure - Virtuous

Arduino (Italian)
Good Friend - Valued Friend
Italian form of Hartwin.

Areeb (Arabic)
Intelligent - Wise
Variants: *Areib, Arib*

Areef (Arabic)
Knowledgeable - Learned - Wise
Variants: *Arif*

Areej (Arabic)
Fragrance
Variants: *Arij*

Areen (Persian)
Member of the Ari People
The Ari people are the people of ancient Persia, also known as Aryans.

Areeq (Arabic)
Deep-rooted - High-born - Noble
Variants: *Ariq*

Areesh (Persian)
Intelligent - Wise
Variants: *Arish*

Areez (Persian)
Dew Drop - Leader
Variants: *Ariz*

Arf (Arabic)
Fragrance - Scent

Arfa (Arabic)
Elevated - Exalted - Great
Variants: *Arfa', Arfaa*

Arfaan (Arabic)
Spiritual Knowledge - Wisdom
Non-standard variant of the name Irfan.
Variants: *Arfan*

Arhab (Arabic)
Gracious - Open-minded
Variants: *Arheb, Arhub, Erheb*

Arham (Arabic)
Compassionate - Kind - Merciful
The name Arham is mentioned in the Quran in verse 12:64.

Arish (Arabic)
Builder - Maker
Variants: *Aarish, Aresh*

Arjasb (Persian)
Keeper of Noble Horses

Arjomand (Persian)
Beloved - Dear - Esteemed - Respected
Variants: *Arjumand*

Arkan (Arabic)
Leaders - Pillars
Variants: *Arkaan*

Arkhun (Persian)
Leader - Lord
Variants: *Arkhon*

Armaghan (Persian, Urdu)
Gift
Variants: *Armagan, Armaghaan*

Arman (Persian)
Desire - Goal - Longing - Purpose
Variants: *Armaan Aarman*

Armeen (Persian)
Name of a character in the Shahnameh, of unknown meaning.

Armin (German)
Army Man

Arnold (English, German)
Eagle Ruler

Aroof (Arabic)
Learned - Skilled - Wise
Variants: *Arouf, Aruf*

Arqam (Arabic)
Snake

Arsalan (Turkish)
Fearless - Lion
Variants: *Arsalaan, Arselan*

Arsam (Persian)
Strong Like a Bear

Arsan (Persian)
Council - Gathering

Arsh (Arabic)
Power - Throne
The name Arsh is mentioned in the Quran.

Arshad (Arabic)
Mature - Well-guided - Wise
Variants: *Arshed*

Arshak (Persian)
Male - Masculine - Virile

Arsham (Persian)
Synonym of Arshama.

Arshama (Persian)
Name of the grandfather of Darius the Great, of unclear meaning.

Arshan (Arabic)
Thrones
Variants: *Arshaan, Arshaan*

Arshan (Persian)
Brave

Arshavir (Persian)
Pure - Virtuous

Arshi (Arabic)
Royal
Literally meaning "worthy of a throne".
Variants: *Arshee, Arshy*

Arshia (Persian)
Throne
From the Zend/Pazend tradition of Persia, not from the Arabic word 'Arsh, which also means "throne".
Variants: *Arshyaa*

Arsin (Persian)
Warrior

Art (English, Irish, Scottish)
Hero - Strong Like a Bear
Short form of Arthur.

Arta (Persian)
Pure - Sacred - Virtuous
Variants: *Aarta, Artaa*

Artaban (Persian)
Guardian - Protector
Synonym of Ardavan.
Variants: *Artabaan*

Artabaz (Persian)
Name of many ancient Armenian kings. Arta means "good", "pure", "virtuous", but the full meaning of the name is unclear.

Artan (Persian)
Doer of Good Deeds - Virtuous

Arteban (Persian)
Guardian - Protector
Synonym of Ardavan.
Variants: *Artebaan*

Artepan (Persian)
Guardian - Protector
Synonym of Ardavan.
Variants: *Artepaan*

Arteshtar (Persian)
Soldier - Warrior
Variants: *Artishar*

Arthur (English)
Hero - Strong Like a Bear

Artin (Persian)
Pure - Virtuous

Arvand (Persian, Urdu)
Agile - Brave - Intelligent
Variants: *Aarvand, Aarwand, Arvend, Arwand*

Arveen (Persian)
Experiment - Test
Variants: *Arvin*

Arya (Persian)
Excellent - Noble
Variants: *Aria, Ariaa, Aryaa*

Aryabod (Persian)
Chief - Leader
Literally "chief of the Arya people", Arya referring to the ancient people of Greater Persia.
Variants: *Ariabod, Aryabud*

Aryaman (Persian)
Comforter - Consoler - Supporter
Variants: *Ariaman*

Aryan (Persian)
Excellent - Noble
Variants: *Aarian, Aaryan, Ariaan, Arian, Aryaan*

Aryano (Persian)
Excellent - Noble - Young
Variants: *Aarianu, Ariano, Arianu, Aryanu*

Aryou (Persian)
Member of the Ari People
The Ari people are the people of ancient Persia, also known as Aryans.

Arz (Arabic)
Breadth - Mountain - Width

Arzhang (Persian)
Name of the illustrated book created by Mani, a pre-Islamic painter from Persia, of unknown meaning.
Variants: *Arzang, Arzgheng*

Asa (Persian)
Adornment - Likeness - Might -

NAMES FOR BOYS

Power - Similarity
Variants: *Aasa, Asaa*

Asaad (Arabic)
Fortunate - Happy
Variants: *As'ad*

Asad (Arabic)
Lion
Variants: *Esed*

Asah (Arabic)
Correct - Healthy - Proper
Variants: *Aseh*

Asar (Arabic)
Mark - Print - Sign - Work
Variants: *Aser, Athat, Ather*

Asbah (Arabic)
Beautiful
Variants: *Esbeh*

Asbat (Arabic)
Deep-rooted - Firmly
Established - Reliable - Steady
Variants: *Athbat*

Aseel (Arabic)
Creative - Deep-rooted - Evening Time - High-born - Nighttime - Original
The name Aseel is mentioned in the Quran.
Variants: *Asil, Assil*

Asfiya (Arabic)
Pure Ones
Variants: *Asfiaa, Asfiyaa*

Asfour (Arabic, Urdu)
Bird
Variant of Arabic Osfur.
Variants: *Asfoor, Asfur*

Asghar (Arabic)
Junior - Smaller - Younger

Asha (Persian)
Adornment - Likeness - Similarity
Synonym of Asa.

Ashaab (Arabic)
Companions - Friends
The name Ashaab is mentioned in the Quran.
Variants: *Ashab*

Ashaar (Arabic)
Fierce
Variants: *Ash'ar, Ashar*

Ashal (Arabic)
Brilliant - Kindled - Radiant
Variants: *Ash'al, Ashaal*

Ashbal (Arabic)
Lion Cubs

Asheeq (Arabic)
Beloved - In Love
Variants: *Ashiq*

Ashhab (Arabic)
Lion

Ashham (Arabic)
Composed - Dignified

Ashhar (Arabic)
Famous - Renowned
Variants: *Ashher*

Ashhub (Arabic)
Shooting Stars
Variants: *Ashhob*

Ashiq (Arabic)
In Love - Obsessed

Ashja (Arabic)
Brave
Variants: *Ashja'*

Ashkan (Persian)
Meaning is "one who belongs to the Ashkan (Parthian) empire", "like Ashk". Ashk was the founder of the Ashkan Empire.

Ashmal (Arabic)
Inclusive

Ashqar (Arabic)
Blond - Fair-skinned
Variants: *Ashqer*

Ashraf (Arabic)
Honorable - Noble

Ashtar (Arabic)
Name of a companion of Ali bin Abi Talib. The meaning is "one whose eyelashes are curved backwards", "one whose eye is torn".

Ashti (Kurdish)
Peace
Variants: *Aashti, Ashtee, Ashty*

Ashwaq (Arabic)
Longing - Yearning
Variants: *Ashuaq, Ashwaaq*

Asif (Arabic)
Fierce - Powerful - Strong
The name Asif is mentioned in the Quran.
Variants: *Aasef, Aasif, Acef, Aceph, Aseph*

Asim (Arabic)
Protector - Rescuer - Shield
The name Asim is mentioned in the Quran.
Variants: *Aasem, Aasim, Asem*

Asjad (Arabic)
Prostrator - Worshiper of God

Askar (Arabic)
Soldier

Aslam (Arabic)
Intact - Safe

Aslan (Turkish)
Lion
Variants: *Aslaan*

Asmar (Arabic)
Brown - Tan
Describes a person whose skin color is not too dark and not too light.

Aso (Kurdish)
Horizon
Variants: *Aaso*

Asrar (Arabic)
Mysteries - Secrets
Variants: *Asraar*

Assab (Arabic)
Gazelle

Aswab (Arabic)
Correct - Rational - Sensible
Variants: *Asuab*

Asyaf (Arabic)
Swords
Variants: *Asiaf, Asyaaf*

Ata (Arabic)
Gift from God
The name Ata is mentioned in the Quran.
Variants: *Ataa*

Ata (Turkish)
Caretaker - Father

Atabak (Persian)
Grandfather - Minister

Ataullah (Arabic)
Gift from God
Variants: *Ata Ullah, Ataaullah*

Ataur Rahman (Arabic)
Gift from God
Variants: *Ataurrahman*

Atbin (Persian)
Doer of Good Deeds - Virtuous

Ateeb (Arabic)
Gentle - Tender

Ateeq (Arabic)
Ancient - Freed - Liberated - Noble
The name Ateeq is mentioned in the Quran.
Variants: *Atiq*

Ateer (Arabic)
Fragrant
Variants: *Atir*

Atf (Arabic)
Affection - Compassion

Atfat (Arabic)
Affection - Compassion

Atheel (Arabic)
Deep-rooted - High-born - Noble
Variants: *Aseel, Asil*

Atheer (Arabic)
Glint - Luster - Radiance - Shimmer
Literal meaning is "shimmer of a sword blade".
Variants: *Aseer, Asir, Atheir, Athir, Esir*

Atif (Arabic)
Affectionate - Sympathetic
Variants: *Aatef, Aatif, Atef*

Atik (Arabic)
Generous - Pure
Variants: *Aatek, Aatik, Atek*

Atila (Turkish)
Agile - Brave
Variants: *Ateela, Atilla*

Atoof (Arabic)
Affectionate - Compassionate - Sympathetic
Variants: *Atouf, Atuf*

Attaf (Arabic)
Affectionate - Compassionate

Attar (Arabic)
Perfume-maker
Variants: *Ataar, Atar, Attaar*

Aubrey (English)
One Who Rules With Elf Wisdom

August (German, Polish)
Majestic - Venerable
German and Polish form of Augustus.

Augustine (English)
Majestic - Venerable
Derived from Augustus.

Auraq (Arabic)
Dust-colored - Sand-colored
Variants: *Awraaq*

Ausan (Arabic)
Relaxed - Resting
Variants: *Awsan*

Austin (English)
Majestic - Venerable
Variants: *Austen*

Avan (Persian)
Guard

Avesta (Persian)
Fellowship - Foundation - Principle
Name of a ancient language of Persia.

NAMES FOR BOYS

Awad (Arabic)
Compassion - Goodness - Kindness
Variants: *Awaad*

Awadil (Arabic)
Fair Ones - Just Ones

Awadili (Arabic)
Fair - Just

Awadini (Arabic)
Eternal - Everlasting

Awamil (Arabic)
Active - Industrious

Awamir (Arabic)
Full of Life - Inhabited

Awamiri (Arabic)
Long-lived

Awan (Arabic)
Moment - Time
Variants: *Awaan*

Awani (Arabic)
Helper - Supporter

Awasim (Arabic)
Fighters of Corruption
Variants: *Awathim*

Awat (Kurdish)
Hope - Wish

Awatif (Arabic)
Emotions - Instincts - Passions
Variants: *Awaatef, Awaatif, Awatef*

Awayed (Arabic)
Habit - Tradition

Awb (Arabic)
Repentance
Variants: *Aub*

Awbi (Arabic)
Repentant
Variants: *Awby*

Awd (Arabic)
Return

Awdaq (Arabic)
Friendly - Genial - Intimate
Variants: *Audaq*

Awfa (Arabic)
Faithful - True
The name Awfa is mentioned in the Quran.
Variants: *Aufa, Awfaa*

Awfar (Arabic)
Plenty
Variants: *Aufar*

Awhad (Arabic)
Unique
Variants: *Auhad*

Awj (Arabic, Persian)
Height - Pinnacle - Top
Variants: *Auj*

Awla (Arabic)
Worthier
Variants: *Aulaa*

Awlan (Arabic)
Returner
Variants: *Aulan*

Awlya (Arabic)
Close Friends - Supporters
Variants: *Auliya*

Awmani (Arabic)
Skilled Swimmer

Awmar (Arabic)
Long-lived

Awmari (Arabic)
Long-lived

Awn (Arabic)
Aid - Friend - Help - Helper
Variants: *Aun*

Awni (Arabic)
Helper - Supporter

Awrad (Arabic)
Rose-colored - Rosy
Variants: *Aurad*

Awsal (Arabic)
Becoming Closer to God
Variants: *Ausaal*

Awsam (Arabic)
Badges of Honor
Variants: *Awsaam*

Awsat (Arabic)
Middle - Moderate
The name Awsat is mentioned in the Quran.

Awshan (Arabic)
Guest
Variants: *Aushan*

Awthal (Arabic)
Dutiful
Variants: *Ausal*

Awwab (Arabic)
Repentant - Virtuous
The name Awwaab is mentioned in the Quran.
Variants: *Auab, Awaab, Awab*

Awwad (Arabic)
Compassionate - Kind

Awwadi (Arabic)
Compassionate - Kind

Awwak (Arabic)
Compassionate - Sympathetic
Variants: *Awak*

Awwal (Arabic)
First
The name Awwal is mentioned in the Quran.
Variants: *Aual, Awal*

Awwalan (Arabic)
Advanced Ones - First Ones
Variants: *Awalaan*

Awwam (Arabic)
Skilled Swimmer
Variants: *Awam*

Awwaz (Arabic)
Restitutioner
Variants: *Awaz, Awwadh*

Ayad (Arabic)
Able - Capable - Powerful
Ayad should not be confused with Ayyad, though both are derived from the same Arabic root.
Variants: *Aiad, Ayaad*

Ayamin (Arabic)
Blessed Ones - Fortunate Ones
Variants: *Ayaamin, Ayamen*

Ayan (Persian)
Inspiration - Long Night
Variants: *Aayaan, Aayan, Ayaan, Ayaan, Ayyan*

Ayan (Arabic)
Era - Time
The name Ayan is mentioned in the Quran in verse 51:12.

Ayaz (Persian, Turkish)
Cool Breeze - Night Breeze
Variants: *Aayaaz, Aayaz, Ayaaz*

Ayd (Arabic)
Power - Strength
Variants: *Aid, Eyd*

Aydarus (Arabic)
Lion
Variants: *Aidaroos, Aidarus*

Aydarusi (Arabic)
Brave
Variants: *Aydaroosy*

Aydeen (Persian)
Radiance

Ayden (Turkish)
Educated - Enlightened - Intellectual
Variants: *Aydin*

Aydi (Arabic)
Hands - Power - Strength
The name Aydi is mentioned in the Quran.
Variants: *Aidi, Aidy, Aydee*

Aydin (Arabic)
Hands - Power - Strength
The name Aydin is mentioned in the Quran in verse 51:47.
Variants: *Aiden, Aidin, Ayden, Eyden, Eydin*

Ayed (Arabic)
Returner - Visitor
Variants: *Aayed, Aayid, Ayid*

Ayeen (Persian)
Creed - Habit

Ayiq (Arabic)
Larkspur
A flowering plant.

Ayish (Arabic)
Alive - Prosperous

Aykon (Arabic)
Nest
Variants: *Aikon, Aikun*

Ayman (Arabic)
Blessed - Fortunate
The name Ayman is mentioned in the Quran.
Variants: *Aiman, Aimen, Aymen*

Aynan (Arabic)
Two Fountains
The name Aynan is mentioned in the Quran.
Variants: *Ainan*

Aysar (Arabic)
Easy - Left-handed - Lenient
Masculine form of Yusra.
Variants: *Aisar, Ayser*

Ayyad (Arabic)
Fortifier - Strengthener - Supporter
Ayyad is an indirect Quranic name for boys that means "able strengthener", a person who is powerful and adds strength to others. It is derived from the Y-D-Y root which is mentioned in many places in the Quran, such as 38:17: Bear with their words patiently. Remember Our servant David, a man of strength who always turned to Us. Ayyad should not be confused with Ayad. Both names are derived from the same root, but they have different, though close, meanings.
Variants: *Ayyaad*

Ayyam (Arabic)
Days
Variants: *Aiam, Ayaam*

Ayyan (Arabic)
Beautiful-eyed - Observant - Perceptive
Variants: *Ayaan, Ayan*

Ayyash (Arabic)
Alive - Prospering
Variants: *Ayash*

NAMES FOR BOYS

Ayyashi (Arabic)
Alive - Prospering
Variants: *Ayashi*

Ayyub (Arabic)
Repentance
Ayyub is the name of one of the prophets mentioned in the Quran.
Variants: *Aiub, Ayoob, Ayub, Ayyoob*

Azaan (Arabic)
Announcement - Call
The name Azaan is mentioned in the Quran.
Variants: *Adhan, Athan, Azan*

Azad (Kurdish, Persian, Urdu)
Free - Sovereign
Variants: *Aazaad, Aazad, Azaad*

Azal (Arabic, Persian)
Eternity - Perpetuity

Azali (Arabic, Persian)
Eternal
Variants: *Azalee, Azaly*

Azarang (Persian)
Brilliant - Shining
Variants: *Aazarang*

Azb (Arabic)
Fresh - Sweet
The name Azbi is mentioned in the Quran.

Azban (Arabic)
Fresh Water

Azeeb (Arabic)
Fresh Water

Azeem (Arabic)
Great - Magnificent
The name Azeem is mentioned in the Quran.
Variants: *Adheem, Adhim, Azim*

Azfaar (Arabic)
Triumphs - Victories
Variants: *Adfaar, Adhfar, Azfar*

Azfar (Arabic)
Overcomer - Victor - Victorious
Variants: *Azfer, Ezfer*

Azhar (Arabic)
Brilliant - Radiant

Azil (Arabic)
Guardian - Protector
Variants: *Aazel, Aazil, Azel*

Azim (Arabic)
Determined - Resolute - Resolved

Aziz (Arabic)
Beloved - Dear - Exalted - Great - Noble
The name Aziz is mentioned in the Quran.
Variants: *Azeez*

Azka (Arabic)
Better - Purer
The name Azka is mentioned in the Quran.
Variants: *Azkaa*

Azm (Arabic)
Aim - Determination - Resolve
The name Azm is mentioned in the Quran.
Variants: *Ezm*

Azmat (Arabic)
Greatness - Importance - Might

Azmi (Arabic)
Brave - Determined - Resolute
Variants: *Azmee, Azmey, Azmy*

Azoom (Arabic)
Determined - Resolved

Azraf (Arabic)
Charming - Intelligent - Witty
Variants: *Adhraf*

Azyan (Arabic)
Adornments - Decorations - Virtues
Variants: *Azian*

Azzam (Arabic)
Lion
Variants: *Azaam, Azam, Azzaam*

Azzami (Arabic)
Fierce - Lion-like

Azzan (Arabic)
Beloved - Cherished - Dear - Excellent - Lofty
Variants: *Azaan, Azzaan*

Azzat (Arabic, Turkish)
Gazelle
Turkish pronunciation of Azzah.

This page intentionally left blank

B

Baadi (Arabic)
Bedouin
Variants: *Bady*

Baashir (Arabic)
Bringer of Good Tidings
Variants: *Basher*

Bab (Arabic)
Door
The name Bab is mentioned in the Quran in verse 12:67.
Variants: *Baab*

Babak (Persian)
Father - Mentor
Variants: *Baabak*

Babar (Turkish)
Leopard

Babr (Persian)
Tiger

Badaah (Arabic)
Plains
Variants: *Baddah*

Badawi (Arabic)
Bedouin

Baddar (Arabic)
Early - On Time - Punctual

Badeed (Arabic)
Example - Sample - Specimen

Badeel (Arabic)
Replacement - Successor
Variants: *Badil*

Badeen (Kurdish, Persian)
Faithful - Religious
Variants: *Badin*

Badhaa (Arabic)
Initiation - Start

Badih (Arabic)
Creative - Intuitive - Witty
Variants: *Badeeh*

Badilayn (Arabic)
Replacements - Substitutes

Badir (Arabic)
Full Moon - Moon
Variants: *Baader, Baadir, Bader*

Badr (Arabic)
Full Moon
This name is mentioned in the Quran.
Variants: *Bedir*

Badr al Din (Arabic)
Supporter of Islam
Literally "full moon of the faith".
Variants: *Badruddin*

Badran (Arabic)
Beautiful - Radiant
Literally "like the full moon".

Badrawi (Arabic)
Handsome - Radiant
Literally "like the full moon".

Badri (Arabic)
Autumn Rain - Fullness of the Moon
In Islamic history this word means "one who took part in the Battle of Badr".
Variants: *Badry*

Baghish (Arabic)
Light Rain

Baha (Persian)
Value - Worth
Variants: *Bahaa, Bahaa*

Baha (Arabic)
Beauty - Brilliance

Baha al Din (Arabic)
Supporter of Islam
Literally "brilliance of the faith".
Variants: *Bahauddin*

Bahadur (Turkish)
Brave - Heroic
Variants: *Bahaador*

Bahamin (Persian)
Spring Season
Variants: *Bahameen*

Bahat (Arabic)
Beauty
Variants: *Bahaat*

Bahat (Arabic)
Pure - Spotless

Baheej (Arabic)
Beautiful - Radiant
Variants: *Bahij*

Baheen (Arabic)
Cheerful

Baheer (Arabic)
Handsome - Radiant - Talented

Bahhas (Arabic)
Researcher - Scholar
Variants: *Bahaas, Bahas*

Bahi (Arabic)
Brilliant - Radiant
Variants: *Bahee, Bahy*

Bahir (Arabic)
Brilliant - Lucid - Renowned
Variants: *Baaher, Baahir, Baher*

Bahiri (Arabic)
Brilliant - Renowned

Bahiriya (Arabic)
Brilliant - Renowned

Bahirun (Arabic)
Brilliant - Lucid - Renowned
Variants: *Baherun*

Bahis (Arabic)
Explorer - Learner - Researcher - Seeker
Variants: *Baahes, Baahis, Bahes, Bahith*

Bahjat (Arabic)
Beautiful - Radiant
Variants: *Behjet*

Bahlul (Arabic)
Cheerful - Smiling
Variants: *Bahlool*

Bahman (Persian)
Avalanche
Also the name of the 11th month of the Persian calendar (Shamsi Hijri calendar).

Bahoos (Arabic)
Researcher - Seeker
Variants: *Bahus*

Bahoosh (Arabic)
Cheerful - Relaxed

Bahr (Arabic)
Ocean - Sea
The name Bahr is mentioned in the Quran.

Bahradin (Arabic)
Knowledgeable - Scholar - Wise
Literally "ocean of the faith".

Bahri (Arabic)
Ocean-like - Vast
Variants: *Bahree, Bahry*

Bahroz (Kurdish)
Fortunate - Lucky
From Persian Behruz.

Bahsa (Persian)
Good - Virtuous
Variants: *Bahsaa, Behsa, Behsaa*

Bahuj (Arabic)
Energetic - Handsome - Lively
Variants: *Bahooj*

Bahur (Arabic)
Brilliant - Lucid
Variants: *Bahoor*

Bahzad (Kurdish)
High-born - Noble
From Persian Behzad.
Variants: *Bahzaad*

Bahzar (Arabic)
Respected - Wise

Baihas (Arabic)
Brave - Lion
Variants: *Bayhas*

Bailul (Arabic)
Freshness - Wetness
Variants: *Baylul*

Baitaar (Arabic)
Expert - Veterinarian

Bajdan (Arabic)
Inhabitant - Resident
Variants: *Bajdaan*

Bajes (Arabic)
Warrior
Variants: *Baajes, Bajis*

Bajli (Arabic)
Cheerful - Happy

Bakeel (Arabic)
Elegant - Good-looking

Bakheet (Arabic)
Fortunate
Variants: *Bakhit*

Bakhit (Arabic)
Fortunate - Lucky

Bakhsh (Persian)
Fortune - Share
Variants: *Baxsh, Beksh*

Bakhshayesh (Persian)
Forgiveness - Pardon

Bakht (Persian)
Fortunte

Bakhtaavar (Persian)
Fortuante

Bakhtaawar (Persian, Urdu)
Fortunate
Variants: *Bakhtaawer*

Bakhtar (Persian)
East - North - Star - West
In Pahlavi (ancient Persian), Bakhtar meant "star".
Variants: *Baakhter*

Bakhtavar (Persian)
Fortunate - Lucky
Variants: *Bakhtaver*

Bakhtawar (Kurdish, Urdu)
Fortunate - Lucky

Bakhti (Arabic)
Fortunate - Lucky

Bakhtiar (Persian)
Blessed - Fortunate

Bakkar (Arabic)
Early Riser

Bakkur (Arabic)
Early - New - On Time

NAMES FOR BOYS

Bakr (Arabic)
New - Untouched - Virgin
Variants: *Bekir*

Bakrun (Arabic)
Fresh - New

Baktash (Turkish)
Chief - Master

Balagh (Arabic)
Announcement - Maturity - Proclamation
Variants: *Balaagh*

Baldwin (English)
Brave Friend

Baleegh (Arabic)
Eloquent - Far-reaching
The name Baleegh is mentioned in the Quran.
Variants: *Baligh*

Balooj (Arabic)
Radiant

Bamdad (Persian)
Dawn
Variants: *Bamdaad*

Bamdat (Persian)
Dawn
Variant of Bamdad.
Variants: *Bamdaat*

Bandar (Arabic, Persian)
Port - Port City
Variants: *Bander*

Bani (Arabic)
Builder - Founder Creator
Variants: *Banee, Bany*

Banna (Arabic)
Builder - Founder
Variants: *Bana, Banaa, Bannaa*

Baqaa (Arabic)
Eternity - Perpetuity
Variants: *Baqa*

Baqee (Arabic)
Enduring - Everlasting
The name Baqee is mentioned in the Quran.
Variants: *Baqi, Baqy*

Baqian (Arabic)
Everlasting - Perpetual

Baqir (Arabic)
Discoverer - Knowledgeable - Lion
Variants: *Baaqir, Baqer*

Baraa (Arabic)
Blameless - Healed - Innocent
The name Baraa mentioned in the Quran.
Variants: *Bara*

Baraaem (Arabic)
Fresh - Innocent - Unopened Flower Bud - Young
Variants: *Bara'im*

Barafi (Aramaic)
Son
Variants: *Barafy*

Barahim (Arabic)
Variant of Ibrahim.

Baraj (Arabic)
Handsome

Barakat (Arabic)
Abundance - Blessings
Variants: *Barakaat*

Baram (Kurdish)
Planet Mars
From Persian Behram.

Barayek (Arabic)
Blessed

Bard (English)
Broad Ford - Broad Wood
Short form of Bradford and Bradley.

Bardia (Persian)
Great - Magnificent

Bareek (Arabic)
Blessed
Variants: *Barik*

Bareeq (Arabic)
Glow - Sheen
Variants: *Bariq*

Bariq (Arabic)
Brilliant - Flashing

Bariz (Arabic)
Prominent - Visible
Variants: *Baarez, Baariz, Barez*

Barizi (Arabic)
Prominent - Visible

Barja (Persian)
Fitting - Stable - Unshakable - Worthy
Variants: *Barjaa*

Barjees (Arabic, Urdu)
Planet Jupiter
Urdu variant of Birjis.
Variants: *Barjis*

Barkhan (Arabic, Turkish)
Great Chief
Variants: *Baarkhan*

Barmak (Persian)
Chief - Leader

Barraq (Arabic)
Brilliant - Radiant - Shining

Barraz (Arabic)
Clear - Prominent

Barzan (Arabic)
Powerful - Prominent - Visible
Variants: *Barzaan*

Basam (Arabic)
Happy - Smiling
Variants: *Basaam, Bassam*

Basar (Arabic)
Eyesight - Insight - Perception - Vision - Wisdom
The name Basar is mentioned in the Quran.

Baseel (Arabic)
Brave - Lion
Variants: *Basil*

Baseer (Arabic)
Discerning - Insightful - Perceptive
The name Baseer is mentioned in the Quran.
Variants: *Basir*

Baseerat (Arabic)
Insight - Perception - Wisdom
Turkish pronunciation of Baseera.
Variants: *Basirat*

Basel (Arabic)
Brave - Lion
Variants: *Baasel, Baasil, Basil*

Basem (Arabic)
Cheerful - Smiling
Variants: *Baasem, Baasim, Basim*

Bashar (Arabic)
Bringer of Good News - Bringer of Good Tidings
Variants: *Bashaar*

Bashash (Arabic)
Charming - Cheerful
Variants: *Bashaash*

Basheer (Arabic)
Bringer of Good News - Bringer of Good Tidings
Variants: *Bashir, Beshir*

Basheesh (Arabic)
Cheerful - Optimistic

Bashiri (Arabic)
Bringer of Good Tidings

Bashirun (Arabic)
Bringers of Good Tidings

Bashu (Arabic)
Cheerful - Optimistic
Variants: *Bashoo*

Bashur (Arabic)
Bringer of Good News
Variants: *Bashoor*

Bashwan (Arabic)
Classy - Good-mannered

Bashwi (Arabic)
Classy - Good-mannered

Basil (English)
Royal

Basili (Arabic)
Brave

Basimi (Arabic)
Happy - Smiling

Basiq (Arabic)
High - Lofty - Soaring - Towering
Variants: *Baaseq, Baasiq, Baseq*

Basit (Arabic)
Friendly - Generous - Kind
The name Basit is mentioned in the Quran.
Variants: *Baaset, Baasit, Baset*

Basmat (Arabic)
Smile
Turkish pronunciation of Basmah.
Variants: *Besmet*

Basmin (Arabic)
Cheerful Ones - Happy Ones - Smiling Ones
Variants: *Basmeen*

Basoom (Arabic)
Cheerful - Smiling

Bassaar (Arabic)
Insightful - Perceptive

Batal (Arabic)
Brave - Hero

Batek (Arabic)
Sharp Sword
Variants: *Baatek, Baatik, Batik*

Bathr (Arabic)
Plain
A type of land.
Variants: *Basr*

Batil (Arabic)
Ascetic - Devoted to God - Virtuous
Variants: *Baatel, Baatil, Batel*

Battaal (Arabic)
Ascetic - Chaste - Modest
Variants: *Bataal*

Bawan (Kurdish)
Beloved - Darling
Variants: *Baawan*

Bayan (Arabic)
Declaration - Elucidation - Exposition - Illustration
Variants: *Baian, Bayaan*

Bayhas (Arabic)
Courageous - Lion
Variants: *Beihas, Beyhas*

Baz (Arabic)
Northern Goshawk
A type of bird of prey.
Variants: *Baaz*

Bazigh (Arabic)
Radiant - Shining
The name Bazigh is mentioned in the Quran.
Variants: *Baazigh*

Bazij (Arabic)
Adorner - Beautifier
Variants: *Baazij*

Bazir (Arabic)
Sower
One who plants seeds
Variants: *Baazir, Bazer*

Bazullah (Arabic)
God's Hawk

Behboud (Persian)
Well-being - Wellness

Behdad (Persian)
Fair - Just

Behnam (Persian)
Reputable - Respected
Variants: *Bahnaam Bahnam Behnaam*

Behrad (Persian)
Generous - Gracious

Behram (Persian)
Planet Mars
Variants: *Behraam*

Behrang (Persian)
Good-looking - Handsome

Behrokh (Persian)
Beautiful - Handsome
Variants: *Behrukh*

Behruz (Persian)
Fortunate - Lucky

Behshad (Persian)
Good - Happy

Behtash (Persian, Turkish)
Good Friend

Behzad (Persian)
High-born - Noble

Benedict (English)
Blessed

Benjamin (English, French, German)
Son of the South

Bennett (English)
Blessed
Synonym of Benedict.
Variants: *Benet, Benett, Bennet*

Benno (German)
Blessed

Bernard (English, French)
Strong Like a Bear

Berthold (German)
Bright Ruler - Famous Ruler

Bertram (English)
Famous Raven

Bertrand (English, French)
Famous Raven
Variant of Bertram.

Berwyn (Welsh)
Fair-skinned - White

Beverley (English)
Beaver Stream
Originally the name of a place in northern England.

Bidar (Arabic)
Earliness - Punctuality

Bidayat (Arabic)
Beginning - Genesis - Inception
Turkish pronunciation of Bidayah.

Bijan (Persian)
Bijan is a variant of the Persian boy name Bizhan, of unknown meaning.
Variants: *Beejan*

Bikr (Arabic)
New - Untouched - Virgin
Variants: *Bekir, Bekr*

Bilal (Arabic)
Water
Variants: *Belaal, Belal*

Bill (English)
Determined Protector
Short form of William.

Birjees (Arabic)
Planet Jupiter
Variants: *Berjees, Berjis*

Biryar (Kurdish)
Decision - Resolution

Bisharah (Arabic)
Good Tidings

Bishr (Arabic)
Cheerfulness - Optimism
Variants: *Beshr*

Bishry (Arabic)
Cheerful - Glad - Optimistic

Bizhan (Persian)
Name of a Persian hero, of

unknown meaning.
Variants: *Beezhan*

Bob (English)
Bright With Fame
Altered short form of Robert.

Bodaad (Arabic)
Fortune - Share

Bokhur (Arabic)
Incense

Bonifacio (Italian, Portuguese, Spanish)
Doer of Good Deeds - Fortunate - Lucky

Borna (Persian)
Brave - Young
Variants: *Burna*

Borumand (Persian)
Powerful - Productive

Borzan (Persian)
Great - Magnificent

Borzou (Persian)
Great - Magnificent

Boshry (Arabic)
Gladness - Happiness

Bozorg (Persian)
Great - Important

Bozorgmehr (Persian)
Gracious - Kind
Variants: *Bozorgmehr*

Bradford (English)
Broad Ford

Bradley (English)
Broad Wood

Brandon (English)
From the Broom Hill
Variants: *Branton*

Brendan (Irish)
Prince

Brian (English, Irish)
High - Noble
Variants: *Bryan, Bryant*

Bruce (English, Scottish)
Elite - Noble
Originally a surname referring to a place.

Bruno (English, German)
Brown

Brychan (Welsh)
Speckled

Bryn (Welsh)
Hill

Brynmor (Welsh)
Large Hill
Originally the name of a place in north-west Wales.

Buck (English)
Male Deer - Robust - Spirited

Bud (English)
Brother - Friend

Budaid (Arabic)
Example - Sample - Specimen

Budaili (Arabic)
Replacement

Budair (Arabic)
Full Moon
Variants: *Bodair*

Budaiwi (Arabic)
Bedouin

Budool (Arabic)
Ascetic - Honored - Respected

Budur (Arabic)
Full Moons
Variants: *Bodoor*

Buhair (Arabic)
Lake

Buhur (Arabic)
Oceans - Seas
Variants: *Bohoor, Buhoor*

Bujaij (Arabic)
Beautiful-eyed - Large-eyed

Bujud (Arabic)
Residence - Stay
Variants: *Bojud*

Bukair (Arabic)
New - Untouched

Bukhari (Arabic, Persian)
One Who Comes From Bukhara
Bukhara is a city and region in modern-day Uzbekistan. Some important Islamic scholars come from this area.

Bukran (Arabic)
Dawn

Bulbul (Arabic)
Nightingale
Variants: *Bolbol*

Bunyan (Arabic)
Buildings - Institutions - Structures
The name Bunyan is mentioned in the Quran.

Buraik (Arabic)
Blessed

Burgess (English)
Freeman of a Borough

Burhan (Arabic)
Demonstration - Evidence - Proof - Proof of God's Greatness
Burhan is used in the Quran in verse 2:111 and others.
Variants: *Borhaan, Borhan, Burhaan*

Burton (English)
Fortified Settlement
Name of various places in England.

Busraq (Arabic)
Yellow Sapphire
Variants: *Busraaq*

Bustan (Persian)
Forest - Garden
Variants: *Bostan, Bustaan*

Buzur (Arabic)
Seeds

This page intentionally left blank

C

Cade (English)
Round

Caerwyn (Welsh)
Blessed Love - Holy Love
Altered form of Carwyn.

Caesar (English)
Emperor

Cahir (Irish)
Warrior

Callisto (Italian)
Fair - Good

Calum (Scottish Gaelic)
Dove

Cameron (Scottish)
Crooked Nose

Canice (Irish)
Handsome

Carl (English, German)
Free Man
German respelling of Karl.

Carlo (Italian)
Free Man
Italian form of Charles.

Carlos (Portuguese, Spanish)
Free Man
Spanish and Portuguese form of Charles.

Carlton (English)
Settlement of Free Peasants
Originally a surname referring to various place names in England.

Carwyn (Welsh)
Blessed Love - Holy Love

Casey (Irish)
Vigilant - Wakeful

Chabuk (Persian)
Agile - Energetic
Variants: *Chabok*

Chaman (Persian)
Greenery - Lawn

Chand (Urdu)
Moon
Variants: *Chaand*

Charles (English, French)
Free Man

Charlie (English, Scottish)
Free Man
Pet form of Charles.

Cheragh (Persian)
Lamp - Lantern - Light
Variants: *Charagh, Cheraagh, Chiragh*

Chester (English)
Legionary Camp
Originally a surname denoting someone from the town of Chester, from Latin castra ("legionary camp").

Cian (Irish)
Ancient

Cillian (Irish)
Strife

Cipriano (Italian)
Cyprian

Ciro (Italian)
Lord
Italian form of Cyrus.

Clay (English)
Settlement
Short form of Clayton.

Clayton (English)
Settlement
Name of various places in England.

Clement (English)
Merciful

Cliamain (Scottish Gaelic)
Merciful

Cliff (English)
Riverbank Ford
Short form of Clifford.

Clifford (English)
Riverbank Ford
The name of many places in England.

Clifton (English)
Riverbank Settlement
Name of many places in England.

Clint (English)
Town on the Hill
Short form of Clinton.

Clinton (English)
Town on the Hill

Clive (English)
Cliff - Slope
Name of various places in England.

Colin (English)
Of the Victorious People
Short form of Nicholas.

Cosmo (English, German, Italian)
Beauty - Order

Craig (English, Scottish)
Rock
From a surname, originally the

name of many places in
Scotland.

Creighton (English, Scottish)
Border Settlement

Curtis (English)
Courteous

Cyril (English)
Lord

Cyrille (French)
Lord
French form of Cyril.

Cyrus (English)
Lord

D

Daaem (Arabic)
Constant - Continual - Perpetual

Dabeer (Persian)
Instructor - Teacher
Variants: *Dabir*

Dabir (Arabic)
Ancestry - Origins - Root
The name Dabir is mentioned in the Quran.

Dadmehr (Persian)
Lover of Justice

Dadvar (Persian)
Arbitrator - Judge

Dadwar (Kurdish)
Arbitrator - Judge

Daeb (Arabic)
Conscientious - Diligent

Daeej (Arabic)
Beautiful-eyed

Dag (Scandinavian)
Day

Dahaa (Arabic)
Intelligence - Sense - Wisdom

Dahban (Arabic)
Gold-plated

Dahee (Arabic)
Clever - Intelligent
Variants: *Dahi*

Dahus (Arabic)
Lion

Dai (Welsh)
Beloved
Welsh pet form of David. Originally of a different origin meaning "to shine".

Dale (English)
Valley

Daleel (Arabic)
Guide - Mentor
The name Daleel is mentioned in the Quran.
Variants: *Dalil*

Dalir (Persian)
Brave

Dalu (Arabic)
Well Bucket
The name Dalu is mentioned in the Quran.

Dan (English)
God is My Judge
Short form of Daniel.

Dan (Biblical)
He Judged
Name of one of the sons of prophet Jacob in the Bible.

Dana (Polish)
Gift from God
Short form of Bogdan.
Variants: *Daana, Daanaa, Danaa*

Dana (Persian)
Experienced - Knowledgeable - Wise

Dane (English)
Valley-dweller
Dialect variant of Dean.

Daneer (Arabic)
Radiant

Danesh (Persian)
Knowledge - Wisdom
Variants: *Daanesh, Daanish, Danish*

Daneshvar (Persian)
Learned - Wise

Daniel (Czech, English, French, German, Jewish, Polish)
God is My Judge
Name of a prophet in the Bible.

Danny (English)
God is My Judge
Pet form of Daniel.

Dante (Italian)
Enduring - Steadfast
Contracted form of Durante.

Daqeeq (Arabic)
Delicate - Fine
Variants: *Daqiq*

Daqr (Arabic)
Thriving Garden

Dara (Kurdish, Persian)
Wealthy
Variants: *Daara, Daraa*

Darab (Persian)
Glory - Power - Wealth
Variants: *Daraab*

Darcy (English)
Originally d'Arcy, borne by a family from Arcy in France. Darcy is the name of the hero of Pride and Prejudice.

Dareeb (Arabic)
Experienced - Trained

Dareeq (Arabic)
Fixer - Mender

Daria (Persian)
Acquirer - Owner - Wealthy
Variants: *Daaria, Darya*

Dario (Italian)
Possessor of Goodness
Originally from Persian.

Daris (Arabic)
Researcher - Seeker of
Knowledge - Student
Variants: *Daares, Daaris*

Dariush (Persian)
Possessor of Goodness
Variants: *Darioosh, Daryoosh, Daryush*

Darkan (Arabic)
Perceptive - Understanding

Darrak (Arabic)
Intelligent - Perceptive
Variants: *Daraak, Darak*

Daruj (Arabic)
Fast - Swift

Dastan (Persian)
Fable - Story

Daulah (Arabic)
Power - State
Variants: *Daula, Dawla, Dawlah*

Daulat (Arabic)
Power - State
Turkish pronunciation of Daulah.
Variants: *Dawlat*

Davar (Persian)
Arbitrator - Judge
Variants: *Daavar, Daver*

David (Biblical)
Beloved
Known as Dawud in Arabic, a prophet mentioned in the Quran and the Bible.

Davood (Persian)
Beloved Friend
Persian pronunciation of Dawood, Arabic form of David.
Variants: *Davud*

Davut (Arabic)
Beloved Friend
Davut is the Turkish form of Dawood, Arabic form of David.

Davy (English, Scottish)
Beloved
Pet form of David.
Variants: *Davey, Davie*

Dawar (Persian, Urdu)
Arbitrator - Judge
Variants: *Daawar, Dawer*

Dawlatyab (Persian)
Leader - Ruler
Literally "founder of state".
Variants: *Dawlat Yah, Dolatyab*

Dawood (Arabic)
Beloved Friend
Originally from Hebrew. The name Dawood is mentioned in the Quran.
Variants: *Daood, Dawoud, Dawud*

Dawub (Arabic)
Conscientious - Diligent
Variants: *Da'ub, Daoob, Daub, Dawood*

Dawwas (Arabic)
Brave - Strong

Dayyar (Arabic)
Inhabitant - Resident

Dayyin (Arabic)
Devout - Religious

Dean (English)
Valley-dweller
Variants: *Deane, Dene*

Deeb (Arabic)
Wolf

Deen (Arabic)
Creed - Religion
The name Deen is mentioned in the Quran.
Variants: *Dean, Dein, Din*

Dehqan (Persian)
Farmer - Village Chief

Del (Persian)
Heart
Variants: *Dil*

Delara (Persian)
Beloved - Darling
Variants: *Delaara, Dilara*

Delaram (Persian)
Peaceful Serene
Variants: *Dilaram*

Delavar (Persian)
Brave - Courageous
Variants: *Delaavar, Delawar, Dilavar, Dilawar*

Delbar (Persian)
Captivating - Charming
Variants: *Dilbar*

Delbaz (Persian)
Captivated - In Love
Variants: *Delbaaz, Dilbaz*

Deldar (Persian)
Beloved - Brave - In Love
Variants: *Deldaar, Dildar*

Delkash (Persian)
Captivating - Enticing
Variants: *Dilkash*

Delnavaz (Persian)
Comforter - Consoler
Variants: *Delnawaz, Dilnawaz*

NAMES FOR BOYS

Delshad (Persian)
Happy - Joyful
Variants: *Delshaad, Dilshad*

Derek (English)
Ruler of the Tribe
From a German form of Theodoric.
Variants: *Derrick*

Desiderio (Italian, Portuguese, Spanish)
Longing
Form of Desiderius.

Desya (Russian)
Moderate - Modest - Obedient
Pet form of the Russian name Modest.

Diakou (Persian)
Name of the first king of the Medes of Persia, of unknown meaning.

Dibaaj (Arabic)
Silk Cloth
A type of silk cloth.

Didar (Persian)
Date - Meet Up - Reunion
Variants: *Deedar, Didaar*

Didier (French)
Longing

Dilf (Arabic)
Bold

Dinar (Arabic)
Gold Coin
The name Dinar is mentioned in the Quran.
Variants: *Deenar*

Diras (Arabic)
Scholar - Student

Dirbas (Arabic)
Lion

Dirgham (Arabic)
Lion

Dirk (Dutch, Flemish)
Ruler of the Tribe
Form of Derek.

Diryas (Arabic)
Lion

Dler (Kurdish)
Brave

Dominic (English, Irish)
Lord

Dominique (French)
Lord
French form of Dominica and Dominic. Used mostly for girls.

Donovan (English, Irish)
Brown-haired Chief

Doost (Persian)
Friend

Doran (Irish)
Stranger - Wanderer

Dosifei (Russian)
Gift from God

Dost (Kurdish)
Friend
From Persian Doost.

Dougal (Scottish)
Dark Stranger
Variants: *Dugal*

Doyle (English, Irish)
Dark Stranger

Drew (Scottish)
Manly - Warrior
Short form of Andrew.

Duane (English, Irish)
Black - Dark
Variants: *Dwane, Dwayne*

Duff (Scottish)
Black - Dark

Duhat (Arabic)
Intelligent - Sensible

Duhr (Arabic)
Noon
Variants: *Dohr*

Duke (English)
Leader - Member of the Nobility

Duncan (English, Scottish)
Dark Warrior

Dunstan (English)
Dark Stone

Duryab (Arabic)
Finder of Pearls
Variants: *Doryab, Duryaab*

This page intentionally left blank

E

Eamon (English, Irish)
Wealthy Protector
Form of Edmund.

Earl (English)
Member of the Nobility -
Nobleman - Prince - Warrior

Edgar (English)
Powerful Spearman

Edmund (English)
Wealthy Protector

Edoardo (Italian)
Wealthy Protector

Eduard (Czech)
Wealthy Protector

Edvard (Czech, Scandinavian)
Wealthy Protector

Edward (English, Polish)
Wealthy Protector

Edwin (English)
Wealthy Friend

Eeda (Arabic)
Commitment - Consignment
Variants: *Idaa'*

Eero (Finnish)
Eternal Ruler

Eetu (Finnish)
Wealthy Protector
Form of Edward.

Eezah (Arabic)
Clarification - Elucidation
Variants: *Izaah*

Egbert (English)
Bright Sword Edge

Egon (German)
Sword Edge

Eid (Arabic)
Celebration - Festival
The name Eid is mentioned in
the Quran.
Variants: *Eed, Eyd*

Eidi (Arabic)
Eid Gift
Variants: *Eedy*

Eifa (Arabic)
Faithfulness - Loyalty
Variants: *Eefaa, Ifaa*

Eihab (Arabic)
To Bestow - To Confer a Gift -
To Endow With
Variants: *Eyhab, Ihaab, Ihab*

Eiham (Arabic)
Fantasy - Illusion
Variants: *Eyham, Iham*

Eiliad (Persian, Turkish)
Memory of the People

Eiliar (Persian, Turkish)
Friend of the People

Eilman (Turkish)
Banner of the People - Symbol
of the People

Eilqar (Persian)
Oath - Promise - Treaty

Eilshan (Turkish)
Leader - Ruler

Eimam (Arabic)
Chief - Leader
Variants: *Eemam*

Einar (Scandinavian)
Lone Warrior

Einas (Arabic)
Comfort - Consolation - Peace
of Mind
Variants: *Eenas*

Einion (Welsh)
Anvil

Eira (Arabic)
Kindling - Starting a Fire
Variants: *Eera, Eiraa, Eyra, Ira*

Eirik (Norwegian)
Eternal Ruler

Eisun (Arabic)
Capable - Competent
Variants: *Esoun, Isoon*

Eisuni (Arabic)
Capable - Competent
Variants: *Isoony, Isuni*

Eithar (Arabic)
Love - Preferring Another
Person to Yourself
Variants: *Isaar, Isar*

Eiwa (Arabic)
Guardianship - Protection
Variants: *Eewaa, Eiwaa, Eywa,
Eywaa, Iwa, Iwaa, Iywa*

Elaf (Arabic)
Safety - Security Promise
The name Elaf is used in the
Quran.
Variants: *Elaaf, Ilaaf, Ilaf*

Eli (Biblical)
Height

Eliar (Persian, Turkish)
Friend of the People

Elias (Arabic)
Yahweh is my God
The name Elias is mentioned in the Quran. It is the name of a prophet mentioned in the Quran, in English known as Elias and Elijah. The meaning of "Yahweh is my God" is acceptable since "Yahweh" is a synonym of "Allah".
Variants: *Eliaas, Elyaas, Elyas, Iliaas, Ilias, Ilyaas, Ilyas*

Elijah (Biblical)
Yahweh is God
Name of a prophet in the Bible and the Quran (known as Ilyas in Arabic).

Eliseo (Italian, Spanish)
God is My Salvation
Biblical prophet known as Elisha in English.

Elliot (English)
Yahweh is God
Originally from Elias (Greek form of Elijhah).
Variants: *Eliot, Eliott, Elliott*

Ellis (English)
Yahweh is my God
Derived from Elias (Elijah in English).

Elmo (Italian)
Helmet - Protection

Emanuel (Scandinavian)
God is With Us
Form of Emmanuel.

Emanuele (Italian)
God is With Us
Italian form of Emmanuel.

Emmanuel (Biblical)
God is With Us

Emyr (Welsh)
King - Lord - Ruler

Endre (Hungarian)
Manly - Warrior
Hungarian form of Andrew.

Enric (Catalan)
Ruler of the House
Catalan form of Henry.

Enrico (Italian)
Ruler of the House
Italian form of Henry.

Enrique (Spanish)
Ruler of the House
Spanish form of Henry.

Eoin (Gaelic)
God is Gracious
Gaelic form of John (Yahya in Arabic).

Erdmann (German)
Brave Man
Altered form of Hartmann.

Erdmut (German)
Brave Spirit
Altered form of Hartmut.

Erhard (German)
Brave and Honorable

Eric (English)
Eternal Ruler

Erkki (Finnish)
Eternal Ruler
Finnish form of Eric.

Erland (Scandinavian)
Foreigner - Stranger
Variants: *Erlend*

Ernest (English)
Determined - Serious

Erwin (German)
Honorable Friend

Esa (Finnish)
God is Salvation
Name of a prophet in the Bible (not mentioned in the Quran), known as Ash'iya in Arabic (different from the the Arabic Esa/Isa, which refers to prophet Jesus son of Mary).

Esfand (Persian)
Holy - Pure

Esfandiar (Persian)
Pure Creation
Variants: *Isfandiar, Isfandyar*

Eshaal (Arabic)
Excitation - Kindling
Variants: *Eshal, Ish'al, Ishaal, Ishal*

Esmond (English)
Grace and Protection

Esteve (Catalan)
Crown - Garland

Etemad (Arabic)
Reliance - Trust
Variants: *I'timad, Itimad*

Ethan (Biblical)
Firmness - Long-lived

Etizaaz (Arabic)
Glory - Greatness - Honor
Variants: *Itizaaz, Ittizaz*

Etzel (German)
Father - Noble
Derived from adal ("noble") or Atta ("father").
Variants: *Edsel*

Eugene (English)
High-born - Noble

NAMES FOR BOYS

Eugenio (Italian, Spanish)
High-born - Noble
Form of Eugene.

Eusebio (Italian, Portuguese, Spanish)
Pious - Respectful

Eutropio (Spanish)
Good-mannered

Evan (Welsh)
God is Gracious
Originally form John.

Evander (Scottish)
Bow Warrior - Good Man
Can either be from Scottish Gaelic Ìomhair or Green Euandros.

Everard (English)
Bear-like in Strength
Variants: *Everett*

Evert (German)
Bear-like in Strength
Form of Eberhard.

Ewan (Irish, Scottish Gaelic)
Born - Yew
Anglicized form of Eóghan.
Variants: *Ewen*

Ewazi (Arabic)
Replacement

Eyazi (Arabic)
Replacement
Variants: *Iyazi*

Ezekiel (Biblical)
God Strengthens
Name of a Biblical prophet, possibly the same as prophet Zul-Kifl who is mentioned in the Quran.

Ezra (Biblical)
Help
Ezra is a Biblical prophet, known as Uzair in Arabic, a person mentioned in the Quran. Some Muslim scholars also consider him a prophet, though the Quran doesn't mention him being one.

This page intentionally left blank

F

Faahim (Arabic)
Intelligent - Understanding
Variants: *Faahem, Fahem, Fahim*

Faaiz (Arabic)
Successful
Variants: *Faaez, Faez, Faiz, Faize, Faizz, Fayez, Fayiz*

Faalan (Arabic)
Productive

Faariq (Arabic)
Differentiator - Judge

Fabil (Arabic)
Heavy Rain

Fabrice (French)
Craftsman

Fadi (Arabic)
Heroic - Self-sacrificing
Variants: *Faady, Fadee, Fady*

Faeq (Arabic)
Excellent - Extraordinary - Superb
Variants: *Faaek, Faaiq, Faiq, Fayeq, Fayik, Fayiq*

Faham (Arabic)
Intelligent - Understanding
Variants: *Fahaam, Faham, Fahham*

Fahd (Arabic)
Leopard

Fahdi (Arabic)
Brave - Leopard-like

Fahduddin (Arabic)
Leopard of the Faith

Fahdullah (Arabic)
Leopard of God

Faheem (Arabic)
Intelligent - Keen - Perceptive - Understanding
Variants: *Fahim, Fehim*

Fahis (Arabic)
Investigator - Tester
Variants: *Faahes, Faahis, Fahes*

Fahm (Arabic)
Comprehension - Understanding

Fahmat (Arabic)
Comprehension - Understanding

Fahmawi (Arabic)
Comprehending - Intelligent

Fahmee (Arabic)
Intelligent - Understanding
Variants: *Fahmi, Fahmy*

Fahmun (Arabic)
Comprehending - Intelligent

Faih (Arabic)
Fragrant - Scent
Variants: *Fayh, Feih*

Faihami (Arabic)
Comprehending - Intelligent

Faihan (Arabic)
Fragrant

Fairuz (Arabic, Kurdish, Persian, Urdu)
Successful - Victor
Variants: *Fairooz, Fayrooz, Fayruz*

Faisal (Arabic)
Decisive
Variants: *Faysal, Feisal, Feysal*

Faitah (Arabic)
Right Guidance

Faiz (Arabic)
Plenty

Faizan (Arabic)
Beneficence - Grace - Philanthropy
Variants: *Faidhaan, Faidhan, Faizaan, Fayzan*

Faizee (Arabic)
Abundance - Gracious - Virtuous
Variants: *Faidhi, Faizy*

Faizullah (Arabic)
Bounty from God

Faizurrahman (Arabic)
Bounty from God

Fajr (Arabic)
Dawn - Daybreak
The name Fajr is mentioned in the Quran.

Fajruddin (Arabic)
Dawn of the Faith

Fajrul Islam (Arabic)
Dawn of Islam

Fakhir (Arabic)
High Quality - Luxurious
Variants: *Faakher, Faakhir, Fakher*

Fakhr (Arabic)
Glory - Honor - Pride
Variants: *Fekhr*

Fakhri (Arabic)
Cause for Pride - Glorious
Variants: *Fakhry*

Fakhrjahan (Arabic)
Pride of the World

Fakhruddin (Arabic)
Supporter of Islam

Literally "pride of the faith".
Variants: *Fakhr al-Din*

Falah (Arabic)
Prosperity - Success
Variants: *Falaah*

Falak (Arabic)
Cosmos - Orbit - Ship - Space
The name Falak is used in the Quran.
Variants: *Felek*

Falaq (Arabic)
Dawn - Daybreak
The name Falaq is used in the Quran.

Faleeh (Arabic)
Successful

Falih (Arabic)
Prosperous - Successful
Variants: *Faaleh, Faalih, Faleh*

Falihi (Arabic)
Successful - Winner

Fallah (Arabic)
Farmer

Falooh (Arabic)
Successful

Fannan (Arabic)
Artist
Variants: *Fanaan, Fanan, Fannaan*

Faqeeh (Arabic)
Expert - Knowledgeable - Learned - Scholar
Variants: *Faqih*

Farahaat (Arabic)
Happiness - Joy
Variants: *Farahat*

Farahmand (Persian)
Magnificent - Majestic

Faraj (Arabic)
Comfort - Ease - Relief

Farajuddin (Arabic)
Relief of the Faith

Farajullah (Arabic)
God's Relief - God's Rescue

Farakh (Persian)
End of Fear - Relief

Faramarz (Persian)
Forgiver of His Enemies

Faramorz (Persian)
Forgiver of His Enemies
Variants: *Faramurz*

Farasat (Arabic)
Acumen - Foresight - Keenness - Vision
Variants: *Faraasat*

Faraz (Persian)
Elevation - High Place - Successful - Top
Variants: *Faraaz*

Farazdaq (Arabic)
Loaf of Bread

Farbad (Persian)
Great - Majestic

Farboud (Persian)
Rightly-guided - Upright

Fardad (Persian)
High-born - Noble

Fardain (Arabic)
Peerless - Unique

Fardan (Arabic)
Unique
Variants: *Fardaan*

Fardun (Arabic)
Peerless - Unique

Fareed (Arabic)
Matchless - Unique
Variants: *Farid*

Fareeman (Persian)
Blessed - Great - Magnificent

Fareeq (Arabic)
Band - Crew - Group
The name Fareeq is mentioned in the Quran.
Variants: *Fariq*

Farehan (Persian)
Great - Majestic

Farhaat (Arabic)
Happiness - Joy
Variants: *Farhat*

Farhad (Persian)
Helper
Variants: *Farhaad, Ferhad*

Farham (Persian)
Possessor of Good Thoughts

Farhan (Arabic)
Happy - Joyous - Rejoicing
Variants: *Farhaan, Ferhan*

Farhand (Arabic)
Full-bodied - Muscular

Farhang (Persian)
Culture - Knowledge - Literature
Variants: *Ferhang*

Farhatullah (Arabic)
Happiness Coming From God

Farheen (Arabic, Urdu)
Happy - Joyous
Variants: *Farhin*

NAMES FOR BOYS

Farhi (Arabic)
Happy

Farhiyyan (Arabic)
Happy

Fariborz (Persian)
Glorious - Majestic - Mighty
Variants: *Fareeborz, Fariburz*

Farih (Arabic)
Happy

Faris (Arabic)
Horseman - Rider

Farivar (Persian)
Correct - Upright

Farjad (Persian)
Wise

Farjam (Persian)
Conclusion - End Result

Farman (Arabic, Persian)
Command - Commandment

Farmanullah (Arabic)
God's Command

Farnad (Persian)
Conclusion

Farnam (Persian)
Respected

Farnoud (Persian)
Clue - Evidence

Farokh (Persian)
Agreeable - Blessed - Fortunate - Good
Variants: *Farrokh, Farrukh, Farukh*

Farood (Arabic)
Peerless - Unique

Farrad (Arabic)
Independent-minded - Original

Farraj (Arabic)
Happy - Joyous

Farrokhzad (Persian)
Blessed - Fortunate

Farrooh (Arabic)
Happy

Farsad (Persian)
Intelligent - Wise

Farshad (Persian)
Glory - Happiness - Joy
Variants: *Farshaad*

Farsheed (Persian)
Majestic

Fartash (Persian)
Being - Existence

Faruq (Arabic)
Differentiator - Distinguisher
Variants: *Farooq*

Farvardin (Persian)
Protector of Good People
Variants: *Farvardeen, Farwardin*

Farwa (Arabic)
Crown - Wealth
Variants: *Farua, Faruah, Farwah*

Farwan (Arabic)
Living in Luxury - Wealthy
Variants: *Faruaan, Faruan, Farwaan*

Faryar (Persian)
Magnificent - Majestic

Farzad (Persian)
High-born - Noble

Farzam (Persian)
Deserving - Worthy

Farzan (Persian)
Calm - Intelligent - Sensible - Wise
Variants: *Farzaan*

Farzin (Persian)
Vizier
Refers to a piece in the game of shtranj (an ancestor of the game Chess).
Variants: *Farzeen*

Faseeh (Arabic)
Eloquent - Fluent

Fateem (Arabic)
Weaned Off Breast Milk

Fateen (Arabic)
Brilliant - Intelligent

Fath (Arabic)
Beginning - Conquest - Guidance
The name Fath is mentioned in the Quran.

Fathan (Arabic)
Conqueror - Guide

Fathi (Arabic)
Conqueror - Guide

Fathuddin (Arabic)
Guidance of the Faith

Fathullah (Arabic)
God's Guidance - God's Help

Fatih (Arabic)
Conqueror - Initiator

Fatihi (Arabic)
Conqueror - Initiator

Fatin (Arabic)
Intelligent - Perceptive
Variants: *Faatin, Faten*

Fatnan (Arabic)
Clever - Keen - Skilled

Fatooh (Arabic)
Conqueror - Guide

Fattah (Arabic)
Conqueror - Victor
The name Fattah is mentioned in the Quran.

Fauz (Arabic)
Victory - Win
The name Fauz is mentioned in the Quran.
Variants: *Fawz, Fouz, Fowz*

Fawaid (Arabic)
Beneficial Things - Benefits

Fawaz (Arabic)
Successful - Winner
Variants: *Fawaaz, Fawwaaz, Fawwaz*

Fawiz (Arabic)
Successful - Winner

Fawzan (Arabic)
Successful
Variants: *Fauzaan, Fauzan, Fawzaan, Fouzan, Fowzan, Fozan*

Fayid (Arabic)
Benefiter - Winner

Fayyaz (Arabic)
Charitable - Doer of Good Deeds
Variants: *Fayaad, Fayaadh, Fayaaz, Fayad, Fayaz, Fayyaaz, Fayyad*

Fazeel (Arabic)
Excellent - Praiseworthy

Fazil (Arabic)
Admirable and Praiseworthy - Exalted - High Status - Noble - Sublime and Superb

Fazl (Arabic)
Courtesy - Noble Deed
The name Fazl is mentioned in the Quran.
Variants: *Fadhl, Fadl*

Fazli (Arabic)
Gracious - Praiseworthy

Fazluddin (Arabic)
Excellence of the Faith

Fazlullah (Arabic)
God's Bounty

Fazlurrahman (Arabic)
God's Bounty

Fedele (Italian)
Faithful
Italian form of Fidel.

Fedosi (Russian)
Gift from God - God-given
Russian form of Teodosio.
Variants: *Feodosi*

Fedot (Russian)
God-given
Russian form of Theodotos.

Fedya (Russian)
Gift from God
Pet form of Fyodor.

Fehredin (Turkish)
Supporter of Islam
Literally "pride of the faith".
Turkish form of the Arabic name Fakhruddin.

Felice (Italian)
Lucky
Italian form of Felix.

Feliciano (Italian, Portuguese, Spanish)
Lucky
Originally derived from Felix.

Felip (Catalan)
Horse-lover

Felipe (Spanish)
Horse-lover

Felix (Latin)
Lucky

Fenton (English)
Marsh Settlement
The name of various places and originally a surname.

Feofil (Russian)
Beloved of God - Lover of God
Russian form of Theophilus.

Feoras (Irish Gaelic)
Rock - Stone
Irish Gaelic form of Piers.

Ferapont (Russian)
Attendant - Servant - Worshiper
From Greek Therapōn.

Ferasat (Persian, Urdu)
Acumen - Foresight - Keenness - Vision
From Arabic Farasat.
Variants: *Feraasat*

Ferdinand (English, French, German)
Brave Voyager - Prepared Journeyer

Fergal (Irish)
Brave Man

Fergus (Irish, Scottish)
Man of Vigor

NAMES FOR BOYS

Fermin (Spanish)
Firm - Steadfast
Spanish form of Firmin.

Fernand (French)
Brave Voyager
French form of Ferdinand

Fernando (Portuguese, Spanish)
Brave Voyager
Spanish and Portuguese form of Ferdinand.

Fidel (Spanish)
Faithful

Fidelis (Latin)
Faithful

Fikr (Arabic)
Concept - Intellect - Thought

Fikrat (Arabic)
Concept - Idea - Thoughts
Turkish pronunciation of Fikrah.

Fikri (Arabic)
Conceptual - Perceptive - Thoughtful

Filat (Russian)
Guarded by God
From Greek Theophylaktos.

Filip (Czech, Polish)
Horse-lover
Polish and Czech form of Philip.

Fio (Italian)
Blossoming - Flourishing
Short form of Fiorenzo.

Firas (Arabic)
Skilled Horseman

Firhad (Arabic)
Full-bodied - Muscular

Firmin (French)
Firm - Steadfast

Firtan (Arabic)
Cool Fresh Water

Firuz (Persian)
Successful - Victor
Variants: *Feeroz, Feeruz, Firooz, Firouz*

Firwad (Arabic)
Independent-minded

Firyal (Persian)
One Who Has a Beautiful Neck

Fizzi (Arabic)
Silvery

Floyd (English)
Gray-haired
Variant of Lloyd.

Foroud (Persian)
Arrival

Forrest (English)
Woodland-dweller

Fortunato (Italian, Portuguese, Spanish)
Fortunate

Foruhar (Persian)
Protection - Shelter

Forutan (Persian)
Down to Earth - Humble

Foster (English)
Forester - Foster-parent - Saddle-tree Maker - Shearer

Francesco (Italian)
French - Frenchman

Francis (English)
French

Franco (Italian)
French

Frank (English)
Frankish
Referring to a member of the tribe of the Franks. The name is also used a short form of Francis, or an Anglicized form of Franco.

Franklin (English)
Frankish - Freeman

Franz (German)
French

Fred (English)
Peaceful Ruler
Short form of Frederick.

Frederick (English)
Peaceful Ruler
In Irish it is used as an Anglicized form of the Gaelic name Feardorcha, meaning "dark man".

Frederik (Danish, German)
Peaceful Ruler
Danish and Low German form of Frederick.

Fredrik (Swedish)
Peaceful Ruler
Swedish form of Frederick.

Frerik (Dutch)
Peaceful Ruler
Dutch form of Frederick.

Friedrich (German)
Peaceful Ruler

Fritz (German)
Peaceful Ruler
Pet form of Fritz.

Fuad (Arabic)
Conscience - Heart
The name Fuad is mentioned in the Quran in verse 28:10.
Variants: *Fo'ad, Foaad, Fowad, Fu'aad, Fu'ad, Fuaad, Fuwaad, Fuwad, Fwaad, Fwad*

Fuhaid (Arabic)
Little Leopard

Fuhaim (Arabic)
Comprehending - Intelligent

Fulaih (Arabic)
Successful

Fulaihan (Arabic)
Successful

Furaij (Arabic)
Relief

Furat (Arabic)
Cool Fresh Water
The name Furat is mentioned in the Quran.

Furhud (Arabic)
Full-bodied - Lion Cub

Fursat (Arabic, Turkish)
Opportunity - Right Time

Furud (Arabic)
Uniqueness

Futaih (Arabic)
Beginning - Conquest - Guidance

Futaim (Arabic)
Weaned Off Breast Milk

Futain (Arabic)
Brilliant - Intelligent

Futooh (Arabic)
Conquests

Fuzail (Arabic)
Excellent - Praiseworthy

Fuzailan (Arabic)
Excellent - Praiseworthy

Fuzzal (Arabic)
Excellent - Praiseworthy

Fyodor (Russian)
Gift from God

G

Gabriel (Biblical)
Man of God
Name of an angel, known as Jibreel in Arabic.

Galen (English)
Calm
Name of a Graeco-Roman writer Claudius Galenus.

Gene (English)
High-born - Noble

Geoffrey (English)
Man of Peace
Variants: *Jeffrey*

George (English)
Farmer

Ghaanim (Arabic)
Winner

Ghadeer (Arabic)
Little Stream

Ghadfan (Arabic)
Generous

Ghadi (Arabic)
Early Riser

Ghadif (Arabic)
Generous

Ghaffari (Arabic)
Forgiver - Forgiving

Ghafir (Arabic)
Forgiving
The name Ghafir is mentioned in the Quran.
Variants: *Ghafer*

Ghafiri (Arabic)
Forgiving

Ghafr (Arabic)
Forgiveness - Pardon

Ghafur (Arabic)
Ghafoor - Ghafour - Ghefur
The name Ghafur is mentioned in the Quran.

Ghafuri (Arabic)
Forgiving

Ghaidan (Arabic)
Delicate - Gentle

Ghailam (Arabic)
Handsome

Ghailum (Arabic)
Handsome

Ghaisullah (Arabic)
God's Bounty

Ghali (Arabic)
Dear - Respected - Valuable

Ghalib (Arabic)
Victor and Winner
The name Ghalib is mentioned in the Quran.

Ghalibi (Arabic)
Victor

Ghallab (Arabic)
Victor

Ghamidi (Arabic)
Sword Sheath

Ghamiq (Arabic)
Black - Dark

Ghaneem (Arabic)
Winner

Ghani (Arabic)
Needless - Rich - Self-sufficient
The name Ghani is mentioned in the Quran.
Variants: *Ghanee, Ghaniy, Ghany*

Ghanimi (Arabic)
Winner

Ghanum (Arabic)
Winner

Ghanyan (Arabic)
Needless - Wealthy

Gharab (Arabic)
Gold - Silver

Gharam (Arabic)
Devotion - Infatuation - Love
The name Gharam is mentioned in the Quran.

Ghareeb (Arabic)
Rare - Strange - Stranger
Variants: *Gharib*

Ghareer (Arabic)
Affluence - Good Manners - Inexperienced - Young

Gharibi (Arabic)
Stranger

Gharisullah (Arabic)
Young Tree Planted by God

Gharras (Arabic)
Tree Planter

Gharsan (Arabic)
Planter of Trees

Ghasasini (Arabic)
Handsome

Ghasharab (Arabic)
Lion

Ghasin (Arabic)
Beautiful - Handsome
Variants: *Ghaasin, Ghasen*

Ghasini (Arabic)
Beautiful

Ghaslan (Arabic)
Forest

Ghassan (Arabic)
Beautiful - Handsome
Variants: *Ghasan*

Ghassani (Arabic)
Handsome

Ghawalib (Arabic)
Victor

Ghawsaddin (Arabic)
Rescuer of the Faith

Ghayat (Arabic)
Aim - End Goal

Ghayid (Arabic)
Gentle - Soft

Ghayoor (Arabic)
Fervent - Protective

Ghays (Arabic)
Rain
The name Ghays is mentioned in the Quran.

Ghayyas (Arabic)
Doer of Good Deeds

Ghazanfar (Arabic)
Lion

Ghazanfari (Arabic)
Lion

Ghazeer (Arabic)
Plenty
Variants: *Ghazir*

Ghazi (Arabic)
Warrior

Ghaziyyat (Arabic)
Enduring - Patient

Ghazni (Arabic)
From Ghazni

Ghazwan (Arabic)
Attacker - Raider

Ghimd (Arabic)
Sword Sheath

Ghufran (Arabic)
Forgiveness - Pardon
The name Ghufran is mentioned in the Quran.

Ghulam (Arabic)
Boy - Young Male Servant
The name Ghulam is mentioned in the Quran.

Ghumair (Arabic)
Saffron

Ghumr (Arabic)
Saffron

Ghur (Arabic)
Fair-skinned - Honored Chief
Variants: *Ghorr*

Ghuraib (Arabic)
Gold - Silver

Ghurais (Arabic)
Newly Planted Tree

Ghurrah (Arabic)
Chief - Leader - Moonrise

Giacomo (Italian)
Heel-grabber
Italian form of James, originally from Greek Iakobos, which is the same as the Arabi name Ya`qub, a prophet mentioned in the Quran and the Bible.

Gianni (Italian)
God is Gracious
Contracted form of Giovanni, Italian form of John (Yahya in Arabic).

Gibran (Arabic)
Consolation - Recompense - Redress
Variants: *Gebran, Gibran, Giybrane, Gybran*

Gilbert (Dutch, English, Flemish, French)
Famous Pledge

Giles (English)
Young
Variants: *Gyles*

Gilles (French)
Young
French form of Giles.

Gillis (Danish, Dutch)
Young
Form of Giles.

Giorgio (Italian)
Farmer
Italian form of George.

Giovanni (Italian)
God is Gracious
Italian form of John.

H

Haaiz (Arabic)
Acquirer - Getter

Haayi (Arabic)
Bashful - Modest

Habaq (Arabic)
Basil - Ocimum
A type of plant.

Habbab (Arabic)
Affectionate - Loving

Habban (Arabic)
Loving

Habib (Arabic)
Beloved - Lover
Variants: *Habeeb*

Habibur Rahman (Arabic)
Loved by God
Variants: *Habeebur Rahman, Habiburrahman*

Habiri (Arabic)
Colorful Clouds

Habqar (Arabic)
Hail

Habr (Arabic)
Blessings - Happiness - Scholars - Virtuous

Habrur (Arabic)
Blessed - Living in Luxury
Variants: *Habroor*

Hadal (Arabic)
Mistletoe
A type of plant.

Haddal (Arabic)
Cooing Pigeon

Hadeed (Arabic)
Iron - Penetrating - Sharp
The name Hadeed is used in the Quran.
Variants: *Hadid*

Hadees (Arabic)
Hadeeth - Hadis - Hadith - Hedis
The name Hadees is mentioned in the Quran.

Hadi (Arabic)
Guide
The name *Hadi* is mentioned in the Quran.
Variants: *Haadi, Haadie, Hadie, Hady*

Hadir (Arabic)
Good-mannered

Hafeel (Arabic)
Plenty

Hafeesh (Arabic)
Candid - Loyal - True-hearted

Haffaz (Arabic)
Protective - Protector

Haib (Arabic)
Seriousness - Solemnity

Haidar (Arabic)
Lion
Variants: *Hayder, Hyder*

Haidaru (Arabic)
Lion

Hairaz (Arabic)
Guardian - Protector

Haizar (Arabic)
Lion

Hajid (Arabic)
Night-long Worshiper - Sleeper

Hajir (Arabic)
Emigrant - Excellent - Migrator

Hakeem (Arabic)
Decisive - Wise
The name *Hakeem* is mentioned in the Quran.
Variants: *Hakeim, Hakim, Hekeem, Hekeime, Hekeimm, Hekiem, Hekim, Hukeem*

Haleef (Arabic)
Ally

Haleej (Arabic)
Rain-Bearing Cloud

Halif (Arabic)
Oath-taker

Halil (Arabic)
Clear - Prominent

Hallam (Arabic)
Enduring - Forbearing - Lenient

Halooj (Arabic)
Cloud That Gives Off Lightning

Halul (Arabic)
Pouring - Torrential

Halyan (Arabic)
Adorned

Hamd (Arabic)
Praise
The name Hamd is mentioned in the Quran.
Variants: *Hemd*

Hamdan (Arabic)
Praise - Praiser
Variants: *Hamdaan*

Hamdat (Arabic, Turkish)
Praise
Turkish pronunciation of Hamdah.

Hamdi (Arabic)
Praise - Praiseworthy
Variants: *Hamdee*

Hamdun (Arabic)
Praise - Praiseworthy

Hameed (Arabic)
Laudable - Praiseworthy
The name Hameed is mentioned in the Quran.
Variants: *Hamed, Hamid*

Hameef (Arabic)
Virtuous

Hameez (Arabic)
Cute - Intelligent - Strong

Hamidat (Arabic)
Praiseworthy
Turkish pronunciation of Hamidah.

Hamim (Arabic)
Close Friend
The name Hamim is mentioned in the Quran.
Variants: *Hameem*

Hammad (Arabic)
Praiser
Variants: *Hamaad, Hamad*

Hammadah (Arabic)
Praiser
Variants: *Hamada*

Hammadi (Arabic)
Praiseworthy

Hammud (Arabic)
Praiseworthy

Hammuzah (Arabic)
Lion

Hamool (Arabic)
Enduring - Patient

Hanafi (Arabic)
Devout Believer - Monotheist

Hanan (Arabic)
Love - Sympathy
The name Hanan is mentioned in the Quran.
Variants: *Hanaan*

Hanif (Arabic)
Devout Believer - Monotheist
Variants: *Haneef*

Hanin (Arabic)
Affectionate - Sympathetic

Haq (Arabic)
Truth
The name Haq is mentioned in the Quran.
Variants: *Hak, Haqq, Haque*

Haqiq (Arabic)
Befitting - Worthy
Variants: *Haqeeq*

Haraz (Arabic)
Guardian - Protector
Variants: *Harraz*

Harees (Arabic)
Desirous - Eager - Keen
The name Harees is mentioned in the Quran.
Variants: *Haris*

Harith (Arabic)
Cultivator - Farmer - Lion
Variants: *Haares, Haareth Haris, Haaris, Haarith, Hares, Hareth, Harith, Harres, Harris*

Haritha (Arabic)
Cultivator - Farmer - Lion
Variants: *Haaretha, Haarethah, Haaritha, Haarithah, Haresah, Haretha, Harethah, Harithah*

Haroona (Arabic)
Mountain
Haroona is the Arabic feminine form of Harun. Harun is not an Arabic word, some Arabic sources say it means "mountain".
Variants: *Haroonah, Haruna, Harunah*

Harun (Arabic)
Mountain
The name Harun is mentioned in the Quran.
Variants: *Haroon, Haroun*

Harz (Arabic)
Guardianship - Protection

Harzan (Arabic)
Guardian - Protector

Hasab (Arabic)
Generosity - Good Deed - Lineage - Pedigree

Hasan (Arabic)
Gentle - Good - Good-mannered - Handsome - Virtuous
The name Hasan is mentioned in the Quran.

Haseef (Arabic)
Judicious - Reasonable
Variants: *Hassif*

Haseem (Arabic)
Assiduous - Diligent - Persevering
Variants: *Hasim*

Haseen (Arabic)
Handsome
Variants: *Hasin*

Hasees (Arabic)
Perceptive - Sensitive
Variants: *Hasis*

NAMES FOR BOYS

Hashaam (Arabic)
Breaker
Variants: *Hashim*

Hashim (Arabic)
Breaker - Destroyer of Evil
Variants: *Haashem, Haashim, Hashem*

Hasil (Arabic)
Acquirer - Harvester - Producer

Hasim (Arabic)
Conclusive - Decisive - Determinate

Hasin (Arabic)
Handsome

Hasoun (Arabic)
Chaste - Virtuous

Hassan (Arabic)
Charitable - Good-mannered - Handsome
Not to be confused with Hasan (name of one of the Prophet's grandsomes PBUH).
Variants: *Hasaan, Hassaan, Hessan*

Hassun (Arabic)
Handsome
Variants: *Hasoon*

Hatim (Arabic)
Decisive - Wise
Variants: *Haatim, Hatem*

Hattab (Arabic)
Woodcutter

Hattal (Arabic)
Heavy Rain

Hawari (Arabic)
Apostle - Follower - Supporter

Hawas (Arabic)
Brave

Hawis (Arabic)
Brave

Hayat (Arabic)
Life
The name Hayat is mentioned in the Quran.
Variants: *Hayaat*

Hayl (Arabic)
Heaped Sand

Hayyan (Arabic)
Alive - Awake - Dignified
n
Variants: *Hayaan, Hayan, Hayyaan*

Hayyee (Arabic)
Bsahful - Modest

Hayyin (Arabic)
Facilitated - Lenient
The name Hayyin is mentioned in the Quran.

Hazar (Arabic)
Cautious - Vigilant
Variants: *Hazzar*

Hazeem (Arabic)
Continuous Rain - Thunder
Variants: *Hazim*

Hazeem (Arabic)
Intelligent - Wise

Haziq (Arabic)
Brilliant - Excellent - Sagacious - Skillful
Variants: *Haazeq, Haaziq, Hadeq, Hadiq*

Hazir (Arabic)
Prepared - Present - Ready
The name Hazir is mentioned in the Quran.

Hazzar (Arabic)
Generous - Laughing

Hedi (Kurdish)
Calm - Serene
Variants: *Hedy*

Hemin (Kurdish)
Calm
Variants: *Hemn*

Herish (Kurdish)
Attack - Onslaught
Variants: *Hersh*

Hezha (Kurdish)
Respected

Hibr (Arabic)
Ink - Scholar - Virtuous
Variants: *Hebr*

Hikma (Arabic)
Wisdom
The name Hikma is mentioned in the Quran.
Variants: *Hekma, Hekmah, Hikmah*

Hikmat (Arabic)
Wisdom
Variants: *Hekmat, Hikmet*

Hilal (Arabic)
Beginning of Rain - Crescent Moon

Hilf (Arabic)
Alliance - Treaty

Hilmi (Arabic)
Enduring - Forbearing - Lenient

Himaa (Arabic)
Harbor - Haven - Hideaway

Himayat (Arabic, Turkish)
Care - Defense - Protection - Safekeeping
Turkish pronunciation of Himayah.

Hirad (Persian)
Amicable - Bringer of Good News - Friendly

Hirbad (Persian)
Mentor - Teacher

Hisham (Arabic)
Gracious - Honorable - Noble
Variants: *Heshaam, Hesham, Hishaam*

Hishmat (Arabic, Turkish)
Modesty - Virtue
Variants: *Heshmat*

Hiwa (Kurdish)
Hope

Hobb (Arabic)
Affectionate - Love
The name Hobb is mentioned in the Quran.

Hoshang (Kurdish)
Awareness - Intelligence
From Persian Houshang.

Hoshiar (Kurdish)
Aware - Bright - Intelligent
From Persian Houshiar.
Variants: *Hoshyaar, Hoshyar, Hushyaar*

Houmaan (Persian)
Good-hearted - Having Good Thoughts
Variants: *Homan, Houman, Humaan, Human*

Houman (Persian)
Good-hearted - Having Good Thoughts
Variants: *Human*

Houshang (Persian)
Awareness - Intelligence
Variants: *Hooshang, Hushang*

Houshiar (Persian)
Aware - Bright - Intelligent
Variants: *Hooshiar, Houshyaar, Hushiar, Hushyar*

Hubaibi (Arabic)
Beloved

Hubair (Arabic)
Ink - Little Scholar
Variants: *Hobair*

Hubbee (Arabic)
Loving

Hufaiz (Arabic)
Protector
Variants: *Hofaidh*

Hulm (Arabic)
Forbearance - Patience

Humaid (Arabic)
Praise

Humaidan (Arabic)
Praiseworthy

Humaisun (Arabic)
Brave

Humam (Arabic)
Elite - Honored - Noble

Hunain (Arabic)
Hunain is the name of a valley between at-Taif and Mecca in which a battle took place. The literal meaning of the word is not known.
Variants: *Honain, Honayn, Hunayn*

Huraira (Arabic)
Cat - Kitten
Variants: *Horaira, Horairah, Hurairah, Hurayrah*

Husaim (Arabic)
Assiduous - Diligent - Persevering
Variants: *Hosaim*

Husam (Arabic)
Sharp Sword - Sword Blade
Variants: *Hosam*

Husni (Arabic)
Good - Handsome
Variants: *Hosnee, Hosni, Husnee, Husny*

Hussein (Arabic)
Gentle - Handsome - Virtuous
Variants: *Hosain, Hosein, Husain, Husein, Hussain*

Hutaim (Arabic)
Judge - Pure
Variants: *Hotaim*

Huveida (Persian)
Apparent - Clear - Lucid - Prominent
Variants: *Hovaida, Hovaidaa, Hoveida, Huveidaa, Huweidaa, Hwaida, Hwaidaa*

Huyai (Arabic)
Alive - Flourishing

Huzaifah (Arabic)
Sheep
Variants: *Hozaifa, Hudhaifa*

Huzair (Arabic)
Laughter

I

Ibad (Arabic)
Servants of Allah
The name Ibad is mentioned in the Quran in verse 20:77.
Variants: *Ebaad, Ebad, Ibaad*

Ibadah (Arabic)
Worship
The name Ibadah is mentioned in the Quran.

Ibadullah (Arabic)
Worshipers

Ibhar (Arabic)
Breadth - Graciousness
Variants: *Ebhar, Ibhaar*

Ibrahim (Arabic)
The name Ibrahim is mentioned in the Quran. It is the name of a Prophet, the same as Biblical Abraham, who is the ancestor of the prophets Isaac, Jacob, Joseph, Moses, John, Jesus and Muhammad (peace be upon them).
Variants: *Ebraheem, Ebraheim, Ebrahim, Ibraaheem, Ibraheem, Ibrahem*

Ibreez (Arabic)
Gold
Variants: *Ebreez, Ebriz, Ibriz*

Ibtihal (Arabic)
Humble Prayer - Supplication
Variants: *Ebtehal*

Ibtisam (Arabic)
Smile
Variants: *Ebetesam, Ebtesaam, Ibtesam, Ibtisaam*

Idris (Arabic)
Idris is the name of one of the prophets mentioned in the Quran. The meaning of the name is not known for certain.
Variants: *Edrees, Edris, Idrees*

Iffat (Arabic)
Chastity - Modesty
Turkish pronunciation of Iffah.

Ifra (Arabic)
Enjoining of Good
Variants: *Efra, Efraa, Ifraa*

Ihdaf (Arabic)
Closeness - Proximity
Variants: *Ihdaaf*

Ihkam (Arabic)
Decisiveness - Mastery
Variants: *Ehkaam, Ehkam, Ihkaam*

Ihlal (Arabic)
Clarity - Radiance
Variants: *Ehlal*

Ihram (Arabic)
Prohibition
The word ihram is used to refer to a pilgrim's entering into a state of prohibition once he starts his pilgrimage, in which many things are prohibited to him, such as hunting or wearing perfume.

Ihsan (Arabic)
Generosity - Good Deeds - Graciousness - Kindness
The name Ihsan is mentioned in the Quran.
Variants: *Ehsaan, Ehsan, Ihsaan, Ihsan*

Ihtiram (Arabic)
Consideration - Esteem - Regard
Variants: *Ehteram, Ehtiram, Ihteram*

Ijlal (Arabic)
Greatness - Majesty
Variants: *Ejlaal, Ejlal, Ijlaal*

Ikha (Arabic)
Brotherhood - Friendship
Variants: *Ekha, Ekhaa, Ikhaa, Ikhaa'*

Ikhlas (Arabic)
Faithfulness - Loyalty - Sincerity
Variants: *Ekhlaas, Ekhlas, Ikhlaas*

Ikhwan (Arabic)
Brothers
The name Ikhwan is mentioned in the Quran.
Variants: *Ekhuan, Ekhwan, Ikhuan, Ikhwaan*

Ikleel (Arabic)
Crown
Variants: *Iklil*

Ikrimah (Arabic)
Female Pigeon
Variants: *Ikrima*

Ilan (Arabic)
Announcement - Proclamation
Variants: *Elaan, Ilaan*

Ilhan (Arabic)
Eloquence
Variants: *Elhaan, Elhan, Ilhaan*

Ilm (Arabic)
Knowledge - Science
The name Ilm is mentioned in the Quran.

Ilya (Arabic)
Great - High in Status - Noble
Variants: *Elia, Eliah, Ilia, Iliah, Ilyah*

Imad (Arabic)
Pillar - Supporter
The name Imad is mentioned in

the Quran.
Variants: *Emaad, Emad, Imaad*

Imad ad-Din (Arabic)
Supporter of Islam
Literally means "pillar of the faith".
Variants: *Imad Uddin, Imaduddin*

Imamuddin (Arabic)
Supporter of Islam
Literally "leader of the faith".
Variants: *Imam Uddin*

Imara (Arabic)
Construction - Revival - Visit
The name Imara is mentioned in the Quran.
Variants: *Emara, Emarah, Imaara, Imaarah, Imarah*

Imdad (Arabic)
Help - Support
Variants: *Emdad, Imdaad*

Imhal (Arabic)
Forbearance - Leniency
Variants: *Emhal, Imhaal*

Imran (Arabic)
The name *Imran* is mentioned in the Quran. It is the name of the father of *Mariam* (Mary), mother of Prophet Isa (Jesus), peace be upon them.
Variants: *Emraan, Emran, Imraan*

Imtiaz (Arabic)
Distinction - Prominence - Superiority
Variants: *Imtyaz*

Imtiazuddin (Arabic)
Supporter of Islam
Literally "superiority of the faith".
Variants: *Imtyaz Uddin*

Imtisal (Arabic)
Adoration - Imitation - To Follow
Variants: *Emtisal*

Inab (Arabic)
Grape
The name Inab is mentioned in the Quran.

Inam (Arabic)
Blessings - God's Favors
Variants: *Enaam, In'am, Inaam*

Inam ul Haq (Arabic)
Gift from God
Literally "blessing from al-Haq". al-Haq means "the Truth" and is one of the names of God.

Inamurrahman (Arabic)
Gift from God
Variants: *Inamur Rahman*

Inbihaj (Arabic)
Cheerfulness - Delight - Mirth
Variants: *Enbihaj, Inbehaaj*

Inbisat (Arabic)
Cheerfulness - Joyfulness - Relaxation
Variants: *Enbisat, Inbesaat*

Infisal (Arabic)
Distance - Divergence - Separation
Variants: *Infesal*

Inhal (Arabic)
Pouring of Rain
Variants: *Enhal*

Injah (Arabic)
Success
Variants: *Injaah*

Injeel (Arabic)
Messenger - The Gospels
The name Injeel is mentioned in the Quran.
Variants: *Enjil*

Ins (Arabic)
Relaxation - Tranquility
Variants: *Ens*

Insaf (Arabic)
Fairness - Justice
Variants: *Insaaf*

Inshad (Arabic)
Chanting - Singing
Variants: *Enshad, Inshaad*

Inshiraf (Arabic)
Glory - Greatness - Honor
Variants: *Insheraaf*

Insijam (Arabic)
Harmony - Symmetry
Variants: *Ensejam, Insejam*

Intiha (Arabic)
Completion - Conclusion - End
Variants: *Intehaa*

Intisar (Arabic)
Triumph - Victory
Variants: *Entisar, Intesaar*

Intishal (Arabic)
Healing - Recovery
Variants: *Entishal, Intishaal*

Intizar (Arabic)
Anticipation - Expectation - Wait
Variants: *Intezaar*

Iqbal (Arabic)
Boldness - Success
Variants: *Eqbaal, Eqbal, Iqbaal*

Iqdam (Arabic)
Boldness
Variants: *Eqdam*

Iqleem (Arabic)
Country - Land - Region - Zone
Variants: *Eqlim, Iqlim*

Iqyan (Arabic)
Gold

Iraj (Persian)
Helper of the Ari People
The Ari people are the people of ancient Persia, also known as Aryans.

Iraq (Arabic)
River Bank - Shore

Irfan (Arabic)
Wisdom - Enlightenment
Variants: *Erfaan, Erfan, Irfaan*

Irmas (Arabic)
Strong - Tough

Irtiqa (Arabic)
Ascension - Ascent - Improvement - Promotion
Variants: *Ertiqa, Ertiqaa, Irteka, Irteqa, Irtika, Irtiqaa*

Isa (Arabic)
God is Salvation
Originally from Hebrew. Arabic form of "Jesus". The name Isa is mentioned in the Quran.
Variants: *Eesa, Eisa, Esa, Esaa, Eysa, Eysaa, Issa*

Isam (Arabic)
Bond - Connection - Promise
Variants: *Esaam, Esam, Isaam*

Ishraq (Arabic)
Daybreak - Emergence - Illumination - Sunrise -
Vividness
The name Ishraq is mentioned in the Quran.
Variants: *Eshraaq, Eshraq, Ishraaq*

Iskandar (Arabic)
Defender of Humanity
Iskandar is the Arabic form of Alexander.
Variants: *Eskander, Iskander*

Islam (Arabic)
Submission
The name Islam is mentioned in the Quran.

Ismaeel (Hebrew)
One Who Hears God
Ismaeel is one of the prophets mentioned in the Quran, son of prophet Ibrahim (Abraham).
Variants: *Ismail*

Israr (Arabic)
Determination - Insistence - Resolve

Istiqlal (Arabic)
Independence - Sovereignty
Variants: *Esteqlal, Estiqlal, Istiqlaal*

Itqan (Arabic)
Mastery - Proficiency - Skill
Variants: *Etqaan, Etqan, Itqaan, Itqan*

Iwazallah (Arabic)
God's Restitution

Iyad (Arabic)
Able - Capable - Powerful
Variants: *Eiaad, Eiaade, Eiad, Eyaad, Eyad, Iyaad*

Iyadi (Arabic)
Consoler - Visitor of the Sick
Variants: *Eyaadi*

Iyan (Arabic)
Era - Time
The name Iyan is mentioned in the Quran. It is an alternate reading of the word Ayyan used in verse 27:65.
Variants: *Eyaan, Eyan, Eyyan, Iyaan, Iyyan*

Iyas (Arabic)
Replacement - Restitution
Variants: *Eyas, Iyaas*

Izaad (Arabic)
Advocacy - Loyalty

Izaan (Arabic)
Acceptance - Obedience - Submission
Variants: *Ezaan, Iz'an*

Izfaar (Arabic)
Help - Support
Literally "to help someone attain victory".
Variants: *Ezfaar, Ezfar, Izfar*

Izzaddin (Arabic)
Honor of the Faith

Izzat (Arabic)
Greatness - Majesty - Might

This page intentionally left blank

J

Jaamil (Arabic)
Handsome

Jaar (Arabic)
Neighbor
Variants: *Jar*

Jaari (Arabic)
Neighborly
Variants: *Jary*

Jabbad (Arabic)
Attractive - Charming

Jabir (Arabic)
Fixer - Improver - Mender
Variants: *Jaaber, Jaabir, Jaber*

Jaboor (Arabic)
Mender - Strong

Jabr (Arabic)
Brave

Jabran (Arabic)
Brave

Jabreel (Arabic)
Gabriel
Variant of Jibreel.

Jadir (Arabic)
Spring Bloom - Spring Sprout
Variants: *Jader*

Jadud (Arabic)
Fortunate - Great - Lucky

Jadur (Arabic)
First Sprout of Spring

Jaed (Arabic)
Generous - Gracious - Torrential Rain
Variants: *Jaaed*

Jafar (Arabic)
River - Stream

Jafaran (Arabic)
Two Rivers

Jafur (Arabic)
River

Jahan (Persian)
World
Variants: *Jahaan, Jehaan, Jehan, Jihaan, Jihan*

Jahd (Arabic)
Strife - Struggle

Jahhad (Arabic)
Striver

Jahid (Arabic)
Striver

Jalee (Arabic)
Clear - Lucid

Jalib (Arabic)
Attractive - Captivating
Variants: *Jaaleb, Jaalib, Jaleb*

Jalis (Arabic)
Sitter

Jalwan (Arabic)
Discoverer of the Truth

Jamal (Arabic)
Beauty
The name Jamal is mentioned in the Quran.
Variants: *Jamaal*

Jameelu (Arabic)
Beautiful - Handsome

Jamiloun (Arabic)
Handsome

Janis (Arabic)
Ripe Fruit

Jaram (Arabic)
Date (fruit) - Kernel - Seed

Jaran (Arabic)
Ally - Neighbor
Variants: *Jaaran*

Jarum (Arabic)
Big-bodied - Fruit Collector

Jaseer (Arabic)
Bold - Brave

Jasim (Arabic)
Hulking - Muscular - Strong
Variants: *Jasem*

Jasir (Arabic)
Bold - Brave
Variants: *Jaser*

Jassar (Arabic)
Bold - Brave

Javan (Persian)
Young

Javanmard (Persian)
Generous - Selfless

Javanshir (Persian)
Lion-like

Jawabir (Arabic)
Mender - Orphan's Caretaker

Jawad (Arabic)
Generous - Gracious - Noble
Variants: *Javad, Jawaad, Jewaad, Jewad*

Jawd (Arabic)
Torrential Rain

Jawdat (Arabic)
Goodness - Virtue

Jawhar (Arabic)
Essence - Jewel - Precious Stone
Variants: *Johar, Jouhar, Jowhar*

Jayed (Arabic)
Generous - Giving

Jayesh (Arabic)
Night Traveler

Jayyid (Arabic)
Good - Gracious

Jazaa (Arabic)
Recompense - Reward
The name Jazaa is mentioned in the Quran.
Variants: *Jaza, Jaza', Jeza, Jezaa*

Jazal (Arabic)
Delight - Happiness

Jazal (Arabic)
Generous - Great

Jazee (Arabic)
Advocate
Variants: *Jazi*

Jazeel (Arabic)
Great - Tremendous

Jazim (Arabic)
Determined - Resolute
Variants: *Jazem*

Jazoon (Arabic)
Advocate
Variants: *Jazun*

Jazub (Arabic)
Attractive - Charming

Jerome (English)
Sacred Name

Jesse (English)
Gift

Jibal (Arabic)
Mountains
The name Jibal is mentioned in the Quran.
Variants: *Jebaal, Jebal, Jibaal*

Jibillah (Arabic)
Nation
The name Jibillah is mentioned in the Quran.

Jibraeel (Arabic)
Gabriel
Variant of Jibreel.

Jibran (Arabic)
Consolation - Recompense - Redress
Variants: *Jebraan, Jebran, Jibraan*

Jibreel (Arabic)
Gabriel
Name of the angel of revelation. The name Jibreel is used in the Quran.

Jibriyal (Arabic)
Gabriel
Variant of Jibreel.

Jihad (Arabic)
Struggle
Jihad is mentioned in the Quran.
Variants: *Jehaad, Jehad, Jihaad*

Jim (English)
Heel-grabber
Short form of James (Ya`qub in Arabic, a prophet).

Joan (English)
God is Gracious
Used as a feminine of John (Yahya in Arabic).

Job (Biblical)
Persecuted
Name of a prophet, known as Ayyub in the Quran.

Jodd (Arabic)
Beach - Coast - Fortunate - Side

Joel (Biblical)
Yahweh is God
Name of a number of characters in the Bible. The meaning is acceptable for Muslims since Yahweh is a synonym of Allah, therefore the name is stressing the fact that Allah is the only true deity.

Johan (German, Scandinavian)
God is Gracious
Form of John.

Johann (German)
God is Gracious
Form of John.

Johd (Arabic)
Strife - Struggle

John (English)
God is Gracious
From Latin Johannes, referring to a Biblical prophet, the same as the Quranic prophet Yahya.

Jonah (Biblical)
Dove
Name of a Biblical prophet, the same as the Quranic prophet Yunus.

Jonathan (Biblical)
God Has Given
Name of several characters in the Bible.

Joris (Dutch, Frisian)
Farmer - Watchful
Form of Georgius or Gregorius.

Josef (Czech, Dutch, German, Scandinavian)
God Shall Add
Form of Jospeh.

NAMES FOR BOYS

Joseph (English, French)
God Shall Add
Name of the son of prophet Jacob/Ya`qub, known as Yusuf in the Quran.

Joshua (Biblical)
God is Salvation
A Biblical character, name of an assistant of prophet Moses (Musa).

Josiah (Biblical)
God Heals
Name of a king of Judah and an ancestor of prophet Jesus (Isa) son of Mary.

Joud (Arabic)
Generosity - Graciousness

Jozafat (Polish)
God Has Judged
From Greek Josaphat, name of a Biblical virtuous king of Judah.

Juan (Spanish)
God is Gracious
Spanish form of John.

Juanito (English)
God is Gracious
Pet form of Juan.

Juayfir (Arabic)
Stream

Jubair (Arabic)
Mender - Unbreaker
Variants: *Jobair, Jobayr, Jubayr*

Jubran (Arabic)
Consolation - Recompense - Redress
Variants: *Jobraan, Jobran, Jubraan*

Juhani (Finnish)
God is Gracious
Finnish form of John.

Jules (English)
Youthful
French form of Julius, or English pet form of Julian.

Julian (English)
Youthful
Derivative of Julius.

Julien (French)
Youthful
French form of Julian.

Julio (Spanish)
Youthful
Spanish form of Julius.

Julius (Latin)
Youthful

Of uncertain derivation, but some sources say it means "youthful".

Jumail (Arabic)
Nightingale

Jumal (Arabic)
Handsome

Junada (Arabic)
Helper - Soldier - Warrior
Variants: *Junaada, Junadah*

Junaid (Arabic)
Soldier - Warrior
Variants: *Jonaid, Jonayd, Junayd*

Juraiw (Arabic)
Cub

Jusair (Arabic)
Bold - Brave

Jusam (Arabic)
Hulking - Muscular

Justin (English)
Fair - Just

Juwaid (Arabic)
Generous - Gracious

This page intentionally left blank

K

Kaabir (Arabic)
Great - Powerful

Kaapo (Finnish)
Man of God
Finnish form of Gabriel.

Kaarim (Arabic)
Excellent - Generous - Gracious - Noble
Variants: *Kaarem, Karem, Karim*

Kaarle (Finnish)
Free Man
Finnish form of Charles.

Kabir (Arabic)
Chief - Great - Powerful
The name Kabir is mentioned in the Quran.
Variants: *Kabeer, Kebir*

Kafi (Arabic)
Sufficient
The name Kafi is mentioned in the Quran.

Kahal (Arabic)
One Who Has Beautiful Dark Eyelids

Kahul (Arabic)
One Who Has Beautiful Black Eyes

Kalamuddin (Arabic)
Supporter of Islam
Literally "speech of the faith", meaning "orator of the faith".

Kalle (Swedish)
Free Man
Pet form of Karl.

Kamal (Arabic)
Completeness - Perfection - Wholeness
Variants: *Kamaal, Kemaal, Kemal*

Kamaluddeen (Arabic)
Virtuous
Literally means "perfection of the faith".

Kamayel (Arabic)
Complete - Perfect - Whole

Kameel (Arabic)
Complete - Perfect - Whole

Kamil (Arabic)
Complete - Perfect - Whole
Variants: *Kaamel, Kaamil, Kamel*

Kamilan (Arabic)
Complete - Perfect - Whole

Kamlan (Arabic)
Complete - Perfect - Whole

Kamush (Arabic)
Bold - Brave

Kanz (Arabic)
Treasure
The name Kanz is used in the Quran.
Variants: *Kenz, Kinz*

Kanzuddin (Arabic)
Treasure of the Faith

Karam (Arabic)
Generosity - Graciousness

Karamullah (Arabic)
God's Graciousness

Karawan (Arabic)
Curlew
A type of bird.

Kareem (Arabic)
Excellent - Generous - Gracious - Noble
The name Kareem is mentioned in the Quran.
Variants: *Karim, Kerim*

Karel (Czech, Dutch)
Free Man
Form of Charles.

Karl (German, Scandinavian)
Free Man
Form of Charles.

Karman (Arabic)
Gracious

Karol (Polish)
Free Man
Polish form of Charles.

Karram (Arabic)
Generous - Gracious

Karrum (Arabic)
Gracious

Kashaaf (Arabic)
Discoverer - Finder
Variants: *Kashshaf, Keshaf*

Kasir (Arabic)
Plenty

Kasoor (Arabic)
Plenty

Kasran (Arabic)
Plenty

Kassab (Arabic)
Earner - Winner

Kathir (Arabic)
Plenty
The name Kathir is mentioned in the Quran.
Variants: *Kaseer, Kasir, Khatheer*

Katib (Arabic)
Intellectual - Scholar - Writer
The name Katib is mentioned in the Quran in verse 2:283.
Variants: *Kaateb, Kaatib, Kateb*

Kattam (Arabic)
Keeper of Secrets

Kawnain (Arabic)
Beings - Existences - Universes

Kayani (Arabic)
Kingly - Royal
Variants: *Kaiani, Kayaani, Kayany*

Kazim (Arabic)
One Who Controls His Own Anger

Kean (Irish)
Ancient
From Gaelic Cian.
Variants: *Keane*

Kelan (Irish)
Slender

Kelemen (Hungarian)
Merciful
Form of Clement.

Kemp (English)
Athlete - Wrestler

Kenelm (English)
Bold Protection - Keen Helmet

Kennard (English)
Bold Guard

Kenya (Russian)
Innocent
Pet form of Innokenti.

Kevin (English, Irish)
Beloved - Comely

Keyan (Persian)
King - Powerful
Variants: *Keyaan, Keyaan, Keyan, Kiaan, Kian, Kian, Kyaan, Kyan*

Keyan (Arabic)
Being - Existence

Khaalud (Arabic)
Immortal

Khabir (Arabic)
Experienced - Expert
The name Khabir is mentioned in the Quran.
Variants: *Khabeer*

Khadamullah (Arabic)
Servant of God

Khadeej (Arabic)
Born Preterm
Variants: *Khadij*

Khafid (Arabic)
Agile - Fast

Khafif (Arabic)
Nimble - Sprightly
Variants: *Khafeef*

Khailad (Arabic)
Immortal

Khair (Arabic)
Good - Wealth
The name *Khair* is mentioned in the Quran.
Variants: *Cair, Caire, Kaire, Kayr, Kayre, Keir, Keire, Ker, Kere, Keyr, Keyre, Khaire, Khayr, Khayre, Kheir, Kheire, Kher, Khere, Kheyr, Kheyre*

Khairullah (Arabic)
God's Blessings

Khaldan (Arabic)
Immortal

Khaldun (Arabic)
Immortal
Variants: *Khaldoon*

Khaleed (Arabic)
Immortal

Khaleef (Arabic)
Leader - Successor
Variants: *Kaleef, Khaleif, Khalif*

Khaleefa (Arabic)
Leader - Successor
The name Khaleefa is mentioned in the Quran.
Variants: *Kalifa, Kalifah, Khaleefah, Khalifa, Khalifah*

Khaleel (Arabic)
Companion - Friend
The name *Khaleel* is mentioned in the Quran.
Variants: *Helil, Kaleel, Kalil, Khalil, Khelil*

Khalees (Arabic)
Brave - Skilled - Vigilant

Khalfun (Arabic)
Successor - Virtuous Son

Khali (Arabic)
Bygone - Solitary

Khalidin (Arabic)
Immortal Ones
The name Khalidin is mentioned in the Quran.
Variants: *Khalideen*

Khalidun (Arabic)
Everlasting - Immortal
The name Khalidun is mentioned in the Quran.
Variants: *Khaledun, Khalidoon*

Khalifat (Arabic)
Successor

NAMES FOR BOYS

Khalis (Arabic)
Pure
The name Khalis is mentioned in the Quran.
Variants: *Khaalis, Khales*

Khalud (Arabic)
Immortal

Khaluq (Arabic)
Good-mannered

Khaseeb (Arabic)
Fertile - Fruitful - Productive

Khashayar (Persian)
Brave

Khassab (Arabic)
Blessed
Variants: *Khasaab*

Khassal (Arabic)
Victor

Khateeb (Arabic)
Orator - Speaker

Khateer (Arabic)
Dangerous - Honorable - Important - Noble
Variants: *Khatir*

Khatir (Arabic)
Heart - Idea - Notion
Variants: *Khaater*

Khattar (Arabic)
Lion - Perfume-maker

Khawatir (Arabic)
Ideas - Notions - Thoughts

Khawli (Arabic)
Chief - Foreman

Khayal (Arabic)
Fantasy - Imagination - Vision

Khayyar (Arabic)
Good - Virtuous

Khayyir (Arabic)
Good - Noble - Virtuous
Variants: *Khayir, Khayyer*

Khazeer (Arabic)
Greenery - Sea

Khazran (Arabic)
Green-colored - Soft Grass

Kheer (Arabic)
Generosity - Honor - Virtue

Khidr (Arabic)
Green
Name of a personality mentioned in the Quran (not by name though), who met prophet Musa (Moses) and taught him.
Variants: *Kheder, Khedr, Khezer, Khezr, Khidhr, Khidir, Khizr*

Khilal (Arabic)
Companionship - Friendship
The name Khilal is mentioned in the Quran in verse 14:31.
Variants: *Kelal, Khelaal, Khelal, Khilaal, Khylal, Kilal*

Khisb (Arabic)
Blessedness - Growth
Variants: *Khesb*

Khitab (Arabic)
Dispatch - Letter - Speech

Khitam (Arabic)
Final - Finale - Seal

Khiyar (Arabic)
Doers of Good Deeds - Virtuous Ones

Khorshid (Persian)
Sun

Khoshnud (Persian)
Cheerful - Content

Khosrau (Arabic, Persian)
King
Variants: *Khosro, Khosrou*

Khoulad (Arabic)
Immortal

Khufaf (Arabic)
Clever - Intelligent
Khufaf is an Arabic name for boys that means "clever", "intelligent".

Khufair (Arabic)
Guardianship - Modesty - Protection

Khulaid (Arabic)
Immortal

Khulaif (Arabic)
Successor

Khulaifah (Arabic)
Successor

Khulum (Arabic)
Devoted Friend

Khuml (Arabic)
Devoted Friend

Khusaib (Arabic)
Fruitfulness - Growth - Productivity

Khusaif (Arabic)
Dust-colored

Khushdel (Arabic)
Happy - Joyful

Khuwailid (Arabic)
Immortal

Khuzaimah (Arabic)
Gabal Elba Dragon Tree
A type of tree.

Kibaar (Arabic)
Great Ones Leaders

Kifah (Arabic)
Strife - Struggle
Variants: *Kefaah, Kefah, Kifaah*

Kifayatullah (Arabic)
God's Contentment
Contentment that is bestowed by God.

Kifl (Arabic)
Example - Fortune - Luck
The name Kifl is mentioned in the Quran.

Kinan (Arabic)
Covering - Veil - Wrap

Kindi (Arabic)
Mountain-dweller

King (English)
King

Kirill (Russian)
Lord
Russian form of Cyril.

Kiswa (Arabic)
Clothing - Garment
Refers to the black silk cloth that covers the Kaaba in Mecca, Saudi Arabia.
Variants: *Keswa, Keswah, Kiswah*

Klaas (Dutch)
Of the Victorious People
Dutch form of Claus.

Klaus (German)
Of the Victorious People
Variant of Claus.

Klemens (Danish, German, Polish, Swedish)
Merciful
Form of Clement.

Klimek (Polish)
Merciful
Pet form of Klemens.

Kliment (Czech, Russian)
Merciful
Russian and Czech form of Clement.

Kohl (Arabic)
Kohl

Kolya (Russian)
Of the Victorious People
Pet form of Nikolai.

Konrad (German, Polish)
Counsel

Kort (Dutch)
Counsel
Dutch form of Kurt.

Kourosh (Persian)
Radiant - Sun-like
Kourosh is known as Cyrus in English.
Variants: *Koorosh, Korush, Kurush*

Kuba (Czech, Polish)
Heel-grabber
Pet form of Jakub (equivalent to Jacob and Ya`qub in Arabic).

Kufah (Arabic)
Mound of Sand

Kumail (Arabic)
Complete - Perfect - Whole
Variants: *Komail, Komayl, Komeil, Kumayl, Kumeil*

Kundas (Arabic)
Magpie
A type of bird.

Kuraiman (Arabic)
Gracious

Kuram (Arabic)
Gracious Ones - Honorable Ones

Kurt (German)
Counsel
Contracted form of Konrad.
Variants: *Curt*

Kyle (English)
Narrow Strait
From a Scottish surname, from the name of a region.

NAMES FOR BOYS

L

Laaiq (Arabic)
Eligible - Qualified - Suitable

Labeeb (Arabic)
Intelligent - Sagacious

Labis (Arabic)
Coverer - Wearer

Lahiq (Arabic)
Following - Reaching

Lahiq (Arabic)
White-colored

Laidan (Arabic)
Gentle - Good-mannered

Lail (Arabic)
Night
The name Lail is mentioned in the Quran.
Variants: *Layl, Leil, Leyl*

Lailan (Arabic)
Two Nights

Laith (Arabic)
Lion

Laithi (Arabic)
Brave - Lion-like

Lajos (Hungarian)
Famous Warrior
Hungarian form of Louis.

Lamaan (Arabic)
Glimmer - Shine

Lambert (Dutch, English, French, German)
Famous Land

Lameek (Arabic)
One Who Has Beautiful Dark Eyelids

Lamees (Arabic)
Smooth - Soft - Sun

Lamis (Arabic)
Toucher

Latafat (Arabic)
Gentleness - Kindness

Lateef (Arabic)
Gentle - Kind
The name Lateef is mentioned in the Quran.
Variants: *Latif*

Latifi (Arabic)
Gentle - Kind

Launo (Finnish)
Of the Victorious People
Finnish form of Claus.

Lawahiz (Arabic)
Eyes - One Who Glances

Layiq (Arabic)
Fitting - Proper - Suitable

Lazim (Arabic)
Desired - Wished For

Leander (Latin)
Lion Man

Lee (English)
Clearing - Wood
From a surname referring to various places.

Leif (Scandinavian)
Descendant - Heir
Variants: *Leiv*

Lelle (Scandinavian)
Brave Like a Lion
Pet form of Lennart.

Len (English)
Brave Like a Lion
Short form of Leonard, Lennox or Lionel.

Lennard (English)
Brave Like a Lion
Form of Leonard.

Lennart (Scandinavian)
Brave Like a Lion
Form of Leonard.

Leo (English)
Lion
From Late Latin.

Leon (English, German, Irish Gaelic)
Lion

Leonard (English)
Brave Like a Lion

Leonardo (Italian, Portuguese, Spanish)
Brave Like a Lion
Form of Leonard.

Leoncio (Spanish)
Lion

Leone (Italian)
Lion
Form of Leo.

Leonid (Russian)
Lion
From Greek Leonidas.

Leonti (Russian)
Lion

Leonzio (Italian)
Lion

Leopold (English)
Brave People

Lev (Russian)
Lion

Lew (Polish)
Lion
Polish spelling of Lev.

Lew (English)
Famous Warrior
Short form of Lewis.

Lewie (English)
Famous Warrior
Variant of Louis or pet form of Lewis.

Lewie (Irish)
Bright - Shining
Anglicized form of Gaelic name Lughaidh.

Lewis (English)
Famous Warrior
Form of Louis.

Lex (English)
Defender of Humanity
Short form of Alex.

Liam (Irish)
Protector
Short form of Uilliam, Gaelic form of William.

Liaqat (Arabic)
Aptitude - Competence - Worthiness

Libor (Czech)
Free

Licerio (Spanish)
Light - Wolf
From Greek lyk ("light") or lykos ("wolf").

Lindon (English)
Hill of Lime Trees
Variant of Lyndon.

Lionel (English)
Lion

Lisanuddin (Arabic)
Supporter of Islam

Lohrasb (Persian)
Owner of Fast Horses

Lou (English)
Famous Warrior
Short form of Louis or Louise.

Louie (English)
Bright - Shining
Variant of Lewie.

Louis (French)
Famous Warrior

Lovell (English)
Wolf-cub

Lowell (English)
Wolf-cub
Variant of Lovell.

Loyal (English)
Faithful - Loyal

Luay (Arabic)
Strong
Variants: *Loae, Loai, Loay, Louay, Loway, Luae, Luai, Luway*

Lubaib (Arabic)
Pure

Luciano (Italian, Portuguese, Spanish)
Illuminated - Radiant

Lucien (French)
Illuminated - Radiant
Derivative of Lucius.

Lucio (Italian, Portuguese, Spanish)
Illuminated - Radiant
Form of Lucius.

Lucius (Latin)
Illuminated - Radiant

Ludiwk (Polish)
Famous Warrior
Polish form of Ludwig.

Ludovic (English, Scottish)
Famous Warrior
Synonym of Louis.

Ludwig (German)
Famous Warrior
The same as Louis.

Luham (Arabic)
Great

Luis (Spanish)
Famous Warrior
Spanish form of Louis.

Luitgard (German)
Protector of the People

Luitpold (German)
Brave People
Form of Leopold.

Lujain (Arabic)
Silver

Luqman (Arabic)
Luqman is the name of a person mentioned in the Quran.
Variants: *Loqmaan, Loqman, Luqmaan*

Lutah (Arabic)
Intelligent - Sensible

Lutaif (Arabic)
Gentle - Kind

Lutf (Arabic)
Gentleness - Kindness - Leniency

Lutfan (Arabic)
Gentleness - Kindness - Leniency

Lutfi (Arabic)
Gentle - Kind

Lutfullah (Arabic)
God's Mercy

Lutfurrahman (Arabic)
God's Mercy

Luwaibid (Arabic)
Little Lion

Luwaih (Arabic)
Apparent - Manifest - Visible

Lyle (English, Scottish)
From the Island

Lyndon (English)
Hill of Lime Trees

Lyov (Russian)
Lion
Variant of Lev.

This page intentionally left blank

M

Maabad (Arabic)
Temple - Worship

Maad (Arabic)
Afterlife - Hereafter - Recurrence
The name Maad is mentioned in the Quran.

Maadil (Arabic)
Method - Road - Way

Maadin (Arabic)
Metal - Mineral

Maadini (Arabic)
Metallic

Maadun (Arabic)
Inhabited - Settled

Maalam (Arabic)
Milestone - Road Sign

Maali (Arabic)
Greatness - Highness of Status

Maamour (Arabic)
Inhabited - Restored
The name Maamour is mentioned in the Quran.

Maan (Arabic)
Beneficial - Helpful
Variants: *Ma'n*

Maany (Arabic)
Meanings - Virtues

Maarif (Arabic)
Knowledge - Wisdom

Maarij (Arabic)
Ascents - Routes of Ascent - Stairs
The name Maarij is mentioned in the Quran.

Maarufi (Arabic)
Doer of Good Deeds

Maas (Dutch)
Twin
Dutch form of Thomas.

Maash (Arabic)
Livelihood - Sustenance
The name Maash is mentioned in the Quran.

Maashar (Arabic)
Folk - Group of People - Kinsfolk
The name Maashar is mentioned in the Quran.
Variants: *Ma'shar*

Maashir (Arabic)
Communities Societies

Maasib (Arabic)
Chiefs - Masters

Maatuq (Arabic)
Freed - Freed From Slavery

Maayish (Arabic)
Livelihood - Sustenance
The name Maayish is mentioned in the Quran.

Maayush (Arabic)
Alive - Prosperous

Maaz (Arabic)
Refuge - Shelter

Maazim (Arabic)
Dignified - Enduring - Patient

Maazir (Arabic)
Excuses

Maazur (Arabic)
Blameless - Excused

Maazuz (Arabic)
Powerful - Strong

Mabkhut (Arabic)
Lucky - Protected
Variants: *Mabkhoot*

Mabruk (Arabic)
Blessed

Mabrur (Arabic)
Blessed - Proper - Valid

Madar (Arabic)
Circuit - Cycle - Orbit

Maddah (Arabic)
Praiser

Madeeh (Arabic)
Praise

Madiar (Persian)
Mother's Helper

Madih (Arabic)
Praiser

Madkhal (Arabic)
Access - Admittance - Entrance - Entry

Maeesh (Arabic)
Life - Lifetime - Livelihood

Mafakhir (Arabic)
Glorious Deed - Glorious Trait

Maftooh (Arabic)
Free - Open
Variants: *Maftuh*

Maghayis (Arabic)
Rainfalls

Maghazi (Arabic)
Content - Essence - Gist - Intent

Magnus (English, Scandinavian, Scottish)
Great

Mahaad (Arabic)
Comforter - Facilitator
Variants: *Mahad*

Mahal (Arabic)
Forbearing - Lenient

Mahbub (Arabic)
Adored - Loved

Mahbur (Arabic)
Affluent - Blessed

Mahd (Arabic)
Cradle - Place of Comfort - Starting Point
The name Mahd is mentioned in the Quran.
Variants: *Mehd*

Mahdi (Arabic)
Well-guided

Maheer (Arabic)
Wise

Mahfuz (Arabic)
Guarded - Protected
The name Mahfuz is mentioned in the Quran.

Mahiar (Persian)
Moon Friend

Mahid (Arabic)
Comforter - Facilitator
Variants: *Maahed, Maahid, Mahed*

Mahir (Arabic)
Adept - Proficient - Skilled

Mahjan (Arabic)
Flourishing - Pure

Mahmand (Persian)
Beloved - Flawless - Good-looking
Literally "possessor of the moon".
Variants: *Maahmand, Mah Mand*

Mahmud (Arabic)
Laudable - Praiseworthy
The name Mahmud is mentioned in the Quran.
Variants: *Mahmood, Mahmoud, Mehmood, Mehmud, Mehmut*

Mahrus (Arabic)
Guarded - Protected

Mahsub (Arabic)
Measured - Quantified

Mahsum (Arabic)
Decided - Determined - Resolved

Mahsun (Arabic)
Beautified - Improved

Mahul (Arabic)
Forbearance - Leniency

Mahzuz (Arabic)
Fortunate - Lucky

Maidan (Arabic)
Arena - Plaza

Maiz (Arabic)
Distinguisher
Variants: *Maaez, Maaiz, Maez*

Majal (Arabic)
Chance - Elbowroom - Opportunity - Space

Majd (Arabic)
Distinction - Glory - Honor
Variants: *Mejd*

Majdan (Arabic)
Glorious - Praiseworthy

Majdi (Arabic)
Laudable - Praiseworthy

Majduddin (Arabic)
Supporter of Islam
Literally "glory of the faith".

Majeed (Arabic)
Glorious - Majestic - Praiseworthy
Variants: *Majid, Mejid*

Majeedan (Arabic)
Glorious - Laudable - Praiseworthy

Majeedi (Arabic)
Laudable - Praiseworthy

Majjad (Arabic)
Glorious - Praiseworthy

Majjadin (Arabic)
Praiseworthy Ones

Majzub (Arabic)
Attracted

Makan (Arabic)
Place
The name Makan is mentioned in the Quran.
Variants: *Makaan*

Makari (Russian)
Blessed
From Late Greek Makarious.
Variants: *Makar*

Makki (Arabic)
Meccan

NAMES FOR BOYS

Makram (Arabic)
Generosity - Honor - Respect

Makrimi (Arabic)
Generosity - Honor

Makrur (Arabic)
Recurring - Repeating

Maktub (Arabic)
Decreed - Recorded - Written

Maleed (Arabic)
Gentle - Soft

Maleeh (Arabic)
Charming - Handsome - Witty
Variants: *Malih*

Maleek (Arabic)
King - Master - Owner
The name Maleek is mentioned in the Quran.

Maleekan (Arabic)
Kings - Masters

Malih (Arabic)
Charming - Handsome - Witty

Malmus (Arabic)
Touchable - Within Reach

Malouf (Arabic)
Beloved - Friend - Well-known
Variants: *Maluf*

Mamdud (Arabic)
Extensive - Great
The name Mamdud is mentioned in the Quran.

Mamduh (Arabic)
Praiseworthy

Mamun (Arabic)
Honorable - Loyal - Trustworthy
Variants: *Ma'mun, Maamun, Mamoon, Mamoun*

Manaf (Arabic)
Great - High in Status

Manafi (Arabic)
Benefits
The name Manafi is mentioned in the Quran.

Manari (Arabic)
Radiant

Manarul Islam (Arabic)
Lighthouse of Islam

Manazir (Arabic)
Flourishing - Radiant

Maneeh (Arabic)
Generous

Manhal (Arabic)
Fountain - Spring - Water Well

Mani (Persian)
Thinker - Thoughtful

Manley (English)
Common Wood - Manly
Originally from a surname meaning "shared wood", "common wood or clearing". Today it is used in association with the adjective manly.

Manoel (Portuguese)
God is With Us
Portuguese form of Emmanuel.

Mansar (Arabic)
Advocacy - Support

Mansur (Arabic)
Backed - Supported - Victor
The name Mansur is mentioned in the Quran.

Mansuri (Arabic)
Victor

Manuchehr (Persian)
From Paradise - Heavenly

Manuel (Spanish)
God is With Us
Spanish form of Emmanuel.

Manzur (Arabic)
Anticipated - Foreseen - Seen - Visible

Maooni (Arabic)
Helper - Supporter

Maqasid (Arabic)
Destinations - Goals - Intentions

Maqbul (Arabic)
Accepted - Approved

Maqdeed (Arabic)
Powerful - Strong

Maqdum (Arabic)
Accepted - Begun - Initiated

Maqdur (Arabic)
Achievable - Doable - Feasible

Maqsud (Arabic)
Desired - Sought

Maraheeb (Arabic)
Generosity - Hospitality - Welcome

Marahi (Arabic)
Exuberant - Lively

Marashid (Arabic)
Right Guidance

Maratib (Arabic)
Ranks - Stations

Marbuh (Arabic)
Earned

Mardin ()
Name of a city in Kurdistan of Turkey, may be from Syriac, meaning "fortress".

Marduf (Arabic)
Followed - Succeeded

Mareekh (Arabic)
Lead Monoxide
A chemical used in Medieval times in alchemy and medicine.

Mareen (Arabic)
Gentle - Lenient

Mareer (Arabic)
Resolved - Strong

Marghab (Arabic)
Desire - Wish

Marin (Arabic)
Forgiving - Lenient

Marooh (Arabic)
Gleeful - Lively

Marshall (English)
Caretaker of Horses - Steward

Marshud (Arabic)
Well-guided

Marshudi (Arabic)
Well-guided

Martia (Persian)
Human

Maruf (Arabic)
Acceptable - Customary - Good
The name Maruf is mentioned in the Quran.
Variants: *Ma'ruf, Maroof, Marouf*

Marukh (Arabic)
Perfume-wearer

Marur (Arabic)
Crossing - Passage

Marwan (Arabic)
Fragrant Tree - Quartz
Variants: *Marwaan*

Marwani (Arabic)
Quartz-like

Marzban (Persian)
Border Guard

Marzi (Arabic)
Approved - Beloved - Chosen - Liked

Marzooq (Arabic)
Blessed - Gifted
Variants: *Marzuq*

Marzun (Arabic)
Calm - Composed - Dignified

Marzuqi (Arabic)
Blessed by God - Given Provision

Marzuqullah (Arabic)
Blessed by God

Masad (Arabic)
Hunting Ground

Masadiq (Arabic)
Faithful - Loyal

Masajid (Arabic)
Mosques - Places of Worship

Masakin (Arabic)
Habitation - Residence
The name Masakin is mentioned in the Quran.

Masari (Arabic)
Path - Road

Masarrat (Arabic)
Gladness - Happiness - Joy

Masbat (Arabic)
Place of Rest - Place of Sleep

Masd (Arabic)
Highland - Plateau

Masduq (Arabic)
Credible - Trusted
Variants: *Masdooq, Masdouq*

Maseeri (Arabic)
Destiny - Fate

Mashahid (Arabic)
Landscapes - Panoramas - Scenes

Mashal (Arabic)
Lantern - Light
Variants: *Mash'al, Mashaal*

Mashar (Arabic)
Honeycomb Cell

Mashariq (Arabic)
East - Eastern Lands - Orient
The name Mashariq is mentioned in the Quran.

Mashawir (Arabic)
Honeycomb Cells

Masheedi (Arabic)
Great - High in Status

Mashhad (Arabic)
Scene - View
The name Mashhad is mentioned in the Quran.

Mashhur (Arabic)
Distinguished - Well-known
Variants: *Mashhoor*

Mashiyat (Arabic)
Will - Willpower

NAMES FOR BOYS

Variants: *Masheat, Masheeat, Mashi'at, Mashiat, Mashiyyat*

Mashkur (Arabic)
Appreciated - Thanked
The name Mashkur is mentioned in the Quran.

Mashkuri (Arabic)
Appreciated - Thanked

Mashqur (Arabic)
Fair-skinned

Mashriq (Arabic)
East - Orient
The name Mashriq is mentioned in the Quran.

Mashriqi (Arabic)
Eastern - Oriental

Mashruh (Arabic)
Explained - Open - Relaxed

Mashta (Arabic)
Winter Resort

Masik (Arabic)
Grasper - Holder

Masir (Arabic)
Destiny - Fate
The name Masir is mentioned in the Quran.
Variants: *Maseer, Massir*

Masjid (Arabic)
Mosque - Place of Worship
The name Masjid is mentioned in the Quran.

Maskun (Arabic)
Inhabited - Occupied

Maso (Italian)
Twin
Form of Tommaso.

Masrur (Arabic)
Glad - Happy
The name Masrur is mentioned in the Quran.

Massimo (Italian)
Greatest
Form of Maxim.

Mastoor (Arabic)
Covered - Hidden - Modest
The name Mastoor is mentioned in the Quran.

Masud (Arabic)
Blessed - Happy - Successful
Variants: *Masood, Masoud*

Masudi (Arabic)
Glad - Happy

Masus (Arabic)
Unripe Date

Mataf (Arabic)
Place of Tawaf - Place of Visitation
Variants: *Mataaf*

Matahir (Arabic)
Cleansers - Purifiers

Matalib (Arabic)
Demands - Desires

Matar (Arabic)
Rain
The name Matar is mentioned in the Quran.

Matari (Arabic)
Rain-like

Matee (Arabic)
Good - Virtuous
Variants: *Mati, Mati'*

Mateer (Arabic)
Rainy

Mateeri (Arabic)
Rain-like

Mathnawi (Arabic)
Binary - Couplet
Usually refers to a type of poetry.

Mathwa (Arabic)
Abode - Home
The name Mathwa is mentioned in the Quran.

Matir (Arabic)
Fast-running Horse - Rainy Day

Matlab (Arabic)
Demand - Desire

Matlub (Arabic)
Desired - Sought
The name Matlub is mentioned in the Quran.

Mattali (Arabic)
Smith - Sword-maker

Matthias (Biblical)
Gift of God
Synonym of Matthew.

Mauddin (Arabic)
Miner

Mauno (Finnish)
Great
Finnish form of Magnus.

Mawfoud (Arabic)
Agent - Delegate - Deputy

Mawhab (Arabic)
Gifted - Given

Mawhad (Arabic)
One - Singular

Mawhub (Arabic)
Bestowed - Gifted - Given Freely

Mawjud (Arabic)
Accessible - Existing - Obtainable

Mawoud (Arabic)
Appointed - Determined - Promisee
The name Mawoud is mentioned in the Quran.

Mawthuq (Arabic)
Trusted - Trustworthy

Max (English, German)
Great
Short form of Maximilian and Maxwell.

Maxim (Russian)
Greatest
From Latin Maximus.

Maximilian (German)
Greatest

Maxwell (English, Scottish)
Great
Originally from a place name meaning "the stream of Mack (form of Magnus)", these days used as an expansion of Max.

Maymun (Arabic)
Blessed - Prosperous
Variants: *Maimoon, Maimun, Maymoon*

Maynard (English)
Strength - Strong

Mazahir (Arabic)
Scenes - Views

Mazamin (Arabic)
Guarantee - Guarantor

Mazeed (Arabic)
Abundance
The name Mazeed is mentioned in the Quran.

Mazhur (Arabic)
Apparent - Clear

Maziar (Persian)
Mountain King

Mazin (Arabic)
Rain-Bearing Cloud
Variants: *Maazen, Maazin, Mazen*

Mazir (Arabic)
Elegant - Witty

Mazkur (Arabic)
Mentioned - Remembered
The name Mazkur is mentioned in the Quran.

Mazman (Arabic)
Bail - Duty - Guarantee - Obligation

Mazmun (Arabic)
Content - Meaning - Significance - Substance

Mehdad (Persian)
Noble - High-born

Mehrad (Persian)
Generous - Selfless

Mehran (Persian)
Affectionate - Kind

Mehrbod (Persian)
Affectionate - Kind

Mehrtash (Persian, Turkish)
Affectionate - Kind

Meical (Welsh)
Who is Like God?
Welsh form of Michael.

Meilyr (Welsh)
Chief - Ruler

Meinard (German)
Strength - Strong
German form of Maynard.
Variants: *Meinhard*

Merry (English)
Cheerful - Mercy - Reward
Form of Mercy, or in association with the word "merry" ("cheerful").

Miad (Arabic)
Appointment

Mibshar (Arabic)
Glad - Happy

Micah (Biblical)
Who is Like (Yahweh)?
Synonym of Michael.

Michael (English, German)
Who is Like God?
Name of an angel, known as Mikhaal in the Quran.

Micolau (Catalan)
Of the Victorious People
Variant of Nicolau (see Nicholas).

Midadi (Arabic)
High - Tall

Midhat (Arabic, Turkish)
Poem of Praise

Midrar (Arabic)
Abundant - Copious - Flowing

Mieshar (Arabic)
One Tenth

Mietaf (Arabic)
Affectionate - Compassionate - Sympathetic

NAMES FOR BOYS

Mietawi (Arabic)
Generous

Mifrah (Arabic)
Happy - Joyous
Variants: *Mefraah, Mefrh, Mifraah*

Miftah (Arabic)
Guide - Key

Miftahuddin (Arabic)
Guide of the Faith

Mifyaz (Arabic)
Gracious

Miguel (Portuguese, Spanish)
Who is Like God?
Form of Michael.

Mihad (Arabic)
Cradle - Place of Comfort - Plain
The name Mihad is mentioned in the Quran.
Variants: *Mehaad, Mehad, Mihaad*

Mihai (Romanian)
Who is Like God?
Form of Michael.

Mihlal (Arabic)
Happy

Mihraz (Arabic)
Fixer - Improver

Mihwar (Arabic)
Axis - Pivot

Mijbar (Arabic)
Improver - Mender

Mijdad (Arabic)
Great - Strong

Mijhan (Arabic)
Young Man

Mikael (Scandinavian)
Who is Like God?
Form of Michael.

Mikhaeel (Arabic)
Mikhaeel is the name that Arab Christians use to refer to the angel Mikaeel/Michael.
Variants: *Mikhael*

Mikkel (Danish, Norwegian)
Who is Like God?
Form of Michael.

Milad (Arabic)
Birth Day - Noble Lineage - Parentage

Milan (Czech)
Favor - Grace
Equivalent of Milena.

Milhaan (Arabic)
Pure White Color
Variants: *Melhaan, Melhan, Milhan*

Milhas (Arabic)
Brave

Minhaj (Arabic)
Clear Path - Clear Way - Curriculum - Method
The name Minhaj is mentioned in the Quran.

Minhajuddin (Arabic)
Curriculum of the Faith - Path of the Faith

Minhal (Arabic)
Generous - Honorable

Minhali (Arabic)
Generous - Honorable

Minsar (Arabic)
Victor - Winner

Miqdad (Arabic)
Powerful - Strong

Miqdadi (Arabic)
Powerful - Strong

Miqdam (Arabic)
Bold - Brave

Miquel (Catalan)
Who is Like God?
Catalan form of Michael.

Miradi (Arabic)
Powerful - Strong

Miraf (Arabic)
Intelligent - Perceptive

Miraj (Arabic)
Ascent - Route of Ascent - Stars
Variants: *Mi'raj*

Mirajuddin (Arabic)
Ascent of the Faith

Mirfiq (Arabic)
Beneficial - Helpful

Mirghad (Arabic)
Doer of Good Deeds

Mirkhas (Arabic)
Gentle - Lenient - Soft

Mirrikh (Arabic)
Planet Mars - Wolf

Mirsab (Arabic)
Forbearing - Lenient

Mirsad (Arabic)
Lookout - Observatory - Place of Ambush

Mirsal (Arabic)
Message-bearer - Messenger

Mirshadi (Arabic)
Well-guided

Mirshaq (Arabic)
Nimble - Sprightly

Mirwaf (Arabic)
Compassionate - Kind

Mirzai (Arabic)
Content - Satisfied

Mirzaq (Arabic)
Affluent

Misam (Arabic)
Beautiful
Variants: *Meesam, Meysam, Miesam, Mysam*

Misaq (Arabic)
Covenant
The name Misaq is mentioned in the Quran.
Variants: *Meesaq, Meethaq, Misaaq, Mithaaq, Mithaq*

Misbah (Arabic)
Lamp - Lantern - Light - Oil Lamp
The name Misbah is mentioned in the Quran.
Variants: *Mesbaah, Mesbah, Misbaah*

Misbahi (Arabic)
Radiant

Misbaq (Arabic)
Advanced - Ahead

Misdad (Arabic)
Faultless - Reasonable - Sensible

Mishal (Arabic)
Lantern - Light
Variants: *Mesh'al, Meshaal, Meshal, Mish'al, Mishaal*

Mishdad (Arabic)
Strong - Tough

Mishkat (Arabic)
Niche
The name Mishkat is mentioned in the Quran.
Variants: *Meshkaat, Meshkat, Mishkaat*

Mishraq (Arabic)
Brilliant - Radiant

Misk (Arabic)
Musk
The name Misk is mentioned in the Quran.

Miski (Arabic)
Musk-like

Misri (Arabic)
Egyptian

Mithal (Arabic)
Ideal - Model

Mizan (Arabic)
Balance - Measure - Scales - Weigth
The name Mizan is used in the Quran.
Variants: *Mezaan, Mezan, Mizaan*

Mizhir (Arabic)
Filled With Flowers

Mizn (Arabic)
Rain-Bearing Cloud - White Cloud

Mizyan (Arabic)
Beautiful

Modya (Russian)
Fellow Traveler
Pet form of Mefodi.

Moein (Arabic)
Helper - Supporter
Variants: *Moeen, Mouin, Mueen, Muin*

Moez (Arabic)
One Who Honors Others - One Who Values Others
Variants: *Moeiz, Muizz*

Mogens (Danish)
Great
Form of Magnus.

Moses (Biblical, English)
Saved
The true meaning of the name is not known, there are various interpretations for it.

Moss (English, Jewish)
Saved
Form of Moses.

Moss (Welsh)
Moss Settlement
Short form of Mostyn.

Mostyn (Welsh)
Moss Settlement

Motya (Russian)
Lady - Twin
The masculine name is from Matthew ("twin") while the feminine name is from Matrona ("lady").

Mouhib (Arabic)
Generous - Giving

Moujab (Arabic)
Amazed - Impressed - Pleased

Moujib (Arabic)
Amazing - Impressive - Pleasing

Moujid (Arabic)
Creator

NAMES FOR BOYS

Moumin (Arabic)
Believer
The name Moumin is mentioned in the Quran.
Variants: *Momin, Mu'min, Mumen, Mumin*

Mouminin (Arabic)
Believers
The name Mouminin is mentioned in the Quran.

Mouminun (Arabic)
Believers
The name Mouminun is mentioned in the Quran.
Variants: *Mu'minun, Muminun*

Moumir (Arabic)
Long-lived

Mouqib (Arabic)
Rewarder

Mourib (Arabic)
Eloquent - Fluent

Mousir (Arabic)
Needless - Wealthy

Moutaaz (Arabic)
Honored - Mighty - Powerful

Moutabir (Arabic)
Introspective - Tester

Moutadil (Arabic)
Balancec - Straight

Moutamad (Arabic)
Aim - Goal - Reliable

Moutamid (Arabic)
Reliant

Moutaq (Arabic)
Freed - Freed Slave

Moutaqad (Arabic)
Belief - Conviction - Faith - Tenet

Moutaqid (Arabic)
Believer - Faithful

Moutasam (Arabic)
Recourse - Refuge

Moutasim (Arabic)
Shelter-taker - Taker of Refuge

Moutaz (Arabic)
Honored - Majestic - Powerful

Moutazim (Arabic)
Determined - Persevering - Resolved

Mouti (Arabic)
Generous

Moutif (Arabic)
Elevated - Great - High in Status

Moutiq (Arabic)
Slave-liberator

Muaddal (Arabic)
Corrected - Reformed - Tuned

Muaddil (Arabic)
Equalizer - Rectifier

Muain (Arabic)
Helper - Supporter

Mualla (Arabic)
Exalted - Raised

Muallam (Arabic)
Educated - Learned - Tauht
The name Muallam is mentioned in the Quran.

Mualli (Arabic)
Exalter - Glorifier - Raiser

Muallim (Arabic)
Teacher
Variants: *Mu'allim*

Muameer (Arabic)
Long-lived
Variant of Muammir.

Muammal (Arabic)
Desired - Hoped For

Muammar (Arabic)
Long-lived

Muarrif (Arabic)
Guide

Muarrifi (Arabic)
Guide

Muashir (Arabic)
Close Friend - Companion - Fellow

Muawini (Arabic)
Helper - Supporter

Muawwal (Arabic)
Dependable - Reliable

Muayyad (Arabic)
Backed - Supported

Muaz (Arabic)
Guarded - Protected

Muazid (Arabic)
Helper - Supporter

Muazzid (Arabic)
Fortifier - Strengthener

Muazzim (Arabic)
Resolute - Resolved

Muazzir (Arabic)
Helper - Supporter

Mubarak (Arabic)
Blessed
The name Mubarak is mentioned in the Quran.

Mubariz (Arabic)
Warrior
Variants: *Mobaariz, Mobarez, Mubaariz*

Mubarrik (Arabic)
Rain-Bearing Cloud

Mubashir (Arabic)
Bringer of Good News - Bringer of Good Tidings
The name Mubashir is mentioned in the Quran.
Variants: *Mobashir, Mubasher*

Mubdih (Arabic)
Praiseworthy

Mubdir (Arabic)
One Who the Full Moon Shines Upon

Mubin (Arabic)
Apparent - Clear - Self-evident
The name Mubin is mentioned in the Quran.
Variants: *Mobeen, Mobin, Mubeen*

Mudassir (Arabic)
Clothed - Covered - Dressed
The name Mudassir is mentioned in the Quran.
Variants: *Modasir, Modasser, Modassir, Modathir, Mudasir, Mudasser, Mudather, Mudathir*

Mueid (Arabic)
Experienced - Skilled

Mueidi (Arabic)
Experienced - Skilled

Mueinuddin (Arabic)
Supporter of the Faith

Mufakkir (Arabic)
Thinker

Mufazzil (Arabic)
Gracious

Mufid (Arabic)
Beneficial

Muflah (Arabic)
Successful

Muflih (Arabic)
Prosperous - Successful
Variants: *Mofleh, Moflih, Mufleh*

Muflihi (Arabic)
Successful

Mufzil (Arabic)
Gracious

Mughamir (Arabic)
Adventurous - Daring

Mugharbal (Arabic)
Chosen - Pure - Select

Mughir (Arabic)
Attacker - Raider

Mughirah (Arabic)
Attacker - Raider

Mughith (Arabic)
Rescuer - Savior

Mughithi (Arabic)
Rescuer - Savior

Mughithuddin (Arabic)
Savior of the Faith

Mughram (Arabic)
In Love - Obsessed

Mughtin (Arabic)
Needless - Rich

Muhab (Arabic)
Fearsome - Mighty - Strong

Muhabbab (Arabic)
Beloved

Muhabbib (Arabic)
Endearer

Muhafaz (Arabic)
Guarded - Protected
Muhafaz is an Arabic name for boys that means "protected", "guarded".

Muhaffiz (Arabic)
Giver of Knowledge

Muhafiz (Arabic)
Conservative - Keeper - Protector

Muhajir (Arabic)
Ascetic - Avoider of Sin - Migrator
The name Muhajir is used in the Quran in verse 29:26.
Variants: *Mohaajer, Mohaajir, Mohajer, Mohajir, Muhaajer, Muhaajir, Muhajer*

Muhammad (Arabic)
Admirable - Noble - Praiseworthy
The name *Muhammad* is mentioned in the Quran.
Variants: *Mohamad, Mohamat, Mohamed, Mohamet, Mohammad, Mohammat, Mohammed, Mohammet, Mohemad, Mohemat, Mohemed, Mohemet, Mohemmad, Mohemmat, Mohemmed, Mohemmet, Muhamad, Muhamat, Muhamed, Muhamet, Muhammat, Muhammed, Muhemad, Muhemat, Muhemed, Muhemet, Muhemmad, Muhemmat, Muhemmed, Muhemmet*

NAMES FOR BOYS

Muhannad (Arabic)
Indian-made Sword

Muhassan (Arabic)
Beautified - Improved

Muhassin (Arabic)
Beautifier - Improver

Muhawwin (Arabic)
Facilitator

Muhazab (Arabic)
Backed - Supported

Muhazib (Arabic)
Advocate - Supporter

Muhazzab (Arabic)
Courteous - Educated - Refined

Muhazzib (Arabic)
Educator - Teacher

Muhazzim (Arabic)
Defeater

Muhib (Arabic)
Lover

Muhibbudin (Arabic)
Lover of the Faith

Muhif (Arabic)
Elevated - Towering

Muhiyyuddin (Arabic)
Reviver of the Faith

Muhiz (Arabic)
Gracious - Honorable

Muhizzat (Arabic, Turkish)
Gracious - Honorable

Muhsad (Arabic)
Sensible - Wise

Muhsin (Arabic)
Doer of Good Deeds
The name Muhsin is mentioned in the Quran.

Muhsinin (Arabic)
Doers of Good Deeds
The name Muhsinin is mentioned in the Quran.
Variants: *Mohsinin*

Muhtad (Arabic)
Well-guided

Muhtadi (Arabic)
Well-guided

Muhtarim (Arabic)
Respectful

Muhtasab (Arabic)
Sufficient

Muhtashim (Arabic)
Chaste - Modest - Virtuous
Variants: *Mohtashem, Mohtashim, Muhtashem*

Muhtasib (Arabic)
Seeker of God's Rewards

Muidd (Arabic)
Preparer

Muinudeen (Arabic)
Supporter of Islam
Variants: *Moeinuddin, Muin Uddin, Muinuddin*

Muir (Scottish)
Rough Grazing
From a surname.

Muizzawi (Arabic)
Enduring - Patient

Mujahid (Arabic)
Striver

Mujammal (Arabic)
Adorned - Beautified - Improved

Mujawir (Arabic)
Neighbor

Mujayed (Arabic)
Praiseworthy

Mujeed (Arabic)
Doer of Good Deeds

Mujeedan (Arabic)
Doer of Good Deeds

Mujeedi (Arabic)
Doer of Good Deeds

Mujfar (Arabic)
Great

Mujib (Arabic)
Answerer - Responder
The name Mujib is mentioned in the Quran.

Mujiran (Arabic)
Protector - Rescuer - Savior

Mujtaba (Arabic)
Chosen - Selected
Variants: *Mojtaba, Mojtabaa, Mujtabaa*

Mujtahid (Arabic)
Striver

Mukabbir (Arabic)
Glorifier of God

Mukafat (Arabic)
Recompense - Reward

Mukaibir (Arabic)
Exalter - Glorifier

Mukairim (Arabic)
Honorable - Respectful

Mukairiman (Arabic)
Honorable - Respectful

Mukallaf (Arabic)
Entrusted - Obligated - Responsible

Mukarram (Arabic)
Honored - Respected

Mukhallis (Arabic)
Chooser - Picker - Purifier - Selector

Mukhlas (Arabic)
Chosen - Purified - Selected
The name Mukhlas is mentioned in the Quran.

Mukhlis (Arabic)
Faithful - Loyal - Sincere
The name Mukhlis is mentioned in the Quran.

Mukhlisi (Arabic)
Faithful - Loyal - Sincere

Mukhtar (Arabic)
Chosen
Variants: *Mokhtaar, Mokhtar, Mukhtaar*

Mukhtari (Arabic)
Chosen - Excellent - Fine - Superior

Muktafi (Arabic)
Content - Needless

Muktamil (Arabic)
Complete - Whole

Muladin (Arabic)
Gentle

Mulahib (Arabic)
Beautiful

Mulaisen (Arabic)
Eloquent - Fluent

Mulatif (Arabic)
Gentle - Kind

Mulayin (Arabic)
Gentle - Kind

Multamas (Arabic)
Desired - Wished For

Multamis (Arabic)
Desirer - Seeker

Muluk (Arabic)
Kings
The name Muluk is mentioned in the Quran.

Mumajjad (Arabic)
Extolled - Glorified

Mumajjid (Arabic)
Extoller - Glorifier

Mumtaz (Arabic)
Excellent - Exceptional

Munaam (Arabic)
Blessed - Given Blessings
Variants: *Mounaam, Mounam, Mun'am*

Munabbahan (Arabic)
Awake - Vigilant - Wakeful

Munadi (Arabic)
Caller
The name Munadi is mentioned in the Quran.

Munajji (Arabic)
Rescuer - Savior

Munal (Arabic)
Giver

Munaqqi (Arabic)
Pure

Munar (Arabic)
Bright - Well-lit

Munawwar (Arabic)
Radiant - Well-lit

Munawwir (Arabic)
Enlightener - Radiant

Mundi (Arabic)
Generous - Giving

Muneeb (Arabic)
One Who Turns to God - Virtuous
The name Muneeb is mentioned in the Quran in verse 75:11.
Variants: *Moneeb, Monib, Muneib, Munib*

Munif (Arabic)
Great - High in Status

Munir (Arabic)
Brilliant - Enlightening - Illuminating - Radiant
The name *Munir* is mentioned in the Quran.
Variants: *Moneer, Monir, Mounir, Muneer, Muner*

Munis (Arabic)
Comforting Friend - Consoling Friend

Muniym (Arabic)
Blessed - Giver of Charity - Wealthy
Variants: *Mounim, Mun'im, Muneim*

Munji (Arabic)
Rescuer - Savior

Munjid (Arabic)
Rescuer - Savior

Munshid (Arabic)
Reciter of Poetry

Munsif (Arabic)
Fair - Just

Muntaha (Arabic)
Aspiration - Goal
The name Muntaha is mentioned in the Quran.

Muntaqa (Arabic)
Chosen - Pure - Purified - Selected

Muntasaf (Arabic)
Middle

Muntasir (Arabic)
Conqueror - Victorious - Winner

Muntazar (Arabic)
Awaited - Expected

Muntazir (Arabic)
Awaiting - Expecting

Munzir (Arabic)
Cautioner - Harbinger - Portent - Warner
The name Munzir is mentioned in the Quran.
Variants: *Monzer, Monzir, Munzer*

Muqaddam (Arabic)
Beginning - Brought Forward - Offered - Start

Muqarab (Arabic)
Brought Close - Muqarrab

Muqassam (Arabic)
Balanced - Symmetric

Muqassim (Arabic)
Distributor - Divider

Muqazi (Arabic)
Arbitrator - Judge - Peace-maker

Muqid (Arabic)
Kindler - Lighter

Muqrin (Arabic)
Brave - Strong - Uniter

Muqsit (Arabic)
Fair - Just

Muqtadir (Arabic)
Capable - Powerful
The name Muqtadir is mentioned in the Quran.

Murabbi (Arabic)
Trainer

Murad (Arabic)
Desired - Wished For
Variants: *Moraad, Morad, Muraad*

Muraffah (Arabic)
Affluent

Muraffal (Arabic)
Respected

Murahiban (Arabic)
Greeter

Muraih (Arabic)
Energetic - Lively

Muraishid (Arabic)
Guide

Murakhas (Arabic)
Authorized - Licensed

Murashih (Arabic)
Mentor - Teacher

Murawwah (Arabic)
Musk-wearer

Murawwih (Arabic)
Perfume-wearer

Murazi (Arabic)
Gainer of Approval - Satisfier

Murdah (Arabic)
Brave

Murdif (Arabic)
Follower - Succeeder

Murdini (Arabic)
Perpetual

Murfiq (Arabic)
Gentle - Lenient

Murghib (Arabic)
Rich - Wealthy

Murid (Arabic)
Desirous - Seeker

Muridan (Arabic)
Desirous - Seeker

Murih (Arabic)
Gentle - Lenient

Murihan (Arabic)
Gentle - Lenient

Murkhi (Arabic)
Affluent

Murkhis (Arabic)
Gentle - Lenient

Mursali (Arabic)
Message-bearer - Messenger

Mursalin (Arabic)
Messengers
The name Mursalin is mentioned in the Quran.
Variants: *Morsalin, Mursaleen*

Murshad (Arabic)
Well-guided

Murshadi (Arabic)
Well-guided

Murshid (Arabic)
Guide

Murshidi (Arabic)
Guide

Mursili (Arabic)
Dispatcher

Murtah (Arabic)
Relaxed

Murtahanullah (Arabic)
God's Chosen Servant

Murtahinullah (Arabic)
Dedicated to God

Murtaqa (Arabic)
Bringer of Greatness

Murtaqi (Arabic)
Great

Murtawi (Arabic)
Quenched (not thirsty)

Murtaza (Arabic)
Gainer of God's Approval
Variants: *Mortaza, Mortazaa, Murtada, Murtadha, Murtadhaa*

Murtazi (Arabic)
Satisfied

Muruj (Arabic)
Green Fields

Murzaq (Arabic)
Blessed - Fortunate

Murzi (Arabic)
Pleaser - Satisfier

Murziq (Arabic)
Giver of Provision

Musa (Arabic)
Saved - Saved from Water - Savior
The name Musa is used in the Quran and it is the Arabic name for Moses. The name is not Arabic and the meanings were taken from non-Arabic scholarly sources.
Variants: *Mousa, Mousaa, Musaa*

Musab (Arabic)
Able - Capable - Strong
Variants: *Mus'ab*

Musabbih (Arabic)
Glorifier of God

Musabi (Arabic)
Capable - Strong

Musabir (Arabic)
Enduring - Patient

Musad (Arabic)
Glad - Happy

Musadan (Arabic)
Glad - Happy

Musaddad (Arabic)
Accomplished - Achieved - Reached

Musaddaq (Arabic)
Believed - Trusted

Musaddid (Arabic)
Accomplisher - Achiever

Musadiq (Arabic)
Acknowledger - Confirmer - Faithful
The name Musadiq is mentioned in the Quran.
Variants: *Mosadeq, Mosadiq, Musaddeq, Musaddiq*

Musaf (Arabic)
Helped - Rescued

Musaghfir (Arabic)
Seeker of God's Forgiveness

Musahib (Arabic)
Companion

Musaid (Arabic)
Helper

Musairi (Arabic)
Egyptian

Musalim (Arabic)
Peace-lover

Musallat (Arabic)
Powerful - Supreme

Musalli (Arabic)
Performer of Salah

Musallim (Arabic)
Obedient - Submissive

Musan (Arabic)
Guarded - Protected

Musannaf (Arabic)
Book

Musannif (Arabic)
Classifier

Musawi (Arabic)
Equal - Equivalent

Musawwir (Arabic)
Designer - Shaper
The name Musawwir is mentioned in the Quran.
Variants: *Mosawir, Mosawwir, Musawer, Musawir, Musawwer*

Musayeib (Arabic)
Powerful - Strong

NAMES FOR BOYS

Musayyab (Arabic)
Free - Unchained

Musayyib (Arabic)
Freer

Musbih (Arabic)
Kindler - Lighter

Musdi (Arabic)
Bestower - Giver - Granter

Musef (Arabic)
Helper - Rescuer

Musfir (Arabic)
Glowing - Radiant

Mushahid (Arabic)
Beholder - Observer - Onlooker

Mushakhis (Arabic)
Differentiator - Discerner

Musharraf (Arabic)
Honorable

Mushawir (Arabic)
Seeker of Advice

Mushaywir (Arabic)
Honeycomb Cell

Mushfiq (Arabic)
Compassionate - Kind - Sympathetic
Variants: *Moshfeq, Moshfiq, Mushfeq*

Mushib (Arabic)
Companion - Friend

Mushidi (Arabic)
Fortifier - Strengthener

Mushir (Arabic)
Gesturer - Guide

Mushqari (Arabic)
Fair-skinned

Mushrif (Arabic)
Elevated - Overseer - Towering

Mushriq (Arabic)
Bright - Well-lit

Mushriqi (Arabic)
Bright - Well-lit

Mushtaq (Arabic)
Desirous - Eager - Yearning

Mushtaqi (Arabic)
Desirous - Eager - Yearning

Musjil (Arabic)
Recorder - Registrar

Musli (Arabic)
Consoler

Muslih (Arabic)
Doer of Good Deeds - Improver - Reformer
The name Muslih is mentioned in the Quran.

Muslim (Arabic)
Muslim
The name Muslim is mentioned in the Quran.

Muslimi (Arabic)
Muslim

Muslimin (Arabic)
Muslims
The name Muslimin is mentioned in the Quran.
Variants: *Moslimin*

Musmih (Arabic)
Forgiving - Lenient

Musnad (Arabic)
Dependable - Reliable

Mustaf (Arabic)
Summer Vacationer

Mustafa (Arabic)
Chosen - Selected
Variants: *Mosftafa, Mostafaa, Mustafaa*

Mustafid (Arabic)
Benefiter - Earner - Winner

Mustahaq (Arabic)
Deserved - Earned

Mustahiq (Arabic)
Deserving - Worthy

Mustahsan (Arabic)
Good - Praiseworthy

Mustahsin (Arabic)
Gentle - Lenient

Mustajab (Arabic)
Accepted - Answered

Mustakfi (Arabic)
Needless

Mustala (Arabic)
Exalted - Raised

Mustali (Arabic)
Exalted - High in Status

Mustaltaf (Arabic)
Adorable - Charming

Mustaneer (Arabic)
Enlightened - Illuminated

Mustansir (Arabic)
Seeker of Help
Variants: *Mostansir*

Mustaqil (Arabic)
Independent - Sovereign

Mustaqim (Arabic)
Correct - Straight
The name Mustaqim is
mentioned in the Quran.
Variants: *Mostaqim, Mustaqeem*

Mustashar (Arabic)
Adviser - Councilor

Mustawi (Arabic)
Even - Flat - Level

Mutaal (Arabic)
Elevated - High in Status -
Sublime
Variants: *Motaal, Muta'al*

Mutahhir (Arabic)
Cleaner - Purifier
The name Mutahhir is
mentioned in the Quran.

Mutahhiran (Arabic)
Cleaner - Purifier

Mutailib (Arabic)
Desired - Sought

Mutair (Arabic)
Rain

Mutairi (Arabic)
Rain-like

Mutalib (Arabic)
Demander - Seeker
Variants: *Mutaalib*

Mutallib (Arabic)
Demander - Seeker

Mutee (Arabic)
Obedient

Muthab (Arabic)
Rewarded

Muthib (Arabic)
Rewarder

Muwaffaq (Arabic)
Prosperous - Successful

Muwaffiq (Arabic)
Successful
Variants: *Mowafeq, Mowaffiq, Muwafeq, Muwafiq*

Muwahid (Arabic)
Monotheist
Variants: *Muwahed, Muwahhid*

Muwaqqa (Arabic)
Brave

Muwaqqit (Arabic)
Time Keeper

Muyassar (Arabic)
Facilitated - Successful

Muyassir (Arabic)
Facilitator - Lenient

Muzaffar (Arabic)
Victor - Winner
Variants: *Mozafar, Mozafer, Muzafar, Muzaffer*

Muzain (Arabic)
Rain-Bearing Cloud

Muzaini (Arabic)
Rain-Bearing Cloud

Muzakir (Arabic)
Reminder
The name Muzakir is mentioned
in the Quran and it means "one
who brings God's remembrance
to people", a person who speaks
about God to people and enjoins
them to follow His
commandments.
Variants: *Mozaker, Mozakir, Muzakker, Muzakkir*

Muzammil (Arabic)
Wrapped in Garments

The name Muzammil is
mentioned in the Quran.
Variants: *Mozammil, Muzamel, Muzamil*

Muzarib (Arabic)
Attacker - Striker
Variants: *Mozaareb, Mozarib, Mudharib, Muzaareb, Muzaarib, Muzareb*

Muzayyan (Arabic)
Adorned - Beautified

Muzayyin (Arabic)
Adorner - Beautifier

Muzdahir (Arabic)
Flourishing - Prospering

Muzhir (Arabic)
Blooming

Muzn (Arabic)
Rain-Bearing Cloud - White
Cloud
The name Muzn is mentioned in
the Quran.

N

Naaim (Arabic)
Peaceful - Serene - Smooth - Soft

Naba (Arabic)
Announcement - News - Tidings

Nabayil (Arabic)
Aristocratic - Brave - Gallant - Highborn - Noble

Nabeel (Arabic)
Dignified - Gracious - Noble
Variants: *Nabil*

Nabhan (Arabic)
Aware - Vigilant - Wakeful

Nabigh (Arabic)
Brilliant - Outstanding

Nabih (Arabic)
Aware - Vigilant - Wakeful

Nabihi (Arabic)
Aware - Honorable - Vigilant - Wakeful

Nabili (Arabic)
Gallant - Gracious - High-born

Nabit (Arabic)
Small New Plant - Sprout

Nadeer (Arabic)
Eloquent - Fluent

Nadir (Arabic)
Rare - Unique

Naeem (Arabic)
Bliss
The name Naeem is mentioned in the Quran.

Nafal (Arabic)
Fragrance - Gifts - Presents

Nafees (Arabic)
Desired - Precious
Variants: *Nafis, Nefis*

Nafih (Arabic)
Charitable - Protector

Nafil (Arabic)
Generous

Nafiz (Arabic)
Influential - Powerful

Naghmat (Arabic)
Melody - Tune

Nahad (Arabic)
Honorable - Mighty - Strong

Nahar (Arabic)
Daytime
The name Nahar is mentioned in the Quran.
Variants: *Nahaar, Nehar*

Nahiz (Arabic)
Diligent - Elevated - Energetic - High - Lofty

Nahran (Arabic)
Rivers

Nahshal (Arabic)
Falcon

Nahum (Biblical)
Comorter
From Hebrew.

Nahwan (Arabic)
Intelligent - Wise

Nahyan (Arabic)
Mature - Wise
Variants: *Nahian, Nahyaan*

Nahzan (Arabic)
Advanced - Growing

Nahzat (Arabic, Turkish)
Advancement - Progress

Naif (Arabic)
Elevated - High - Towering

Naimurrahman (Arabic)
God's Bliss

Naizak (Arabic)
Meteor - Shooting Star - Short Spear

Najah (Arabic)
Success

Najat (Arabic)
Rescue - Salvation
The name Najat is used in the Quran.
Variants: *Najaat*

Najd (Arabic)
Highland - Plateau

Najdat (Arabic)
Bravery - Rescue

Najeed (Arabic)
Lion

Najeemuddin (Arabic)
Radiance of the Faith

Naji (Arabic)
Rescued - Survivor

Najib (Arabic)
Excellent - High-born
Variants: *Najeeb*

Najid (Arabic)
Rescuer - Supporter

Najjad (Arabic)
Rescuer - Savior

Najlan (Arabic)
Beautiful-eyed

Najm (Arabic)
Star
The name Najm is mentioned in the Quran.
Variants: *Nejm*

Najmuddin (Arabic)
Star of the Faith

Najud (Arabic)
Intelligent - Sensible - Wise

Nakheel (Arabic)
Date Palms

Nakhlan (Arabic)
Pure - Purified

Namdar (Persian)
Famous - Great

Nameer (Arabic)
Fresh Water

Nami (Arabic)
Developing - Growing - Increasing

Nami (Persian)
Beloved - Famous - Well-known

Namiq (Arabic)
Adorner - Decorator - Embellisher

Namir (Arabic)
Leopard

Namjur (Persian)
Famous

Namran (Arabic)
Leopard-like

Nanne (Swedish)
Daring Wolf

Also used as a pet form of Anders.

Naoum (Arabic)
Blessed

Naqeeb (Arabic)
Leader - Representative
The name Naqeeb is mentioned in the Quran.
Variants: *Nakib, Naqib*

Naqeel (Arabic)
Flood - Stranger

Naqi (Arabic)
Pure

Naqil (Arabic)
Copyist - Transporter

Naqqad (Arabic)
Critic - Reviewer
Variants: *Naqaad, Naqad*

Nariman (Persian)
Brave

Nasayir (Arabic)
Helper - Supporter

Naseeb (Arabic)
Fitting - Gentlemanly - Proper
Variants: *Nasib, Nesib*

Naseef (Arabic)
Secretly Spoken Words
Variants: *Naseif, Nasif, Nesif*

Naseel (Arabic)
Pure

Naseem (Arabic)
Gentle Breeze
Variants: *Nasim*

Naseer (Arabic)
Helper - Supporter
The name Naseer is mentioned

in the Quran.
Variants: *Nasir*

Nashid (Arabic)
Praiser - Reciter of Poetry

Nashwan (Arabic)
Delirious - Ecstatic
Variants: *Nashuan, Nashwaan*

Nasih (Arabic)
Giver of Advice - Guide
The name Nasih is mentioned in the Quran.

Nasik (Arabic)
Worshiper

Nasikh (Arabic)
Clerk - Copyist - Editor

Nasir (Arabic)
Helper - Supporter
The name Nasir is mentioned in the Quran.

Nasiruddin (Arabic)
Supporter of the Faith

Nasooh (Arabic)
Faithful - Loyal
The name Nasooh is mentioned in the Quran.

Nasr (Arabic)
Victory
The name Nasr is mentioned in the Quran.
Variants: *Nassr*

Nasrat (Arabic)
Help - Support

Nasruddin (Arabic)
Supporter of the Faith
Variants: *Nasraddin*

Nasrullah (Arabic)
God's Help

NAMES FOR BOYS

The name Nasrullah is mentioned in the Quran.

Nassah (Arabic)
Giver of Good Advice - Guide

Nassar (Arabic)
Helper - Supporter

Nathan (Biblical)
He (God) Has Given

Nathaniel (English)
God Has Given

Natiq (Arabic)
Articulate - Clear - Interlocutor - Manifest - Spokesman

Nattaj (Arabic)
Fruitful - Productive

Naum (Russian)
Comforter
Russian form of Nahum.

Navid (Persian)
Good News - Good Tidings

Nawafil (Arabic)
Gifts - Presents

Nawf (Arabic)
Greatness - Highness

Nawfal (Arabic)
Generous - Gracious - Handsome - Ocean - Sea

Nawfan (Arabic)
Great - High

Nawhan (Arabic)
Elevated - Exalted - Great

Nawl (Arabic)
Generosity - Nobleness

Nawras (Arabic, Persian)
Blossoming - Budding - Young

Nawroz (Kurdish, Persian)
New Day
Name of the Persian New Year's Day.
Variants: *Nawrooz, Norooz, Noruz, Nouroz*

Nawwab (Arabic)
Delegate - Representative

Nawwaf (Arabic)
Elevated - High - Lofty

Nawwar (Arabic)
Glowing - Radiant

Nawyan (Arabic)
Determined - Intending

Nayel (Arabic)
Acquirer - Brave - Courageous - Finder - Winner
Variants: *Na'il, Naael, Naail, Naayel, Naayil, Nael, Nayil*

Nayem (Arabic)
Calm - Tranquil

Nayir (Arabic)
Brilliant - Radiant

Nazeef (Arabic)
Clean - Virtuous

Nazeem (Arabic)
Orderly - Organized

Nazeer (Arabic)
Cautioner - Harbinger - Portent - Warner
The name Nazeer is mentioned in the Quran.
Variants: *Nazir, Nezir*

Nazhan (Arabic)
Chaste - Virtuous

Nazih (Arabic)
Rain

Nazim (Arabic)
Arranger - Organizer
Variants: *Naazem, Naazim, Nazem*

Nazir (Arabic)
Beautiful - Radiant

Nazmi (Arabic)
Orderly - Organized - Systematic

Nazzar (Arabic)
Observer - Spectator

Neacal (Scottish Gaelic)
Of the Victorious People
Form of Nicholas.

Ned (English)
Wealthy Protector
Short form of Edward.

Neekan (Persian)
Good Ones - Virtuous Ones

Neem (Arabic)
Affluence

Neerumand (Persian)
Powerful - Strong

Nehrin (Arabic, Turkish)
River
Variants: *Nehreen*

Neimat (Arabic)
Blessing

Niamullah (Arabic)
God's Blessings - God's Favors

Nihad (Arabic)
Mighty - Strong
Variants: *Nehad*

Nihad (Persian)
Creed - Essence - Nature

Nijat (Urdu)
Rescue - Salvation
Variant of Najat.
Variants: *Nejaat, Nejat, Nijaat*

Niknam (Persian)
Honored - Respected

Nikrouz (Persian)
Blessed - Fortunate

Nikzad (Persian)
High-born - Virtuous

Nils (Swedish)
Of the Victorious People
Swedish form of Nicholas.
Variants: *Nels*

Nima (Persian)
Army Commander - Powerful - Strong
Variants: *Neema*

Nimatullah (Arabic)
God's Blessings - God's Favors

Nino (Italian)
God is Gracious
Short form of Giannino, pet form of Gianni, contracted form of Giovanni, common Italian form of John.

Nisbat (Arabic)
Connection - Harmony - Relationship

Nisbi (Arabic)
Comparative - Proportional

Nismat (Arabic, Turkish)
Soft Breeze

Nisse (Swedish)
Of the Victorious People
Pet form of Nils.

Nitaj (Arabic)
Fruit - Product - Profit

Niyazi (Arabic)
Beloved - Desired

Nizal (Arabic)
Strife - Struggle

Nizam (Arabic)
Arrangement - Rule - System

Nizamuddin (Arabic)
System of the Faith

Nizamul Haq (Arabic)
System of Truth

Nizar (Arabic)
Rare - Unique

Noah (English)
Name of the Biblical prophet known as Nooh/Nuh in the Quran.

Noam (Jewish)
Delight - Joy - Pleasantness

Nobakht (Persian)
Young and Blessed

Noble (English)
High-born - Noble - Praiseworthy

Nolan (Australian, English, Irish)
Descendant of a Champion

Norman (English)
Norseman - North Man

Norris (English)
From the North

Noum (Arabic)
Affluence

Nouman (Arabic)
Blood

Novin (Persian)
Fresh - New

Nowzar (Persian)
Mythical Persian hero, may mean "young".

Nuaim (Arabic)
Delicate - Soft

Nubugh (Arabic)
Brilliance - Talent

Nudair (Arabic)
Rare - Unique

Nuh (Arabic)
Comfort - Noah - Rest
Nuh is the name of one of the prophets mentioned in the Quran, known as Noah in the Bible.
Variants: *Nooh, Nouh*

Nuhuz (Arabic)
Advancement - Rise - Rising

Nujaid (Arabic)
Highland

Nujaim (Arabic)
Little Star

Nukhail (Arabic)
Little Palm Tree

Numair (Arabic)
Little Leopard
Numair is an Arabic name for boys that means "little leopard", being the diminutive form of Namir.

NAMES FOR BOYS

Numou (Arabic)
Growth - Increase

Nur (Arabic)
Light - Radiance
The name *Nur* is mentioned in the Quran.
Variants: *Noor, Nour*

Nuraddeen (Arabic)
Light - Radiance - Supporter of Islam
Variants: *Noraddeen, Noraddin, Noradin, Nur Addin, Nur Uddin, Nur al-Din, Nuraddeen, Nuradeen, Nuradin, Nuruddin*

Nurahan (Arabic, Persian, Turkish)
Good Tidings - Radiant King

Nuri (Arabic)
Brilliant - Good - Radiant

Nuril (Aramaic)
Light of God

Nurshah (Arabic)
Light of the King

Nurulislam (Arabic)
Light of Islam

Nurullah (Arabic)
Light of God

Nusaib (Arabic)
Fitting - Gentlemanly - Proper
Variants: *Nosaib, Nosayb, Nusayb*

Nusaim (Arabic)
Breath - Soft Breeze

Nusair (Arabic)
Triumph - Victory

Nushad (Persian)
Happy Young Person

Nushur (Arabic)
Resurrection
The name Nushur is mentioned in the Quran.

Nusur (Arabic)
Vultures

Nutou (Arabic)
Elevation - Greatness - Loftiness

Nuwaib (Arabic)
Chief - Leader

Nuwaidir (Arabic)
Rare - Unique

Nuwair (Arabic)
Light - Radiance

Nuwairan (Arabic)
Light - Radiance

Nuwaisir (Arabic)
Helper - Supporter

Nuzair (Arabic)
Cautioner - Warner

Nuzhan (Persian)
Pine Tree
Variants: *Nouzhan*

Nuzhat (Arabic, Turkish)
Chastity - Virtue

Nuzhi (Arabic)
Chaste – Virtuous

This page intentionally left blank.

O

Obadiah (English)
Servant of God
Name of a Biblical prophet, synonym of Arabic Abdullah.

Octavian (English)
Eighth
From Latin.

Octavius (English)
Eight
From a Latin family name.

Okko (Finnish)
Friend of Deer

Oktai (Turkish)
Elite - Famous

Oleg (Russian)
Prosperous - Successful

Oleksander (Ukrainian)
Defender of Humanity
Form of Alexander.

Oliver (English)
Olive Tree

Omaijid (Arabic)
Glorious - Noble - Praiseworthy
Variants: *Umayyed*

Omidvar (Persian)
Hopeful

Onays (Arabic)
Consoler - Good Friend
Variants: *Onais, Unais*

Ons (Arabic)
Gladness
Variants: *Uns*

Onsi (Arabic)
Bringer of Calm and Gladness
Variants: *Unsi*

Oraib (Arabic)
Intelligent - Keen - Perceptive
Variants: *Uraib*

Oraibi (Arabic)
Intelligent - Keen - Perceptive
Variants: *Uraibi*

Orang (Persian)
Throne

Orell (Swiss)
Golden
Form of Aurelius.

Orhan (Turkish)
Great Leader
Variants: *Orhaan*

Orkhan (Turkish)
Great Leader
Variants: *Orkhaan*

Orlando (Italian)
Famous Land
Italian form of Roland.

Orson (English)
Bear-cub

Orz (Arabic)
Proximity - Side

Osborn (English)
Bear of God - Warrior of God
Variants: *Osborne, Osbourne*

Oscar (English, Irish)
Friend of Deer

Osheen (Irish)
Little Deer

Osip (Russian)
(God) Shall Add (Another Son)
Form of Joseph.

Osmond (English)
Protected by God
Variants: *Osmund*

Oswald (English)
Rule of God

Oswin (English)
Friend of God

Ottavio (Italian)
Eighth
Form of Octavius.

Otto (German)
Prosperous

Ovadia (Jewish)
Servant of God
Modern Hebrew form of Obadiah.

Owaib (Arabic)
Repentant
Variants: *Uwaibah*

Owais (Arabic)
Little Wolf
Variants: *Oways, Uwais, Uways*

Owaisi (Arabic)
Brave - Warrior
Variants: *Uwaisi*

Owaiz (Arabic)
Replacement

Ozhan (Persian)
Thrower

This page intentionally left blank

P

Paavo (Finnish)
Small
Finnish form of Paul.

Pablo (Spanish)
Small
Spanish form of Paul.

Paco (Spanish)
French
Variants: *Paquito*

Paivand (Persian)
Connection - Kin - Oath - Promise
Variants: *Payvand*

Paolino (Italian)
Small
A form of Paulino.

Paolo (Italian)
Small
Italian form of Paul.

Pastor (Spanish)
Shepherd

Patrick (English, Irish)
Noble - Patrician

Patya (Russian)
Best - Highest
Pet form of Ipati.

Paul (English, French, German)
Small

Paulino (Portuguese, Spanish)
Small
From a derivative of Paulus, from which Paul is also derived.

Pearce (English, Irish)
Rock - Stone
Variant of Pierce.

Pedr (Welsh)
Rock - Stone

Pelle (Swedish)
Rock - Stone
Pet form of Per, Scandinavian form of Peter.

Pellegrino (Italian)
Foreigner - Stranger
Italian form of Peregrine.

Per (Scandinavian)
Rock - Stone
Form of Peter.

Perce (Irish)
Rock - Stone
Variant of Pierce.

Peregrine (English)
Foreigner - Stranger

Perry (English)
Foreigner - Stranger
Pet form of Peregrine, or from a surname meaning "one who lives by a pear tree".

Peter (English, German, Scandinavian)
Rock - Stone
Name of one of the apostles of prophet Jesus son of Mary.

Philbert (English, French)
Bright Love - Very Bright - Very Famous

Philip (English)
Horse-lover

Philo (English, German)
Loving

Piaras (Irish Gaelic)
Rock - Stone
From Piers.

Pierre (French)
Rock - Stone
French form of Peter.

Piers (English)
Rock - Stone
Middle English form of Peter.

Piet (Dutch, Flemish, German)
Rock - Stone
Form of Peter.

Pietro (Italian)
Rock - Stone
Italian form of Peter.

Pio (Italian, Portuguese, Spanish)
Honorable - Pious - Respectful
From Latin Pius.

Porfirio (Italian, Spanish)
Purple Dye

Porifirio (Italian, Spanish)
Purple Dye

Poul (Danish)
Small
Danish form of Paul.

Primo (Italian, Portuguese, Spanish)
First

Primrose (English)
Primrose

Prince (English)
Prince

Prokopi (Russian)
Progress - Success

Prosper (English, French)
Fortunate - Prosperous
From Latin Prosperus.

Prospero (Italian, Portuguese, Spanish)
Fortunate - Prosperous

Prudencio (Portuguese, Spanish)
Provident - Prudent

Prudenzio (Italian)
Provident - Prudent

Prym (Polish)
First
Polish form of Primo.

Pyotr (Russian)
Rock - Stone
Russian form of Peer.

Q

Qaaid (Arabic)
Chief - Leader

Qabil (Arabic)
Accepter - Approver - Endorser
The name Qabil is mentioned in the Quran.

Qabis (Arabic)
Acquirer of Knowledge - Educated - Learned - Wise
Variants: *Kaabes, Kabis, Qaabes, Qaabis, Qabes*

Qablan (Arabic)
Accepter - Advancer

Qabool (Arabic)
Acceptance - Approval

Qaddar (Arabic)
Arranger - Organizer

Qaddur (Arabic)
Able - Capable - Powerful
Qaddur is an Arabic name for boys that means "capable", "powerful", "able".

Qadeer (Arabic)
Able - Capable - Powerful
The name Qadeer is mentioned in the Quran.
Variants: *Qadir, Qedir*

Qadim (Arabic)
Advancer - Comer

Qadiman (Arabic)
Age-old - Ancient - Time-honored
Variants: *Qadeeman*

Qadimi (Arabic)
Advancer - Comer

Qadir (Arabic)
Able - Capable - Powerful
The name Qadir is mentioned in the Quran.
Variants: *Qaader, Qaadir, Qader*

Qadoom (Arabic)
Bold - Brave

Qadri (Arabic)
Able - Powerful

Qaleeb (Arabic)
Water Well

Qamar (Arabic)
Moon
The name Qamar is mentioned in the Quran.
Variants: *Qemer*

Qamari (Arabic)
Moon-like

Qamaruddin (Arabic)
Supporter of Islam

Qamarullah (Arabic)
Moon of God

Qamarurrahman (Arabic)
Moon of God

Qamarussalam (Arabic)
Moon of Peace

Qamrani (Arabic)
Moonlit

Qamrun (Arabic)
Moon

Qareen (Arabic)
Companion - Friend
The name Qareen is mentioned in the Quran.

Qari (Arabic)
Reader - Reciter

Qarib (Arabic)
Near
The name Qarib is mentioned in the Quran.
Variants: *Kareeb, Qareeb*

Qarni (Arabic)
Bright - Sharp

Qaseet (Arabic)
Fair - Just

Qasheeb (Arabic)
Clean - Fresh

Qasim (Arabic)
Generous - Handsome
Variants: *Qaasem, Qaasim, Qasem*

Qasimi (Arabic)
Distributor - Divider - Spreader

Qasmun (Arabic)
Handsome

Qaswar (Arabic)
Lion - Strong

Qaswari (Arabic)
Brave - Lion-like

Qateef (Arabic)
Flower Picker - Fruit Picker

Qawi (Arabic)
Powerful - Strong
The name Qawi is mentioned in the Quran.
Variants: *Qawee, Qawiy*

Qayyam (Arabic)
Stander

Qayyim (Arabic)
Good - Proper - Upright

Qiblah (Arabic)
Direction - Direction of the Kaaba

The name Qiblah is mentioned in the Quran.

Qindil (Arabic)
Oil Lamp

Qirni (Arabic)
Able - Capable

Qirtas (Arabic)
Paper - Parchment

Qismat (Arabic)
Fortune - Luck

Qiyam (Arabic)
Night-long Worship
The name Qiyam is mentioned in the Quran.

Qobad (Persian)
Beloved King

Qudaiman (Arabic)
Bold - Brave

Qudair (Arabic)
Decree - Reckoning

Qudratullah (Arabic)
God's Power

Quentin (English, French)
Fifth

Quinton (English)
Fifth
Variant of Quentin.

Qulaib (Arabic)
Conscience - Heart

Qumr (Arabic)
Fair-skinned

Qunbar (Arabic)
Turnstone
A type of bird.

Qurb (Arabic)
Closeness - Nearness

Qurum (Arabic)
Chief - Leader

Qusait (Arabic)
Fair - Just

Qutb (Arabic)
Chief - Leader

Qutbuddin (Arabic)
Leader of the Faith

Qutbullah (Arabic)
Leader in the Service of God

Quwa (Arabic)
Strength
The name Quwa is mentioned in the Quran.
Variants: *Qowa, Quah, Quwwa, Quwwah*

R

Raad (Arabic)
Explorer - Scout

Raafi (Arabic)
Elevated - Exalted - Great
The name Raafi is mentioned in the Quran in verse 3:55.
Variants: *Raafei, Raafiy, Rafi, Rafi'*

Rabeeh (Arabic)
Earner - Winner

Rabih (Arabic)
Earner - Winner

Rabooh (Arabic)
Earner - Winner

Rad (Persian)
Free - Generous - Selfless - Wise

Radeen (Persian)
Free

Radman (Persian)
Generous - Selfless

Radmehr (Persian)
Generous - Radiant

Radooh (Arabic)
Bold - Brave

Radvin (Persian)
Generous - Noble

Raed (Arabic)
Guide - Leader - Pioneer
Variants: *Ra'ed, Ra'id, Raaed, Raaid*

Raees (Arabic)
Chief - Leader
Variants: *Rais, Rayis*

Rafaaq (Arabic)
Affectionate - Gentle

Rafaat (Arabic)
Glory - Greatness - Highness of Status
Variants: *Raf'at, Rafat*

Rafael (Portuguese, Spanish)
God Heals
Spanish and Portuguese form of Raphael.

Rafal (Polish)
God Heals
Polish form of Raphael.

Rafee (Arabic)
Elevated - Exalted - Great
The name Rafee is mentioned in the Quran in verse 40:15.
Variants: *Rafee', Rafei, Rafi, Rafie*

Rafeeq (Arabic)
Companion - Gentle - Kind
Variants: *Rafeek, Rafiq*

Rafeq (Arabic)
Companion - Gentle - Kind
Variants: *Raafek, Raafeq, Raafik, Raafiq, Rafik, Rafiq*

Raffaele (Italian)
God Heals
Italian form of Raphael.
Variants: *Raffaello*

Rafid (Arabic)
Helper - Supporter
Variants: *Raafed, Raafid, Rafed*

Raghib (Arabic)
Aspiring - Desirous - Seeking

Raghibun (Arabic)
Aspiring Ones - Seeking Ones

Rahayim (Arabic, Aramaic)
Compassionate - Merciful

Rahbah (Arabic)
Vast Expanse of Land

Rahbat (Arabic)
Vast Expanse of Land

Rahd (Arabic)
Delicate - Soft

Raheef (Arabic)
Gentle - Tender
Variants: *Rahif*

Raheel (Arabic)
Departure - Journey
Variants: *Rahil*

Raheem (Arabic)
Kind - Merciful - Tenderhearted
The name Raheem is mentioned in the Quran in many places, such as 2:128.
Variants: *Rahim, Rehim*

Rahil (Arabic)
Journeyer - Traveler
Variants: *Raahel, Raahil, Rahel*

Rahim (Arabic)
Kind - Merciful - Tenderhearted

Rahmatullah (Arabic)
God's Mercy
The name Rahmatullah is mentioned in the Quran.

Raif (Arabic)
Compassion - Kind - Softhearted
Variants: *Raaef, Raaif, Raef, Raefe, Rayf, Rayif, Rayife*

Raika (Persian)
Adored - Beloved

Rajab (Arabic)
7th Month of the Hijri Calendar
Literally "great", "tremendous".

NAMES FOR BOYS

Rajhan (Arabic)
Sensible - Wise

Rajih (Arabic)
Predominant - Superior

Rakeed (Arabic)
Tranquil

Rakeen (Arabic)
Composed - Dignified

Rakhs (Arabic)
Delicate - Soft

Rakhwan (Arabic)
Ease of Living - Luxury

Ram (Persian)
Happy - Joyous

Ramak (Persian)
Happy - Joyous

Raman (Persian)
Happy - Joyous

Rambod (Persian)
Comforter - Soother

Rameen (Persian)
Happy - Joyous - Jubilant

Rami (Persian)
Happy - Joyous

Ramiar (Persian)
Shepherd

Ramlat (Arabic, Turkish)
Grain of Sand

Ramz (Arabic)
Gesture - Mark - Symbol
The name Ramz is mentioned in the Quran.

Ramzi (Arabic)
Gesture - Sign - Symbl
Variants: *Ramzee, Ramzy*

Ranin (Arabic)
Buzz - Resonance
Variants: *Raneen*

Ransu (Finnish)
French
Finnish form of Francis.

Raphael (English, French, German)
God Heals

Raqeem (Arabic)
The name Raqeem is mentioned in the Quran.
Variants: *Rakeem, Rakim, Raqim*

Raqian (Arabic)
Elevated

Raqqah (Arabic)
Flat Land With Soft Dust

Raseen (Arabic)
Deep-rooted - Stable - Upstanding
Variants: *Rasin*

Rashad (Arabic)
Right Guidance - Right Path

Rashdan (Arabic)
Rightly-guided - Wise
Variants: *Rashdaan*

Rashid (Arabic)
Mature - Rightly-guided - Wise
Variants: *Raashed, Raashid, Rashed*

Rasteen (Persian)
Upright - Virtuous

Rastgar (Persian)
Free - Unhindered

Rateeq (Arabic)
Imrpover - Mender

Rauf (Arabic)
Compassionate - Kind - Lenient - Merciful
Variants: *Ra'uf, Raoof, Raouf, Reouf*

Rawsan (Arabic)
Light Rain
Variants: *Rausan*

Rayhan (Arabic)
Fragrance
The name Rayhan is mentioned in the Quran.
Variants: *Raihaan, Raihan, Rayhaan, Reehan, Reihan, Reyhan, Rihan*

Rayyan (Arabic)
Quenched - Watered
Name of one of the gates of Paradise.
Variants: *Raiaan, Raian, Rayaan, Rayan, Reyan, Reyyan, Ryan*

Rayyih (Arabic)
Fragrant
Variants: *Rayeh*

Rayyis (Arabic)
Chief - Leader
Variants: *Rayes*

Razaan (Arabic)
Calm - Composed - Dignified

Razaani (Arabic)
Composed - Dignified

Razeem (Arabic)
Lion's Roar
Razeem is an Arabic name for boys that means "lion's roar".

Razeen (Arabic)
Calm - Composed - Dignified

NAMES FOR BOYS

Razhan (Persian)
Sleep

Razni (Arabic)
Composed - Dignified

Razwan (Arabic)
Chosen - Desired - Selected

Rehab (Arabic)
Generous - Open-hearted - Open-minded - Spacious - Vast
Variants: *Rehaab, Reihaab, Reihab, Reyhaab, Reyhab, Rihaab, Rihab, Ryhab*

Reid (English, Scottish)
Red-haired - Ruddy-complexioned

Resa (Persian)
Eloquent - Well-guided - Wise

Reuel (Biblical)
Friend of God

Rex (English)
King
From Latin rex ("king").

Reyah (Arabic)
Power - Scents - Victory - Winds
Variants: *Reyaah, Riah, Riyaah, Riyah, Ryah*

Riaz (Arabic)
Gardens
Variants: *Riaaz, Riyaadh, Riyadh, Riyaz, Ryaaz, Ryaz*

Rich (English)
Powerful Ruler
Short form of Richard.

Richard (Czech, English, French, German)
Powerful Ruler

Richie (Australian, English, Scottish)
Powerful Rule
Pet form of Richard.
Variants: *Ritchie*

Riddees (Arabic)
Strong - Tough

Ridfan (Arabic)
Day and Night Cycle

Riel (Czech)
Man of God
Short form of Gabriel.

Rieti (Finnish)
Peaceful Ruler
Finnish form of Frederick.

Rifaah (Arabic)
Greatness - Highness of Status

Rifaat (Arabic)
Greatness - Highness of Status

Rifal (Arabic)
Affluence

Rifaq (Arabic)
Companions - Friends

Rifqat (Arabic, Turkish)
Gentleness - Leniency
Turkish pronunciation of Rifqah.

Rifqi (Arabic)
Gentle - Kind - Lenient

Rikard (Scandinavian)
Powerful Ruler
Scandinavian form of Richard.

Rinad (Arabic)
Agarwood - Aloeswood
Any tree that has a good scent.

Riordan (Irish)
King's Poet
Variants: *Rearden*

Riqqah (Arabic)
Gentleness - Kindness - Leniency

Risl (Arabic)
Gentleness - Leniency

Riza (Arabic)
Contentment - Having God's Approval
Variants: *Reda, Redaa, Redha, Redhaa, Reza, Rida, Ridaa, Ridha, Ridhaa, Rizaa*

Rizwan (Arabic)
Contentment - Having God's Approval
The name Rizwan is mentioned in the Quran in verse 57:20.
Variants: *Redhwan, Rezwaan, Rezwan, Ridhwaan, Ridhwan, Ridwaan, Ridwan, Rizwaan*

Roald (Norwegian)
Famous Ruler

Robert (English, French, Scandinavian, Scottish)
Bright With Fame

Robin (English)
Bright With Fame - Robin
Pet form Robert, or a reference to the bird.

Rocco (Italian)
Rest

Roderick (English)
Famous Ruler

Rodolf (Danish, German)
Famous Wolf
Variant of Rudolf.

Rodolfo (Italian, Spanish)
Famous Wolf
Variant of Rudolf.

Rodolphe (French)
Famous Wolf
French form of Rudolf.

Rodrigo (Spanish)
Famous Ruler
Cognate of Roderick.

Roelof (Dutch)
Famous Wolf

Roger (English, French)
Famous Spear
Variants: *Rodger*

Roland (English, French, German, Scandinavian)
Famous Land
Variants: *Rowland*

Rolf (English, German, Scandinavian)
Famous Wolf

Rollo (Latin)
Famous Wolf
Latinized form of Roul, form of Rolf.

Roque (Portuguese, Spanish)
Rest
Form of Rocco.

Rosendo (Spanish)
Famous Path

Rouzba (Persian)
Blessed - Fortunate
Variants: *Ruzbeh*

Rowan (English)
Little Red One

Roy (Scottish)
Red

Rozhbin (Kurdish)
Enlightener - Guide
Variants: *Rozhbeen*

Rozhyar (Persian)
Daytime
Variants: *Rozhiar*

Rubaih (Arabic)
Earner - Winner

Rudi (German)
Famous Wolf
Short form of Rudolf.

Rudolf (Czech, Dutch, English, German, Polish, Scandinavian)
Famous Wolf

Rufah (Arabic)
Affectionate - Sympathetic
Variants: *Roofa*

Rufino (Italian, Portuguese, Spanish)
Red-haired
From Rufus.
Variants: *Ruffino*

Rufus (English)
Red-haired

Ruhab (Arabic)
Forbearing - Generous - Open-minded
Variants: *Rohaab, Rohab, Ruhaab*

Ruhail (Arabic)
Departer - Journeyer
Variants: *Rohail, Ruhayl*

Ruhan (Arabic)
Kind - Spiritual
Variants: *Rohaan, Rohan, Rouhaan, Rouhan, Ruhaan*

Rujhan (Arabic)
Intelligent - Wisdom

Rukain (Arabic)
Pillar - Support

Rukn (Arabic)
Pillar - Prop - Support
The name Rukn is mentioned in the Quran.

Rumaiz (Arabic)
Gesture - Sign - Symbol

Rune (Scandinavian)
SecretLore

Rupert (Dutch, English, German)
Bright With Fame
Form of Robert.

Ruqaihan (Arabic)
Earner - Mender

Ruqaim (Arabic)
Mark - Seal

Ruqee (Arabic)
Elevated - Raised

Rurik (Russian)
Famous Ruler
From Roderick.

Rushaid (Arabic)
Rightly-guided

Rushd (Arabic)
Maturity - Right Guidance

Rushdan (Arabic)
Right Guidance - Rightly-guided

Russ (English)
Little Red One
Short form of Russell.

Russell (English)
Little Red One

Rustam (Persian)
Hulking - Strong - Tall

Rusul (Arabic)
Little Girl - Messengers

Rutger (Dutch)
Famous Spear

Ruwaid (Arabic)
Leniency - Soft Breeze
Variants: *Rowaid*

Ruwaihim (Arabic)
Compassionate - Kind
Variants: *Rowayhim*

Ruwaiq (Arabic)
Pure
Variants: *Rowaiq*

Ruwais (Arabic)
Chief - Leader
Variants: *Rowais*

Ruwaishid (Arabic)
Rightly-guided
Variants: *Rowaishid*

Ruwayfi (Arabic)
Elevated - Exalted - High
Variants: *Ruwaifi, Ruwaifi'*

Ruzm (Arabic)
Lion

Ryszard (Polish)
Powerful Ruler
Form of Richard.

This page intentionally left blank.

S

Saabih (Arabic)
Clear - Handsome

Saad (Arabic)
Blessedness - Hapiness
Variants: *Sa'ad, Sa'd*

Saadad (Arabic)
Rationality - Sense
Variants: *Sa'dad*

Saadan (Arabic)
Happy - Successful
Variants: *Sa'dan*

Saadat (Arabic)
Leaders - Lords

Saadi (Arabic)
Blessed - Successful
Variants: *Sa'di, Saady*

Saadoon (Arabic)
Happy - Successful
Variants: *Sa'dun*

Saaeb (Arabic)
Intelligent - Rational - Sensible

Saaed (Arabic)
Great - Majestic
Variants: *Sa'ed, Saed*

Saaf (Arabic)
Pure

Saafin (Arabic)
Pure Ones

Saaie (Arabic)
Effort - Labor
Variants: *Sa'i*

Saaigh (Arabic)
Jewelry Maker

Saaih (Arabic)
One Who Fasts
Variants: *Saaeh, Saayih, Saih, Sayeh, Sayih*

Saair (Arabic)
Avenger - Excited - Revolutionary
Variants: *Thair*

Saayed (Arabic)
Hunter
Variants: *Saayid, Sayed*

Saayed (Arabic)
Chief - Dominant

Sabalan (Persian)
Name of a mountain range in north-western Iran.

Sabbagh (Arabic)
Dyer

Sabbaq (Arabic)
Racer
Variants: *Sabaaq, Sabaq*

Sabbar (Arabic)
Enduring - Patient
The name Sabbar is mentioned in the Quran.

Sabeeh (Arabic)
Handsome - Radiant
Variants: *Sabih*

Sabeel (Arabic)
Path - Road - Way
The name Sabeel is mentioned in the Quran in verse 27:24 and others.
Variants: *Sabil, Sabyll, Sebil, Sebill, Sybil*

Sabeer (Arabic)
Enduring - Patient

Sabeeri (Arabic)
Enduring - Patient

Sabi (Arabic)
Affectionate

Sabigh (Arabic)
Dyer

Sabihi (Arabic)
Bright - Handsome

Sabiq (Arabic)
Advanced - Ahead
Variants: *Saabeq, Saabiq, Sabeq*

Sabir (Arabic)
Enduring - Patient
The name Sabir is mentioned in the Quran.

Sabit (Arabic)
Firm - Reliable - Stable
The name Sabit is mentioned in the Quran.
Variants: *Saabet, Saabit, Sabet, Thaabit, Thabet, Thabit*

Sabr (Arabic)
Enduring - Patience
The name Sabr is mentioned in the Quran.

Sabri (Arabic)
Enduring - Patient

Sabur (Arabic)
Enduring - Patient

Saburi (Arabic)
Enduring - Patient

Sacha (French)
Defender of Humanity
From a Russian pet form of Alexander.

Sadaad (Arabic)
Rationality - Sense
Variants: *Sadad*

Sadan (Arabic)
Prudent - Reasonable - Sensible

Sadeeq (Arabic)
Friend

Sadiq (Arabic)
Devoted - Faithful - Honest - Sincere - Truehearted
The name Sadiq is mentioned in the Quran.
Variants: *Saadeq, Saadiq, Sadeq*

Sadiqin (Arabic)
Truthful Ones
The name Sadiqin is mentioned in the Quran.
Variants: *Sadiqeen*

Sadqan (Arabic)
Sincere - Truthful

Saeed (Arabic)
Happy - Successful
Variants: *Sa'id*

Saeedan (Arabic)
Happy - Successful
Variants: *Sa'idan*

Safee (Arabic)
Pure
Variants: *Safi, Safy*

Safeen (Arabic)
Ships
Variants: *Safin*

Safeer (Arabic)
Ambassador

Safih (Arabic)
Forgiving

Safiyyaddin (Arabic)
Best of the Faith

Safuh (Arabic)
Forgiving - Lenient

Safwan (Arabic)
Pure - Rock
The name Safwan is mentioned in the Quran.
Variants: *Safwaan*

Safwat (Arabic)
Best - Finest - Prime

Sahabah (Arabic)
Companions

Sahand (Persian)
Name of a volcanic mountain in the Eastern Azerbaijan province of Iran.

Sahari (Arabic)
Deserts

Sahbah (Arabic)
Companionship - Friendship

Sahbal (Arabic)
Brave

Sahban (Arabic)
Companion - Friend

Sahbi (Arabic)
Companion - Friend

Saheer (Arabic)
Caretaker

Sahhah (Arabic)
Flawless - Whole

Sahi (Arabic)
Awake - Sober - Vigilant

Sahib (Arabic)
Companion - Friend

The name Sahib is mentioned in the Quran.

Sahil (Arabic)
Beach - River Bank - Shore
The name Sahil is mentioned in the Quran.
Variants: *Saahel, Sahel*

Sahir (Arabic)
Unsleeping - Wakeful
Variants: *Saaher, Saahir*

Sahl (Arabic)
Easy - Lenient

Sahm (Arabic)
Arrow
Variants: *Sehm*

Sahwan (Arabic)
Awake - Sober - Vigilant

Sahwi (Arabic)
Awake - Sober - Vigilant

Saibal (Arabic)
Heavy Rain - Spike of Corn

Saif (Arabic)
Sword
Variants: *Sayf, Sayf, Seif*

Saif (Arabic)
Summer
The name Saif is mentioned in the Quran.

Saifaddin (Arabic)
Sword of the Faith

Saiful Haq (Arabic)
Sword of Truth

Saiful Islam (Arabic)
Sword of Islam

Saim (Arabic)
One Who Fasts

Variants: *Sa'im, Saaem, Saaim, Saayim, Saem, Sayem, Sayim*

Sajeed (Arabic)
Prostrator - Worshiper

Sajid (Arabic)
Prostrator - Worshiper of God
The name Sajid is mentioned in the Quran.
Variants: *Saajed, Saajid, Sajed*

Sakheei (Arabic)
Generous - Noble
Variants: *Sakhi*

Sakhr (Arabic)
Boulder - Rock
The name Sakhr is mentioned in the Quran.

Sakou (Persian)
Tree-less Mountain

Salaat (Arabic)
Litany - Prayer
The name Salaat is mentioned in the Quran.

Salah (Arabic)
Faithfulness - Piety - Purity

Salahaddin (Arabic)
Reformation of the Faith - Uprightness of the Faith

Salahan (Arabic)
Devoted - Good - Upright

Salam (Arabic)
Peace - Safety - Security
The name Salam is mentioned in the Quran in verse 5:16 and others.
Variants: *Salaam, Selaam, Selam*

Salama (Arabic)
Safety - Security

Variants: *Salaama, Salaamah, Salamah*

Salar (Persian)
Chief - Leader - Sovereign
Variants: *Saalaar, Saalar, Salaar*

Saleef (Arabic)
Advanced - Preceding

Saleem (Arabic)
Intact - Righteous - Whole
The name Saleem is mentioned in the Quran.
Variants: *Salim*

Salees (Arabic)
Flowing - Gentle - Pleasant - Soft

Saleet (Arabic)
Eloquent

Sali (Arabic)
Amused - Cheerful
Variants: *Saly*

Salif (Arabic)
Preceding
Variants: *Salef*

Salih (Arabic)
Virtuous
The name *Salih* is mentioned in the Quran.
Variants: *Saaleh, Saalih, Saleh, Salih, Saulih, Solley, Soulih*

Salihan (Arabic)
Pious - Virtuous

Salihin (Arabic)
Pious - Virtuous
The name Salihin is mentioned in the Quran.

Salim (Arabic)
Intact - Righteous - Whole

Saloof (Arabic)
Advancer

Saloom (Arabic)
Safe - Unharmed

Salsabil (Arabic)
Refreshing and Tasy Drink
Variants: *Salsabeel*

Sam (English)
He (God) Has Hearkened
Short form of Samuel.

Sam (Persian)
Precious

Samaan (Arabic)
Hearer

Saman (Persian)
Capacity - Power - Wealth
Variants: *Saaman*

Samawah (Arabic)
Elevation - Greatness

Samawi (Arabic)
Heavenly

Samd (Arabic)
Composure - Determination - Perseverance

Samee (Arabic)
Hearer - Perceptive
The name Samee is mentioned in the Quran.
Variants: *Samee'*

Sameeh (Arabic)
Forgiving - Gracious - Lenient

Sameek (Arabic)
Elevated - High in Status - Majestic
Variants: *Samik*

Sameen (Persian)
Precious - Valuable

Sameer (Arabic)
Friend - Night Conversation Partner
Variants: *Sameir, Samir*

Samer (Arabic)
Friend - Night Conversation Partner
The name Samer is mentioned in the Quran.
Variants: *Samir*

Samh (Arabic)
Leniency - Pardon

Samhaan (Arabic)
Forgiving - Gracious - Lenient

Samhun (Arabic)
Forgiving - Lenient

Sami (Arabic)
Great - Lofty - Sublime
Variants: *Saami, Saamy, Samee, Samy*

Samiar (Persian)
Wealthy

Samid (Arabic)
Firm - Steadfast

Samih (Arabic)
Forgiving - Gracious
Variants: *Sameh*

Samihi (Arabic)
Forgiving - Gracious - Lenient

Samik (Arabic)
Elevated - High in Status - Majestic

Samil (Arabic)
Constant - Firmly Established - Fixed
Variants: *Samel, Thamel, Thamil*

Samit (Arabic)
Silent - Wise
Variants: *Saamet, Saamit, Samet*

Saml (Arabic)
Endurance - Perseverance

Sammad (Arabic)
Determined - Persevering - Steadfast

Samood (Arabic)
Determined - Persevering - Steadfast

Samooh (Arabic)
Forgiving - Lenient

Samoor (Arabic)
Night Conversation

Samoyla (Russian)
He (God) Has Hearkened
Form of Samuel.

Samran (Arabic)
One Who Continues Conversation Long Into the Night

Samson (English)
Sun
Variants: *Sampson*

Samuel (Biblical)
He (God) Has Hearkened

Sanaauddin (Arabic)
Supporter of Islam
Literally "greatness of the faith".

Sanan (Arabic)
Tradition - Way of Life

Sandar (Arabic)
Bold - Brave

Sandro (Italian)
Defender of Humanity
Short form of Alessandro (Italian form of Alexander).

Saniar (Persian)
Dignified - Honored

Sannee (Arabic)
Exalted - High in Status

Sansone (Italian)
Sun
Italian form of Samson.

Sanubar (Arabic)
Cypress

Sanya (Russian)
Defender of Humanity
Pet form of Alexander and Alexandra.

Saqib (Arabic)
Piercing - Sharp
The name Saqib is mentioned in the Quran.
Variants: *Thaqib*

Saqqar (Arabic)
Falconer

Saqr (Arabic)
Falcon

Saqri (Arabic)
Falcon-like

Saqrun (Arabic)
Falcon

Saraab (Arabic)
Mirage
The name Saraab is mentioned in the Quran.
Variants: *Sarab*

Sarafraz (Persian)
Dignified - Honored

NAMES FOR BOYS

Sarang (Persian)
Starling
Type of bird.

Sardar (Persian)
Chief - Leader

Sardee (Arabic)
Like Light Rain
Variants: *Thardi*

Saree (Arabic)
Stream
Variants: *Sari*

Sareem (Arabic)
Firm Decision - Resolution
Variants: *Sarim*

Sarfaraz (Persian)
Dignified - Honored

Sarih (Arabic)
Shepherd - Successful
Variants: *Sareh*

Sarim (Arabic)
Brave - Decisive - Strong
Variants: *Saarem, Saarim, Sarem*

Sarou (Persian)
Starling
Type of bird.

Sarraan (Arabic)
Happy - Pleased
Variants: *Saraan, Saran*

Sarraw (Arabic)
Honorable - Noble
Variants: *Sarau*

Sarvar (Persian)
Chief - Leader

Sarwar (Kurdish)
Chief - Leader

Sarwat (Arabic, Kurdish, Persian, Turkish, Urdu)
Affluence - Fortune - Wealth
Turkish pronunciation of Sarwah.
Variants: *Tharwat*

Sasha (English)
Defender of Humanity
Pet form of Alexander or Alexandra.

Satal (Arabic)
Type of Bird
An eagle or something similar to it.

Sattar (Arabic)
Hider
Variants: *Satar*

Saud (Arabic)
Blessed - Fortunate - Happy
Variants: *Sa'ud, Saood, Saoud*

Savak (Persian)
Gentleness

Saviz (Persian)
Friendly - Good-mannered

Sawab (Arabic)
Repentant - Reward
Variants: *Thawab*

Sawahil (Arabic)
Coasts - River Banks - Shores

Sawalan (Arabic)
Ascendancy - Domination - Power

Sawdan (Arabic)
Glorious - Great

Sawin (Arabic)
Guardian - Protector

Sawni (Arabic)
Maintainer - Protector

Sawrat (Arabic)
Revolution - Uprising
Turkish pronunciation of Sawrah.
Variants: *Thawrat*

Sawwan (Arabic)
Protector - Quartz

Sawyl (Welsh)
He (God) Has Hearkened
Welsh form of Samuel.

Sayalan (Arabic)
Effusion - Flooding - Flow

Saydad (Arabic)
Rationality - Sense

Sayhan (Arabic)
Sayhan is the name of a river in the Levant and its meaning may be "journeyer", "traveler".
Variants: *Sayhane, Seehan, Seihan, Seyhan, Seyhane, Sihan*

Saytar (Arabic)
Hiding

Sayyidah (Arabic)
Chief - Lady

Seef (Arabic)
Coast - Shore

Seepan (Kurdish)
Snow-capped Mountain

Seid (Arabic)
Lion - Wolf

Semyon (Russian)
Hearkening
Russian form of Simon.

Senan (Irish)
Old - Wise

Sendid (Arabic)
Brave Chief - Forbearing Master

Seneen (Arabic)
Years

Senya (Russian)
Hearkening - Male - Virile
PEt form of Arseni and Semyon.

Sepahdar (Persian)
Army Commander - Chief

Sepanta (Persian)
Pure - Virtous

Sepehr (Persian)
Sky

Serir (Arabic)
Bringer of Joy
Variants: *Sirrir*

Servaas (Dutch)
Redeemed - Saved

Seth (Biblical)
Appointed - Placed
Name of the third son of
prophet Adam.

Seve (Spanish)
Severe - Stern
Pet form of Severiano and
Severino.

Severiano (Italian, Portuguese, Spanish)
Severe - Stern

Severino (Italian, Portuguese, Spanish)
Severe - Stern

Severo (Italian, Portuguese, Spanish)
Severe - Stern

Shaalah (Arabic)
Kindler

Shaan (Arabic)
Greatness - Rank - Status
The name Shaan is mentioned in the Quran.
Variants: *Sha'n, Shan*

Shab (Arabic)
Young Person

Shabab (Arabic)
Young Age - Youth

Shaban (Arabic)
8th Month of the Hijri Calendar
Literal meaning may be "branching out".

Shabeeb (Arabic)
Young Age - Youth

Shabir (Arabic)
Handsome

Shaddad (Arabic)
Firm - Severe - Strong

Shaddan (Arabic)
Gazelle

Shadi (Arabic)
Seeker of Knowledge

Shadid (Arabic)
Intense - Severe - Strong
The name Shadid is mentioned in the Quran.
Variants: *Shadeed*

Shadli (Persian, Turkish)
Happy

Shadman (Persian)
Happy

Shaeef (Arabic)
Strongly in Love

Shafaq (Arabic)
Affection - Dawn - Pity - Sympathy - Twilight

Shafaqatullah (Arabic)
God's Mercy

Shafeef (Arabic)
Translucent - Transparent

Shafeei (Arabic)
Cured

Shafi (Arabic)
Healer

Shafiq (Arabic)
Compassioante - Sympathetic
Variants: *Shafeeq*

Shaghaaf (Arabic)
Strongly in Love

Shaghf (Arabic)
Strong Love

Shah (Persian)
King
Variants: *Shaah*

Shahab (Arabic)
Meteor - Shooting Star
Non-standard pronunciation of Shihab.
Variants: *Shahaab*

Shahada (Arabic)
Martyrdom - Testimony
The name Shahada is mentioned in the Quran.
Variants: *Shahadah*

Shahbaz (Arabic, Urdu)
Eagle - Eastern Imperial Eagle
Variants: *Shaahbaz, Shahbaaz*

Shahd (Arabic)
Witness

Shahdad (Persian)
Created by God - Gift from God

Shaheeb (Arabic)
Gray-colored

Shaheed (Arabic)
Martyr - Witness
The name Shaheed is mentioned in the Quran in verse 28:75 and others.
Variants: *Shaheid, Shahid, Shehid*

Shaheer (Arabic)
Distinguished - Well-known
Variants: *Shaher, Shahir*

Shahid (Arabic)
Witness
The name Shahid is mentioned in the Quran in verse 33:45 and others.
Variants: *Shaahed, Shaahid, Shahed*

Shahir (Arabic)
Populizer

Shahm (Arabic)
Intelligent - Rational - Sensible

Shahnam (Persian)
Kingly - Royal

Shahou (Persian)
Precious Pearl

Shahpur (Persian)
Prince

Shahr (Arabic)
Month
The name Shahr is mentioned in the Quran.

Shahraan (Arabic)
Famous - Moon-like
Variants: *Shahran, Shehraan, Shehran*

Shahrad (Persian)
Gracious - King

Shahram (Persian)
Trusty Soldier of the King

Shahrdad (Persian)
City-born - Cosmopolitan

Shahriar (Persian)
Chief - King

Shahrokh (Persian)
Handsome

Shahroud (Persian)
Beloved Son

Shahsavar (Persian)
Royal Knight

Shaidan (Arabic)
Great - High in Status

Shaigan (Persian)
Precious - Valuable - Worthy

Shail (Arabic)
Greatness - Highness of Status

Shajar (Arabic)
Tree
The name Shajar is mentioned in the Quran.

Shakeeb (Persian)
Patience - Perseverance

Shakir (Arabic)
Appreciative - Thankful
The name Shakir is used in the Quran.
Variants: *Shaaker, Shaakir, Shaker*

Shakira (Arabic)
Appreciative - Thankful
Variants: *Shaakera, Shaakerah, Shaakira, Shaakirah, Shakera, Shakerah, Shakirah*

Shakirullah (Arabic)
Thankful Toward God

Shakkar (Arabic)
Thankful

Shakur (Arabic)
Appreciative - Thankful
Variants: *Shakoor*

Shalan (Arabic)
Brilliant - Lit - Radiant
Variants: *Sha'lan, Shaalan, Shalaan*

Shaleel (Arabic)
Gorge - Ravine

Shamakh (Arabic)
Great - High in Status

Shamees (Arabic)
Bright - Sunny

Shamehr (Persian)
Happy - Kind

Shamikh (Arabic)
Great - High - Lofty - Towering
Variants: *Shaamikh, Shamekh*

Shamir (Hebrew)
End of a Rope - Flint Stone
Variants: *Shameer*

Shamis (Arabic)
Bright - Sunlit

Shammam (Arabic)
Muskmelon

Shams (Arabic)
Light and Radiance
The name *Shams* is mentioned in the Quran.

Shamsaddin (Arabic)
Supporter of Islam
Literally "sun of the faith".
Variants: *Shamsadeen, Shamsuddin, Shamsudeen*

Shamsan (Arabic)
Bright - Sunlit

Shannaf (Arabic)
Intelligent

Shapur (Persian)
Prince

Shaqeer (Arabic)
Fair-skinned

Shaqeeri (Arabic)
Fair-skinned

Shaqir (Arabic)
Fair-skinned

Shaqoor (Arabic)
Fair-skinned
Variants: *Shaqur*

Shaqroon (Arabic)
Fair-skinned

Sharaf (Arabic)
Dignity - Honor

Shareeq (Arabic)
East - Place of Sunrise

Sharfan (Arabic)
High in Status - Honorable

Sharif (Arabic)
Glorious - High in Status - Honored

Shariq (Arabic)
Variants: *Glowing, Radiant*

Sharrah (Arabic)
Explainer - Interpreter

Sharuf (Arabic)
Glorious - Honored - Noble

Sharveen (Persian)
Eternal - Immortal
Sharveen is a Persian name for boys that means "immortal", "eternal".

Shaswar (Kurdish, Persian)
Royal Knight

Shatb (Arabic)
Slim - Tall

Shati (Arabic)
Beach - Coast - Side
The name Shati is mentioned in the Quran.

Shaun (Irish Gaelic)
God is Gracious
Anglicized spelling of Seán, form of John.

Shawal (Arabic)
Great - High in Status

Shawamikh (Arabic)
Great - High in Status

Shawas (Arabic)
Courage

Shaweef (Arabic)
Adornment - Observation

Shaweer (Arabic)
Handsome

Shawn (Irish Gaelic)
God is Gracious

Anglicized spelling of Seán, form of John.

Shawqan (Arabic)
Desirous - Longing

Shawqi (Arabic)
Desirous - Longing

Shawr (Arabic)
Honey

Shayan (Kurdish)
Deserving - Worthy
Variants: *Shaayan, Shayaan*

Shayif (Arabic)
Observer

Shayraf (Arabic)
Great - Honorable

Shayyir (Arabic)
Handsome

Shayyir Ali (Arabic)
Great - Handsome

Sheaaf (Arabic)
Short Shower of Rain - Strong Love

Sheeban (Arabic)
Snow - White
Variants: *Shibaan, Shiban*

Shervan (Persian)
Cypress
A type of tree.

Shibl (Arabic)
Lion Cub

Shifa (Arabic)
Cure - Healing - Remedy
The name Shifa is mentioned in the Quran.
Variants: *Shefa, Shefaa, Shifaa*

NAMES FOR BOYS

Shifaullah (Arabic)
God's Healing

Shihab (Arabic)
Meteor - Shooting Star
Variants: *Shehaab, Shehab, Shihaab*

Shuaif (Arabic)
Strong Love

Shufaiq (Arabic)
Mercy - Pity

Shuhaib (Arabic)
Little Shooting Star

Shuhaid (Arabic)
Witness

Shuhair (Arabic)
Famous - Month

Shuhrokh (Persian)
Kingly - Majestic - Stately

Shuhud (Arabic)
Witnesses
The name Shuhud is mentioned in the Quran.

Shujaa (Arabic)
Brave

Shujaat (Arabic)
Bravery - Courage
Variants: *Shojaat, Shuja'at*

Shukr (Arabic)
Thankfulness
Shukr is an Arabic name for boys and girls that means "thankfulness", "appreciation".. The name Shukr is mentioned in the Quran.

Shukrullah (Arabic)
Thankfulness Toward God

Shulaykhan (Arabic)
Handsome

Shuqair (Arabic)
Fair-skinned

Shuqairah (Arabic)
Fair-skinned

Shuqairy (Arabic)
Fair-skinned

Shuqur (Arabic)
Blondness - Fairness of Skin
Variants: *Shoqur*

Shuraa (Arabic)
Consultation - Council - Honeycomb Cell - View

Shuraif (Arabic)
Glory - Honor

Shuraim (Arabic)
Bay - Gulf - Inlet
Variants: *Shoraim*

Shuraiq (Arabic)
East - Place of Sunrise

Shuruq (Arabic)
Sunrise

Shuwair (Arabic)
Handsome

Siamak (Persian)
Black-haired

Siarl (Welsh)
Free Man
Welsh form of Charles.

Siavash (Persian)
Keeper of Black Horses

Siba (Arabic)
Childhood - Emotion - Enthusiasm - Youthfulness
Variants: *Seba, Sebaa, Sibaa, Syba*

Sibagh (Arabic)
Dye - Paint

Siddiq (Arabic)
Devoted - Loyal - True Friend - Truthful
The name Siddiq is mentioned in the Quran.
Variants: *Seddiq, Sediq, Siddeeq, Siddique, Sideeq*

Sidqi (Arabic)
Sincere - Truthful

Sidratul Muntaha (Arabic)
Lote Tree of the Utmost Boundary
The name Sidratul Muntaha is mentioned in the Quran. It is the name of a tree in or near Paradise.
Variants: *Sidrat Ul Muntaha, Sidratulmuntaha*

Sigurd (Scandinavian)
Guardian of Victory

Sihab (Arabic)
Deep Water Well

Sihah (Arabic)
Faultless - Healthy

Sihlal (Arabic)
Gentle - Lenient

Sikandar (Arabic)
Defender of Humanity
Variant of Iskandar.

Silaam (Arabic)
Peace-making
Variants: *Selam*

Silas (Biblical)
Wood
From Latin.

Silvano (Italian)
Wood

Silver (English)
Fair-haired - Silver

Silvester (English, German)
Of the Woods
Variants: *Sylvester*

Simab (Persian)
Mercury
Refers to the liquid metallic element.
Variants: *Seemab*

Simar (Arabic)
Night Conversation

Simeon (Biblical)
Hearkening
Also known as Simon.

Simon (English)
Hearkening
Usual English form of Simeon.

Sina (Arabic)
Mountain Sinae

Sinan (Arabic)
Leopard - Spearhead

Sineen (Arabic)
Mountain Sinai
The name Sineen is mentioned in the Quran.
Variants: *Senin, Sinin*

Sinwan (Arabic)
Multiple Trees Growing From the Same Root
The name Sinwan is mentioned in the Quran.

Siraj (Arabic)
Cresset - Lamp - Light
Variants: *Seraa, Seraj, Siraaj*

Siraj al-Haq (Arabic)
Lamp of Truth
Variants: *Sirajulhaq*

Sirajaddin (Arabic)
Supporter of Islam
Literally "lamp of the faith".
Variants: *Sirajuddin*

Sirat (Arabic)
Path
The name Sirat is mentioned in the Quran.
Variants: *Serat, Siraat*

Sirhan (Arabic)
Lion - Wolf
Variants: *Serhan*

Sirvan (Kurdish, Persian)
Name of a river in Eastern Iraq and Western Iran.
Variants: *Sirwan*

Siyadah (Arabic)
Glory - Greatness - Honor - Leadership

Siyam (Arabic)
The name Siyam is mentioned in the Quran.
Variants: *Fasting*

Siyaq (Arabic)
Articulation - Context

Sobaan (Arabic)
Repentance
Variants: *Sawbaan, Sawban, Sowbaan, Sowban, Thowban, Thuban*

Sohrab (Persian)
Red Water
Name of a mythical Persian hero, son of Rustam.

Solomon (Biblical)
Peaceful
Name of a king of Israel and a prophet mentioned in the Quran.

Solwi (Arabic)
Comfort - Consolation

Soran (Kurdish)
Name of a region of Kurdistan of Iraq.

Soren (Scandinavian)
Severe - Stern
Form of Severinus.

Soroush (Kurdish, Persian)
Inspiration - Messenger - Revelation

Spencer (English)
Dispenser
From a surname.

Spiridon (Russian)
Soul - Spirit

Staffan (Swedish)
Crown - Garland
Form of Stephen.

Stanley (English)
Stone Clearing

Steaphan (Scottish Gaelic)
Crown - Garland
Form of Stephen.

Stefan (German, Scandinavian)
Crown - Garland
Form of Stephen.

Stefano (Italian)
Crown - Garland
Italian form of Stephen.

Steffan (Welsh)
Crown - Garland
Welsh form of Steffan.

Steffen (German)
Crown - Garland
Form of Stephen.

Sten (Swedish)
Stone

Stenya (Russian)
Crown - Garland
Pet form of Stepan, from Stephan.

Stepan (Russian)
Crown - Garland
Russian form of Stephan.

Stephen (English)
Crown - Garland
Variants: *Stephan, Steven*

Steve (English)
Crown - Garland
Short form of Stephen and Steven.

Steven (English)
Crown - Garland
Variant of Stephen.

Stevie (English)
Crown - Garland
Pet form of Stephen and Stephanie.

Stewart (English)
Steward
Variant of Stuart.

Stian (Scandinavian)
Wanderer

Stiana (Irish Gaelic)
Crown - Garland
Form of Stephen.

Stig (Scandinavian)
Wanderer
From Stígr, short for Stígandr ("wanderer").

Storm (English)
Storm

Styopa (Russian)
Crown - Garland
Pet form of Stepan, from Stephan.

Suaidan (Arabic)
Happy - Successful
Variants: *Su'aidan*

Subah (Arabic)
Flame of a Lamp - Handsome

Subaih (Arabic)
Handsome - Radiant
Variants: *Sobaih, Sobayh, Subayh*

Subail (Arabic)
Pouring Rain - Spike of Corn
Variants: *Sobail*

Subair (Arabic)
Enduring - Patient

Subayyaah (Arabic)
Morning

Subh (Arabic)
Morning
The name Subh is mentioned in the Quran.

Subhi (Arabic)
Bright

Sudain (Arabic)
Maintainer of the Kaaba
Variants: *Sodain*

Sudaiq (Arabic)
Sincere - Truthful

Sudair (Arabic)
Alder Buckthorn
A type of tree.
Variants: *Sodair*

Sudairi (Arabic)
Alder Buckthorn
A type of tree. The name is an attribution to said tree.
Variants: *Sodayri*

Sudais (Arabic)
One Sixth - Sixth
Variants: *Sodais, Sodays, Sudays*

Sudur (Arabic)
Hearts
The name Sudur is mentioned in the Quran.
Variants: *Sodur, Sudoor*

Sufan (Arabic)
Amadou

Sufian (Arabic)
Agile - Nimble
Variants: *Sofiaan, Sofian, Sufiaan, Sufyaan, Sufyan*

Sufyan (Arabic)
Slender - Slim

Suhaib (Arabic)
Red-brown-haired

Suhaibun (Arabic)
Red-brown-haired

Suhaid (Arabic)
Handsome

Suhail (Arabic)
Easy - Lenient
Variants: *Sohail*

Suhaim (Arabic)
Arrow
Variants: *Sohaim, Soheim, Suhaym, Suhayme, Suheim*

Suhair (Arabic)
Unsleeping - Wakeful
Variants: *Sohair, Suhayr*

Suhbah (Arabic)
Companionship - Friendship

Suhban (Arabic)
Companion - Friend

Suhbani (Arabic)
Companion - Friend

Sukkar (Arabic)
Sugar
Variants: *Sokar, Sukar*

Sulaaf (Arabic)
Predecessors
Variants: *Solaf*

Sulaif (Arabic)
Advanced - Preceding

Sulaikan (Arabic)
Follower of a Path

Sulaim (Arabic)
Safe - Unharmed

Sulaiman (Arabic, Hebrew)
Peace - Peaceful
Sulaiman is one of the prophets mentioned in the Quran, known as Solomon in the Bible.
Variants: *Solaiman, Solaymaan, Solayman, Sulaimaan, Sulayman*

Sulaytan (Arabic)
King - Power - Ruler

Sulh (Arabic)
Ceasfire - Peace
The name Sulh is mentioned in the Quran.

Suloof (Arabic)
Advancement

Sultan (Arabic)
King - Power - Ruler
Variants: *Soltan*

Sumaih (Arabic)
Forgiving - Gracious - Lenient

Sumair (Arabic)
Friend - Night Conversation Partner
Variants: *Somair, Someir, Sumeir*

Sumama (Arabic)
Rescue - Salvation
Variants: *Sumamah, Thumama, Thumamah*

Sumood (Arabic)
Composure - Determination - Perseverance

Sumou (Arabic)
Elevation - Greatness

Sumran (Arabic)
Tan-skinned

Sunain (Arabic)
Leopard - Spearhead

Sunan (Arabic)
Traditions - Ways of Life
The name Sunan is mentioned in the Quran.

Sunayyan (Arabic)
Exalted - High in Status - Radiant

Sunud (Arabic)
Climb - Dependence - Reliance

Suqaib (Arabic)
Neighbor

Suqair (Arabic)
Little Falcon

Sureen (Persian)
Powerful - Strong

Sushiant (Persian)
Helper - Rescuer

Suwaib (Arabic)
Reward
Variants: *Thuwaib*

Suwaibih (Arabic)
Bright - Fresh

Suwaibir (Arabic)
Enduring - Patient

Suwaidan (Arabic)
Great - Noble - Respected

Suwaidin (Arabic)
Maintainer of the Kaaba

Suwaif (Arabic)
Enduring - Patient

Suwaih (Arabic)
One Who Fasts

Suwaihir (Arabic)
One Who Stays Up During the Night

Suwailih (Arabic)
Good - Pious

Suwailim (Arabic)
Safe - Unharmed - Whole

Suwaim (Arabic)
Bamboo - Gold

Suwar (Arabic)
Fragrance - Musk Container

Suwayhil (Arabic)
Gentle - Lenient

Sven (Swedish)
Boy - Lad

Sylvain (French)
Wood
French form of Silvanus.

This page intentionally left blank

T

Taal (Arabic)
Ascending - Come
The name can be a command ("come!") or a description of the state of something that ascends.

Taavi (Finnish)
Darling
Finnish form of David.

Taazaz (Arabic)
Honor - Might - Power

Tabarak (Arabic)
Blessed

Tabarruk (Arabic)
Blessedness

Tabith (Aramaic)
Gazelle

Tabseer (Arabic)
Education - Enlightenment

Tadbir (Arabic)
Contrivance - Organization - Procurement

Tadris (Arabic)
Research - Study

Taeb (Arabic)
Repenting - Virtuous
Variants: *Taaeb, Taaib, Taeib, Taib, Tayeb*

Tafaf (Arabic)
Sundown

Tafali (Arabic)
Sundown - Sunup

Tafheem (Arabic)
Elaboration - Illustration
Variants: *Tafhim, Tefhim*

Tafli (Arabic)
Delicate - Gentle - Soft

Taghlib (Arabic)
The Win - They Defeat Their Enemies

Taha (Arabic)
Taha is the name of chapter 20 of the Quran and is also the word that the chapter starts with. The meaning of this word is not known, some people think it is another name for the Prophet Muhammad (peace and blessings of Allah upon him).

Tahani (Arabic)
Congratulations

Tahannud (Arabic)
Friendliness - Gentleness

Tahir (Arabic)
Pure
Variants: *Taaher, Taahir, Taher*

Tahmeed (Arabic)
Praising of God
Variants: *Tahmid, Tehmid*

Tahrir (Arabic)
Liberation

Tahsin (Arabic)
Beautification - Improvement
Variants: *Tahseen, Tehsin*

Tahzeeb (Arabic)
Edification - Purification - Rectification - Refinement

Taif (Arabic)
Circumambulator - Visitation
The name Taif is used in the Quran.
Variants: *Taaef, Taaif, Taef*

Taihan (Arabic)
Vast
Variants: *Taihaan, Tayhaan, Tayhan, Teihan, Teyhan*

Taimaz (Turkish)
Established - Firm

Tajammul (Arabic)
Beautification
Variants: *Tajammol, Tajamol, Tajamul*

Tajdar (Persian)
Crowned

Takleef (Arabic)
Assignment - To Give Someone a Duty

Takreem (Arabic)
Graciousness - Honor - Respect
Variants: *Takrim, Tekrim*

Talaab (Arabic)
Desired - Sought After

Talaat (Arabic, Turkish)
Aspect - Countenance - Face
Turkish pronunciation of Talaah.

Talab (Arabic)
Demand - Desire - Seeker
The name Talab is mentioned in the Quran.

Talal (Arabic)
Coater
One who puts a coat of varnish or dye on something.

Talha (Arabic)
Banana Tree
Variants: *Talhah*

Talib (Arabic)
Pursuer - Seeker - Seeker of Knowledge
The name Talib is mentioned in the Quran.
Variants: *Taaleb, Taalib, Taleb*

Talibullah (Arabic)
Seeker of God

Tam (Scottish)
Twin
Short form of Thomas.

Tamanna (Arabic)
Hope - Wish
Variants: *Tamana, Tamanaa, Tamannaa*

Tamassuk (Arabic)
Adherence

Tamasul (Arabic)
Similarity

Tamheed (Arabic)
Facilitation - Preparation

Tami (Arabic)
Elevated - Exalted - High

Tamir (Arabic)
Date Merchant

Tammam (Arabic)
Complete - Whole

Tammar (Arabic)
Date Merchant

Tamur (Arabic)
Variants: *Tamoor*

Taneem (Arabic)
Blessedness
Variants: *Tan'im, Taneim, Tanim*

Taneli (Finnish)
God is My Judge
Finnish form of Daniel.

Taqadum (Arabic)
Advancement - Progress

Tarashud (Arabic)
Guidance

Tareef (Arabic)
Exquisite - Quaint - Rate

Tareem (Arabic)
Humble Supplicator

Tarheeb (Arabic)
Graciousness - Spaciousness - Vastness

Tariq (Arabic)
Star
The name *Tariq* is mentioned in the Quran.
Variants: *Taarek, Taareq, Taarik, Taariq, Tarek, Tareq, Tarik*

Tarkheem (Arabic)
Mellowing - Softening

Tarooq (Arabic)
Star

Tasafi (Arabic)
Loyalty - Sincerity

Tasahir (Arabic)
Vigils

Tasamuh (Arabic)
Forbearance - Forgiveness - Pardon

Taseen (Arabic)
Unknown
Taseen is a Quranic name for boys. Chapter 27 of the Quran starts with the two Arabic letters Ta and seen, which together are read as Taseen, the meaning of which is not known.
Variants: *Taaseen, Taasin, Tasin*

Taskeen (Arabic)
Tranquility

Tasmir (Arabic)
Blossoming - Flourishing - Producing
Variants: *Tathmir*

Tasneem (Arabic)
Falling Water - Fountain in Paradise
Variants: *Tasnim*

Tasteer (Arabic)
To Author - To Write

Tasweer (Arabic)
To Describe - To Paint - To Picture

Tatheer (Arabic)
Purification
The name Tatheer is mentioned in the Quran.
Variants: *Tateheer, Tathir*

Tauno (Finnish)
Great - Magnificent
Finnish form of Augustine.

Tavana (Persian)
Able - Powerful

Tawab (Arabic)
Repentant
The name Tawab is mentioned in the Quran.
Variants: *Tawwab*

Tawadud (Arabic)
Affection - Love

Tawaf (Arabic)
Circumambulation
Variants: *Tawaaf, Tewaf*

NAMES FOR BOYS

Tawafiq (Arabic)
Success

Tawakkul (Arabic)
Reliance Upon God
Variants: *Tauakkul, Tawakkol, Tawakol, Tawakul*

Tawaqur (Arabic)
Calmness - Composure - Solemnity

Tawazou (Arabic)
Humility

Taweel (Arabic)
Long - Tall
The name Taweel is mentioned in the Quran.

Tawfeeq (Arabic)
Success
The name Tawfeeq is used in the Quran.
Variants: *Taufeeq, Taufiq, Taufique, Tawfeeque, Tawfiq*

Tawheed (Arabic)
Belief in God's Oneness
Variants: *Tauheed, Tauhid, Tawhid*

Tawkeel (Arabic)
Reliance Upon God
Variants: *Taukeel, Taukil, Tawkil*

Tawl (Arabic)
Might - Power - Strength
The name Tawl is mentioned in the Quran.

Tawlan (Arabic)
Elevated - Great - Mighty
The name Tawlan is mentioned in the Quran.

Tawqan (Arabic)
Desirous

Tawus (Arabic)
Beautiful - Peafowl

Tawwad (Arabic)
Affection - Love

Tayil (Arabic)
Great - Powerful

Taylor (English)
Tailor

Taymur (Arabic, Persian, Turkish)
Iron - Steel
Originally from Turkic.

Taysir (Arabic)
Ease - Facilitation

Tayyib (Arabic)
Good - Pure - Virtuous
The name Tayyib is mentioned in the Quran.
Variants: *Taeib, Taib, Tayeb, Tayib, Tayyeb*

Tazayyun (Arabic)
Adornment - Beautification

Tazeen (Arabic)
Adornment - Beautification
Variants: *Tazieen, Tazyeen, Tazyin*

Teague (Irish)
Philosopher - Poet
From Gaelic Tadhg.
Variants: *Teigue*

Teeb (Arabic)
Perfume

Teodosio (Italian, Portuguese, Spanish)
Gift of God

Teofilo (Italian, Portuguese, Spanish)
Lover of God
Form of Theophilus.

Terry (English)
Power of the Tribe

Thaalab (Arabic)
Fox
Variants: *Saalab, Salab*

Thameen (Arabic)
Precious - Valable
Variants: *Sameen*

Thamir (Arabic)
Fruit-bearing - Productive - Profitable
Variants: *Saamir, Samer, Samir, Thaamir, Thamer*

Thayeb (Arabic)
Repentant
Variants: *Sayeb, Sayib, Thaayeb, Thaib*

Theodoor (Dutch)
Gift of God
Form of Theodore

Theodor (German)
Gift of God
Form of Theodore.

Theodore (English)
Gift of God
Originally from Greek.

Theophilus (English)
Friend of God

Thomas (Biblical)
Twin

Thuailib (Arabic)
Fox
Variants: *Suaylib*

Tibaq (Arabic)
Equivalent - Similar

The name Tibaq is mentioned in the Quran.

Tibhaj (Arabic)
Beauty - Radiance

Tibr (Arabic)
Gold Ore

Tilal (Arabic)
Exquisite - Light Rain - Rare

Tim (English)
One Who Honors God
Short for Timothy.

Timothy (English)
One Who Honors God

Tinjal (Arabic)
Beauty of the Eyes

Tireem (Arabic)
Honey - Tall - Thick Clouds

Tirhab (Arabic)
Graciousness - Spaciousness - Vastness

Tobias (Biblical)
God is Good
From Hebrew Tobiah.

Toby (English)
God is Good
Vernacular form of Tobias.

Tom (English)
Twin
Short form of Thomas.

Tomos (Welsh)
Twin
Welsh form of Thomas.

Trevor (Welsh)
Large Settlement
From a Welsh surname, from various place names.

Truman (English)
Trustworthy - Trusty
Variants: *Trueman*

Tufan (Arabic)
Cataclysm - Deluge - Flood
The name Tufan is mentioned in the Quran.

Tufayl (Arabic)
Beautiful - Gentle - Little Child - Soft

Tullaab (Arabic)
Seekers - Students

Tumaim (Arabic)
Little Sea

Turaj (Persian)
Brave

Turas (Arabic)
Inheritance
The name Turas is mentioned in the Quran.

Tuwaij (Arabic)
Little Crown

Tuwailib (Arabic)
Seeker of Knowledge - Student

Tyler (English)
Roof Tiler

U

Ubad (Arabic)
Worshipers

Ubadah (Arabic)
Worshipers

Ubai (Arabic)
Father
Diminutive form of Ab ("father").
Variants: *Obay, Obayy, Ubay, Ubayy*

Ubaid (Arabic)
Servant of God
Variants: *Obaid, Obayd, Ubayd*

Ubaidullah (Arabic)
Servant of God
Variants: *Ubaydullah*

Udai (Arabic)
Warrior
Variants: *Odai, Oday, Uday*

Udail (Arabic)
Fair - Just

Udo (German)
Prosperous

Ufair (Arabic)
Brave

Ugo (Italian)
Heart - Mind - Spirit
Italian form of Hugh.

Uhaid (Arabic)
Covenant - Promise

Uhdawi (Arabic)
Guardian - Protector
Variants: *Ohdawi*

Uhud (Arabic)
Name of a mountain near Medina where a battle took place.
Variants: *Ohud*

Uilleam (Scottish Gaelic)
Determined Protector
Form of William.

Ujab (Arabic)
Amazement - Wonder
The name Ujab is mentioned in the Quran.

Ulf (Danish, Swedish)
Wolf

Ulla (Scandinavian)
Power of Prosperity
Form of Ulrika.

Ulric (English)
Power of Prosperity - Powerful Wolf
Cognate of either Wulfric or Ulrich.
Variants: *Ulrick*

Ulrich (German)
Power of Prosperity

Ulv (Norwegian)
Wolf

Umaijid (Arabic)
Glorious - Majestic
Variants: *Omaijed*

Umair (Arabic)
Life - Long-lived
Variants: *Omayr, Umayr Omair*

Umairi (Arabic)
Long-lived

Umaizar (Arabic)
Strong
Variants: *Omaizar*

Umar (Arabic)
Life - Long-lived
Variants: *Omar, Omer, Umer*

Umberto (Italian)
Famous Bear-cub
Italian form of Humbert.

Umrah (Arabic)
Minor Pilgrimage - Overhaul - Restoration - Revival
The name Umrah is mentioned in the Quran.

Uraif (Arabic)
Good Scent

Urban (Czech, Danish, English, Polish, Swedish)
City-dweller

Urrab (Arabic)
Eloquent - Fluent

Urs (German)
Bear

Urwah (Arabic)
Ever-green Tree - Handhold - Lion
The name Urwah is mentioned in the Quran in verse 31:22.
Variants: *Orwa, Orwah, Urwa*

Usaim (Arabic)
Guardian - Protector - Refuge
Variants: *Osaim, Osaym, Usaym*

Usman (Arabic)
Baby Houbara - Baby Snake

Utaib (Arabic)
Gentleness - Softness

Utaif (Arabic)
Affectionate - Compassionate

Utaiq (Arabic)
Generosity - Virtue

Utayk (Arabic)
Good - Noble - Pure

Uwaim (Arabic)
Year

Uwain (Arabic)
Helper - Supporter
Variants: *Owain, Uwayn*

Uwaiz (Arabic)
Restitution

Uwaymir (Arabic)
Life - Long-lived
Variants: *Owaimir, Owaymir, Uwaimir*

Uzaib (Arabic)
Fresh Water

Uzaina (Arabic)
Listener - Obedient
Variants: *Odaina, Odayna, Ozaina, Udaina, Uzaina*

Uzair (Arabic)
God Helped
The name Uzair is mentioned in the Quran, known as Ezra or Azariah in the Bible.

Uzaiz (Arabic)
Honor - Might - Power

V

Val (English)
Healthy - Strong
Short form of Valerie or Valentine.

Valter (Scandinavian)
Army Commander

Vanya (Russian)
God is Gracious
Pet form of Ivan, form of John.

Vasili (Russian)
Royal
Form of Basil.

Vaughan (English, Welsh)
Small

Velten (German)
Healthy - Strong
Form of Valentine.

Venedikt (Russian)
Blessed

Venya (Russian)
Son of the South
Pet form of Venyamin.

Venyamin (Russian)
Son of the South
Form of Benjamin.

Vere (English)
Alder
From a surname referring to places in northern France.

Vester (German)
Of the Woods
Short form of Silvester.

Vicente (Spanish)
Conquering
Form of Vincent.

Victor (English)
Conqueror

Vidal (Spanish)
Alive
Form of Vitale.

Vilhelm (Scandinavian)
Determined Protector
Form of William.

Vilmos (Hungarian)
Determined Protector
Form of William.

Vince (English)
Conquering
Short form of Vincent.

Vincent (Danish, Dutch, English, French)
Conquering
From Latin Vincens.

Vittore (Italian)
Conqueror
Form of Victor.

Vittorio (Italian)
Conqueror
From a derivative of Victor.

Viv (English)
Alive
Short form of Vivian and Vivien.

Vivian (English)
Alive
Variants: *Vyvyan*

Vladimir (Russian)
Powerful - Ruler of the World

Volker (German)
Warrior of the People

Volkmar (German)
Famous People

This page intentionally left blank

W

Waad (Arabic)
Promise
The name Waad is mentioned in the Quran.
Variants: *Wa'd, Wad*

Waali (Arabic)
Governor - Prefect - Ruler
Variants: *Waaly, Walee, Wali*

Waazi (Arabic)
Distributor - Protector
Variants: *Waazy, Wazi*

Wad (Arabic)
Affection - Love

Waddeen (Arabic)
Loving Ones

Wadeed (Arabic)
Affectionate - Loving
Variants: *Wadid*

Wadi (Arabic)
Valley
The name Wadi is mentioned in the Quran.
Variants: *Waadi, Wady*

Wadid (Arabic)
Affectionate - Loving
Variants: *Waaded, Waadid, Waded*

Wadood (Arabic)
Affectionate - Loving
The name Wadood is mentioned in the Quran.

Wael (Arabic)
Seeker of Refuge - Tribe
Variants: *Waael, Waail, Wail*

Waf (Arabic)
Faithful - Loyal - Perfect - Whole

Wafa (Arabic)
Completion - Faithfulness - Fulfillment - Loyalty

Wafaee (Arabic)
Complete - Faithful - Loyal

Wafee (Arabic)
Faithful - Loyal
Variants: *Wafi, Wafiy*

Wafeeq (Arabic)
Appropriate - Companion - Friend - Harmonious

Wafeer (Arabic)
Plenty

Wafi (Arabic)
Faithful - Loyal
Wafi is an indirect Quranic name for boys that means "faithful", "loyal". It is derived from the Quranic W-F-Y root. This name is different from Wafee, they have the same meaning but different pronunciations.

Wafiq (Arabic)
Waafeq - Waafiq - Wafeq
Wafiq is an indirect Quranic name for boys that means "successful". It is derived from the W-F-Q root which is used in the Quran.
Variants: *Successful*

Wahb (Arabic)
Bestowal - Blessing - Gift

Wahban (Arabic)
Generous - Giving

Wahbi (Arabic)
Bestowal - Gift

Wahbullah (Arabic)
Gift from God

Wahdan (Arabic)
Peerless - Unique

Wahdat (Arabic)
Wahdat is the Turkish pronunciation of Wahdah.

Waheeb (Arabic)
Bestowal - Gift

Waheebullah (Arabic)
Gift from God

Waheed (Arabic)
Alone - Peerless - Singular - Unique
The name Waheed is mentioned in the Quran.
Variants: *Wahid, Wehid*

Wahhab (Arabic)
Bestower - Giver
The name Wahhab is mentioned in the Quran.

Wahib (Arabic)
Bestower - Giver

Wahid (Arabic)
One - Unique
The name Wahid is mentioned in the Quran.

Wajeed (Arabic)
Affectionate - Loving

Wajeeh (Arabic)
Honorable - Noble - Prestigious

Wajeehan (Arabic)
Honorable - Noble - Prestigious

Wajib (Arabic)
Duty
Variants: *Waajeb, Waajib, Wajeb*

Wajid (Arabic)
Acquirer - Finder - Loving

Wakib (Arabic)
Gentle Walker

Wakil (Arabic)
Agent - Deputy - Trustee
The name Wakil is mentioned in the Quran.
Variants: *Wakeel*

Wal (Arabic)
Helper - Master

Waldamar (Dutch, German, Scandinavian)
Famous Rule

Walee (Arabic)
Friend - Guardian - Patron - Protector
The name Walee is mentioned in the Quran.
Variants: *Walee, Walei, Wali*

Waleed (Arabic)
Baby - Boy - Infant - Newborn

Walenty (Polish)
Healthy - Strong
Form of Valentine.

Walentyna (Polish)
Healthy - Strong
Feminine of Walenty.

Waliyuddin (Arabic)
Supporter of Islam
Variants: *Wali Uddin*

Wallace (English, Scottish)
Celtic - Foreign

Walter (English, German, Scandinavian)
Army Commander

Waqar (Arabic)
Composure - Dignity - Self-respect
Variants: *Waqaar*

Waqid (Arabic)
Brilliant - Kindled
Variants: *Waaqed, Waaqid, Waqed*

Waqqas (Arabic)
Breaker - Destroyer

Waqur (Arabic)
Composed - Dignified

Ward (Arabic)
Flower - Rose
Variants: *Werd*

Ward (English)
Guard - Watchman
From a surname.

Wardaa (Arabic)
Flower - Rose
Variants: *Warda*

Wardi (Arabic)
Rose-like - Rosy

Wareef (Arabic)
Blooming - Flourishing

Warid (Arabic)
Aware - Experienced - Learned
Variants: *Waared, Waarid, Wared*

Warish (Arabic)
Agile - Sprightly

Warith (Arabic)
Inheritor - Long-lived
Variants: *Waares, Waareth, Waaris, Waarith, Wareth, Waris*

Warshan (Arabic)
Pigeon

Wasaaf (Arabic)
Describer - Praiser
Variants: *Wasaf, Wassaaf, Wassaf*

Waseem (Arabic)
Handsome
Variants: *Wasim*

Waseeq (Arabic)
Firm - Strong - Trustworthy
Variants: *Wasiq, Watheeq, Wathiq*

Wasfi (Arabic)
Praiseworthy
Variants: *Wasfee, Wasfy*

Washan (Arabic)
Elevated Land - Highland

Wasif (Arabic)
Describer - Praiser
Variants: *Waasef, Waasif, Wasef*

Wasil (Arabic)
Connected - Friend
Variants: *Waasel, Waasil, Wasel*

Wasl (Arabic)
Attachment - Connection - Juncture - Receipt

Wathaq (Arabic)
Home - Solemn Promsie
Variants: *Wasaaq, Wasaq, Wathaaq*

Wathiq (Arabic)
Certain - Sure

Wayel (Arabic)
Clan - Tribe

Wayne (English)
Carter - Cartwright

Wazee (Arabic)
Clean - Handsome

Wazian (Arabic)
Clean - Handsome

Wazin (Arabic)
Collator - Comparer - Weigher

Wazir (Arabic)
Assistant - Helper - Minister
Variants: *Wazeer*

Waziran (Arabic)
Ministers - Viziers

Wazn (Arabic)
Gauge - Measure - Weighing - Weight

Wazzah (Arabic)
Clear - Handsome

Wesly (English)
Western Meadow - Western Wood
From a surname referring to a place name.

Wiam (Arabic)
Concord - Harmony - Peace - Rapport
Variants: *Wi'am, Wiaam*

Wid (Arabic)
Affection - Harmony - Love
Variants: *Widd*

Widad (Arabic)
Affection - Harmony - Love
Variants: *Wedaad, Wedad, Widaad*

Widadi (Arabic)
Affectionate - Loving

Wifaq (Arabic)
Harmony - Sympathy - Unity
Variants: *Wefaaq, Wefaq, Wfaaq*

Wijdan (Arabic)
Affection - Conscience - Fondness - Soul - Tenderness
Variants: *Wejdaan, Wejdan, Wijdaan*

Wildan (Arabic)
Boys
The name Wildan is mentioned in the Quran. It is the plural of Walad ("boy", "child").
Variants: *Weldaan, Weldan, Wildaan*

Wilhelm (German)
Determined Protector
Form of William.

Will (English)
Determined Protector
Short form of William.

William (German)
Determined Protector

Wirad (Arabic)
Flowers - Roses
Variants: *Werad, Wiraad*

Wisal (Arabic)
Communion - Reunion
Variants: *Wesal, Wisaal*

Wisam (Arabic)
Handsome
Variants: *Wesaam, Wesam, Wisaam*

Wolfram (German)
Wolf Raven

Woodrow (English)
Originally a name for someone who lived by a row of houses by a wood.

Wuhaib (Arabic)
Bestowal - Gift

Wuraid (Arabic)
Little Flower

Wyn (Welsh)
Blessed - White

This page intentionally left blank

Y

Yahya (Arabic)
Alive
The name Yahya is mentioned in the Quran in verse 3:39.
Variants: *Iahea, Ieahia, Yahea, Yaheaa, Yahia, Yahiaa, Yahya, Yahyaa, Yehea, Yeheaa, Yehia, Yehiaa, Yehya, Yehyaa*

Yamaan (Arabic)
Blessed - Yemeni

Yamam (Arabic)
Dove
Variants: *Yamaam*

Yamar (Arabic)
Alive - Life - Long-lived
Variants: *Ya'mar, Yaamar, Yaamer, Yamer*

Yameen (Arabic)
Blessedness - Power - Right Hand
The name Yameen is mentioned in the Quran.
Variants: *Yamein, Yamin, Yemin*

Yaqeen (Arabic)
Certainty
The name Yaqeen is mentioned in the Quran.
Variants: *Yaqin*

Yaqub (Arabic)
Heir - Successor
The name Yaqub is mentioned in the Quran.
Variants: *Ya'qub, Yaqob, Yaqoob, Yaqoub*

Yaroq (Turkish)
Brilliant - White

Yasar (Arabic)
Affluence

Yaseer (Arabic)
Blessed - Easy
Variants: *Yasir*

Yashal (Arabic)
Brilliant - Radiant
Variants: *Yash'al*

Yasir (Arabic)
Blessed - Lenient
Variants: *Yaaser, Yaasir, Yaser*

Yawer (Persian)
Companion - Friend
Variants: *Yawar*

Yazar (Turkish)
Writer

Yazeed (Arabic)
Growing - Increasing - Prospering
The name Yazeed is mentioned in the Quran.
Variants: *Yazid, Yezid*

Yelena (Russian)
Shining Light
Russian form of Helen.

Yevgeni (Russian)
High-born - Noble

Yunus (Arabic)
Yunus is the name of a Prophet mentioned in the Quran, such as in verse 10:88.
Variants: *Yonos, Yoones, Yoonis, Younes, Younis, Younos, Younous, Younus, Yunis*

Yuri (Russian)
Farmer
Russian form of George.

Yusr (Arabic)
Gentleness - Needlessness

Yusri (Arabic)
Living in Luxury - Needless - Rich
Variants: *Yosree, Yosri, Yusree, Yusry*

Yusrullah (Arabic)
God's Blessing

Yusuf (Arabic)
God Gives
The name Yusuf is mentioned in the Quran.
Variants: *Yoosuf, Yosof, Yosuf, Yousof, Yousuf, Yusof*

Yves (French)
Yew
Yew is a type of tree.

This page intentionally left blank

Z

Zaaef (Arabic)
Hospitable

Zaakher (Arabic)
Rich - Wealthy - Wise
Variants: *Zaakhir, Zakher, Zakhir*

Zaaki (Arabic)
Blessed - Virtuous
Variants: *Zaky*

Zaal (Persian)
White-haired
Name of the father of Rustam, the Persian mythical hero.
Variants: *Zal*

Zaatar (Arabic)
A type of herb.
Variants: *Zatar*

Zabeer (Arabic)
Handsome - Intelligent - Witty
Variants: *Zabir*

Zabi (Arabic)
Gazelle

Zaboor (Arabic)
Brave - Lion
Variants: *Dhaboor, Zabur*

Zabreen (Persian)
Highest - Lofty
Variants: *Zabrin*

Zachary (English)
God Has Remembered
Refers to the father of John, known as prophet Zakariyya in the Quran.

Zack (English)
God Has Remembered
Variants: *Zak*

Zaeem (Arabic)
Guarantor - Leader - Resolute
The name Zaeem is mentioned in the Quran.
Variants: *Za'eem, Za'im, Zaeim, Zaeym, Zaim*

Zafar (Arabic)
Triumph - Victory - Win
Variants: *Dafar, Dhafar, Zafer*

Zafaruddin (Arabic)
Triumph of the Faith

Zafeer (Arabic)
Successful
Variants: *Dhafeer, Dhafir, Zafir, Zefir*

Zafir (Arabic)
Successful
Variants: *Dhafir, Zaafer, Zaafir, Zafer*

Zaghlul (Arabic)
Baby Pigeon
Variants: *Zaghlool*

Zagros (Persian)
Name of a mountain range in Western Iran and Eastern Turkey and Iraq.

Zahaar (Arabic)
Florist
Variants: *Zahhar*

Zahanat (Arabic, Turkish)
Intelligence - Keeness
Turkish pronunciation of Zahanah.
Variants: *Dahanat, Zahaanat*

Zahauddin (Arabic)
Supporter of Islam
Literally "radiance of the faith".
Variants: *Zaha Uddin*

Zaheel (Arabic)
Sure of Heart
Variants: *Zahil, Zahil*

Zaheel (Arabic)
Sure of Heart

Zaheen (Arabic)
Intellectual - Intelligent - Sagacious
Variants: *Dahin, Zahin, Zehin*

Zaheer (Arabic)
Blossoming - Flourishing - Glowing
Variants: *Zahir*

Zahi (Arabic)
Beautiful - Breeze - Handsome - Radiant
Variants: *Zahee*

Zahian (Arabic)
Bright Day - Brilliant
Variants: *Dhahian, Zahiaan, Zahyaan, Zahyan*

Zahid (Arabic)
Ascetic
Variants: *Zahed*

Zahir (Arabic)
Bright - Glowing

Zahirulhaq (Arabic)
Visible Truth
Variants: *Zaahirul Haq, Zaherol Haq*

Zahl (Arabic)
Confidence - Sureness of Heart

Zahou (Arabic)
Beautiful View - Blooming Plant
Variants: *Zahu, Zahu*

Zahou (Arabic)
Beautiful View - Blooming Plant

Zahran (Arabic)
Blossoming - Radiant
Variants: *Zahraan, Zehraan, Zehran*

Zahri (Arabic)
Flower-like
Variants: *Zahry*

Zahrun (Arabic)
Blossom - Flower
Variants: *Zahroon*

Zahuk (Arabic)
Happy - Laughing

Zahun (Arabic)
Intelligent
Variants: *Zahoon*

Zahur (Arabic)
Radiant
Variants: *Zahoor*

Zahyan (Arabic)
Brilliant - Luminous

Zaifullah (Arabic)
God's Guest - Protected by God

Zakaa (Arabic)
Intelligence - Keenness
Arabic for "intelligence", "cleverness".
Variants: *Zaka*

Zakariyya (Hebrew)
God Has Remembered
The name Zakariyya is mentioned in the Quran. It is the name of a prophet. It is the Arabic form of a Hebrew name, spelled as Zechariah in English.
Variants: *Zakaria, Zakariaa, Zakariya, Zakariyaa, Zekaria*

Zakat (Arabic)
Alms - Purification
The name Zakat is mentioned in the Quran.
Variants: *Zakaat, Zekat*

Zakawat (Arabic, Turkish)
Intelligence - Keenness
Turkish pronunciation of Zakawah.
Variants: *Zakaawat*

Zaki (Arabic)
Blessed - Pious - Pure - Righteous
Variants: *Zakee, Zaky*

Zakou (Arabic)
Growth - Increase
Variants: *Zaku*

Zakwan (Arabic)
Brilliant - Intelligent
Variants: *Zakwaan, Zekwan*

Zaleeq (Arabic)
Eloquent - Fluent
Variants: *Zaliq*

Zaluj (Arabic)
Nimble - Sprightly
Variants: *Zalooj*

Zamaair (Arabic)
Consciences - Hearts - Minds
Variants: *Zamaaer, Zamaer, Zamair*

Zamaan (Arabic)
Age - Era - Time
Variants: *Zaman*

Zameel (Arabic)
Colleague - Companion

Zameer (Arabic)
Conscience - Heart - Mind
Variants: *Dameer, Dhamir, Zamir, Zemir*

Zamil (Arabic)
Follower

Zamin (Arabic)
Guarantor - Surety
Variants: *Damin, Dhaamin, Zaamen, Zaamin, Zamen*

Zamr (Arabic)
Lion's Roar

Zaraafat (Arabic)
Intelligence - Talent
Arabic for "intelligence", "cleverness", "talent".
Variants: *Zarafat, Zerafat*

Zarab (Persian)
Colloidal Gold - Golden Water
Variants: *Zaraab*

Zarar (Arabic)
Experienced - Intelligent
Variants: *Zaraar*

Zardasht (Persian)
Zoroaster
Zardasht refers to the prophet Zoroaster, who is considered a true prophet sent by God by some Muslim scholars.

Zareeb (Arabic)
Attacker - Likeness - Similarity
Variants: *Dharib, Zarib*

Zareef (Arabic)
Charming - Intelligent - Witty
Variants: *Dharif, Zarif*

Zareer (Persian)
Fragrant Plant - Intelligent
Name of a fragrant plant known as Reseda in English. It is also the name of a character mentioned in the Shahnameh.
Variants: *Zarir*

Zargham (Arabic)
Brave - Lion - Warrior
Can be pronounced with a long

NAMES FOR BOYS

or short second "a" sound.
(Zarghum or Zarghaam)

Zargoon (Persian)
Beautiful - Percious
Literally "gold-colored", "like gold".
Variants: *Zargun*

Zarib (Arabic)
Attacker - Striker

Zarin (Persian)
Golden
Variants: *Zareen*

Zariyan (Arabic)
Dispersed

Zarnab (Arabic, Persian)
Fragrant Plant
Scientific name: Taxus baccata.
Variants: *Zarnaab*

Zartash (Persian)
Gold-carver
Variants: *Zartaash*

Zaryab (Persian)
Colloidal Gold - Finder of Gold - Wealthy
Variants: *Zariaab, Zariab, Zaryaab*

Zaryan (Urdu)
Gold Finder
Variants: *Zarian, Zaryaan*

Zaufishan (Arabic, Persian)
Radiant - Spreader of Light
Variants: *Zaufeshan, Zaufishaan, Zofishan, Zowfishan*

Zauq (Arabic)
Enthusiasm - Joyfuless
Variants: *Dhawq, Zawq*

Zawal (Arabic)
Sundown
Variants: *Zawaal*

Zaweel (Arabic)
Motion - Movement
Variants: *Zawil*

Zawqi (Arabic)
Enthusiastic - Joyful
Variants: *Zawqee, Zawqy, Zowqi*

Zawri (Arabic)
Intelligent
Variants: *Zauri*

Zayd (Arabic)
Growth - Increase - Progress
The name *Zayd* is mentioned in the Quran.
Variants: *Zaed, Zaid, Zaide, Zeid, Zeyd*

Zayed (Arabic)
Increasing - Progressing - Prospering
Variants: *Zaayed, Zaayid, Zaied, Zayid*

Zayef (Arabic)
Hospitable
Variants: *Dayef, Dayif, Dhaye, Dhayif, Zaayef, Zaayif, Zayif*

Zayir (Arabic)
Roaring Lion
Variants: *Zayer*

Zayn (Arabic)
Adornment - Beauty - Excellence - Grace - Virtue
Variants: *Zain, Zaine, Zane, Zayne, Zein, Zeine, Zeyn, Zeyne*

Zaynul Abidin (Arabic)
Supporter of Islam
Literally meaning "adornment of the worshipers".
Variants: *Zaynulabidin*

Zayyan (Arabic)
Adorner - Beautifier - Decorator
Variants: *Zaiaan, Zaian, Zaiane,*

Zayaan, Zayan, Zayyaan, Zayyaane, Zayyane, Zeyan, Zeyyan

Zeb (English)
Exaltation
Short form of Zebulun, name of the sixth son of Leah and Jacob.

Zechariah (Biblical)
God Has Remembered
Name of a prophet, known as Zakariyya in the Quran. The prophet Zakariyya in the Quran is commonly known as Zachary in English, while the name Zechariah is reserved for a different Biblical prophet (even though Zakariyya, Zachary and Zechariah are all the same name).

Zed (English)
Justice of Yahweh
Short for Zedekiah, the name of a number of characters in the Bible.

Zeeshan (Arabic)
Dignified - Respected
Variants: *Zishan*

Zehn (Arabic)
Intellect - Psyche - Reason
Variants: *Zihn*

Zeke (English)
God Strengthens
Short form of Ezekiel.

Zeph (English)
Hidden by God
Short for Zephaniah, name of a prophet in the Bible.

Zewar (Kurdish, Persian)
Adornment - Beautification

Zhenya (Russian)
High-born - Noble

Pet form of Yevgeni (male) and Yevgenia (female).

Zhobin (Persian)
Small Spear
Also pronounced with a "Z".
Variants: *Zhobeen, Zobeen, Zobin*

Ziauddin (Arabic)
Radiance of the Faith

Zidan (Arabic)
Growth - Increase - Progress
Variants: *Zedaan, Zedaane, Zedan, Zedane, Zeedan, Zeedane, Zeeidaan, Zeeidan, Zeeydaan, Zeeydan, Zeidaan, Zeidan, Zeidane, Zeydaan, Zeydan, Zidaan, Zidaane, Zidan, Zidane, Ziedaan, Ziedan, Ziedane, Ziydaan, Ziydan, Ziydane, Zydaan, Zydaane, Zydan, Zydane*

Zihni (Arabic)
Intellectual - Reasonable - Understanding
Arabic for "intellectual", "understanding", "reasonable", "deep thinker".
Variants: *Dhehni, Zehni, Zihnee, Zihny*

Zikr (Arabic)
Mention - Remembrance
The name Zikr is mentioned in the Quran.
Variants: *Dhekr, Dhikr, Dikr, Zekr*

Zil Allah (Arabic)
God's Mercy - God's Protection
Literally meaning "shade of God".
Variants: *Zell Allah, Zilallah*

Zil Elahi (Arabic, Urdu)
God's Mercy - God's Protection
Literally meaning "shade of God".
Variants: *Zill Elahi*

Zil Yazdan (Arabic, Persian, Urdu)
God's Mercy - God's Protection
Literally meaning "shade of God".
Variants: *Zil Yazdaan*

Zilal (Arabic)
Shade
The name Zilal is mentioned in the Quran.
Variants: *Zelaal, Zelal, Zilaa, Zylal*

Zill (Arabic)
Shade - Shadow
Variants: *Zel, Zell, Zil*

Zimr (Arabic)
Brave

Zirar (Arabic)
Warrior
The name of a Sahabi, whose full name is Zirar bin al-Azwar.
Variants: *Zerar, Ziraar*

Ziyad (Arabic)
Growth - Increase - Progress
Ziyad is an indirect Quranic name with the same meaning as Zayd and Zidan: growth, progress, increase, and being blessed by Allah. Ziyad is derived from the Z-Y-D Quranic root which is used in a number of places in the Quran, such as in 10:26: Those who do good works shall have a good reward and a surplus. No darkness and no ignominy shall cover their faces. They are destined for Paradise wherein they shall dwell forever.
Variants: *Zeyaad, Zeyad, Ziaad, Ziad, Ziyaad, Zyaad, Zyad, Zyead*

Zoomeer (Arabic, Persian, Urdu)
Radiant

Literally "king of light".
Variants: *Zoumeer, Zumir*

Zoraiz (Arabic, Persian)
Enlightener - Spreader of Light
Variants: *Dhuraiz, Zoreez, Zoriz, Zouraiz, Zuriz*

Zryan (Kurdish)
Storm
Variants: *Zriaan, Zrian, Zryaan*

Zuaib (Arabic)
Guide
Variants: *Zoaib*

Zubaid (Arabic)
Gift from God
Variants: *Zobaid, Zubayd*

Zubair (Arabic)
Firm - Intelligent - Powerful - Wise
Variants: *Zobair, Zobayr, Zubayr*

Zufar (Arabic)
Brave
Variants: *Dhufar, Zofar, Zofer, Zufer*

Zufunoon (Arabic)
Skilled - Talented
Literally "possessor of many arts".
Variants: *Dhufunoon, Zufunun*

Zuhain (Arabic)
Intelligent
Variants: *Zohain*

Zuhair (Arabic)
Blossom - Flower
Variants: *Zohair, Zohayr, Zuhayr*

Zuhdi (Arabic)
Ascetic
Variants: *Zohdi*

NAMES FOR BOYS

Zuhni (Arabic)
Intelligent - Wise

Zulfateh (Arabic)
Guided

Zulfiqar (Arabic)
Name of the sword that was given to Ali bin Abi Talib by Prophet Muhammad ﷺ. The word literally means "that which has vertebrae".
Variants: *Zulfeqar, Zulfiqaar*

Zulghaffar (Arabic)
Forgiving

Zulghina (Arabic)
Wealthy

Zulhijjah (Arabic)
12th Month of the Hijri Calendar

Zulhimmah (Arabic)
Resolute - Resolved

Zulikram (Arabic)
Gracious - Honored
Variants: *Zolikram*

Zuljalal (Arabic)
Majestic - Mighty
The name Zuljalal is mentioned in the Quran.
Variants: *Zul Jalal, Zuljalaal*

Zulkifl (Arabic)
One of the prophets mentioned in the Quran (peace be upon him). He is the same as the Biblical Ezekiel.
Variants: *Dhulkifl, Zul Kifl, Zulkefl*

Zulnoon (Arabic)
Literally "possessor of the whale", a nickname for prophet Yunus. The name Zulnoon is mentioned in the Quran.

Zulnoorain (Arabic)
Radiant
Zulnoorain was the nickname of Uthman ibn Affan, may Allah be pleased with him, literally meaning "possessor of two lights".
Variants: *Dhulnurain, Zul Nurain*

Zulqadr (Arabic)
Composed - Dignified

Zulqarnain (Arabic)
Two-horned
The name Zulqarnain is mentioned in the Quran.

Zultan (Arabic, Urdu)
King - Leader
Urdu variant of Arabic Sultan.
Variants: *Zultaan*

Zumail (Arabic)
Companion - Friend
Ancient Arabic name without a clearly defined meaning, may be pet form of Zameel, meaning "colleague", "friend", "companion".

Zumar (Arabic)
Groups - Throngs
The name Zumar is mentioned in the Quran.
Variants: *Zomar, Zomer, Zumer*

Zuraib (Arabic)
Eloquent
Variants: *Dhuraib, Zoraib, Zorayb, Zurayb*

Zuraib (Arabic)
Attacker - Striker

Zuwail (Arabic)
Motion - Movement
Variants: *Zowail, Zowayl, Zuwayl*

Zuwayhir (Arabic)
Radiant
Variants: *Zowaihir*

Zyan (Arabic)
Adornment - Beautification - Decoration
Variants: *Zeyan, Ziyaan, Ziyan, Zyaan*

Zyaud Deen (Arabic)
Supporter of Islam
Literally "radiance of the faith".
Variants: *Zya Uddin, Zyaauddin, Zyauddin*

Zyauddeen (Arabic)
Supporter of Isam
Literally "brilliance of the faith".
Variants: *Diaudin, Dyauddin, Zya Uddin, Zyaaudin*

Printed in the USA
CPSIA information can be obtained
at www.ICGtesting.com
LVHW041632301023
762577LV00002B/13

9 781980 380900